Social Practices in Higher Education

Social Practices in Higher Education

A Knowledge Framework Approach to Linguistic Research and Teaching

Edited by Tammy Slater

SHEFFIELD UK BRISTOL CT

Published by Equinox Publishing Ltd.

UK Office 415, The Workstation, 15 Paternoster Row, Sheffield, South Yorkshire S1 2BX
USA ISD, 70 Enterprise Drive, Bristol, CT 06010

www.equinoxpub.com

First published 2023

British Library Cataloguing-in-Publication Data

A catalogue record for this book is available from the British Library.

ISBN-13 978 1 78179 740 2 (hardback)
978 1 78179 741 9 (ePDF)
978 1 80050 410 3 (ePub)

Library of Congress Cataloging-in-Publication Data

Names: Slater, Tammy, editor.
Title: Social practices in higher education : a knowledge framework approach to linguistic research and teaching / edited by Tammy Slater.
Description: Sheffield, South Yorkshire ; Bristol, CT : Equinox Publishing Ltd, 2023. | Includes bibliographical references and index. | Summary: "This book addresses Mohan's (1986) concept of a social practice, an educational activity that can be considered as action in a frame of meaning, or a "knowledge framework" (KF). The KF, grounded in systemic functional linguistics, is a heuristic that provides both a theoretical framework for researching the language of social practices and a springboard for organizing lessons that can help teachers bring explicit language development into content teaching. This volume brings together the latest research on using Mohan's SFL-based theory at institutions of higher learning"-- Provided by publisher.
Identifiers: LCCN 2023016388 (print) | LCCN 2023016389 (ebook) | ISBN 9781781797402 (hardback) | ISBN 9781781797419 (pdf) | ISBN 9781800504103 (epub)
Subjects: LCSH: Language and education--Social aspects. | Language and languages--Study and teaching (Higher)--Social aspects. | LCGFT: Essays.
Classification: LCC P40.8 .S619 2023 (print) | LCC P40.8 (ebook) | DDC 418.0071--dc23/eng/20230725
LC record available at https://lccn.loc.gov/2023016388
LC ebook record available at https://lccn.loc.gov/2023016389

Typeset by Sparks – www.sparkspublishing.com

Contents

1 A Knowledge Framework Approach to Linguistic Research and Teaching

Tammy Slater

Abstract

The Knowledge Framework (KF) is a heuristic that allows educators, materials/curriculum developers, and researchers to explore in creative ways the integration of language, content, thinking skills, and key visuals. Grounded in Systemic Functional Linguistics, the KF revolves around the concept of an educational activity or social practice. Participating successfully in an activity or social practice involves both *doing* (actions or practice) and *knowing* (theory or understandings that inform what we do). The KF heuristic is drawn as a set of six boxes, with the bottom three relating to the top three in this doing/knowing relationship. This chapter begins by documenting the history of the creation of the KF and continues with a detailed description of the heuristic and its value when teaching, especially teaching English language learners. Following this, the existing literature is summarized according to its use in the various content areas, offering what is likely the most comprehensive review to date of the available literature on the KF. The chapter ends with a snapshot of each of the chapters in the current volume.

Keywords: Knowledge Framework; literature review; classroom research; materials development; linguistic analysis

The Beginnings of the KF

It has been over 35 years since Bernard A. Mohan published his seminal work on integrating language and content (Mohan, 1986). His book discussed the concept of a social practice, an educational activity that can be considered as action in a *frame of meaning* that highlights the integration of content and language. Mohan's brainchild, this "Knowledge Framework," began with his doctoral research (Mohan, 1969), carried out under the guidance of Michael Halliday. Mohan explored the Systemic Functional Linguistic (SFL) concept of "context of situation" using a mixed-methods approach using the card game of *Blackjack*. He worked with five triads (each with two experts and one novice) in which the game was taught and then played. His SFL analysis showed how the language of teaching and learning the game was much more complex than the language of playing the game, results which were statistically significant in all cases. This early work showed how teaching the game makes explicit the context of situation around the playing of the game. Mohan argued that the learner learns this context of situation and applies it implicitly in order to play the game. Thus, teaching and learning of how to play Blackjack illustrates a social practice with both theory and practice coming together as a knowledge framework. The teaching and learning of the game semantically involve the CLASSIFICATION of cards, the rules and causes and effects of the actions (PRINCIPLES), and the EVALUATION of the hands. Playing the game semantically involves the DESCRIPTION of the cards, the CHOICE of actions, and the SEQUENCE of plays.

Under a decade later, Mohan (1977) discussed the differences between the structural approach to language teaching and the situational approach, commenting that the practice at that time tended to organize the course either structurally, choosing situations that may illustrate the structure best, or situationally, choosing structures that can be used within the situation. Mohan suggested adapting Lawrence's (1972) *logical methods of organization,* which Mohan grouped into four classes—descriptive class, sequence class, decision-making class, and generalization class—to help organize a situational curriculum. Mohan argued in this paper that each of these classes could be related to structure as well as semantic notions and language-constructed concepts. Similar to Mohan (1977), Mohan (1978) discussed common ways in which one can examine the integrated teaching of language and content and presented a table that outlined various discourse categories from more specific concepts to more general ones, a classification that reflected to a great extent the paired cognitive categories of the KF. This early thinking helped conceptualize his ideas for the publication of his 1986 book, *Language and Content,* in which the Knowledge Framework was detailed in full.

Reinforcing the message in his 1986 book, Mohan (1989) stated that research on language-and-content learning had moved from a theoretical perspective on second language learning to a focus on learning as a linguistic process. He examined connections between text structures (a linguistic category) and knowledge structures (a cognitive category), suggesting that "the knowledge structures of a situation are reflected in the macrostructures of the expository texts of that situation" (p. 103), offering an example of how the classification of plants in gardening is similar to a classification of statistics, and presenting three studies to argue how knowledge structures go across content areas, both in discourse and in graphics. In a 1990 publication, Mohan offered a systematic review of the research on the integration of language and content and argued that knowledge structures underlie content-area knowledge as well as knowledge about texts. Mohan suggested that bringing students' awareness to these knowledge structures and information patterns can improve students' comprehension of texts as well as their ability to write. He encouraged more research on the connections between knowledge structures and student learning tasks, concluding that these are "complementary ways of looking at the integration of language learning and content learning" (p. 147) that would benefit from further examinations of how they complement each other.

The Knowledge Framework is a heuristic approach to the analysis of human activities and their meanings. Mohan (Chapter 6) draws attention to the analysis of human activities by the Greek philosopher Aristotle and emphasizes the importance of relating work on the Knowledge Framework to this very longstanding tradition. Aristotle's work had a major impact on the European Middle Ages and indirectly became critical in the development of modern philosophy as well as European law and theology. Aristotle's influence declined in the 17th century, attacked by authors such as Francis Bacon, but in recent years, according to Curren (2010), there has been an Aristotelian renaissance in the philosophy of education which may have led to an increase in interest in linguistic evidence in educational interactions relevant to that tradition of ethics. Central to the discussion of ethical questions is the issue of CHOICE, one of the six knowledge structures in the Knowledge Framework. CHOICE and EVALUATION/deliberation has thus become a growing and important part of the linguistic analysis offered through the Knowledge Framework and has played an important role in Mohan's presentation of theory/practice connections. His work in this volume reflects this interest.

At the same time as Mohan's *Language and Content* was being published, the authors of Early, Thew, and Wakefield (1986) were examining Western Canadian textbooks and curriculum handbooks. They found that the six identified knowledge structures occurred with regularity through the educational resources, both as examples of language texts and of the thinking skills that were targeted for development throughout pre-K to twelfth-grade schooling. This finding was followed by a large-scale action research project, described in Early, Mohan, and Hooper (1988; see also Early, 2001; Early & Hooper, 2001), in which teams of ESL and content teachers in eight elementary and four secondary schools (more than 100 educators) used the KF to produce and implement thematic units for teaching English language learners as well as tested out the applicability and utility of the KF within these contexts. This project was a university/school board collaboration that, rather than following any top–down model of a method, engaged teams of teachers in conversations that supported them as creative designers of learning using the KF as they imagined best. Teachers were free to choose interests and contexts, and many graduate school projects detailed these endeavors, as this chapter will show.

Since that time, there have been numerous articles written around the world about the Knowledge Framework, both detailing what the KF is and its implementation. Regarding what it is, Mohan (2001) highlighted the primary aspects of his KF for teaching ESL, and Mohan (2007) described the KF and reviewed research in the field to show how the KF connects with SFL, critical thinking, and computer resources, suggesting that the framework offers possibilities for all levels of teaching. Slater and Gleason (2011) also described the KF in usable detail and reviewed some of the early work on the KF in teaching, summarizing strategies for designing a KF-based unit plan. More recently, Slater and Mohan (2019) also offered a short piece detailing the highlights of the KF.

This chapter brings together all the available literature about the KF by first describing what the Knowledge Framework (KF) is and follows this by summarizing the literature that has appeared since Mohan's 1986 book was published. The chapter concludes with an overview of the various studies that make up this volume.

What is the KF?

The Knowledge Framework is a theoretical framework anchored in Systemic Functional Linguistics. It can be used as an organizer for creative and innovative curriculum planning as well as for researching language use and development within the concept of activity, as suggested in the previous section. Figure 1.1 shows the KF model in its basic representation. Across the top from left to right are CLASSIFICATION, PRINCIPLES, and EVALUATION, and across the bottom are DESCRIPTION, SEQUENCE, and CHOICE.

Conceptually, the two levels (top and bottom) are connected in a theory–practice dynamic. Simply put, CLASSIFICATION relates to DESCRIPTION in the sense that when we use language to describe something (in practice), we infer various classifications (our understandings of theory). For example,

CLASSIFICATION	PRINCIPLES	EVALUATION
DESCRIPTION	SEQUENCE	CHOICE

Figure 1.1 The Knowledge Framework

if we were to describe a particular tree we were impressed by, at a basic level we would need to have a classification of colors that we can draw from as well as information related to size and shape. These are quite commonplace classifications that are taught and learned very early in the lives of native speakers and are also presented early in English language classes. These simple classifications allow us to say that a particular tree is tall and bushy and green, or short and round and red. If we were learning about trees, however, we would be learning how to describe trees using much more scientific classifications and thus our more "educated" descriptions may sound or look very different, although they would still be descriptions based on our conceptual understandings and our use of classifications. English language learners (ELLs) who have already learned the conceptual information in their first language would also need to acquire the appropriate language to talk about these classifications in English.

The same theory–practice connection exists with PRINCIPLES and SEQUENCE. Notice that you can sequence what you see as you talk about the rain that falls and how a puddle disappears when the sun comes out (e.g., After it rains, the sun comes out and soon the puddles go away until the ground is dry again). But you would need to be able to understand cause and effect and the theory of the water cycle to be able to explain (PRINCIPLES) this process, and so your language would sound or look very different, not only in your choice of vocabulary, but very likely in your grammar as well. Finally, when you make a choice linguistically (e.g., I'd like coffee, please), you do so because of the values you hold (e.g., you value coffee for its flavor or for the caffeine), and thus EVALUATION and CHOICE also make a theory–practice pair. Once again, you do something (your practice) because you hold theories about that something (your knowledge/theories).

These six knowledge structures (KSs) all include categories of thinking skills. CLASSIFICATION refers to the thinking skills of classifying, grouping, and defining. DESCRIPTION encompasses thinking skills such as identifying, labeling, comparing, contrasting, and describing. Examples of thinking skills that involve PRINCIPLES are predicting, explaining, concluding, interpreting data, establishing hypotheses, and developing generalizations about cause and effect, means/end, rules, reasons, and results. Those in SEQUENCE concern, for example, ordering things and ideas, following directions, and noting changes over time. EVALUATION involves ranking, appreciating, judging, justifying preferences and opinions, and deciding on values, goals, and evaluation criteria. Finally CHOICE revolves around such thinking skills as selecting, making decisions, and proposing alternatives.

From a linguistic perspective, Mohan and his followers have argued that there is language associated with these six boxes individually, with some patterns found that distinguish the three pairs rather than individual KSs. With regards to the commonality amongst the pairs, broadly speaking, CLASSIFICATION and DESCRIPTION make use of verbs of *being* and *having* while PRINCIPLES and SEQUENCE use action verbs, including verbs that suggest sequence (e.g., *start, begin, finish, end, follow, precede, proceed, continue*) and cause (e.g., *cause, make, produce, lead to, result in*). The knowledge structures of EVALUATION and CHOICE typically use verbs that show more mental states, or sensing verbs, such as *like, want, prefer, choose*, and *want* for CHOICE, and for EVALUATION, verbs such as *rank, evaluate, value, approve, recommend*, and *judge*.

There is also characteristic language of KSs that reflect parts of speech other than verbs. Both CLASSIFICATION and DESCRIPTION make use of additive conjunctions such as *and*, but whereas DESCRIPTION makes use of the language of comparison and contrast (e.g., *the same as, similar to, like, different from*) and attributive lexis such as adjectives of color and size, CLASSIFICATION involves taxonomic and part–whole lexis such as *types, classes, kinds, categories*, and *ways*. The language of PRINCIPLES includes consequential conjunctions and adverbials such as *since, due to, in order to, consequently, because, thus*, and *if*-clauses as well as cause–effect lexis (e.g., *cause, effect, result*). SEQUENCE language has temporal conjunction and adverbials (e.g., *after, since, as, initially, firstly, finally*, and *when*- and *as*-clauses) and also includes sequential lexis such as *beginning* and *end* and *summary*. EVALUATION includes lexis such as *best, worst, good, bad, right, wrong, boring*, and *acceptable*. The alternative conjunction "or" is a linguistic characteristic of CHOICE, as are appositional choice lexis (e.g., *choice, option*, and *which* + noun).

Beyond verbal language, there are key visuals (KVs) that are associated with the six KSs. CLASSIFICATION can be visualized in a tree diagram or a web while DESCRIPTION can be an image, a Venn diagram, or even bar graphs and pie charts. Key visuals for PRINCIPLES can be cause–effect chains, cycles, and problem–solution charts, while SEQUENCE can be illustrated in timelines, action strips, and flow charts. Key visuals associated with EVALUATION are rating grids and evaluation charts, whereas decision trees and other visuals that show the generation of alternatives represent the KS of CHOICE.

From a teaching perspective, the KF can have tremendous value. As stated by Early (1990a, p. 569), "the ways in which knowledge is structured are similar from situation to situation. This raises possibilities for the transfer of certain language and thinking skills across different content areas and situations." Because these knowledge structures have been found to occur in all activities and all areas of the curriculum, teachers can help students—especially ELLs—develop their language simultaneously within the various content areas, reinforcing the language as it occurs and reoccurs throughout the school day. Teachers can use the KF to create unit plans based on a theme or topic, and divide their lessons to address questions that target each of the various KSs to ensure that students have plenty of opportunities to be exposed to, learn, and use the language associated with the types of thinking skills each lesson in the unit targets while learning the content at the same time. As Mohan (1986) argues, the KF can be used in the same way for mainstream students, school-based ELLs, and adult English language classes, given that the "integration of language and subject areas is relevant to all teachers, whether they teach language or subject matter, and whether they teach second language learners or native speakers" (Mohan, 1986, p. iv).

From a researcher's perspective, the KF can offer a useful tool for the discourse analysis of social practices, including unravelling the patterns that are associated with the teaching of content at various grade levels, or the patterns in political speeches, or any other social practice of interest. Which knowledge structures are prevalent, and do they occur in regular patterns or cycles that can help inform the field by offering insight into what might be predictable for understanding the social practice? Along these lines, Mohan (2011) reviewed four different social practices—young children learning magnetism, graduate students participating in online discussion, secondary students learning cooperatively, and action research on a process of learning—to illustrate the concept of a social practice as a framework of ideational meanings, or a register. Mohan argued that the study of social practices as units of linguistic meaning can provide a link between "social" and "linguistic" approaches to literacy, can speak to the needs of L2 learners who must develop academic discourse in content areas, and can point towards forms of formative assessment that take greater account of meaning-making by learners. Relatively little has been done in areas such as these, although this volume attempts to address this gap. However, as the following comprehensive literature review reveals, using the KF in pre-K to 12 teaching and learning contexts has been a main focus over the years across a wide variety of content areas.

What Are the Content Areas the KF Has Been Used In?

Since the onset of the Vancouver School Board project in or around 1986, research has been carried out in various classrooms where the focus has been on specific subject areas. The following sections briefly summarize these subject-focused studies, highlighting the KF's ability to allow for creativity of design and implementation.

Science

Science classrooms have provided one of the most popular contexts for teaching and researching the language using the KF, and as the following review indicates, articles involving these contexts have consistently shown how students have developed academic language and content understanding through the use of the heuristic. Early (1989), working with K–12 students in a variety of content areas, offered illustrations of mammal CLASSIFICATION and a compare/contrast (DESCRIPTION) chart for whales to argue the value of using KF-organized key visuals to help students understand academic texts. The author offered student quotes to corroborate how both ESL and native English-speaking students found the key visual helpful in their learning of these science concepts. Similarly, Early (1990a) detailed a thematic unit on fish, taught to a class of fourth and fifth grade ELLs using key visuals and focusing on CLASSIFICATION and DESCRIPTION while also suggesting tasks for CHOICE and EVALUATION. She concluded that the KF in thematic units helps support ELLs—even those at low English levels—to "produce texts of which they can be proud" (p. 574). Early (1990b) examined an elementary school beginner's English as a second language (ESL) class in which 20 students aged 10 to 13 learned how animals live using a KF approach combined with an adapted language experience approach. The goal of the teacher, successfully met and enjoyed by the students, was to teach subject matter knowledge as well as help her students develop their writing and reading ability.

In a mixed-methods design that included surveys and a pre- and posttest, Liew (1994) compared the results of 60 eleventh-grade biology students' lab reports after the students were taught using either a KF or genre-based approach. He found that the two approaches were complementary, and both were difficult for students to learn, but the KF approach was more effective in improving the quality of the lab reports for both mainstream and ESL students. The author stated that the KF provided a useful organizational tool for focusing on the linguistic resources needed to write their reports.

A 12-week-long qualitative and quantitative action research project for a master's degree (Hawkes, 1996) examined the use of key visuals of KSs to enhance ELLs' learning in a sixth-grade science class. Her study revealed that students with lower language abilities relied more on KVs to show their understanding of content, and that all participants became more aware of KVs in knowledge creation because of the unit. Furthermore, in another master's project that explored digital learning in science, Moore (1998) explored the use of the KF to help 10- to 11-year-old ELLs use internet information to develop their knowledge and language about marine mammals. He found that by implementing tasks which included KS-based key visuals and language choices as well as point-form notes rather than spaces for full sentences, students produced more texts that were authentic rather than copied. In other words, Moore suggested that the use of the KF and key visuals when searching online has the potential to help students write authentic texts from information they research on the internet.

Huang and Morgan (2003) used knowledge structure analysis to evaluate the development of science writing, specifically CLASSIFICATION, by 29 high school ELLs. A classification tree was used not only to present the new science content but also as a prompt for students to use to write a classification text. Students were also introduced to classification language. Altogether, students wrote three drafts, the first using a model text, the second after instruction on the language of CLASSIFICATION and various class activities and discussions, and the third after peer review. The authors concluded that the third writing sample was much more elaborate than the earlier drafts and offer examples of this development in language ability. Their findings showed how students appeared to learn content that was exhibited in their key visuals as well as the metalanguage of CLASSIFICATION. Similarly, in a five-week case study of 35 ELLs in grades eight to ten, Huang (2004) examined a KF approach that aimed to teach about the composition of matter, again focusing primarily on CLASSIFICATION. Her goal was to help students understand the content and to develop their linguistic ability to write their understandings. Between the students' first and third drafts, both the content detail improved, and students used more linguistic resources of CLASSIFICATION, suggesting a successful socialization into this type of science discourse. Along a similar vein, but looking at knowledge transfer across languages, Tong (2004) focused on the KS of CLASSIFICATION and its use in science, showing how 14 high school Chinese students used their background knowledge of the taxonomy of living organisms, acquired through their L1, combined with organizational displays of the knowledge (their KVs) and the KS-appropriate language features, to create well developed classification texts with a variety of language features in both their L1 and English. Her results reinforced the potential of using the KF in bilingual education contexts, where content can be introduced in the first language, and with the teaching of the KF, students can better show their knowledge when writing in their second.

Using data from Slater (2004), which focused on the development of causal discourse (the language of PRINCIPLES), Mohan and Slater (2004a) argued that teachers need to attend to the patterns of meaning and how they are developed linguistically to scaffold their students' learning. These patterns of meaning, the authors pointed out, are well detailed in the KF. Also based on Slater (2004), Mohan and Slater (2005) examined the teaching of magnetism to a class of young (6/7 years old) ESL students, focusing on the use of the KF to connect theory to practice. The authors showed how the teacher built up a basic theory of magnetism, linked technical terms to students' practical experience, and helped students use the theory to explain their evolving understanding of magnetism. A similar argument with the magnetism data was presented in German for the German readership in Mohan and Slater (2013). Mohan and Slater (2006) reported on an ethnographic case study which examined a high school science class, detailing the unit from the introduction of the topic and theory to the problem-solving activities that illustrated the students' understanding of the topic. The authors' look at this social practice of learning about matter highlighted the role of language and the development of science discourse alongside the development of theoretical understanding. Also based on Slater (2004), Slater and Mohan (2010a) compared ESL and science teachers' work on teaching science at the high school level, showing how each developed KSs in similar ways to help their students develop academic language and understandings, despite their noticeable differences in content.

Explaining causal connections is a critical aspect of expressing science knowledge, as argued in Halliday and Martin (1993), but being able to construct causality goes beyond science itself into the development of academic discourse in general. Mohan and Van Naerssen (1997) focused on the knowledge structure of PRINCIPLES to illustrate how causal language and meaning interact, or the connection between what is said and how that reflects the theoretical model of causality the speaker may hold. Slater (1998) focused on five explanations of the water cycle selected from a total of 50 texts, showing how there was patterned variation in the way different people constructed their explanations, with some leaning towards sequential explanations and others towards texts that utilized resources that were strongly causal (PRINCIPLES). Slater's study, reported in Mohan and Slater (2004b), has important implications for assessment as it argued that raters intuitively noted a difference between the sequentially constructed water cycle and the causal construction, admitting that the causal line was more "sophisticated" or at "a higher caliber" (p. 265), but that their traditional language-based rubric could not account for this difference. Mohan and Slater recommended that tools to assess causal discourse be based on a theory that views language as resource rather than language as rule. Also making use of water cycle texts written from a visual prompt, Mohan et al. (2006) looked comparatively at the linguistic features of the knowledge structures of SEQUENCE and PRINCIPLES in their discussion of 36 texts written in English, Japanese, and Mandarin. The authors argued that texts that reflect causal meanings (i.e., PRINCIPLES) exemplify the features of scientific discourse more than do texts that show sequential meanings, and that in all three of these languages there were examples of both causal and sequential texts. Their study points to the value of looking at common language features in the first and target languages as well as the content being taught and the multimodal possibilities that can link the various languages.

Many of these observations closely connect to the concept of a developmental path of cause, as presented in Mohan, Slater, Luo, and Jaipal, 2002, and described in Slater and Mohan (2010b). This path was hypothesized as a result of a corpus examination of the linguistic resources of causality appearing in a 70,000- to 75,000-word sample from a science encyclopedia for eight- to fourteen-year-old children and the same sized sample from one designed for adult readers. Slater and Mohan (2010b) used this developmental path of cause to examine students' oral explanations and argued that they followed a similar path. The authors analyzed the language features of various oral explanations to see how they reflected sequence, cause, and proof.

This developmental path of cause was further put to the test through a mixed-methods study by Ma and Slater (2015), which examined 58 essays and compare scores by *Criterion*® (an automated writing evaluation system) with the path. Their findings led credence to having teachers use the path with their students to help align classroom assessment with *Criterion*. The same authors (Ma and Slater, 2016) used a mixed-method approach to compare AWE scores to ratings based on teachers' intuitions as well as to scores based on the course assignment rubric. The qualitative aspect, which utilized focus group interviews, suggested that the developmental path of cause can help teachers justify their intuitions about the language of PRINCIPLES. The quantitative data showed that teachers trained to use the path supported the scores generated by AWE (*Criterion*) better than did the scores based on the rubric.

With regards to modeling causal discourse in teaching within science content, Mohan and Beckett (2003) analyzed the causal discourse that occurred among a teacher and three Japanese exchange students in an intensive English program (IEP) at a Western Canadian university as they talked about "the brain." The authors showed how the teacher used functional recasts to scaffold students in their development of more sophisticated causal explanations.

Mathematics

One of the first studies that examined the use of the KF in math classes was an MA study carried out at the University of British Columbia during the Vancouver School Board project. Hunter (1990) collected and analyzed ESL students' questions in a high school ESL math class designed to transition students into mainstream math classes. In examining the context of the discourse, the author looked at the form of the question and its intended meaning and categorized each one based on the type of knowledge (the knowledge structure) sought. His findings shed light on how students were learning math and how they could be helped to ask better questions that may assist in further developing their math knowledge.

Most of the later publications targeting the research on math from a KF perspective have been led by Jingzi Huang. Huang, Normandia, and Greer (2005) examined the knowledge structures that were constructed by a teacher and her 25 students (two blocks of classes with 12 students in one and 13 in the other) in the talk of a secondary math class. Their findings showed that although all six KSs appeared in the teacher discourse, mostly DESCRIPTION, SEQUENCE, and CHOICE (the KSs of action) appeared in the oral discourse of the students. Moreover, efforts by the teacher to elicit the theory-level KSs (CLASSIFICATION, PRINCIPLES, and EVALUATION) were largely unsuccessful.

Moving from oral to written discourse, Huang and Normandia (2007) examined the writing produced by 11 students in a secondary math class, focusing on two texts: one with the lowest score and the other with the highest. The authors offered evidence that the "expression of conceptual understanding and procedural knowledge requires the use of certain linguistic features" (p. 309), and thus the lack of these features may impact a student's ability to express their mathematical understandings. The authors recommended that teachers make these features explicit for students. In Huang and Normandia (2008), the authors presented an alternative to taking a key-word approach to understanding and solving mathematical word problems. They advocated having teachers use a set of seven questions derived from the KF to help students find connections between language and content (mathematical) knowledge. Finally, Huang, Berg, Siegrist, and Damsri (2017) used a knowledge structure analysis approach to examine the discourse of student writing collected by six teachers in a professional development program that aimed to raise the teachers' linguistic sensitivity. Their findings indicated that this analysis and the training not only added to the teachers' knowledge and skills but was directly transferred from these teachers to their students, who showed growth in the use of academic language.

Social Studies and Related Fields

Whereas the science fields set the context for much of the research on teaching the KF, the areas that reflect social studies content—history, geography, political science, sociology—were also notable in number, especially in the early days of the KF. Early and Tang (1991) used history content to illustrate how to develop and use key visuals (KVs), arguing that their results with three contexts of students (eighth grade, eleventh grade, and transitional ESL science) in two secondary schools suggested that using KVs can help ELLs read and write content-based texts. At roughly the same time, Tang (1991a) carried out a two-part study on the value of KF-based key visuals in a seventh-grade social studies class in which students were learning about systems of government. The first part utilized a pretest–posttest nonequivalent-control group quasi-experimental design, and the second carried out semi-structured interviews with 45 students, 22 in the experimental group and 23 in the control group. She found that teaching students how to construct KVs from texts helped the students understand the content presented and recall more of it. The interviews also showed that the majority of students agreed that the KVs helped them in their learning.

Tang (1992a) focused on the KS of CLASSIFICATION with sixth- and seventh-grade students, using a tree for one group (graphic group) to recap a text about the system of government in various countries, and highlighting vocabulary along with an oral review of the text for the non-graphic group. Her findings supported her argument that the use of graphics helped facilitate comprehension of the content, and the majority of the students found KVs helpful. Similarly, Tang (1997a; see also Tang, 1992b) outlined the procedure for using the KF and KVs in a seventh-grade social studies class, arguing that adopting such an approach can help students understand the content and develop the language to read and write academic texts.

A qualitative year-long study by Sampson (1998) compared the teaching of the KF by two experienced trained-in-KF teachers (one seventh-grade content teacher in social studies and one ESL support teacher) to one novice KF social studies teacher to explore the role of experience in teaching the KF, and how content teachers and language teachers can collaborate more easily and to the benefit of the students, using the KF as an organizational heuristic. Her findings suggested that whereas the experienced KF teachers used the KF in their long-term planning in the four skills (reading, writing, listening, and speaking) and used it to collaborate with each other, the teacher who was less familiar with the KF was more likely to use parts of the KF for specific short-term writing tasks.

Beckett, Gonzalez, and Schwartz (2004) made use of the KF to design an advanced-level IEP writing course integrated with a first-year sociology course. In analyzing the course requirements from a KF perspective, the ESL instructors came to the understanding that the sheltered writing courses they were familiar with were inadequate in content-based language teaching due to their focus on sentence-level grammar practice. The teachers also realized the usefulness of KF-based key visuals in their teaching.

Finally, Thorley and Vasquez (2011) briefly described the implementation of the KF in a Year 7 geography class in West London (UK). The authors listed the benefits of the approach for students as giving them opportunities to produce well-structured and original texts with appropriate vocabulary. Teachers found that the KF provided a systematic way to focus on the integration of language and content, and highlighted the role of language in learning and the strategies needed to develop students' academic language ability.

Literature

Although there has been some work that has suggested a KF approach to literature teaching (see, for example, Early & Marshall, 2008), the research explicitly making use of the KF to teach this subject is quite limited. Early (1991) advocated combining the KF with wordless picture books to develop primary school-aged ESL students' oral and written language across various text types. She argued that the books encourage students to work with language in a coherent, cohesive way that fosters confidence.

Early, Potts, and Mohan (2005) presented an example of the collaboration between an ESL teacher and a sixth-grade classroom teacher as they designed and taught a unit that would help students develop and language and content knowledge regarding literature, specifically *The Lion, the Witch, and the Wardrobe* (Lewis, 1950) and two versions of *The Three Little Pigs*. The authors discussed the unit in terms of the KF, which they heralded as a tool to examine the *what* of the unit (the language and content) and the Teaching and Learning Model (building background knowledge on prior understandings, interacting the new knowledge socially and critically, and consolidating new knowledge in discourse) to examine the *how*. They offered examples that showed how students were able to acquire both a deep understanding of the content and the language required to talk about these understandings.

For her MA thesis research, Bingham Brunner (2016) carried out a qualitative case study to examine KF-based activities designed to teach adult ELLs about the book *The Giver* (Lowry, 1993), focusing on the students' perceptions of these activities. The analysis was based on 16 students who completed workshops, a survey, and an interview. Her findings suggested that the level of student ability seemed to correlate with the perception of difficulty of the KS, with the CHOICE activity presenting more problems for lower-level students than for higher-level ones. Overall, the author heralded the explicit instruction of the language of the knowledge structures to help the students articulate their ideas.

As the final example of using the KF for teaching literature, Javed (2011) questioned whether the explicit teaching of KSs could facilitate poetry reading by two secondary ESL students. The author detailed the steps taken in the unit plan and concluded that the use of the KF helped teach integrated language and content, and the key visuals aided in the students' comprehension.

Combining Subject Areas

Examining the subject areas across the K–12 curriculum and highlighting the demands of various content areas was an important step in the development of the KF, as mentioned earlier in this chapter. As stated in the early section of this chapter, Early, Thew, and Wakefield (1986) examined the curriculum guidelines from the province of British Columbia and many of their recommended textbooks and found that the six KSs occurred regularly, both in texts and as thinking skills that teachers needed to develop in their students. Fourteen years later, Huang and Mullinix (2002) compared the various content areas of the New Jersey Core Curriculum Content Standards of 1996 and 2002 using the KF and progress indicators. Their analysis revealed that the Standards required students to be able to use all six knowledge structures across the content areas, with high demands for the theory-level knowledge structures of PRINCIPLES and EVALUATION over SEQUENCE and CHOICE. The authors recommended ensuring that teachers be aware of the language needs of these knowledge structures and provide activities for their students to engage in the language and literacy demands of the various content areas.

The existence of these KSs across curricular content have prompted some researchers to look at a variety of content areas or to examine classes in which teachers were teaching different subjects. For example, in her doctoral dissertation research, Tang (1989) explored the use of KVs in two seventh-grade ESL multi-subject classes (n=56), using both an ethnographic approach and a pretest–posttest nonequivalent-control group design. Her results indicated that students needed teacher guidance to realize the potential of key visuals of the KSs to improve comprehension. This finding was also noted in Tang (1991b), which focused on ELLs' use of key visuals in both reading and presenting. She reported that not only did students **not** typically attend to the visuals in their reading materials, they also chose **not** to use them in their presentations.

Tang (1994a) examined the collaborative teaching of a KF unit that combined the learning of the novel *Alone on the Atlantic: The Clare Francis Story* (Vincent, 1982) and developing computer literacy. Eleven secondary ESL students were able to understand and enjoy the novel, improve their ability to use language to show their understanding of the novel, and learn computer skills at the same time. A similar study based on data from seventh-grade social studies classes and secondary science/computer science classes (Tang, 2001) detailed how teachers used the KF, concluding that the KF allowed for the successful learning of language and content in both cases, as the teacher explicitly focused on knowledge structures, the linguistic resources used to signal them, and the visual representations of these knowledge structures.

Tang (1997b) reported on a study carried out in a Hong Kong prevocational secondary school that offered a wide variety of academic and technical subjects such as accounting, fashion design, and metalwork. She demonstrated that KSs and the graphics that represent them are common across both English and Cantonese textbooks and thus Hong Kong students were able to understand meaning through graphics when the content was presented in English. Tang concluded that if the use of graphics facilitated content understanding, they could be used successfully to teach the discourse of that content in any language, be it Cantonese or English. As mentioned earlier, Tong (2004) worked with a similar concept, examining how high school students could learn in their first language and improve their ability to construct CLASSIFICATION knowledge in the second.

Henry (1989) used a qualitative analysis of classroom discourse to examine vocabulary teaching in a sixth-grade ESL classroom, focusing on the KSs of CLASSIFICATION and DESCRIPTION, both as they were used in specific contexts as well as explicitly teaching the metalanguage of the two KSs. Among other results, the author found that when the teachers used language associated with a particular KS, the students were better able to learn the content-relevant words within the discourse.

In her MA study, Grant (1995) carried out action research with sixth- and seventh-grade ELLs using the KF to learn various content areas. She revealed that students found key visuals easier to use than text samples when working with knowledge structures, and that they found it easier to construct a key visual from a text than to create a text from a key visual. Overall, Grant found that students at that age level can benefit from being introduced to the KF, an observation that was also argued by McPherson (2007), who advocated the use of Mohan's KF by teacher-librarians working with ELLs so that they could help familiarize them with the types of knowledge being constructed by academic texts.

Evans (2000) documented a qualitative case study that examined a class of fifth- and sixth-grade students being taught patterns in math and characterizations in literature. The units were designed collaboratively by a content teacher and an ESL resource teacher using the KF. The author found that students had more trouble with the patterns (math) unit, speculating that prior classroom experience and the link between everyday and technical language were critical issues, given that a similar KS (DESCRIPTION) was being examined. In other words, whereas students had little trouble drawing on everyday experience and language to describe characters, they needed to know technical language when describing patterns in math.

Slater and Butler (2015) used the KF and the concept of a social practice to compare the oral discourse of teaching and learning in a sixth-grade physical education class with that of two science classes, one at the primary school level (Mohan & Slater, 2005) and one at the secondary level (Mohan & Slater, 2006). The authors noted that because both physical education and science involve the idea of "activity" and with the carefully planned teaching of these activities, both could be analyzed in terms of knowledge structures that follow similar patterns across content areas. They argued that focusing on similarities rather than differences, which the KF advocates, can help ELLs master content while developing language.

Mohan, Slater, Beckett, and Tong (2015) discussed the development of language through activity as a social practice (doing and knowing) in both a magnetism unit for young children and a marketing unit for adults in a community college in Hong Kong. The authors argued that student activities—consistent with Dewey's view of activity as socio-semantic and meaning-making and within the concept of "field"—assist in improving students' understanding of the content as well as their ability to produce discourse that shows that understanding.

Gleason, Berg, and Huang (2018) used oral data from middle and high school math, science, social studies, and language arts classrooms to explore the differences in both teacher and student discourse, and to examine how knowledge is constructed through oral interactions. The authors focused on the knowledge structures of CHOICE and EVALUATION, recognizing that whereas CHOICE can be easy for students to enact, justifying these choices requires more theoretical knowledge. There were fewer student examples of EVALUATION discourse in the math and science data than in the social studies and language arts data. The authors argued that students need opportunities to produce the language of EVALUATION so as to be able to position themselves as experts as well as to show their understanding of the theory that supports the practical tasks they are engaged in.

In What Other Ways Has the KF Been Examined?

Collaboration

With the Vancouver School Board project requiring ESL resource specialists to work with classroom teachers, early work carried out by graduate students looked at the role of the KF in the collaborative process. Mention has already been made of Tang (1994a) in which there was mutual cooperation and support between an ESL teacher and a content teacher in the creation and teaching of a secondary school unit. Another example is Dempsey (1994), who offered a qualitative examination of the collaborative planning of KF-based units by an ESL specialist and six content teachers over a four-month period (within a two-year study). The author addressed this planning within the frame of school cultures and systemic demands, reflecting on the need to identify broad goals and create a shared vision. She established that successful collaboration worked best when it was voluntary and had support with trust and joint sharing. She also listed *enjoyable* as an important feature in the successful collaboration around the creation of KF units.

Also in a qualitative case study, Hurren (1994) examined the collaborative planning process between a classroom teacher and an ESL specialist. She documented a consistent focus on goals throughout the planning process, with key visuals playing a major organizational role. The author stated that the KF provided a useful structure for planning tasks and key visuals, concluding that the KF is effective at both the unit-planning and task-planning levels.

Materials Development

As noted above, Hurren (1994) observed that the KF provided a useful visual for planning tasks and units when collaborating. Others have made similar claims. For example, working from a Japanese college context in an introductory course about political science, Stewart (1997) noted that "in normal circumstances it is not overly time consuming to plan units with the KF" (p. 11). The author continued: "By creating and examining our activities through the KF, we found it easier to isolate and present content and language points for each" (p. 12). He concluded by saying "The knowledge framework gives instructor teams from different disciplines a way to discuss and plan common lessons in a comprehensive way. This leads to highly structured lessons where content and language learning are naturally combined. The final result of this process is the development of a fully integrated classroom in which it is often not clear who is the language instructor and who is the content instructor" (p. 18).

Hooper (1996) detailed a seven-lesson KF-based unit plan on the classification of vertebrates for a seventh-grade class of 28 students, 18 of whom were categorized as ELLs. The unit was taught by a classroom teacher and an ESL support teacher. The author not only presented a description of each lesson and its tasks, but also offered examples of the relevant student discourse as groups carried out the tasks. Hooper also offered suggestions for improving the unit for future use.

Several graduate students have produced KF-based unit plans as part of their MA programs. Bensend (2011) used the KF as an organizational tool for her English language immersion program materials targeted towards sixth- to eighth-grade non-English-speaking students. Pan (2011) developed a five-lesson unit based on the KF to teach static electricity to secondary ELLs. Walton (2013) created a 21-lesson KF-based unit designed for a blended online (Google Docs) and face-to-face delivery to intermediate-level students in a university intensive English program. The focus of the unit was on both the development of writing skills and technology use, with an emphasis on student collaboration. McCulloch (2015) developed 15 lessons plus five additional KF-based activities for a literature unit designed to teach language and *The Giver* (Lowry, 1993) to Korean EFL undergraduates. And finally, Turley (2016) developed KF-based materials to teach ESL parents how to enroll their children in grade school. Moreover, in their book on teaching language across the curriculum, Cummins and Early (2015) offer valuable suggestions and ideas for lessons that can help develop language and content knowledge within language arts, math, science, and social studies. Each chapter includes teaching vignettes that offer ideas for teaching as well. The final chapter offers a template for instructional planning that teachers or materials developers can use in planning KF-based units.

At the higher education level, Slater and Beckett (2019) detailed a project-based unit plan that emphasizes the integration of language, content, and technology to teach international students how to apply for US graduate school programs. The authors argued that by combining the Project Framework (Beckett & Slater, 2005) and Mohan's KF, students can clearly see how their language is developing through their engagement in the application project.

Finally, Early (1989) offers a step-by-step approach to creating KF-based key visuals from texts as well as how to use them to teach their ESL students.

Professional Development

Whereas there has been much professional development on the KF over the past 35 years, there has been surprisingly little actually published on the topic. Bucking this trend and using a mixed-methods approach, Berg and Huang (2015) researched the use of the KF in teachers' professional development. Twenty-three teachers (13 in K–6 and 10 in 7–12) with experience varying between one and twelve years participated. The authors found that after the training, the teachers' unit plans and instructional practice showed that they were paying more attention to students' language development—not just vocabulary but at the sentence and discourse level—in the process of content teaching. They stated that the KF "serves both as a theoretical base for systematic integration of language and content and as a practical guide to academic task analysis, instructional design and assessment implementation" (p. 4). Added to this was previously mentioned Huang, Berg, Siegrist, and Damsri (2017), in which teachers' linguistic sensitivity was raised through training and the KF analysis of their students' texts, Huang and Laskowski (2014), and Huang, Berg, Romero, and Walker (2016).

From an EFL teaching perspective, Kong (2008) described work that blended the KF, text structures, and language objectives in an effort to teach late immersion secondary students successfully in Hong Kong. The work focused on highlighting teachers' awareness of content/language relationships and how form is connected to meaning, a necessary understanding for teachers to successfully carry out content-based instruction. Kong stated, "A language aware teacher can use **and** explicitly draw students' attention to the key language… A planned and targeted approach to language use of this kind provides students with focused language input that supports content-language learning" (p. 126–27; emphasis in original).

Project-based Learning

Bringing the KF into project-based language teaching is a recent development. Slater (2020) examined a technology-integrated project-based intensive English program at a Midwestern university, showing that although the students could easily see how much content they were learning, they struggled to identify any explicit teaching of language, an observation that had been made previously (see Beckett, 1999; Beckett & Slater, 2018). Slater highlighted how the instructors were in fact using the language of the KF in their tasks, arguing that had they been more familiar with the approach, they might have helped the students see how language was being developed through their participation in projects. In other words, Slater was advocating for the inclusion of a functional linguistic theory within project-based learning. Slater and Beckett (2019), offering a potential unit plan to show how this can be done, advocated combining the KF with project-based learning.

Slater, Beckett, and Aufderhaar (2006) offered the KF as a way to *assess* project-based learning by summarizing literature that focused on the various knowledge structures and offering data examples to illustrate their ideas. The authors argued that because doing a project means being involved in a social practice, and a social practice can be analyzed through the KF, analyses can be used to assess students' development of both language and content understanding. The chapter offers potential graphics for use in evaluating this development and calls for educators to put the assessment model to the test in classrooms. Also focusing on the assessment of project-based learning and teaching, Chen and Hirch (2020) involved the KF as a way to evaluate critical thinking competence in their model for assessing technology-infused project-based language learning. They encouraged teachers using a project-based approach to consider the types of knowledge structures the various tasks in the project involve and the language required to successfully work with these tasks. As with Slater, Beckett, and Aufderhaar (2006), the authors here encouraged the assessment of tasks as process as well as the products that students create through the project approach.

Online Teaching

Despite the popularity of CALL and online delivery, there has been a dearth of research on the use of the KF with computers and the internet. As mentioned earlier, Moore (1998) used key visuals associated with knowledge structures to help develop students' knowledge as they searched the internet and took notes. Other than that, Mohan and Luo (2005) presented online discussion as a relatively new social practice that the authors argued cannot be sufficiently well researched using a second language acquisition perspective but can benefit greatly from an examination using SFL in general and the KF specifically. Reviewing a number of recent studies, they suggested that a functional perspective can allow educators and researchers to track the development of academic discourse in new social practices and registers, such as those occurring within CALL.

Assessment

As mentioned above, the KF has been addressed as a way to assess project-based language teaching (e.g., Slater, Beckett, & Aufderhaar, 2006; Chen & Hirch, 2020) and to evaluate academic discourse—particularly causal—in writing (e.g., Ma & Slater, 2015, 2016) through the concept of the developmental path of cause (see Slater & Mohan, 2010b). Outside of causal discourse assessment is Mohan and Huang (2002), which reported on a qualitative study of 73 fifth- and sixth-grade (aged 9–11) students who were mostly native speakers of English learning Chinese as a foreign language twice a week, with data collected over an eight-month period. The unit concerned the theme of personal information and the analysis of student writing examined specifically the KSs of SEQUENCE and CLASSIFICATION. The discourse analysis offered examples that can inform educators about how they can use the KF to assess students' meaning-making ability with these two KSs.

There has also been mention of the issues involved in testing, presented in Mohan and Slater (2004b), where rubrics were unable to reveal what raters intuitively noticed about the sophistication of the texts. Also raising questions about issues in assessment that a KF analysis can reveal, Mohan (1998) analyzed eight examples of the OPI (Oral Proficiency Interview) using the KF, showing how an examination of knowledge structures can reveal issues with the assessment of the interview and in the ways that the discourse is co-constructed between the interviewer and the test-taker.

Moving from a more standardized testing format to classroom formative assessment, Leung and Mohan (2004) focused on the KS of CHOICE in data collected in two multi-ethnic fourth-grade classes near London, England, showing how a KS analysis of classroom discourse can provide a theoretically informed approach to assessment.

Cotos and Chung (2019) used the KF to ascertain whether an assessment tool (the TOEFL iBT® speaking test) elicited the same or similar types of functional language that international teaching assistants (ITA) use in labs, recitations, and lectures. Their findings from a quantitative analysis of the two corpora supported the assumption that the tasks in the speaking test indeed prompted the same kinds of language apparent in the ITA discourse (see also Cotos & Chung, 2018).

Cross-cultural Understanding

There has been some work done that highlights potential cross-cultural understandings as similarities or differences. One early study (Tang, 1994b) used the KF to examine the function of textbook illustrations in social studies textbooks from the seventh-grade level across three languages (Hong Kong Chinese, Japanese, and Mexican Spanish), then compared the illustrations in the Hong Kong textbook to a Canadian English textbook from the same level and content. Tang found that all textbooks were highly illustrated, with DESCRIPTION being by far the most common KS represented (89% to 94% across the four languages), and SEQUENCE and CLASSIFICATION represented only occasionally (1% to 7.5% and 1.5% to 5% respectively). PRINCIPLES, CHOICE, and EVALUATION were not represented as KVs in any of the four texts examined. These differences were not statistically significant at the 0.05 level, suggesting that the four languages used illustrations in very similar ways. Tang concluded that the similarities in KVs used across these four textbooks should compel teachers to make use of these graphics to enhance their ELLs' learning of content. She argued that students from these countries may already understand the function of the KVs presented in their first language and thus teachers can use these KVs to activate their students' memory schemata to facilitate learning in their second language.

Another examination of cross-cultural research using the KF was presented in Mohan et al. (2006) in their comparison of water cycle texts from English, Japanese, and Mandarin Chinese. Their findings lent support for a *language of science*, a form of discourse that had similar features across the three quite structurally and lexically different languages. Looking at resumé-writing practices of North Americans, Japanese, and Russians, Semenova (2000) focused on the knowledge structures of CHOICE and EVALUATION, noting that writers' choices strongly connected to the cultural and personal values they held.

Finally, Levis, Muller Levis, and Slater (2012) made use of the KF to analyze and compare the discourse of four American, four Indian, and six

Chinese teaching assistants at a large Midwestern university as they adapted a paragraph on energy into a short (four- to six-minute) lecture of the content. The analysis helped to highlight salient differences that can help educators clarify for international teaching assistants how the content has been organized by the original textbook so they may be able to parallel that structure in their lectures. The authors' analysis also illustrated differences in the linguistic resources used by the various teaching assistant groups to construct the relevant knowledge structures.

These two previous sections have offered summaries of the various articles that have been uncovered about the Knowledge Framework through a rigorous search of the literature. Findings of these articles together have shown the potential of the KF in teaching and researching various social practices that relate to education. Within these two sections, it can be seen that the vast majority of the articles have targeted teaching and learning at the kindergarten to twelfth-grade levels, including some that have looked at professional development for teachers at these levels. Relatively few have examined the use of the KF outside of these contexts. It is this lack of research that has prompted the creation of this volume. The next section will describe new work that focuses on the various ways the KF has been explored or implemented in contexts that involve higher academic participants and texts.

What is in this Volume?

In **Chapter 2**, Elena Cotos builds on her experience with her two oral language corpora (see Cotos & Chung, 2018, 2019) to describe in detail the methodological challenges of annotating the spoken texts produced by adult non-native speakers of English in teaching and testing contexts. She argues that the promise of KF-base corpus studies is huge, as such work can highlight the functional language that these speakers may require to improve their ability to communicate effectively as teachers.

Feedback plays a role in each of the next two chapters. In **Chapter 3**, Constant Leung analyzes a sample of student writing alongside tutor comments to argue that although there are no fixed or universal templates for teaching and learning disciplinary literacy, genre (e.g., Swales, 1990), argument (e.g., Toulmin, 1958/2003), and knowledge structures (e.g., Mohan, 1986) are concepts whose criteria are useful to provide insight into the construal of academic writing. Automated feedback is the focus of **Chapter 4**, which examines how university-level students perceive feedback in their writing of causal texts, discourse that falls within the knowledge structure of PRINCIPLES, although some writers also rely heavily on the linguistic resources of SEQUENCE (see, for example, Mohan & Slater, 2004b; Slater, 1998). In this chapter, authors Saricaoglu, Chukharev-Hudilainen, and Feng describe the differences perceived between text-level and sentence-level feedback with the aim of improving automated writing evaluation tools.

Carolyn Kristjánsson and Bernard A. Mohan in **Chapter 5** examine the role of CHOICE and EVALUATION in the social practice of academic coaching. Their chapter details two analyses; a macro-analysis examines the overall shape of the coaching session, highlighting choices/decisions and whether these are made or abandoned, drawing on the KF to guide the identification of the knowledge structures. A micro-level analysis is also presented, using Appraisal (Martin & White, 2005) to track potential connections between emotion and the ethical/moral dimension in the decision-making process.

CHOICE and EVALUATION are also at the core of **Chapter 6**, in which Mohan uses the KF to examine the social practice of voting from both the perspective of voter suppression and the Aristotelian political tradition of the voter as an engaged and responsible individual who uses ethical thought and purpose to choose a candidate. Mohan's objective is to show how a linguistic analysis can reveal values and evidence in the media and thus how it can play an important role in civics education at the adult level.

In **Chapter 7**, Zhi Li reveals disciplinary differences by examining lecture slides from six undergraduate courses in two broadly defined content areas: Engineering and Social Sciences. His analysis of the slides' text-based and visual-based knowledge structures shows that whereas there are differences in the frequencies of the knowledge structures across these two disciplines, there are similarities in their distributions. Given the importance of lecture slides in assisting students with content comprehension, Li's findings offer important implications for educators.

Also connecting lectures to text, Kim Becker and Xiaoping Liang offer a discourse analysis of a physics lecture given by a Chinese professor, comparing the causal meaning constructions to the same content as it is presented in the English-medium textbook being used in the course. Focusing on the knowledge structure of PRINCIPLES and using an up–down metaphor, **Chapter 8** reveals the variety of causal linguistic resources that the professor made use of in his primarily downward functional recasts to help explicate the content of the course textbook. The authors offer implications for the use of the KF when teaching international teaching assistants.

Continuing on the topic of functional recasts, Masaki and Emi Kobayashi examine the role of teacher's functional recasts in Japanese undergraduate students' constructions of the knowledge structure of PRINCIPLES in a content-based EFL course on intercultural communication. Building on Mohan and Beckett (2003), **Chapter 9** compares the efforts at uptake when the functional recasts were offered in oral contexts versus on written work and the differences are discussed with regards to key visuals, oral presentations, and language levels of the recasts.

The next four chapters examine the use of the KF in preservice and in-service teacher development programs. In **Chapter 10**, Stephanie Link and Jesse Gleason address the potential of online materials development in combination with the KF along with the teaching–learning cycle to heighten teachers' understanding of form–function connections and question whether this type of opportunity as a professional development program would transfer over into teachers' planning of curriculum. In the chapter, the authors evaluate the impact of such a program on ten participants in a graduate-level literacy development course. In **Chapter 11**, Jingzi Huang and Margaret Berg present findings from a mixed-methods approach to look at change over time in teachers' linguistic sensitivity and cultural responsiveness through training with the KF. The teachers in their study were regular classroom teachers in a variety of content areas who did not generally consider the teaching of language to be their responsibilities. Their findings strengthen the arguments in favor of including linguistic and cultural awareness in professional development programs. In **Chapter 12**, Jesse Gleason and Elena Schmitt track 19 graduate-level preservice teachers as they engaged in ethnographic observations in K–12 contexts after they had been trained to use the KF. The preservice teachers transcribed and analyzed the discourse they had collected during their observations and reflected on what they had noticed. Findings across the 19 ethnographers revealed patterns of knowledge structures that are used in constructing knowledge and teaching. The authors offer implications for using the KF in tandem with classroom observations in teacher training programs. **Chapter 13** has Amy Walton and Gulbahar H. Beckett adopting a qualitative case study approach to examine a preservice teacher development program in which a group of 17 undergraduate students participated in a four-week unit on learning the KF by using it to create a project-based unit of their choosing. The authors discuss the students' reflections on their understandings of project-based teaching with the KF and highlight the issues and challenges that arose, offering implications for future teaching of KF-informed project-based teaching and learning.

The next two chapters in this volume examine the use of the KF in foreign language contexts in which explicit focus on aspects of the KF was carried out. In **Chapter 14**, Esther Ka-man Tong, Cecilia Fung-Kan Pun, and Phoebe Siu discuss the effectiveness of using the KF to carry out a needs analysis for the academic literacy demands of an Engineering program in an English-medium college in Hong Kong. A knowledge structure analysis was used to identify the cognitive, linguistic, and multimodal needs of Engineering students and then to plan instruction for these program-specific needs. In **Chapter 15**, Hong Ma and Jian Zhou report on a qualitative case study of a class of 39 medical students as they took a one-semester course which explicitly taught the KF and select SFL-based concepts. Using the linguistic features of the KF and an SFL-informed discourse analysis of the students' writing samples composed before, during, and after the instruction of the KF, the authors argued that such instruction was effective in moving the students towards more academic ways of constructing their understandings.

To complete the volume, Diane Potts moves the KF from its previous work on K–12 unit planning to a curriculum design tool for higher education courses, illustrating this through examples from both English as a second language and English as a foreign language contexts. **Chapter 16** employs the concept of textual trajectories (Maybin, 2017) and highlights the KF's relevance to issues associated with this concept.

The present chapter has offered the most comprehensive and up-to-date summary of the various articles, chapters, and graduate products that have been published on the KF from countries such as Canada, China, Germany, Japan, Korea, the UK, and the US. It has accentuated the KF's power to promote and support creativity in the design and implementation of integrated language-and-content teaching and research. The following 15 chapters further aim to bring up to date our understanding of the myriad ways in which the KF has been used—and continues to be used—within higher education contexts, reinforcing its ability for versatility. This latest work opens up exciting new frontiers for the KF in areas such as project-based language learning, corpus analysis and its applications, needs analyses, writing instruction/feedback, and teaching with/through technology as well as new information on less explored social practices such as voting and coaching. The hope of the volume is to spark further interest in researching how, with the help of Mohan's KF, various social practices both inside and outside of educational activities are linguistically constructed so that we and future educators can help our students understand how our expanding language resources can help us become socialized into whatever social practices we hope to engage in.

References

Beckett, G.H. (1999). *Project-based instruction in a Canadian secondary school's ESL classes: Goals and evaluations.* Unpublished doctoral dissertation. University of British Columbia. Retrieved from https://circle.ubc.ca/bitstream/id/24487/ubc_1999-463176.pdf

Beckett, G.H., Gonzalez, V., & Schwartz, H. (2004). Content-based ESL writing curriculum: A language socialization model. *NABE Journal of Research and Practice, 2*(1), 161–175.

Beckett, G.H., & Slater, T. (2005). The project framework: A tool for language, content, and skills integration, *ELT Journal, 59*(2), 108–116.

Beckett, G.H., & Slater, T. (2018). Project-based learning and technology. In J. Liontas (Ed.), *The TESOL encyclopedia of English language teaching.* John Wiley and Sons, Inc. DOI:10.1002/9781118784235.eelt0427

Bensend, A. (2011). *Tales from English Island: A task-based English language immersion program.* Unpublished Creative Component, Iowa State University, Ames, Iowa.

Berg, M.A., & Huang, J. (2015). Improving in-service teachers' effectiveness: K–12 academic literacy for the linguistically diverse. *Functional Linguistics, 2.* DOI 10.1186/s40554-015-0017-6

Bingham Brunner, H. (2016). The Giver *as content-based reading instruction: Student beliefs about using literature for ESL.* Unpublished MA study, Iowa State University, Ames, Iowa.

Chen, M., & Hirch, R.R. (2020). A research-based framework for assessing technology-infused PBLL. In G.H. Beckett & T. Slater (Eds.), *Global perspectives on project-based language learning, teaching, and assessment: Key approaches, technology tools, and frameworks* (pp. 224–243). Routledge.

Cotos, E., & Chung, Y-R. (2018). *Domain description: Validating the interpretation of the TOEFL iBT® speaking scores for international teaching assistant screening and certification purposes.* (TOEFL Research Report No. RR-85). Educational Testing Service. https://doi.org/10.1002/ets2.12233

Cotos, E., & Chung, Y-R. (2019). Functional language in curriculum genres: Implications for screening international teaching assistants. *Journal of English for Academic Purposes, 41,* 100766.

Cummins, J., & Early, M. (2015). *Big ideas for expanding minds: Teaching English language learners across the curriculum.* Pearson Canada Inc.

Curren, R. (2010). Aristotle's educational politics and the Aristotelian renaissance in philosophy of education, *Oxford Review of Education, 36*(5), 543–559.

Dempsey, J.L. (1994). *Collaborative planning to integrate language and content instruction: A case study.* Unpublished MA study, University of British Columbia, Vancouver, Canada. https://dx.doi.org/10.14288/1.0099128

Early, M. (1989). Using key visuals to aid ESL students' comprehension of content classroom texts. *Reading–Canada–Lecture, 7*(4), 202–212.

Early, M. (1990a). Enabling first and second language learners in the classroom. *Language Arts, 67*, 567–575.

Early, M. (1990b). ESL beginning literacy: A content-based approach. *TESL Canada Journal, 7*(2), 82–93.

Early, M. (1991). Using wordless picture books to promote second language learning. *ELT Journal, 45*(3), 245–251.

Early, M. (2001). Language and content in social practice: A case study. *The Canadian Modern Language Review, 58*(1), 156–179.

Early, M., & Hooper, H. (2001). Implementation of the Vancouver School Board's ESL initiatives. In B. Mohan, C. Leung, & C. Davison (Eds.), *English as a second language in the mainstream: Teaching, learning, and identity* (pp. 138–150). Pearson Education Limited.

Early, M., & Marshall, S. (2008). Adolescent ESL students' interpretation and appreciation of literary texts: A case study of multimodality. *The Canadian Modern Language Review, 64*(3), 377–397.

Early, M., Mohan, B.A. & Hooper, H.R. (1988). The Vancouver School Board language and content project. In J.M. Esling (Ed.), *Multicultural education and policy: ESL in the 90s* (pp. 107–125). Ontario Institute for Studies in Education.

Early, M., Potts, D., & Mohan, B. (2005). Teachers' professional knowledge in scaffolding academic literacies for English language learners. *Prospect, 20*(3), 63–76.

Early, M., & Tang, G.M. (1991). Helping ESL students cope with content-based texts. *TESL Canada Journal, 8*(2), 34–44.

Early, M., Thew, C., & Wakefield, P. (1986). *Integrating language and content instruction K-12: An E.S.L. resource book, Vol. 1.* Victoria, B.C. Ministry of Education, Modern Language Services Branch.

Evans, P.D. (2000). *Language and content in language arts and math: A case study.* Unpublished MA study, University of British Columbia, Vancouver, Canada. https://dx.doi.org/10.14288/1.0078178

Gleason, J., Berg, M., & Huang, J. (2018). Patterns of oral choice and evaluation across secondary content areas. *Language and Education, 32*(2), 93–111. doi.org/10.1080/09500782.2017.1391279

Grant, L.M. (1995). *Developing student awareness of knowledge structures: An exploratory teacher action study.* Unpublished MA study, University of British Columbia, Vancouver, Canada.

Halliday, M.A.K., & Martin, J.R. (1993). *Writing science: Literacy and discursive power.* The Falmer Press.

Hawkes, A.C. (1996). *Creating meaning within the process of integrating language and content: The action of using graphic representations of knowledge structures to adapt content to meet the needs of English second language learners.* Unpublished MA study, University of British Columbia, Vancouver, Canada. https://dx.doi.org/10.14288/1.0078127

Henry, D.A. (1989). *A case study of the acquisition of vocabulary by a group of ESL students examined from the perspective of knowledge structures.* Unpublished MA study, University of British Columbia, Vancouver, Canada. https://dx.doi.org/10.14288/1.0078309+

Hooper, H. (1996). Mainstream science with a majority of ESL learners: Integrating language and content. In J. Clegg (Ed.), *Mainstreaming ESL: Case studies in integrating ESL students into the mainstream classroom* (pp. 217–236). Multilingual Matters.

Huang, J. (2004). Socializing ESL students into the discourse of school science through academic writing. *Language and Education, 18*(2), 97–123.

Huang, J., Berg, M., Romero, D., & Walker, D. (2016). In-service teacher development for culturally and linguistically diverse responsive pedagogy. *Journal of the world Federation of Associations of Teacher Education, 1*(1), 80–101.

Huang, J., Berg, M., Siegrist, M., & Damsri, C. (2017). Impact of a functional linguistic approach to teacher development on content area student writing. *International Journal of Applied Linguistics, 27*(2), 331–362. doi: 10.1111/ijal.12133

Huang, J., & Laskowski, T. (2014). Developing linguistic sensitivity of ESL teacher candidates for linguistically responsive instruction, *The International Journal of Literacies, 20*(2), 29–50.

Huang, J., & Morgan, G. (2003). A functional approach to evaluating content knowledge and language development in ESL students' science classification texts. *International Journal of Applied Linguistics, 13*(2), 234–262.

Huang, J., & Mullinix, B.B. (2002). *Content literacy and language development across the curriculum: What do core curriculum content standards have to say?* Paper presented at the National Reaching Conference 52nd Annual Meeting, Miami, Florida. ERIC Reproduction Number ED479206.

Huang, J., & Normandia, B. (2007). Learning the language of mathematics: A study of student writing. *International Journal of Applied Linguistics, 17*(3), 294–318.

Huang, J., & Normandia, B. (2008). Comprehending and solving word problems in mathematics: Beyond key words. In Z. Fang & M.J. Schleppegrell (Eds.), *Reading in secondary content areas: A language-based pedagogy* (pp. 64–83). University of Michigan Press.

Huang, J., Normandia, B., & Greer, S. (2005). Communicating mathematically: Comparison of knowledge structures in teacher and student discourse in a secondary math classroom. *Communication Education, 54*(1), 34–51. http://dx.doi.org/10.1080/14613190500044002

Hunter, L.M. (1990). *The ESL student in the mathematics classroom: Student questions as a mode of access to knowledge.* Unpublished MA study, University of British Columbia, Vancouver, Canada. https://dx.doi.org/10.14288/1.0078245

Hurren, P.J. (1994). *How do an ESL specialist and a classroom teacher collaboratively plan instruction which integrates language and content demands of tasks?* Unpublished MA study, University of British Columbia, Vancouver, Canada. https://dx.doi.org/10.14288/1.005486

Javed, S. (2011). Facilitating ESL poetry reading through knowledge structures. *The Free Library*. Retrieved from https://www.thefreelibrary.com/FacilitatingESLPoetryReadingThroughKnowledgeStructures.-a0306324544

Kong, S. (2008). Late immersion in Hong Kong: A pedagogical framework for integrating content-language teaching and learning. *The Journal of Asia TEFL, 5*(3), 107–132.

Lawrence, M. (1972). *Writing as a thinking process*. The University of Michigan Press.

Leung, C., & Mohan, B. (2004). Teacher formative assessment and talk in classroom contexts: Assessment *as* discourse and assessment *of* discourse. *Language Testing, 21*(3), 335–359.

Levis, J., Muller Levis, G., & Slater, T. (2012). Written English into spoken: A functional discourse analysis of American, Indian, and Chinese TA presentations. In G. Gorsuch (Ed.), *Working theories for TA and ITA development* (pp. 529–572). New Forums Press.

Lewis, C.S. (1950). *The lion, the witch and the wardrobe*. Geoffrey Bless.

Liew, E.C.Y. (1994). *Two approaches to writing laboratory reports in senior science: The Knowledge Framework and the Genre-based Approach to literacy*. Unpublished MA study, University of British Columbia, Vancouver, Canada. https://dx.doi.org/10.14288/1.0078124

Lowry, L. (1993). *The giver*. Houghton Mifflin.

Ma, H., & Slater, T. (2015). Using the developmental path of cause to bridge the gap between AWE scores and writing teachers' evaluations. *Writing and Pedagogy, 7*(2–3), 395–422. DOI:10.1558/wap.v7i2-3.26376

Ma, H., & Slater, T. (2016). Connecting Criterion scores and classroom grading contexts: A systemic functional linguistic model for teaching and assessing causal language. *CALICO Journal, 33*(1), 1–18. DOI:10.1558/cj.v33i1.26562

Martin, J. & White, P. (2005). *The language of evaluation: Appraisal in English*. Palgrave Macmillan.

Maybin, J. (2017). Textual trajectories: Theoretical roots and institutional consequences. *Text & Talk, 37*(4), 415–435. doi: 10.1515/text-2017-0011

McCulloch, M. (2015). *Using* The Giver *as a medium for content-based language learning*. Unpublished Creative Component, Iowa State University, Ames, Iowa.

McPherson, K. (2007). Fostering content area literacy. *Teacher Librarian, 35*(1), 65–68.

Mohan, B.A. (1969). *The relation between language and situational factors*. Unpublished PhD dissertation. University of London, UK.

Mohan, B.A. (1977). Towards a situational curriculum. In H.D. Brown, C.A. Yorio, & R.H. Crymes (Eds.), *Teaching and learning English as a second language: Trends in research and practice. On TESOL '77* (pp. 250–257). Teachers of English to Speakers of Other Languages.

Mohan, B.A. (1978). Relating language teaching and content teaching. *TESOL Quarterly, 13*(2), 171–182.

Mohan, B.A. (1986). *Language and content*. Addison-Wesley Publishing Company.

Mohan, B.A. (1989). Knowledge structures and academic discourse. *Word, 40*(1–2), 99–115, DOI: 10.1080/00437956.1989.11435799

Mohan, B.A. (1990). LEP students and the integration of language and content: Knowledge structures and tasks. Proceedings of the research symposium on limited English proficient students' issues (pp. 113–160). Office of Bilingual Education and Minority Language Affairs. ERIC No. 314 264.

Mohan, B. (1998). Knowledge structures in oral proficiency interviews for international teaching assistants. In R. Young & A.W. He (Eds.), *Talking and testing: Discourse approaches to the assessment of oral proficiency* (pp. 173–204). John Benjamins Publishing Company.

Mohan, B.A. (2001). The second language as a medium of learning. In B. Mohan, C. Leung, & C. Davison (Eds.), *English as a second language in the mainstream: Teaching, learning, and identity* (pp. 107–126). Pearson Education Limited.

Mohan, B. (2007). Knowledge structures in social practices. In J. Cummins & C. Davison (Eds.), *International handbook of English language teaching, Volume 15* (pp. 303–315). Springer.

Mohan, B. (2011). Social Practice and Register: Language as a Means of Learning. In E. Hinkel (Ed.), *Handbook of research in second language teaching and learning, Vol. 2* (pp. 57–74). Taylor & Francis.

Mohan, B., & Beckett, G.H. (2003). A functional approach to research on content-based language learning: Recasts in causal explanations. *Modern Language Journal, 87*(3), 421–432.

Mohan, B., & Huang, J. (2002). Assessing the integration of language and content in a Mandarin as a foreign language classroom. *Linguistics and Education, 13*(3), 405–433.

Mohan, B., & Luo, L. (2005). A systemic functional linguistics perspective on CALL. In J.L. Egbert & G.M. Petrie (Eds.), *CALL research perspectives* (pp. 86–96). Routledge.

Mohan, B., & Slater, T. (2004a). A knowledge framework for relating language and "content". *NALDIC Quarterly, 2*(1), 13–15.

Mohan, B., & Slater, T. (2004b). The evaluation of causal discourse and language as a resource for meaning. In J.A. Foley (Ed.), *Language, education, and discourse: Functional approaches* (pp. 255–269). Continuum.

Mohan, B., & Slater, T. (2005). A functional perspective on the critical "theory/practice" relation in teaching language and science. *Linguistics and Education, 16*(2), 151–172,

Mohan B., & Slater, T. (2006). Examining the theory/practice relation in a high school science register: A functional linguistic perspective. *Journal of English for Academic Purposes, 5* (2006), 302–316.

Mohan, B., & Slater, T. (2013). Systemisch-funktionales Lernen von Sprache und Fachinhalt: Aufbau sozialer Praxen. [Systemic-functional Learning of Language and subject content: Building of Social Practices]. In I. Gogolin, I. Lange, & H.H. Reich (Eds.), *Herausforderung Bildungssprache* [Academic Language as a Challenge] (pp. 257–271). FörMig-Edition 9. Waxmann Verlag.

Mohan, B., Slater, T., & Beckett, G., & Tong, E. (2015). Tasks as meaning-making activities: A functional approach. In M. Bygate (Ed.), *Domains and directions in the development of task-based language teaching: A decade of plenaries from the international conference* (pp. 157–192). John Benjamins Publishing Company.

Mohan, B., Slater, T., Kobayashi, M., Luo, L., Kobayashi, E., & Ji, K. (2006). Multimodal scientific representations across languages and cultures. In T. Royce & W. Boucher (Eds.), *New directions in the analysis of multimodal discourse* (pp. 275–298). Lawrence Erlbaum Associates.

Mohan, B., Slater, T., Luo, L., & Jaipal, K. (2002). *Developmental lexicogrammar of causal explanations in science.* Paper presented at the International Systemic Functional Linguistics Congress (ISFC29), Liverpool, UK.

Mohan, B. & Van Naerssen, M. (1997). Understanding cause–effect: Learning through language. *English Teaching Forum, 35*(4), 22–29.

Moore, R.R. (1998). *Supporting ESL learners' language and content development in a digital environment.* Unpublished MA study, University of British Columbia, Vancouver, Canada. https://dx.doi.org/10.14288/1.0078155

Pan, N. (2011). *Empowering ESL students in science through Knowledge Framework.* Unpublished Creative Component, Iowa State University, Ames, Iowa.

Sampson, B.L. (1998). *How three elementary teachers integrated language and content using the Knowledge Framework and how their LEP students responded.* Unpublished MA study, University of British Columbia, Vancouver, Canada. https://dx.doi.org/10.14288/1.007818

Semenova, D. (2000). *Resumes and choices: Analyzing the discourse of a decision-making activity.* Unpublished MA study, University of British Columbia, Vancouver, Canada.

Slater, T. (1998). *Evaluating causal discourse in academic writing.* Unpublished MA study, University of British Columbia, Vancouver, Canada. DOI:10.14288/1.0078184

Slater, T. (2004). *The discourse of causal explanations in school science.* Unpublished doctoral dissertation, University of British Columbia, Vancouver, Canada. DOI:10.14288/1.0078228

Slater, T. (2020). The Knowledge Framework: An organizational tool for highlighting the "LL" in technology-integrated PBLL. In G.H. Beckett & T. Slater (Eds.), *Global perspectives on project-based language learning, teaching, and assessment: Key approaches, technology tools, and frameworks* (pp. 185–203). Routledge.

Slater, T., & Beckett, G.H. (2019). Integrating language, content, technology, and skills development through project-based language learning: Blending frameworks for successful unit planning. *MEXTESOL Journal, 43*(1), 1–14. Retrieved from www.mextesol.net/journal/index.php?page=journal&id_article=5557

Slater, T., Beckett, G.H., & Aufderhaar, C. (2006). Assessing projects as second language and content learning. In G.H. Beckett & P. Chamness Miller (Eds.), *Project-based second and foreign language education: Past, present, and future* (pp. 241–260). Information Age Publishing, Inc.

Slater, T., & Butler, J.I. (2015). Examining connections between the physical and the mental in education: A systemic functional linguistic analysis of PE teaching and learning. *Linguistics and Education, 30,* 12–25.

Slater, T., & Gleason, J. (2011). Integrating language and content: The Knowledge Framework. *The Conference Proceedings of MIDTESOL: Gateway to Global Citizenship.* Retrieved from http://www.midtesol.org/docs/MIDTESOLProceedings_2011.pdf

Slater, T., & Mohan, B. (2010a). Cooperation between science teachers and ESL teachers: A register perspective. *Theory into Practice, 49*(2), 91–98.

Slater, T., & Mohan, B. (2010b). Towards systematic and sustained formative assessment of causal explanations in oral interactions. In A. Paran & L. Sercu (Eds.), *Testing the untestable in language education* (pp. 256–269). Multilingual Matters.

Slater, T., & Mohan, B. (2019). The Knowledge Framework approach to developing language and content. In J.I. Liontas (Ed.), *The TESOL encyclopedia of English language teaching.* John Wiley and Sons, Inc. DOI: 10.1002/9781118784235.eelt0965

Stewart, T. (1997). *Integrating language and content instruction: A framework to guide cross-disciplinary team teaching.* Miyazaki International College. (ERIC Document Reproduction Service No. ED 403 751.

Swales, J. (1990). *Genre analysis: English in academic and research settings.* Cambridge University Press.

Tang, G.M. (1989). *Graphic representation of knowledge structures in ESL student learning.* Unpublished doctoral dissertation, University of British Columbia, Vancouver, Canada. https://dx.doi.org/10.14288/1.0055217

Tang, G.M. (1991a) The role and value of graphic representation of knowledge structures in ESL learning: An ethnographic study. *TESL Canada Journal, 9*(1), 29–41.

Tang, G.M. (1991b). ESL student perception of student-generated graphics a reading strategy. *Reflections on Canadian Literacy, 9*(1), 2–9.

Tang, G.M. (1992a). The effect of graphic representation of knowledge structures on ESL reading comprehension. *Studies in Second Language Acquisition, 14,* 177–195.

Tang, G.M. (1992b). Teaching content knowledge and ESOL in multicultural classrooms. *TESOL Journal, 2,* 8–12.

Tang, G.M. (1994a). Teacher collaboration in integrating language and content. *TESL Canada Journal, 11*(2), 100–116.

Tang, G.M. (1994b). Textbook illustrations: A cross-cultural study and its implications for teachers of language minority students. *The Journal of Educational Issues of Language Minority Students, 13,* 175–194.

Tang, G.M. (1997a). Teaching content knowledge and ESL in multicultural classrooms. In M.A. Snow & D.M. Brinton (Eds.), *The content-based classroom* (pp. 69–77). Longman.

Tang, G. (1997b). From graphic literacy across languages to integrating English and content teaching in vocational settings. *Hong Kong Journal of Applied Linguistics, 2*(1), 97–114.

Tang, G. (2001). Knowledge Framework and classroom action. In B. Mohan, C. Leung, & C. Davison (Eds.), *English as a second language in the mainstrea m: Teaching, learning, and identity* (pp. 127–137). Pearson Education Limited.

Thorley, P., & Vasquez, M. (2011). Classroom practice and pedagogy: Using the Knowledge Framework approach in the classroom. *NALDIC*. Retrieved from https://www.naldic.org.uk/Resources/NALDIC/Teaching%20and%20Learning/Documents/Using_Knowledge_Framework.pdf

Tong, E.K-M. (2004). *Science register across Chinese and English: The relation between learners' language production of scientific classification discourse in Chinese and English*. Unpublished MA study, University of British Columbia, Vancouver, Canada. https://dx.doi.org/10.14288/1.0078224

Toulmin, S. (1958/2003). *The uses of argument*. Cambridge University Press.

Turley, V. (2016). *Teaching adult ESL literacy and grade school enrollment using the Knowledge Framework*. Unpublished Creative Component, Iowa State University, Ames, Iowa.

Vincent, M. (1982). *Alone on the Atlantic: The Clare Francis story*. Heinemann.

Walton, A. (2013). *Blending learning, language, and knowledge: A unit for collaboration and academic writing with Google Docs*. Unpublished Creative Component, Iowa State University, Ames, Iowa.

About the Author

Tammy Slater, Associate Professor Emerita at Iowa State University, draws upon analytic methods from Systemic Functional Linguistics, including Mohan's Knowledge Framework, to investigate and understand the development of academic language through content-based and project-based teaching and learning, particularly in ways that inform and advance the field of literacy education for English language learners. She has published in several journals, including *Linguistics and Education* and *Theory into Practice*, and has co-authored chapters in several books. With Gulbahar H. Beckett, she edited *Global Perspectives on Project-based Language Learning, Teaching, and Assessment: Key Approaches, Technology Tools, and Frameworks* (2020).

2 Corpus-based Knowledge Framework Analysis: A Deliberation of Methodology and Outcomes

Elena Cotos

Abstract

The promise of the Knowledge Framework is immense, and its potential can be further realized through corpus studies. To obtain compelling and conclusive corpus-based findings, however, it is important to attend to major methodological challenges inherent to applying this framework to the analysis of large collections of text data. One such challenge is posed by qualitative corpus annotation, especially when the corpus is composed of spoken learner language. As a starting point to a scholarly forum on streamlining the methods and laying the groundwork for replicability and reproducibility of Knowledge Framework analysis, this chapter describes the methodology of a corpus-based project investigating the knowledge structures and language functions in spoken discourse produced by non-native speakers of English in two different types of situations—teaching and testing. In parallel with that, it provides rationales for specific procedural steps in view of latent challenges. The methodological rigor pursued in this study resulted in a set of tangible outcomes applicable to future research, including descriptors of functional realizations and linguistic instantiations of the knowledge structures and an annotation protocol. Additionally, these outcomes have important implications for language teaching and assessment, as they are indicative of the functional language ability that non-native English speakers need in order to be effective communicators in instructional settings.

Keywords: knowledge structures; language functions; spoken corpora; corpus annotation and analysis

Mohan's (1986) Knowledge Framework, grounded in Systemic Functional Linguistics (SFL), has motivated a wide array of studies that explored language and content by analyzing "doing" in the discourse related to thinking skills. Within the extensive scope of using the framework in teaching and language learning and assessment, much research has focused on classroom discourse produced by native and non-native speakers (Leung & Mohan, 2004; Levis, Levis, & Slater, 2012; Mohan & Beckett, 2003; Slater & Mohan, 2010). More recently, this framework has begun to make headway into advanced computational applications such as automated assessment (Gleason, 2014). Judging by the works presented in this volume, the promise of this framework is substantial, but to realize its full potential for technological innovations, it has to be applied to large amounts of linguistic data. Compiled in context-specific corpora, such data can represent register language varieties as well as verbal strategies used to accomplish the social purposes of genres and can thus enable analyses bridging the situation-based and text-based approaches distinguished by Mohan (1989).

Obtaining compelling findings from large collections of text data requires merging research methods in SFL and corpus linguistics. As these perspectives are rooted in different epistemologies, it is important to make principled decisions, establish valid analytic criteria, and carefully consider potential caveats that may arise when methods are integrated. Scholarly deliberations, similar to Moreno and Swales (2018) who reflect on the methodological challenges of corpus-based genre analysis, are thus needed to inform researchers interested in pursuing corpus-based Knowledge Framework analysis.

On a broader scale, thorough methodological accounts are important for conducting replicable and reproducible research, long-established themes of experimental science—replicability referring to the application of original methods to generate "new data, which can then ostensibly be analyzed for either confirmation or disconfirmation of previous results," and reproducibility referring to providing "access to the original data for independent analysis" for the same purpose (Berez-Kroeker et al., 2018, p. 4). The notion of reproducibility, which emerged as a primary concern for scientific rigor in computer science (Claerbout & Karrenbach, 1992; Donoho, 2010), is currently gaining prominence in linguistics as a data-driven social science, where linguists draw inferences about human cognition and social structure from studies of language use (Berez-Kroeker et al., 2018). Corpus-based Knowledge Framework analysis is in essence one such data-driven approach, and the research employing this approach should be both replicable and reproducible.

As a starting point to a scholarly forum on streamlining the methods and laying the groundwork for replicability and reproducibility of this up-and-coming research agenda, the current chapter describes the methodology of a corpus-based project investigating knowledge structures (KSs) and language functions (LFs) in spoken discourse produced by non-native speakers of English in two different types of situations—teaching and testing. In parallel with that, it provides rationales for specific procedural steps in view of latent challenges. Due to its main emphasis on methodology, the chapter is not a traditional research manuscript formally reporting results. Instead, it presents select outcomes that are applicable to future research and demonstrates the nature of the insights that can be generated from a corpus-based Knowledge Framework analysis driven by specific research objectives.

Project Background

This project was conducted at Iowa State University for the TOEFL® COE Research Program of the Educational Testing Service (ETS). It bridges SFL-driven discourse analysis and language assessment through a corpus-based investigation aimed to obtain validity evidence that would support a secondary use of the TOEFL iBT® Speaking test. Secondary use here refers to using scores from this test for the purpose of screening or certification of international teaching assistants (ITAs) in English-medium universities. Because the test scores need to be interpreted in relation to the target domain (i.e., whether the speaking skills used in instructional contexts are elicited by TOEFL tasks), obtaining validity evidence requires an understanding of ITA language use in the instructional domain to which inferences about TOEFL test-takers' ability to use language would need to be generalized. Therefore, the research focused on examining authentic ITA discourse and test-taker responses to TOEFL iBT® Speaking tasks, compiled in two respective corpora.

An important inference regarding the ITA domain that has not been previously addressed in TOEFL validation research is related to the use of functional language, an ability needed for oral knowledge construction in ITAs' encounters with their undergraduate students. To address this gap, the analysis of the two corpora focused on identifying the KSs and LFs characteristic of ITA discourse and obtaining evidence to answer a series of questions:

1. How do ITAs use functional language to impart knowledge to undergraduate students in lab, recitation, and lecture settings?
    a. Which KSs and LFs do they use?
    b. How do KSs and LFs compare in terms of frequency of occurrence, relative associations, and linguistic instantiations?

2. How do test-takers use functional language to construct responses to TOEFL iBT® Speaking independent and integrated tasks?
   a. Which KSs and LFs do they use?
   b. How do KSs and LFs compare in terms of frequency of occurrence, relative associations, and linguistic instantiations?
3. Are the KSs and LFs used in English-medium ITA instructional contexts identifiable in test-takers' responses elicited by the TOEFL iBT® Speaking tasks? If so, how do they compare in terms of frequency of occurrence, relative associations, and linguistic instantiations?

Given that the Knowledge Framework has been employed as a heuristic for describing functional language use in classroom discourse, and given its inherent relation to teaching, this framework was adopted for the purpose of analyzing the two corpora. The section that follows elaborates on key procedural phases of this two-year project: (1) compilation or relevant corpora, (2) testing the Knowledge Framework on ITA and test-taker discourse, (3) developing a coding protocol through pilot annotation, (4) micro-level functional annotation of the corpora, and (5) analysis of the annotated corpus data.

Deliberation of Methods

Compilation and Preparation of Corpora

The corpora used in the project were the ITA Speech Corpus and the TOEFL iBT® Speech Corpus. Because appropriate corpora were not readily available, how to design the corpora (such that they support the inquiry into the situation–text interface) was an essential methodological consideration. One of the most critical aspects of corpus design is representativeness. In practice, corpus representativeness is a malleable concept, as it must be linked to research goals. This is partially why "there is no objective way to balance a corpus or measure its representativeness" (McEnery, Xiao, & Tono, 2006, p. 30). Nevertheless, factors contributing to representativeness and how those factors aligned with the purpose of this corpus study had to be considered to the extent possible. To begin with, it was necessary to consider corpus type—general or specialized. Both corpora had to be created for a specific purpose; that is, both corpora had to be specialized. While they could be small size-wise (as specialized corpora typically are), they had to be focused on the target domain and appropriate in terms of balance and size. As such, their design posed inherent limitations and required careful forethought.

ITA Speech Corpus. Considering the focus on domain specificity, the speech samples for the ITA Speech Corpus had to be recorded in authentic instructional settings representative of the ITA teaching domain. As for any corpus, the spoken texts had to be selected based on external criteria, which should be defined situationally in terms or register or genre (Biber, 1993). The range of registers or genres in a corpus is what constitutes balance, a criterion that contributes to the representativeness of corpora (Sinclair, 1995). Therefore, the ITA Speech Corpus included three subsets of typical curriculum genres representing ITA pedagogic discourse: lab, recitation, and lecture.

Balance is closely associated with sampling from a representative population. Ideally, for a corpus to be considered representative, the number of samples across text categories should be proportional to their frequency in the target population. "However, it can be notoriously difficult to define a population or construct a sampling frame, particularly for spoken language, for which there are no ready-made sampling frames" (McEnery et al., 2006, pp. 1–20). That being said, in corpus design a population can be defined in terms of language production. In this case population sampling should be demographically oriented focusing on the individuals who produce language. It can also be defined as language as a product, then sampling can be organized based on text category or genre of language data.

Per McEnery et al., demographic sampling is more appropriate for spoken data. Therefore, the design of this corpus relied on demographic sampling by recruiting ITAs who not only produced language in domain-specific settings, but also taught a variety of disciplinary courses in a range of academic departments that commonly employ ITAs. Moreover, demographic sampling included the language proficiency criterion because ITAs at Iowa State University are generally assigned particular teaching assistantship roles based on their scores on the institutional Oral English Certification Test (OECT). The role of independent instructor who lectures requires the highest Level 1, recitation leader—Level 2, and lab assistant—Level 3. Level 4 is sufficient for grading and other teaching duties that do not entail direct oral communication with students, which is why ITAs with Level 4 OECT scores were not recruited. Once the spoken data were collected and transcribed, the texts were internally organized based on the curriculum genres they pertained to, thus to some degree accounting for language as a product.

Along with composition, representativeness can be determined by the size of the corpus, which is also linked to sampling. Of the two general approaches to text sampling, proportional (representing "groups to the extent that they occur in the larger population") and stratified (representing "the full range of linguistic variation that exists in a language, not the proportions of variation"), Biber and Jones recommend the latter for studies of linguistic variation and use because "[i]n a stratified corpus, the researcher begins by identifying the text categories that are the focus of research; texts are then selected from each of those categories so that each category is adequately represented" (2009, p. 1288). With that in mind, the initial intent for the size of the ITA Speech Corpus was to record at least 180 spoken texts obtained from at least 90 participants: 30 teaching lectures, 30 holding recitations, and 30 providing support to students during lab sessions. Each participating ITA had to be audio-recorded performing their instructional duties twice (30 ITAs * 3 curriculum genres * 2 instructional sessions = 180 speech samples). However, recruiting the necessary number of ITAs was not possible within the time frame allocated for this phase of the project. As the corpus was insufficiently large, stratified sampling from the genre-based subsets was not advisable. (This is likely to be a very common problem for domain-specific specialized corpora, especially spoken corpora). A major question thus was what is a workable corpus size? Biber (1993) demonstrated that ten 2000-word text samples per category can be sufficient. The genre-based subsets within the corpus had to at least satisfy this minimum size criterion for the curriculum genres in as many disciplines as possible, and also representative of various language backgrounds. For this reason, the collection of spoken data had to be extended from one to two semesters (from 4.5 to 9 months).

In this time frame, 52 ITA participants (31 male and 21 female) were recruited from Aerospace Engineering; Apparel, Events, & Hospitality Management; Biology; Chemistry; Computer Engineering; Computer Science; Construction Engineering; Economics; Engineering Mechanics; English; Food Science; Mathematics; Mechanical Engineering; Physics; Speech Communication; and Statistics. This target population sample included 18 native speakers of Indo-Aryan, 15 of Chinese, 5 of Persian, 4 of Korean, 4 of Spanish, 2 of Turkish, 2 of Vietnamese, 1 of Slavic languages, plus one unknown. Most participants held only lab sessions (21), some were independent course instructors (13), some led only recitations (9), and some taught both lab and recitation sessions (9). The majority of ITAs (49) were audio-recorded twice on a small, portable digital audio-recorder.

In preparation for transcription, the audio files were pre-processed. First, any discourse produced before and after the teaching session was removed. The audio files were then saved as de-identified files, the name of each file containing the type of curriculum genre, ID number, and month and year when the spoken text was recorded (e.g., rec-01-2-nov2015). At the same time, the transcribers received training and guided practice in applying the transcription conventions. The conventions were adopted from ETS because the transcription of the ITA Speech Corpus had to be consistent with that of the TOEFL iBT® Speech Corpus. The transcribers transcribed ITA talk only, leaving out student talk. Additionally, they added a time stamp for unclear utterances, which later made it possible for the annotators to easily identify audio segments and listen for clues whenever needed. The transcribed genre-based subsets included 25 Lecture texts (64681 words), 35 Recitation texts (93956 words), and 59 Lab texts (152976 words). The resulting corpus contained 119 texts (311613 words total; 2619 words on average).

TOEFL iBT® Speech Corpus. The second corpus did not require collecting discourse data because ETS provided the audio files and the transcriptions of 2,879 test-taker responses to TOEFL iBT® Speaking tasks. The size of this dataset did not present an issue. However, this dataset was not a corpus per se, so design considerations were critical in this case as well in order to compile the test data into a corpus responsive to the needs of the study. Specifically, this corpus had to be used not only for the purpose of identifying KSs and their LFs, but also for comparison with the target ITA domain of language use.

The speech samples from TOEFL iBT® represented responses to test prompts that were designed to elicit academic language. As a more general domain, academic language may include instructional discourse, and thus it would be reasonable to expect both similarities and differences with the three curriculum genres included in the ITA Speech Corpus. Similarities would be expected in the ways in which instructional discourse is generalizable to academic registers. Differences would mark the aspects of instructional discourse that are not characteristic of general academic discourse, as well as the ways in which the two corpora are representative of each form of discourse (for instance, the TOEFL iBT® Speech Corpus might underrepresent interactional aspects of academic discourse). Admittedly, although both corpora contain academic language, they may not be as comparable as one would wish. This is another possible caveat for future research using more than one corpus. Relevant corpus design considerations, however, can enable a reasonable level of comparability, although it should be acknowledged that it could still be somewhat loose.

The first factor to consider for the TOEFL iBT® Speech Corpus was text category. Given that the ITA Speech Corpus was organized based on texts pertaining to a certain genre category, the TOEFL corpus had to be organized based on text categories with shared characteristics. Along with text type, the characteristics had to be appropriate for Knowledge Framework-based comparison. Note that the Knowledge Framework is theorized relying on the concept of activity, which is accomplished through an action guided by a theoretical understanding. This theory/action dyad corresponds to background knowledge (knowing) and action knowledge (doing). The degree to which ITAs and TOEFL test-takers draw on background and action knowledge varies depending on the task. Instructional tasks in a lab generally require more action knowledge, as ITAs often draw upon their discipline-specific (facilitated by expertise) practical experience of doing things. TOEFL independent Tasks 1 and 2 also require the test-takers to draw entirely on their own ideas and experiences. In both scenarios, the speakers have no supporting materials to prepare their impromptu responses. On the other hand, in recitations and lectures ITAs draw more upon focal content, which can be considered integral to background knowledge, and use instructional materials to prepare. This may be considered similar to how test-takers respond to integrated Tasks 3–6 where they have to describe, explain, or summarize the content of reading passages and audio clips that are provided as supporting materials to prepare the response. Therefore, this conceivable distinction served as a criterion for organizing the TOEFL spoken texts based on test task type categories: independent and integrated, with the assumption that these two categories are roughly comparable with lab and recitation/lecture texts, respectively. Parenthetically, it should be pointed out that the interpretation of the findings should consider differences that may be due to the general-purposes nature of the assessment (i.e., background knowledge is not considered relevant to what is being tested) and the domain (i.e., background knowledge is relevant to performance). Such differences are justified by the test developers given the original intended use of TOEFL iBT® and also given fairness concerns.

Apart from this internal organization of texts that in part accounted for language as a product, language production in terms of demographically oriented population sampling was also attempted to maintain consistency with the design of the ITA Speaking corpus. Clearly, the characteristics of the population sample could not be directly comparable between the two corpora. Nonetheless, the first languages of the speakers in the ITA sample were also represented in the TOEFL iBT® Speech Corpus: 59 native speakers of Indo-Aryan, 69 of Chinese, 70 of Korean, 45 of Spanish, 14 of Turkish, 4 of Vietnamese, and 11 of Russian. The only language not represented was Persian. Additional language backgrounds included Arabic (32), Japanese (32), German (21), French (13), Tagalog (13), Thai (10), and 29 other languages represented by fewer than 10 speakers. In total, 481 test-takers contributed to the TOEFL iBT® Speech Corpus, of whom 217 were males and 206 were females (the gender of 58 test-takers was not provided).

Additionally, it was possible to approximate the level of language proficiency of both ITAs and test-takers, as the English-speaking ability of the former was assessed through OECT and of the latter through TOEFL iBT®. (See the description of TOEFL iBT® scaled section scores at https://www.ets.org/toefl/ibt/scores.) It was determined that the lowest converted TOEFL iBT® Speaking score of participating ITAs (i.e., ITAs who obtained Levels 1–3 on OECT) was 15, which is why this score was established as the cut-off score. Consequently, responses with raw scores of 2, 3, and 4 for individual speaking tasks were included because this score range could include converted final scores of 15 and higher. Not all of the 2,879 speech samples provided by ETS were thus included in the corpus. The Task 1–2 subset contained 924 texts (88,589 words), and the Task 3–6 subset contained 1,814 texts (222,981 words). Overall, the TOEFL iBT® Speech Corpus had a much higher number of texts (2,738 texts) than the ITA Speech Corpus. The texts in the TOEFL corpus were much smaller (114 words on average), but it was comparable in terms of total word count (311,570 words).

Testing and Refining the Knowledge Framework

The KSs of the Knowledge Framework were put forth by Mohan (1986) as starting blocks for teachers to organize instructional tasks such that they integrate language development into content teaching. Given its focus on language and content, it was also useful as a heuristic applied to the analysis of classroom discourse, revealing how teachers use functional language in content-area instruction. While this framework was deemed applicable to the analysis of ITA discourse, its suitability for the analysis of TOEFL spoken texts was not apparent. Therefore, a preliminary analysis to test the applicability of the framework was necessary. Preliminary analysis was important for two more reasons: a) it could inform further manual annotation of the corpora, which had to use KSs and LFs as coding categories, and b) it could help the annotators better understand the nature of learner language data at hand.

Since KSs are reflected in the macrostructures of texts (Mohan, 1989), it was reasonable to approach the preliminary analysis from a top-down perspective (Biber, Connor, & Upton, 2007). In short, beginning with a close reading of sample texts (3 ITA and 7 TOEFL), functional segments were identified and categorized into functional units using the KS and LF categories defined by Mohan (1986) and used by Levis et al. (2012). It was precisely this attempt to apply the framework when considerable challenges surfaced in the project.

The first difficulty was distinguishing among certain KSs and LFs, for existing definitions of the Knowledge Framework categories were not sufficiently specific. The definitions turned out to be too generic for the task at hand, referring to the same language features as examples for different KSs and LFs. For instance, features such as general reference, relational processes, and additive conjunction were listed as descriptive of the *classification* and *definitions* functions of KS CLASSIFICATION as well as of *description*, *comparison/contrast*, *quantification*, and *spatial order* functions of KS DESCRIPTION (Mohan, 1986). Admittedly, Mohan aligned the linguistic features based on KS pairs in view of his theoretical interpretation of the theory/action dyad. Such a description serves its purpose when applied to teaching. Corpus annotation, however, required more precise functional and linguistic descriptors.

For this purpose, the research team (principal investigator, post-doctoral associate, and graduate research assistants) analyzed a large sample of texts from both corpora over a period of six months. In the process of identifying and attempting to categorize functional segments, the researchers worked with texts independently and then participated in weekly meetings devoted to:

- explicit rationalizing of why a particular text segment carries a particular function,
- clarifying ambiguous or unclear segments,
- explaining unclear functional categories,
- discussing segments that did not seem to fit within existing functional categories,
- addressing overlap and duplication of functional categories, and
- compiling representative examples of linguistic instantiations of functional categories.

It must be noted that the team also interacted with an expert consultant, Dr. Tammy Slater, who advised during the process and confirmed the tentative and final version of the framework. As a result of these long-term systematic deliberations, a comprehensive record of the realizations of LFs was created. New functions emerged from the data as well: *exemplifying* in KS DESCRIPTION, *conceiving ideas* in KS EVALUATION, and *making choices*, *presenting options*, *expressing desire*, *advising*, and *presenting arguments* in KS CHOICE. This, in essence, supports Mohan's idea that the six KSs were the core that could serve as an appropriate starting point for functional analysis, and that other categories could be added to realize the full complexity of the theory-practice fusion. Overall, the qualitative analysis phase yielded a refined

Knowledge Framework with more comprehensive functional and linguistic descriptors, which are presented below as the first main outcome.

Outcome 1: Descriptors of Knowledge Framework Categories. Tables 2.1 to 2.6 summarize the descriptors of the LFs within each KS in terms of distinct functional and linguistic realizations.

Table 2.1 KS CLASSIFICATION

Functions	Functional realizations	Example linguistic realizations
Classifying	• arrange concrete or abstract concepts in sets/classes/ categories pertaining to a broader group	• classify (as/into), divide (into), organize (into), categorize (as/into), sort (into)
	• place in an aggregate/set/group/ class/category of concrete or abstract concepts	• include, incorporate (in), be a kind/type of
	• distinguish from an aggregate/ set/group/class/category of concrete or abstract concepts	• exclude, except (for), other (than), apart from, aside from, leaving out, besides
	• have as contents or part of the contents, and/or indicate whole/ part relations	• comprise, constitute, made up of, contain, have
	• specify or refer to a type of category/class/group/set	• Assignment 3, Question 7
	• indicate a part or whole of an equation/formula/chemical compound and the like	• equal, X is Y, number plus number equals number
	• indicate belonging or possession	• my, your/s, own, have, possess, belong, be in possession of
Defining	• assign a term, name, or role to something/someone	• be referred to as, be called, be defined as
	• provide a definition; state precisely the meaning of something	• denote, mean, stand for, connote

Table 2.2 KS DESCRIPTION

Functions	**Functional realizations**	**Example linguistic realizations**
Describing	• describe attributes, characteristics, or state of something/someone	• tall, rich, strong, this, that, these, those, conserved
	• indicate presence/existence or lack of something/someone	• there is/are/was/were, used to be, exist, lacking, missing, have
	• describe physical/intellectual ability or emotional state/experience	• feel, suffer, enjoy, be able to, can, have a pain
	• indicate a connection/association/relation to/with/between/among something	• concerning, about, pertinent to, relevant to, related to, regarding, correlate with, correspond to, relate to, meet (a condition), satisfy (a condition)
	• illustrate something/someone (possibly with reference to a visual)	• show, depict, illustrate, portray, sketch, picture, outline, describe, represent (meaning "depict"), indicate, seem, appear
	• add supplementary information	• and, also, in addition, additionally, another, plus
Comparing	• note factual similarities between characteristics/attributes (possibly using metaphor/simile/analogy)	• (look) like, resemble, similar to, bear resemblance to, compare
	• note factual differences between characteristics/attributes (possibly using metaphor/simile/analogy)	• unlike, different, distinct, dissimilar, discrepant
	• make a factual comparison with/between/among something/somebody	• taller, richer, younger, less similar, as brave as
	• set or present a criterion or norm against which a comparison can be made	• to the extent that, as far as, to some degree

(Continued)

Table 2.2 (*Continued*)

Functions	Functional realizations	Example linguistic realizations
Exemplifying	• provide information that supports a statement or helps better convey something	• for example, for instance, such as, like (this or that), give an example
	• indicate situational or abstract reference	• in this case, in the case of, in A's case
Quantifying	• specify quantity in terms of measures/ amount (precise or generic)	• five, a plethora of, some, several, many, numerous, enough (time), everything, something,
	• specify numbers, counting, or listing numbers	• 1, 2, 3, 4, etc.
Spatial positioning	• indicate location within a space/ area or spatial relations	• in, on, under, below, inside, in front of, etc.

Table 2.3 KS PRINCIPLES

Functions	Functional realizations	Example linguistic realizations
Explaining	• provide clarifying details to make something clear and understandable (e.g., what a concept is, how it is applied, etc.)	• explain, point out, clarify, shed light (on), provide/ give insight (into), that is, namely, in other words, imply
	• supply a reason or rationale for something	• because, reason, why, as, since, now that, by virtue of
	• supply judgment or evidence to make an inference or support a conclusion	• based on, drawing on/from, depending on, on account of, in a sense that, given (that), according to
Predicting	• express possibility, probability, or certainty for an outcome (or lack thereof), often accompanied with a true/untrue conditional (if)	• will, be going to, can, may, would, should, must, maybe, probably, likely, likelihood, (it) seems/ appears
	• forecast an outcome (or lack thereof)	• predict, expect, foretell, forecast, anticipate, envision, foresee, supposed to, guarantee

(*Continued*)

Table 2.3 (*Continued*)

Functions	Functional realizations	Example linguistic realizations
Concluding	• summarize or synthesize information into a logical deduction or reasoning (not a consequence)	• in conclusion, to sum up, thus, therefore, hence, in short, in a nutshell, so, conclude, deduce, basically (in a summative sense)
Hypothesizing	• make an assumption about something possible, yet currently non-existing	• assume, surmise, presume, suppose (that), provided (that), speculate, perhaps, as if, even if, if… (then), should (you) ... (then)
	• present a (hypothetical) condition or presumptive assumption	• in case that, given that, on a condition that, as long as, provided that
Demonstrating cause-effect	• indicate that a triggering action/event/factor (cause/ reason) produces a certain response/action in the form of another action/event (effect/ consequence) + problem-solving	• so, consequently, led to, as a result of, because (of), on account of, cause, bring about, end up with, depend on, rely on, affect, allow something/ somebody to (verb)
Setting rules	• establish or clarify rules/ regulations/principles of behavior or belief	• the rule says/is that (…) • "Students do not speak loudly in the library."
	• indicate theoretical/conceptual discipline-specific rules/ principles	• If you have a current going clockwise, you use the right hand rule.
Specifying means	• indicate a manner/method/way used to accomplish something	• how, this way, by means of, using, with, on purpose, objectively
	• indicate a manner/way in which something is achieved	• carefully, together
Specifying ends	• indicate an end goal/purpose/ target	• in order to, for, for the sake of, conducive to, in the interest of, so/such that

Table 2.4 KS SEQUENCE

Functions	**Functional realizations**	**Example linguistic realizations**
Reporting	• retell information available from elsewhere or conveyed by someone else	• say, ask (if/whether), restate, according to
Indicating order	• indicate temporal relationships (a succession related to a particular time sequence/cycle/chronology, a point in time, duration)	• every (day/minute), when, while, during, for hours, as, since, before, after, prior to, beginning, end, previous, most of the time, still, eventually, then (="after that"), as long as, finally
	• indicate general observations based on frequencies of occurrence	• always, usually, generally, commonly, typically, often, rarely
	• indicate a rank/importance/topical order	• first(ly), second(ly), next, last
Indicating process	• indicate processes that require time to be completed	• begin, start, finish, complete, continue, handle, treat, take care of, achieve, accomplish, process, proceed, try, become
	• indicate physical actions	• go, walk, run, return, lift, see, look, listen, turn
Instructing	• solicit an action (authoritatively/imperatively or not), give directions	• instruct, direct, command, tell somebody to (verb) • imperatives
	• solicit a response through a question, ask for a comprehension check	• yes/no questions; wh-questions • "sorry?", "pardon me?", "excuse me?"
	• address the interlocutor/audience (e.g. greetings)	• good morning, bye • "see you later"
Narrating	• recount events/experiences	• narrate, recount, recite, give an account of
	• communicate descriptive information	• tell, talk about, mention, state, answer, refer to (meaning "mention")
	• direct quotes of a text or saying	• "early birds catch the worms"

Table 2.5 KS EVALUATION

Functions	Functional realizations	Example linguistic realizations
Evaluating	• determine or judge the quality, significance, or worth of something/somebody	• good, bad, excellent, exciting, boring, useful, harmful, deserve, make sense, work
	• compare/contrast based on a subjective/objective appraisal of something/somebody	• better, worse, the most helpful, likewise, however, but, whereas, while, meanwhile, although
	• express emotion/affect with regards to something/somebody	• be sorry, feel guilty, love, like, loathe, worry, be concerned, care about
	• state a need	• need, necessitate, be necessary
	• express approval/disapproval or confirmation of something/ somebody	• dislike, hate, disapprove, reject, it's ok, that's fine, sure, yes
	• express negative connotation	• no, not, not at all, no more
	• indicate a particular process, method, or outcome for assessing knowledge/skill/behavior/activity	• assess, grade, score, evaluate, make a mistake, verify, make sure
	• Indicate lack of restriction or referring to a thing, person, entity, phenomenon, etc.	• lack, no matter, whatever, whichever, whoever, however (pretty...), wherever, ever, regardless of
Conceiving ideas	• form a notion or understanding of something/somebody (generally expressed with verbs denoting mental actions/cognitive activities)	• know, understand, comprehend, learn, believe, conceive, consider, perceive, discern, ponder over/upon, reflect, remember, forget, on/ upon, think (of/about), guess, find (=to perceive, recognize), discover (=become aware of), recognize, notice
	• indicate how something/ somebody impacts/affects one's understanding/knowledge	• confuse, misinform, mislead, disorient, obscure
Making judgments	• form an intellectual, rational opinion/appraisal about something/somebody based on evidence/circumstances presented to the mind	• judge, criticize, suspect, doubt, determine, appraise, adjudicate

Table 2.6 KS CHOICE

Functions	Functional realizations	Example linguistic realizations
Making choices	• select from a number of possibilities by preference and/or decision	• choose, select, prefer, opt, refuse, resist, abandon, decide, plan, promise, elect, would rather
Presenting options	• indicate alternative options	• otherwise, or, either…or, neither…nor, instead of, (something) else, whether (…or), if (=whether)
Expressing desire	• indicate willingness/intention to do something	• will, want to, need to, intend to, be willing to, intention, let me (verb)
	• express a desire, wish, or hope either for something possible or unrealistic	• wish, desire, crave, pray, aspiration, hope, longing, want
	• express gratitude or accept gratitude	• thank, appreciate
	• express an apology	• excuse me, sorry, apologize
Advising	• offer a suggestion, recommendation, or advice	• advise, recommend, suggest, encourage, propose to, let's, why don't (you/we), how about, can, (you) may want to, might want to
	• indicate an obligation/necessity	• should, have to, must, ought to, might want to/could, demand, command • Please!
	• indicate a permission or request	• ask, request
	• urge someone to be careful or do something	• warn, forewarn, flag, caution, alert, put on guard
Expressing opinions	• express a personal view or attitude	• In my opinion, in fact, (I/she) (don't/doesn't) think/believe (that), as far as I am concerned, from my point of view • oppose, object, agree, disagree, complain
	• indicate a personal emphasis	• actually, really, anyway, just, so (nice), particularly, do/does, exactly, certainly, it is certain that, only, of course, not only, that's it, basically
	• elicit someone's view, tag questions asking for confirmation	• right? isn't it? don't they? OK?

(Continued)

Table 2.6 (*Continued*)

Functions	Functional realizations	Example linguistic realizations
Presenting arguments	• support something/ somebody by providing reasoning/rationale/evidence	• argue, claim, maintain, uphold, prove, support, discuss
	• defend something/ somebody as warranted or well-grounded	• justify, advocate, defend, acquit
	• provide reasoning/rationale/ evidence to contradict or uncover something	• counter-argue, refute, rebut, debate, discredit, disprove

Pilot Annotation

As with any coding schema, the refined framework had to be applied in a pilot annotation phase to develop a protocol for corpus annotation. Again, all the members of the research team were involved. Randomly selected texts were first annotated individually, then the annotations were compared in group meetings (at least three meetings per week). Even though at this stage the researchers had more precise functional and linguistic descriptors, the nature of the corpus data posed challenges for segmentation and classification.

Segmenting texts into functional segments was difficult because spoken learner language contained errors as well as inappropriate, ambiguous, and incomplete utterances. Addressing this issue required thorough consideration of the notion of "functional segment" as the unit of annotation. The annotators had to be able to determine the boundaries of functional segments in a dependable manner. The group concurred that the unit of annotation should be the finite clause, as it was the syntactic unit whose boundaries could be identified with a higher level of consistency. In the example provided further below, the boundaries are marked by a vertical bar.

Classifying the units of annotation in turn required specifications for how to determine the KS and LF. In this respect, questions arose about how to ensure consistency in various instances when the speakers' lexicogrammatical choices required the annotators to infer the functional meaning and could lead to multiple interpretations. Another classification issue was related to units that appeared to be multi-functional; that is, a clause contained explicit linguistic realizations that were descriptive of different LFs. In such instances, the annotators chose one LF based on which function they perceived as being most prominent, given the context. Because it became evident that the functional strength of the LFs contained in the same clause was not the same, this observation was translated to the concept of primary and secondary functions. This was an insightful distinction that was then attempted in the ongoing pilot annotation. However, as the project timeline was impacted by extending the framework testing phase, a trade-off had to be made. Annotating texts with both primary and secondary tags was much more time consuming; plus, the unit of secondary function coding could not be the same clause (distinguishing the linguistic realizations of primary and secondary functions would have been a daunting task). Therefore, the compromise was to annotate only for primary functions employing a two-tier KS/LF classification as illustrated in the following example from the TOEFL iBT® Speech Corpus (text ID SP-F2-i3-S4-20072148):

> The woman totally disagrees with Mr. Wilson | KS CHOICE; *LF expressing opinions*
> because she says | KS PRINCIPLES; *LF explaining*
> that he graduated from Oakdale twenty-five years ago | KS SEQUENCE; *LF indicating process*
> when people at that times were not exposed to computers yet. | KS SEQUENCE; *LF indicating order*

A number of other concerns were identified as well, including different types of clauses, missing subject or verb, fragments, embeddings, close repetitions, consequent imperatives, self-repairs, language errors, quoted excerpts, and so on. A log containing incremental decisions regarding how to address these concerns was continually updated following each group meeting. It became the source used to formulate annotation guidelines, which are detailed next as the second usable outcome.

Outcome 2: Annotation Protocol. The general annotation followed the procedure below.

- Segment sentences/utterances into units of annotation.
  - ⇒ Locate the subject and the predicate of the clause.
  - ⇒ Determine its boundaries.
- Annotate the unit with the respective KS and LF.
  - ⇒ Identify the linguistic feature/s indicative of LF/s.
  - ⇒ To determine the KS and LF of the annotation unit, identify which feature is indicative of the primary function based on the context (other features may be indicative of secondary functions).

Segmentation Guidelines:

- Segment a fragment as an independent unit if the subject or predicate of a clause is missing but easily inferred from the context.
- Segment a fragment together with the adjacent clause if the subject or/and predicate of a fragment is missing and cannot be inferred from the context.
- Segment a larger clause as one unit if it contains an embedded clause.
- Segment close repetitions as one unit.
- Segment a self-repair together with the following clause.
- Segment a false start that takes the form of a clause as an independent unit.
- Segment [unclear] together with the adjacent word or phrase (e.g., outside [unclear]).
- Segment "Yes." and "No." and "OK." when followed by a period separately and annotate with the LF that can be determined based on the context.
- Segment "Yes," and "No," when followed by a comma as part of the adjacent clause.
- Segment independent and embedded "wh"-clauses separately from the main clause.
- Segment the preposition together with the "wh"-clause if it introduces the clause.
- Segment verbs like "suppose," "assume," and "imagine" separately if they are followed by a "that"-clause.
- Segment the "that" complementizer together with the following noun clause unless another adverbial (e.g., "if" or "when") introduces an embedded clause, or unless the subordinate clause is separated by another inserted clause.
- Segment two (or more) verb phrases that refer to the same subject together as a single unit if their LF is the same; segment such verb phrases as separate units if they have different LFs.
- Segment two consecutive imperatives (e.g., "square them and add them up") as a single unit.
- Segment two consecutive clauses that refer to the same adverbial conjunction together. If more than two clauses seem to be conjoined but reference to the same adverbial conjunction is unclear, segment them separately.
- Do not segment adjectival phrases (presumably reduced relative clauses) as independent units.
- Do not segment fillers (e.g., "you know", "I mean", "so") as independent units.

Annotation Guidelines

- Annotate (restrictive) relative clauses with the primary tag of DESCRIPTION/*Describing* because they provide descriptive information about a noun. If a relative clause is non-restrictive, annotate it based on its function.
- Annotate quoted excerpts as SEQUENCE/*Narrating*.
- Annotate a perception verb indicating a sense of sight, hearing, taste, or touch (e.g., saw him) as SEQUENCE, *indicating process*.
- Annotate a perception verb indicating a mental activity (e.g., I see your point) as EVALUATION, *conceiving ideas*.
- If a clause contains linguistic features that signal different LFs, annotate with the function that occurs first in the clause.
- If a clause begins with a frequency adverb, consider the meaning of the adverb to determine the primary function of the clause. (If a frequency adverb is placed inside a clause, it may not always indicate a primary function.)
- Even if a cause-effect relationship between two conjoined clauses may be possible, but no cause-effect linguistic feature is present, annotate with the LF that is explicitly conveyed.
- If a language error is critical to annotation, flag it for discussion and clarification.
- If a text is missing too many verbs (which may be marked as unclear), flag it for discussion and clarification.

Annotating the Corpora

Annotator training is of utmost importance when text data is to be manually coded. Insufficient, inadequate, or lack of training is bound to lead to creating a dataset that has no empirical value. In this project, the integral participation of all members of the research team in the development of detailed functional and linguistic descriptors and annotation guidelines helped the annotators acquire a shared understanding of the theoretical underpinnings, procedural steps, and analytic strategies, as well as a feel for what the text data was like. Still, once the guidelines were specified, the annotators exercised them through group practice annotation, individual annotation, and adjudication sessions with the principal investigator.

For the annotation task, the choice fell on an open-source software called Callisto by the MITRE Corporation (http://mitre.github.io/callisto). It was suitable not only because it allows for multi-layered annotation of the same text segments, but also because the user interface afforded a color visual

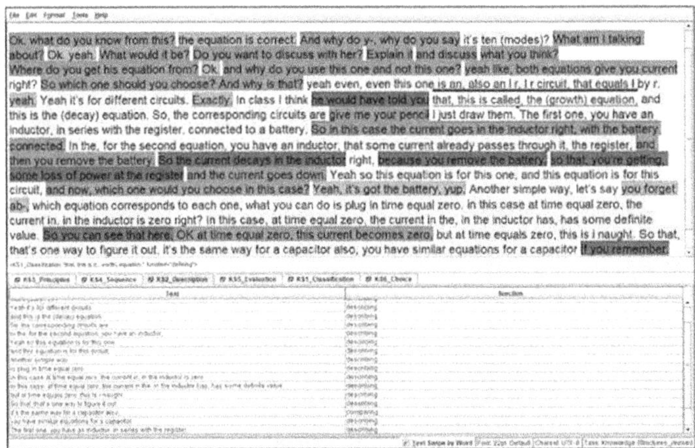

Figure 2.1 Example of annotated text in Callisto, modified from color to greyscale

display of both the full text and the Knowledge Framework categories assigned to individual segmented units. Figure 2.1 illustrates a shaded screenshot of an excerpt from an annotated Recitation text from the ITA Speech Corpus (025 rec-04-2-oct2015). The different shades indicate the first layer of annotation—the KSs—and are unique to individual KSs. Seeing that each segment is colored was a convenient way for the annotators to ensure that there are no gaps in annotation. Once a segment was color coded, it was then tagged with an LF of the respective KS. Tabs appear at the bottom of the screen, under which the annotated segments and their functions are shown. This interface feature helped verify the annotations per LF.

Each annotator was assigned different sets of ITA and TOEFL iBT® texts for independent annotation to avoid developing bias towards a particular text type. As a formal measure of agreement among the annotators, a protocol was established for annotating the same sets of texts by all the annotators and for holding weekly adjudication sessions. A total of 26 sets of the same texts were used for this purpose. Each set contained 3–4 texts from the TOEFL iBT® Speech Corpus (avg. 393 words) and an excerpt from an ITA text (avg. 439 words). The annotations were manually entered into an Excel document in a format that showed how the segments were coded by each annotator (Fig. 2.2).

The disagreement was marked in terms of unit boundaries and functions. Boundary disagreement (**bd** and lighter font in Fig. 2.2) was marked when one or more annotators segmented annotation units differently because of fragmentation, semantic ambiguity, grammatical inaccuracy, inappropriate

Text ID	KS function	Boundary	A1_clause	A1_KS function	A2_clause	A2_KS function	A3_clause	A3_KS function	Adjudicated KS function	Adjudicated boundary
SP-F2-14-52-200732 50			like uh if you are, you, you have [2 unclear words] in the football game.	hypothesizing	like uh if you are, you, you have [2 unclear words] in the football game.	hypothesizing	if you are, you, you have [2 unclear words] in the football game.	hypothesizing	hypothesizing	
SP-F2-14-52-200732 50		bd	Uh although the football game is not very good for, uh not very uh what, what you	evaluating	Uh although the football game is not very good for.	evaluating	Uh although the football game is not very good for, uh not very uh	evaluating	evaluating	Uh although the football game is not very good for, uh not very uh
SP-F2-14-52-					uh not very uh what, what you watching.	indicating_process	what, what you watching.	indicating_process	indicating_process	what, what you watching.
SP-F2-14-52-200732			But you still watching in, uh uh but uh you still watching uh of	indicating_process	But you still watching in, uh uh but uh you still watching uh of [unclear],	indicating_process	But you still watching in, uh uh but uh you still watching uh of	indicating_process	indicating_process	
SP-F2-14-52-200732	pd		in fact uh the football game i you can watch from your tv.	expressing_opinions	in fact uh the football game i you can watch from your tv.	predicting	in fact uh the football game i you can watch from your tv.	expressing_opinions	expressing_opinions	
SP-F2-14-52-200732	pd		Uh maybe you are very, more happier than watching tv.	comparing	Uh maybe you are very, more happier than watching tv.	predicting	Uh maybe you are very, more happier than watching tv.	predicting	predicting	

Figure 2.2 Example of working document for adjudication of disagreement

word choice, and so on. Table 2.7 lists the number of annotated and agreed on units per set along with the percent agreement.

Functional disagreement was marked when one or more annotators labeled a given unit with different KS/LF tags. When annotating LFs, it was very important to bear in mind multifunctionality. Therefore, the reliability protocol focused on both primary and secondary functions. For example:

Annotated segment: *Instead of this, it moves a little bit more up because of different kind of, hyrb-, hybrid orbitals.*
Primary function: KS CHOICE; *presenting options* (signaled by *instead of this)*
Secondary functions: KS SEQUENCE; *indicating process* (signaled by *moves*)
KS PRINCIPLES; *explaining* (signaled by *because of)*

Consequently, functional disagreement was marked as partial (**pd** in Figure 2.2) if one or two annotators coded a given segment based on the linguistic signals indicative of its secondary functions, and complete (**cd**) if none of the annotators coded a given clause based on the linguistic signals indicative of its primary function. Consider the following examples:

Partial functional disagreement:
Annotated unit: *Uh the man is skeptical about the library's uh plan...*
Annotator 1: KS DESCRIPTION, *describing* (signaled by *is*)
Annotator 2: KS EVALUATION, *evaluating* (signaled by *skeptical*)
Annotator 3: KS EVALUATION, *evaluating* (signaled by *skeptical*)
Adjudication: KS EVALUATION, *evaluating* (signaled by *skeptical*)

Table 2.7 Inter-annotator agreement on annotation unit boundaries

Text sets	Number of units	Number of units agreed	Percent of units agreed
Set 1	101	91	90%
Set 2	99	92	93%
Set 3	98	86	88%
Set 4	68	56	82%
Set 5	84	75	89%
Set 6	83	75	90%
Set 7	78	69	88%
Set 8	84	77	92%
Set 9	97	90	93%
Set 10	105	97	92%
Set 11	132	119	90%
Set 12	99	94	95%
Set 13	90	84	93%
Set 14	88	75	85%
Set 15	104	99	95%
Set 16	29	25	86%
Set 17	106	92	87%
Set 18	112	104	93%
Set 19	105	99	93%
Set 20	104	93	89%
Set 21	330	310	94%
Set 22	29	25	86%
Set 23	106	92	87%
Set 24	112	104	93%
Set 25	104	93	89%
Set 26	330	310	94%
Total	2877	2626	90%

Complete functional disagreement:

Annotated unit:	*but today we are also going to calculate the [unclear] energy*
Annotator 1:	KS PRINCIPLES, *predicting* (signaled by *going to*)
Annotator 2:	KS SEQUENCE, *indicating order* (signaled by *today*)
Annotator 3:	KS PRINCIPLES, *predicting* (signaled by *going to*)
Adjudication:	KS EVALUATION, *evaluating* (signaled by *but*)

The rate of complete disagreement among the annotators was 3.7% across all the text sets; 17% of the disagreements were partial. The discrepancies and inconsistencies were identified, discussed, and adjudicated as a group. In this process, the LF descriptors continued to be fine-tuned. The final adjudications served as data for calculations of inter-annotator reliability, which was determined using several measures: Cohen's Kappa was calculated for pairs of annotators (.75), Light's Kappa coefficients were calculated to check the overall agreement patterns among the three annotators (.82), and Conger's Kappa coefficients were calculated to estimate the percent chance agreement among the annotators (.82). These measures were also used to measure agreement with regards to the final adjudications. Listing the coefficients for all texts sets would take more space than permitted, so Table 2.8 shows the inter-annotator reliabilities against the final adjudications at different intervals.

Table 2.8 Adjudication-based inter-annotator reliability measures

Text sets	Annotators-Adjudication	Cohen's Kappa	Light's Kappa	Conger's Kappa
Set 1	A1-ADJ	.73		
	A2-ADJ	.78		
	A3-ADJ	.90		
	A1-A2-A3-ADJ		.76	.77
Set 4	A1-ADJ	.90		
	A2-ADJ	.80		
	A3-ADJ	.82		
	A1-A2-A3-ADJ		.79	.79
Set 8	A1-ADJ	.78		
	A2-ADJ	.76		
	A3-ADJ	.86		
	A1-A2-A3-ADJ		0.77	.77
Set 12	A1-ADJ	.84		
	A2-ADJ	.86		
	A3-ADJ	.84		
	A1-A2-A3-ADJ		.81	.81
Set 16	A1-ADJ	.91		
	A2-ADJ	.72		
	A1-A2-ADJ		.78	.78
Set 21	A1-ADJ	.91		
	A2-ADJ	.82		
	A1-A2-ADJ		.83	.83
Set 26	A1-ADJ	.90		
	A2-ADJ	.85		
	A1-A2-ADJ		.84	.84

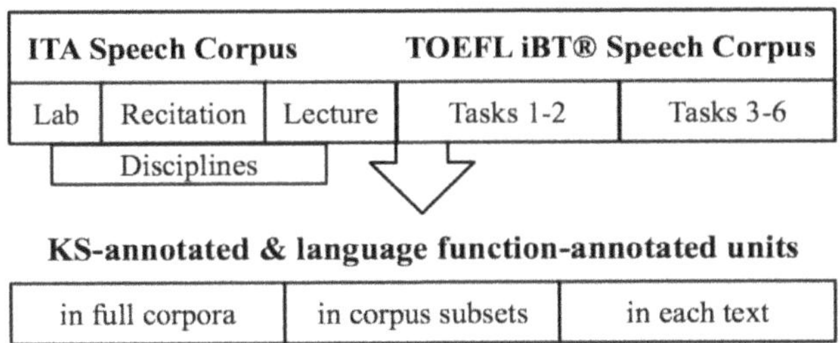

Figure 2.3 Annotated corpus datasets

Outcome 3: Annotated Corpora. Once annotated, the corpus data were extracted to enable creating multiple combinations of annotated datasets needed to address the research objectives. As shown in Figure 2.3, the datasets were extracted per corpus, per subsets within each corpus (including per discipline for the ITA Speech Corpus), and per text.

Analyzing the Annotated Corpora

The annotated corpus datasets presented rich opportunities for frequency-based scrutiny (Figure 2.4). Descriptive analyses of KSs and LFs, quantified in terms of percentages, provided results indicating the distribution of the macro- and micro-level functional categories at the level of full corpora and at the level of subsets within each corpus. For comparative purposes, the frequencies of occurrence were used in statistical analyses. Multivariate correspondence analysis (CA) was employed to examine the relative associations among the subsets of the two corpora and the functional categories in the Knowledge Framework. CA, or reciprocal averaging, compares multiple categorical variables together and at the same scale based on the frequency of each category relative to their respective totals (for more about CA, see Clausen, 1998, and Yelland, 2010). N-gram analysis allowed for a gain in insights about the language choices that were used to realize specific functional

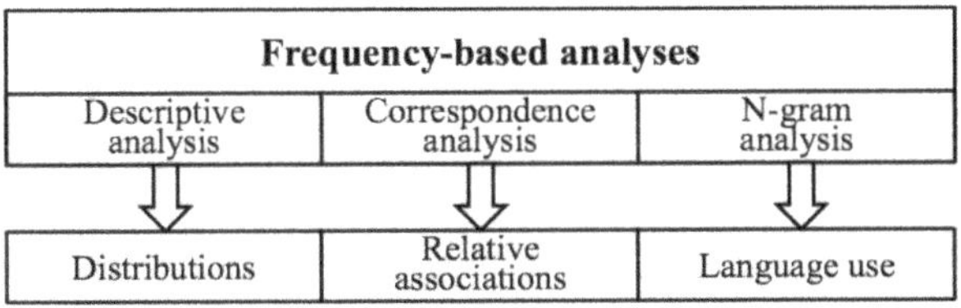

Figure 2.4 Data analysis

meanings. More specifically, n-grams, or "strings of adjacently positioned lexical items" (McCarthy, Watanabe, & Lamkin, 2012, p. 315), of length ranging from one lexical item (uni-grams) to five (five-grams) were used in Principal Component Analysis to examine patterns in language use between the two corpora. The results were aggregated into bootstrap consensus trees. The tree nodes for which there was a sufficiently large consensus among the individual cluster analyses were visualized such that the similarities between texts across different frequency bands could be detected (for more information, see Eder, Rybicki, & Kestemont, 2016).

Outcome 4: Research Insights from Corpus-based KF Analysis. Select findings demonstrate the nature of the insights focusing on identifying and comparing the occurrence of KSs and LFs in the ITA Speech and in the TOEFL iBT® Speech Corpora, their relative associations, and linguistic instantiations (for detailed findings, see Cotos & Chung, 2018, 2019). Briefly, the descriptive analyses revealed that both ITA discourse and TOEFL iBT® Speaking responses contained all six KSs and all 29 LFs, albeit with varied frequencies. Tables 2.9 and 2.10 summarize the percent proportions of each functional category. Overall, the frequency patterns were similar, except for one considerable difference—KS3 PRINCIPLES (especially *explaining*) being more frequent in TOEFL iBT® responses, and KS 4 SEQUENCE (especially *instructing*) in ITA talk.

Tables 2.9 and 2.10 indicate a similar magnitude of percentages across the subsets of the ITA Speech and TOEFL iBT® Corpora, but they do not render a meaningful comparison of the frequency of multiple functional categories. The CA results summarized in Table 2.11 do that, suggesting important distinctions in terms of associational relationships based on the data structured into a matrix that expressed the frequency-based relative values of each KS in each subset of the two corpora (the matrix is too large to be included here). The CA results supported the initial assumption at the stage of corpus design

Table 2.9 KSs in the subsets of the ITA speech and TOEFL iBT® Corpora

Knowledge Structure	Lab	Recitation-Lecture	Tasks 1–2	Tasks 3–6
KS1 CLASSIFICATION	1.43%	2.29%	0.25%	1.68%
KS2 DESCRIPTION	19.46%	21.17%	20.45%	21.55%
KS3 PRINCIPLES	19.62%	19.81%	26.37%	29.36%
KS4 SEQUENCE	29.06%	28.82%	18.25%	19.60%
KS5 EVALUATION	15.02%	11.46%	17.39%	13.62%
KS6 CHOICE	15.40%	16.45%	17.27%	14.19%

Table 2.10 LFs in the subsets of the ITA Speech and TOEFL iBT® Corpora

Functions	Lab	Recitation-Lecture	Tasks 1–2	Tasks 3–6
KS1_classifying	0.95%	1.80%	0.23%	0.43%
KS1_defining	0.48%	0.49%	0.02%	1.25%
KS2_comparing	0.98%	1.02%	1.61%	0.99%
KS2_describing	12.78%	14.57%	14.61%	15.80%
KS2_exemplifying	0.68%	0.99%	1.77%	2.61%
KS2_quantifying	2.84%	3.16%	2.03%	1.74%
KS2_spatial positioning	2.19%	1.42%	0.44%	0.42%
KS3_concluding	2.40%	2.61%	3.40%	3.39%
KS3_demonstrating cause-effect	1.38%	1.23%	3.14%	3.92%
KS3_explaining	3.16%	3.65%	9.14%	7.34%
KS3_hypothesizing	2.95%	3.52%	1.76%	2.80%
KS3_predicting	8.20%	7.46%	7.68%	10.89%
KS3_setting rules	0.08%	0.10%	0.01%	0.03%
KS3_specifying ends	0.89%	0.63%	0.41%	0.26%
KS3_specifying means	0.57%	0.61%	0.84%	0.73%
KS4_indicating order	7.96%	6.06%	10.91%	9.20%
KS4_indicating process	5.70%	5.48%	6.64%	7.60%
KS4_instructing	14.96%	15.75%	0.29%	0.42%
KS4_narrating	0.17%	0.86%	0.27%	0.62%
KS4_reporting	0.28%	0.68%	0.15%	1.76%
KS5_conceiving ideas	1.18%	1.23%	1.24%	1.27%
KS5_evaluating	13.84%	10.24%	16.16%	12.33%
KS5_making judgments	0.00%	0.02%	0.01%	0.00%
KS6_advising	3.81%	3.73%	2.69%	3.36%
KS6_expressing desire	1.31%	1.29%	0.63%	1.10%
KS6_expressing opinions	9.36%	10.18%	12.51%	6.92%
KS6_making choices	0.05%	0.07%	0.43%	0.66%
KS6_presenting arguments	0.02%	0.05%	0.04%	0.14%
KS6_presenting options	0.87%	1.12%	0.98%	2.01%

regarding the comparability of the subset components of the two corpora. In other words, close associations were detected between ITA Lab discourse and the responses to Tasks 1–2, and between Recitation-Lecture and Tasks 3–6 responses. More importantly, as shown in Table 2.11, the analysis helped detect strong relationships among four KSs and individual ITA and TOEFL subsets. Weak associations indicate that the respective KSs were relatively common in other subsets. For example, KS2 DESCRIPTION had a weak association

Table 2.11 Associations between KSs and subsets of the ITA speech and TOEFL iBT® Corpora

	Associational relationship	
Knowledge Structure	*Strong*	*Weak*
KS1 CLASSIFICATION	Recitation-Lecture	
KS2 DESCRIPTION		Tasks 3–6
KS3 PRINCIPLES	Tasks 3–6	
KS4 SEQUENCE	Lab and Recitation-Lecture	
KS5 EVALUATION	Tasks 1–2	
KS6 CHOICE		Lab

with Tasks 3–6, but it was similarly frequent in Recitation-Lecture. The same inference can be made about the relation of KS6 CHOICE to Lab and Recitation-Lecture discourse. Interestingly, despite the similarity in frequency distributions, ITA genre discourse appeared to be different from the TOEFL responses in terms of KS associations, as no strong associations were detected between the same KSs and comparable subsets of the two corpora.

The complexity of the CA results on LFs can be gleaned from Figure 2.5, which illustrates the perceptual map of the relationships between the individual functions and the ITA and TOEFL subsets. The circle nearest to the border of Dimension 2 indicates that the LFs in Lab and Recitation-Lecture

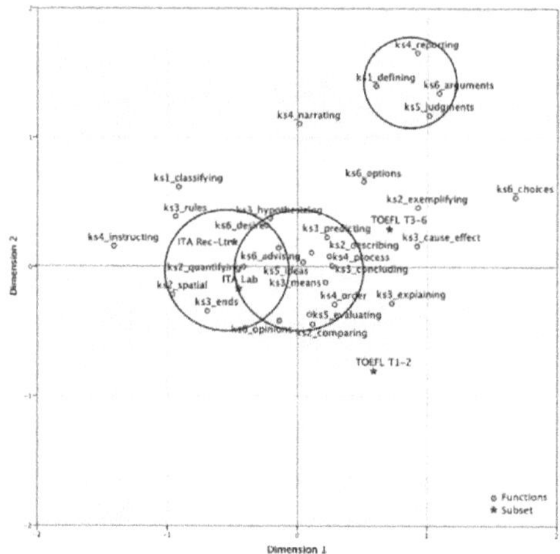

Figure 2.5 Associations among LFs and subsets of the ITA speech and TOEFL iBT® Corpora

plotted closer together, which means that they were common across the curriculum genres. Given that many functions clustered within the circle in the center area of the map, this figure also indicates that they were frequently used by both ITAs and test-takers. The LFs in the responses to Tasks 3–6 were more dispersedly positioned on the map, suggesting stronger associations with such functions as KS4 *reporting*, KS1 *defining*, KS6 *presenting arguments*, and KS5 *making judgments* encircled in the top corner.

Developing the descriptors of the Knowledge Framework categories presented in Outcome 1 above provided a more comprehensive understanding of the linguistic instantiations of functional discourse. For instance, it was interesting to observe that some language choices were the same for different LFs. This observation was supported by the n-gram analysis results. While many uni-grams did represent linguistic features that realized the functional meanings of a given KS (e.g., taxonomic lexis for CLASSIFICATION, demonstrative and relative pronouns for DESCRIPTION, consequential adverbials for PRINCIPLES, temporal adverbials for SEQUENCE, evaluative lexis for EVALUATION; alternative conjunctions for CHOICE), some of the same uni-grams placed among the most frequent ones. For instance, the uni-grams in Table 2.12 were among the top 30 most frequent ones; underlined are the uni-grams that occurred in more than one KS.

Another relevant observation was that the longer the n-gram was, the more it reflected the nature of the content that was communicated for a given purpose. For the sake of brevity, Table 2.13 refers only to KS1 CLASSIFICATION

Table 2.12 Examples of most frequent uni-grams per KS

KS	Examples of most frequent uni-grams
KS1 CLASSIFICATION	*mean; call; kind; type; <u>someth</u>; contain; famili; part; bodi; <u>one</u>, equal; <u>two</u>; minus; plus; time; number; <u>have</u>; divid; multipli; root*
KS2 DESCRIPTION	*exampl; <u>like</u>; also; this; that; thing; <u>someth</u>; anoth; and; <u>one</u>; <u>two</u>; <u>have</u>; here; there; which; what; some; your; where; how*
KS3 PRINCIPLES	*can; will; think; get; <u>someth</u>; <u>take</u>; use; expect; gonna; know; might; <u>want</u>; becaus; would; about; if; then; start; <u>first</u>; since*
KS4 SEQUENCE	*<u>first</u>; give; second; time; help; make; use; year; now; when; after; put; <u>take</u>; next; last; into; befor; did; with; for*
KS5 EVALUATION	*but; <u>import</u>; good; problem; <u>like</u>; better; best; ever; yes; dont; alright; sure; just; correct; yup; veri; exact; matter; great; <u>realli</u>*
KS6 CHOICE	*think; <u>want</u>; <u>realli</u>; opinion; need; prefer; agre; suggest; <u>import</u>; <u>like</u>; thank; should; point; either; whether; actual; know*

Table 2.13 Examples of most frequent bi-, tri-, four-, and five-grams of CLASSIFICATION

KS1 CLASSIFICATION	**Examples of most frequent n-grams**
bi-grams	*kind of; is the; is a; is called; called the; it's called; are called; this is; reciprocity is; generalized reciprocity; reciprocity means*
tri-grams	*is called the; this is called; this kind of; generalized reciprocity is; is equal to; to the minus; equal to the; to the power; the power of*
four-grams	*to the power of; is equal to the; this is equal to; this is called the; generalized reciprocity is a; the exchange of goods; is the money sunk; and balanced reciprocity is*
five-grams	*sunk cost is the money; to the power of two; this is equal to the; generalized reciprocity and balanced reciprocity; is the exchange of goods; e to the minus x; is equal to probability of*

n-grams. Bi-grams such as *kind of*, *is a*, and *is called* seem to capture functional language choices that are not necessarily dependent on text type (curriculum genre or test-task response). On the other hand, n-grams like *to the power*, *to the power of*, and *to the power of two* are common for curriculum genres, while *generalized reciprocity is, and balanced reciprocity is*, and *generalized reciprocity and balanced reciprocity* were clearly determined by the TOEFL prompt. This observation and the one above reinforce the importance of not only identifying linguistic signals, but also interpreting their function in the context.

The n-gram analysis results plotted as bootstrap consensus trees in Figure 2.6 further show a conspicuous difference stemming from the use of language choices that realized the KSs. This can be seen in the two clear bifurcations between the n-grams in the TOEFL iBT® and ITA Speaking Corpora. Considering the frequencies of occurrence, differences were expected for KS3 PRINCIPLES and KS4 SEQUENCE, and some similarities were expected for the other four KSs. However, KS2 DESCRIPTION, KS3 PRINCIPLES, KS4 SEQUENCE, KS5 EVALUATION, and KS6 CHOICE in the two corpora branched out on opposite dimensions. If the linguistic choices were similar, the branches representing the TOEFL and ITA data would have clustered closer together, as is the case of tri-grams representing KS1 CLASSIFICATION (grey triangle in Figure 2.6).

It must be noted that although KS1 CLASSIFICATION tri-grams plotted almost ideally next to each other, this KS was the sparsest category in both corpora, and so the inference that the linguistic instantiations of

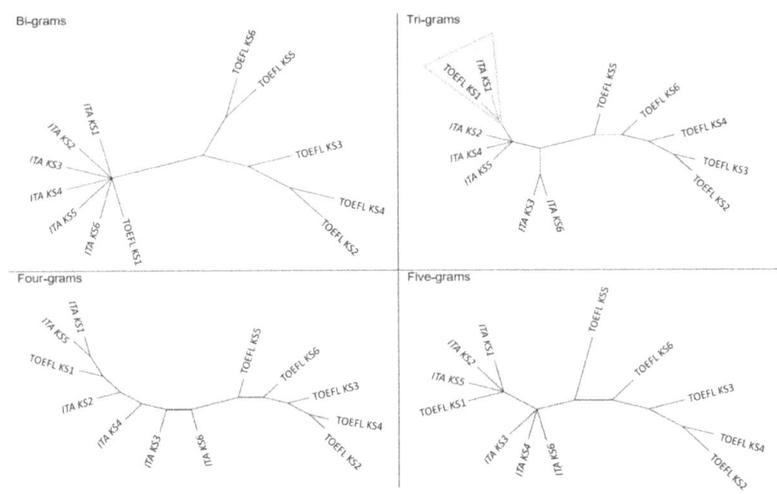

Figure 2.6 Comparison of n-grams per KS in TOEFL iBT® and ITA Speaking Corpora

CLASSIFICATION in ITA and test-taker speech are similar should be viewed as tentative. With regards to KS2 DESCRIPTION, both corpora included frequent *be* n-grams; however, ITAs used relational *be* verbs and clauses to describe concepts and attributive processes, while TOEFL test-takers used *be* mostly with *there* as dummy subject. KS5 EVALUATION was realized largely through confirmation checks, answers to Yes/No questions, and evaluative lexis in ITA discourse, while TOEFL test-takers used words of appraisal and comparison. Interestingly, because ITAs also need to formatively assess their students' actions and responses, they tended rather frequently to use *I think* as KS5 EVALUATION, possibly trying to mitigate an authoritative tone in their appraisal. KS6 CHOICE expressions used by ITAs conveyed desire, advice, opinions, and emphasis. Those used by TOEFL test-takers contained verbs indicating mental processes. In general, it would be fair to say that ITAs' language choices largely reflected the nature of interpersonal communication, plus disciplinary content. The functions and language choice patterns observed in the TOEFL iBT® Speaking Corpus appeared to be determined to a great extent by the task prompts.

Conclusion

This chapter recounts and reflects upon the methodological choices of an investigation of KSs and LFs in ITA and test-taker discourse. Overall, by determining the extent to which relevant functional language abilities are measured in the TOEFL, the study has direct implications for language assessment and ITA training, which are addressed in other publications (Cotos & Chung, 2018, 2019). The focus on methodological rigor here offers a preface to articulating principles for corpus-based Knowledge Framework research, exemplifying the potential of merging SFL and corpus linguistics research methods, and at the same time reflecting on essential research procedures and sharing usable outcomes. Additionally, some challenges and natural limitations encountered in this work can serve as valuable lessons learned. Far from being exhaustive yet helpful are the recommendations in Table 2.14, which are provided in parallel with the key procedural phases described throughout the chapter.

These recommendations may seem to offer an "ideal" approach; however, the reality may impose practical considerations and require many departures that can impact the generalizability of findings. This chapter illustrated and

Table 2.14 Methodological challenges and suggested recommendations for corpus-based Knowledge Framework research

Challenges	Recommendations
Compiling and preparing corpora	
• Using spoken texts provided by an external source for comparative analysis with target discourse	Ensure consistency of transcription protocol.
• Collecting spoken texts in natural settings	Reduce factors that may affect the authenticity of discourse and record metadata. Plan more time for corpus compilation and text processing; if possible, begin new tasks concurrently with data collection to ensure efficiency and timely progress.
• Designing specialized corpora for comparative analyses	Establish appropriate balance and sampling criteria; stratified sampling, although desired, may not be possible.
Adopting/adapting an analytic framework	
• Applying an existing framework to a new research task	Determine whether the framework categories are sufficiently clear for the task; if not, conduct additional analysis to generate suitable and comprehensive framework descriptors. Determine and define the unit of annotation.

(*Continued*)

Table 2.14 (*Continued*)

Challenges	Recommendations
• Applying an existing framework to new types of data	Test the framework on random samples of target discourse (e.g., curriculum genres and test-elicited responses) to determine the extent to which the framework categories apply to the data at hand; if needed, expand the range of categories to capture the nature of the data.
Annotating corpora	
• Applying the framework as an annotation schema	Provide substantial training for annotators; if possible, engage the annotators in testing and refining the analytic framework. Conduct pilot annotation and develop a rigorous protocol with specific segmentation and annotation guidelines.
• Annotating corpus texts	Choose appropriate software for linguistic coding; if possible, one that visualizes the annotated data. Ensure that the annotators consistently consult/apply/fine-tune the annotation schema and follow the annotation guidelines. Continue updating the annotation protocol throughout the entire annotation process.
• Monitoring the quality and reliability of annotation	Establish a protocol for identifying and resolving disagreements among annotators. Conduct ongoing adjudication sessions and record initial and adjudicated annotations. Choose appropriate measures of reliability (e.g., between/among annotators; between annotators and final adjudication).
Analyzing annotated corpus data	
• Processing the data	Extract annotated data into different datasets to allow multiple types of analysis.
• Examining the data	Select quantitative analysis measures appropriate for the size and composition of the corpora. Triangulate results obtained from different types of analysis.

justified some points of departure, to the extent possible considering the factors contributing to representativeness and how those factors aligned with the purpose of this corpus study. It may be worth adding here that, given the variation in how domains may be structured, it would have been ideal to compile a domain-specific corpus that would extend across many geographically bound ITA communities at different universities, not only at Iowa State University. This limits generalizability, as it leaves open the question of how representative the corpus is of ITA language use in general. Furthermore, although sampling issues were considered and rationalized in terms of corpus size, adequate variability (including first language and gender) is critical to representativeness. A larger number of speech samples per category would have been desired to account for the true variation inherent in the ITA population at Iowa State and the ITA population elsewhere.

More broadly, this chapter has attempted to reiterate the importance of advancing a discipline-wide culture of replicable and reproducible data-driven linguistic research. To increase verification and accountability in linguistic research, we must thus prioritize "transparency about methods of data collection and analysis, and transparency about the status of source data" (Berez-Kroeker et al., 2018, p. 8). This chapter has described key methodological procedures and outcomes in order to illustrate the degree of transparency needed for corpus-based Knowledge Framework research. Details about methods of data collection included the conditions under which text samples were collected, participants from whom the texts were obtained, and criteria established for a principled design of the two corpora. Details about methods of data analysis covered the steps prerequisite to the application of the analytic framework (testing/refining) and to the annotation of the corpora (pilot annotation and coding guidelines), as well as the types of analyses (descriptive, CA, n-gram) undertaken to answer the research questions based on the frequency of occurrence, relative associations, and linguistic instantiations of KSs and LFs. While prioritizing transparency in these realms, similar to Moreno and Swales (2018), particular attention was paid to the reliability of creating the annotated corpus datasets (inter-annotator agreement at unit boundary and function levels).

Arguably, working with language data can pose inherent constraints, which are generally acknowledged and not deemed too controversial, especially in methodologically eclectic studies. Nevertheless, "they do not relieve us of the obligation of scientific accountability" (Berez-Kroeker et al., 2018, p. 5). According to Gawne et al. (2017), mechanisms for increasing transparency are greatly needed, as many linguistic studies do not describe the methods or data sources explicitly enough. Thus, accounting for methodological transparency (including how complications are addressed) and generating peer-accepted guidelines should become essential requisites for replicability in corpus-based Knowledge Framework research. Reproducibility is a more ambitious endeavor because it calls for providing the disciplinary community with access to personally created corpus data; however, it is not unrealistic considering the data sharing possibilities afforded by continuously advancing technologies (e.g., Maxwell, 2012; Thieberger, 2009; Thieberger & Berez, 2012).

To conclude, the methods of inquiry should be replicable, provided that sufficient procedural and data-specific details are supplied so that the same procedures could be repeated. The results should be reproducible, provided that the same results from other studies with methods as closely matched to an original study as possible are obtained. Ultimately, the same deductions from replication studies or reanalyzes of the original study should be drawn, which would allow for inferential reproducibility (Goodman, Fanelli, & Ioannidis, 2016).

Acknowledgements

This research was funded by the TOEFL® Committee of Examiners 2015 Research Program, Educational Testing Service. Gratitude is expressed to the anonymous reviewers and the Technical Editor for their helpful comments, and to the research team for their substantial contributions to the project.

References

Berez-Kroeker, L.G., Smythe Kung, S., Kelly, B.F., Heston, T., Holton, G., Pulsifer, P., Beaver, D.I., Chelliah, S., Dubinsky, S., Meier, R.P., Thieberger, N., Rice, K., & Woodbury, A.C. (2018). Reproducible research in linguistics: A position statement on data citation and attribution in our field. *Linguistics, 56*(1), 1–18.

Biber, D. (1993). Representativeness in corpus design. *Literary and Linguistic Computing, 8*(4), 243–257.

Biber, D., Connor, U., & Upton, T. (2007). *Discourse on the Move: Using corpus analysis to describe discourse structure*. John Benjamins.

Biber, D., & Jones, J.K. (2009). Quantitative methods in corpus linguistics. In A. Lüdeling and M. Kytö (Eds.), *Corpus linguistics: An international handbook* (pp. 1286–1304). Walter de Gruyter.

Claerbout J.F., & Karrenbach M. (1992). Electronic documents give reproducible research a new meaning. *SEG Technical Program Expanded Abstracts* (pp. 601–604).

Clausen, S.E. (1998). *Applied correspondence analysis.* A SAGE University Paper.

Cotos, E., & Chung, Y. (2018). Domain description: Validating the interpretation of TOEFL iBT® Speaking scores for ITA screening and certification purposes. (TOEFL iBT Research Report No. RR-85). Educational Testing Service. Org/10.1002/ets2.12233

Cotos, E., & Chung, Y. (2019). Functional language in curriculum genres: Implications for screening international teaching assistants. *Journal of English for Academic Purposes, 41*, 100766.

Donoho, D.L. (2010). An invitation to reproducible computational research. *Biostatistics, 11*, 385–388.

Eder, M., Rybicki, J., & Kestemont, M. (2016). Stylometry with R: A Package for computational text analysis. *R Journal, 8*(1), 107–121.

Gawne, L., Kelly, B.F., Berez-Kroeker, A.L., & Heston, T. (2017). Putting practice into words: The state of data and methods transparency in grammatical descriptions. *Language Documentation & Conservation, 11*, 157–189.

Gleason, J. (2014). Meaning-based scoring: A systemic functional linguistics model for automated test tasks. *Hispania, 97*(4), 466–488.

Goodman, S.N., Fanelli, D., & Ioannidis, J.P.A. (2016). What does research reproducibility mean? Science Translational Medicine, *8*(341), 1–6. Retrieved from http://stm.sciencemag.org/content/8/341/341ps12/tab-pdf.

Levis, J., Levis, G.M., & Slater, T. (2012). Written English into Spoken: A functional discourse analysis of American, Indian, and Chinese TA presentations. In G. Gorsuch (Ed.), *Working theories for teaching assistant development: Time-tested & robust theories, frameworks, & models for TA & ITA learning* (pp. 529–573). New Forums.

Leung, C., & Mohan, B. (2004). Teacher formative assessment and talk in classroom contexts: Assessment as discourse and assessment of discourse. *Language Testing, 20*, 335–359.

Maxwell, M. (2012). Electronic grammars and reproducible research. In S. Nordhoff (Ed.), *Electronic grammaticography* (Language Documentation & Conservation Special Publication, No. 4) (pp. 207–234). University of Hawai'i Press,

McCarthy, P.M., Watanabe, S., & Lamkin, T.A. (2012). The Gramulator: A tool for the identification of indicative linguistic features. In P.M. McCarthy & C. Boonthum (Eds.), *Applied natural language processing and contend analysis: Identification, investigation, and resolution* (pp. 311–332). IGI Global.

McEnery, T., Xiao, R., & Tono, Y. (2006). *Corpus-based language studies: An advanced resource book.* Routledge.

Mohan, B. (1986). *Language and content.* Addison-Wesley.

Mohan, B. (1989). Knowledge structures and academic discourse. *Word, 40*, 99–115.

Mohan, A., & Beckett, G.H. (2003). A functional approach to content-based language learning: Recasts in causal explanations. *The Modern Language Journal, 87*,421–432.

Moreno, A.I., & Swales, J.M. (2018). Strengthening move analysis methodology towards bridging the function-form gap. *English for Specific Purposes, 50*, 40–63.

Sinclair, J. (1995). From theory to practice. In G. Leech, G., Myers, and J. Thomas (Eds.). *Spoken English on Computer* (pp. 99–112). Longman.

Slater, T., & Mohan, B.A. (2010). Cooperation between science teachers and ESL teachers: A register perspective. *Theory into Practice, 49*(2), 91–98.

Thieberger, N. (2009). Steps toward a grammar embedded in data. In P. Epps & A. Arkhipov (Eds.), *New challenges in typology: Transcending the borders and refining the distinctions* (p. 389–408). Mouton de Gruyter.

Thieberger, N., & Berez, A.L. (2012). Linguistic data management. In N. Thieberger (ed.), *The Oxford handbook of linguistic fieldwork* (pp. 90–118). Oxford University Press.

Yelland, P.M. (2010). An introduction to correspondence analysis. *The Mathematica® Journal, 12*, 1–21.

About the Author

Elena Cotos is an associate professor in the Applied Linguistics Program and graduate faculty in the Human Computer Interaction Interdisciplinary Program at Iowa State University. She is also the Director of the Center for Communication Excellence of the Graduate College. She investigates written and spoken discourse, automated writing evaluation, the application of corpus-based genre analysis to applied natural language processing tasks, and computer-assisted language learning and assessment.

3 Student Academic Writing: Situated Enactment of Genre, Argument, and Knowledge Structure

Constant Leung

Abstract

Academic writing is widely acknowledged to be challenging for students. In this chapter I will focus on the situated nature of academic writing, taking account of discipline-relevant content and intellectual sensibilities. I will also pay attention to Toulmin's informal logic of argument and Mohan's knowledge structures that can be used to help analyze the compositional interiority found in a good deal of academic discourse. The pedagogic relevance of this orientation will be illustrated through an analysis of a sample of student writing and tutor comments through the lens of genre, argument, and knowledge structure. It will be argued that just as there is no one finite way of knowing and doing academic literacy, there are no fixed universal templates for academic writing across different disciplines in different teaching–learning contexts; but the concepts of genre, argument, and knowledge structure can be used as criterial considerations to provide insight into how academic writing is construed and enacted.

Keywords: academic literacy; academic writing; disciplinary sensibility; knowledge structure; informal logic of argument

This chapter focuses on academic literacy in higher education, with particular reference to writing. The use of language for academic communication is widely acknowledged to be a complex phenomenon. The effective use of written language for academic purposes is a particular challenge for both teachers and students at all levels of education. It is commonly acknowledged that writing is the one of the locales where difficulties in emulating expert practice show up most clearly. A good deal of research in the past thirty years or so has explored the nature of this kind of language use at all levels of education, often with a view to applying research findings to teaching. In educational contexts where the student population is linguistically diverse, the challenges of academic language for those with an additional/second language background are well acknowledged. Indeed, universities often have special academic language support provision for international students, although debates continue on what counts as appropriate provision in terms of conceptualization of academic literacy and modes of delivery (e.g., Lea & Street, 1998; Lillis & Scott, 2007; Wingate, 2016).

The backdrop to the discussion in this chapter is the disciplinary and rhetorical interiority of academic writing at university as it impacts on students' attempts to appropriate expert practice. The discussion will try to show the educationally and socially situated nature of academic writing, taking account of both discipline-relevant content and intellectual sensibilities as well as informal logic of argument and knowledge structures that are academic community-wide. The compositional interiority is illustrated by a sample of student writing and tutor comments through the lens of genre, argument, and knowledge structure. It is argued that just as there is no one finite way of knowing and doing academic literacy, there are no fixed universal templates for academic writing across different disciplines in different teaching–learning contexts; but the concepts of genre, argument, and knowledge structure can be used as criterial considerations to provide insight into how academic writing is construed and enacted. The main aim of this chapter is to offer a close-up view, analytically speaking, of the interiority of academic writing, as seen through tutors' evaluation and feedback comments, with reference to the concepts of genre, argument, and knowledge structure. While it is not the main focus of this discussion, it will be seen that the analytic approach adopted here is potentially relevant to formative assessment in so far as it can help identify individual students' learning needs.

The chapter is organized in four main parts. The first part will draw on Street's (1984, among others) concept of literacy practice to frame the complex uses of language and literacy for academic purposes in terms of his ideological model. The ideological model alerts us to the need to recognize disciplinary specificities in academic writing in terms of content and rhetorical sensibility. The next part locates academic and language and literacy within an ideological perspective, taking account of the heuristic value of genre analysis (e.g., Swales, 1990) as it relates to academic disciplines. After that I will explore writing at university as an academic disciplinary practice. The work of Toulmin on argument (e.g., 1958/2003) and Mohan on knowledge structure (e.g., 1986) are invoked, in addition to the idea of genre, to provide an analytic lens to look into the interiority of academic writing. In the final part, a sample of student writing accompanied by tutor comments will be used to show the analytic purchase of the triumvirate of genre, argument, and knowledge structure. The chapter will close with some brief concluding comments on the heuristic value of examining student writing and tutor comments as a window into the interiority of academic writing in context. For reasons of focus and rhetorical economy, the term academic literacy in this discussion refers to reading and writing primarily, but it assumes that listening and speaking are often involved.

Academic Language and Literacy—An Evolving Understanding

At school education levels the conceptual distinction between Basic Interpersonal Communication Skills (BICS) and Cognitive Academic Language Proficiency (CALP) proposed by Cummins (1992, 2008, among others) has served as a useful heuristic frame for analytic and pedagogic purposes. At university education level the work by researchers such as Hyland (e.g., 1999, 2004), Ivanič (e.g., 1998, 2004), Nesi and Gardner (2012) and Swales (e.g., 1990, 2004) have shed a good deal of light on different aspects of academic writing in terms of discipline-sensitive content components and structuring, use of language at lexical and clause levels, and authorial voice and stance. A good deal of this work is associated with the concept of "genre". The concept itself has been developed with reference to different theoretical orientations (e.g., Bazerman, Bonini, & Figueiredo, 2009; Martin & Rose, 2008; Swales, 1990). Generally speaking, genre studies have provided analytic information on content structuring, rhetorical styling, and text organization. It has been pointed out that much of genre-based knowledge is primarily referenced to selected "model" sample texts (on whatever criteria). However, there does not seem to be any delimitation to the range of possible samples because writing, as any other mode of communication, is an open, recursive, and always emergent phenomenon. For this reason selected samples tend to appeal to specific niches. Furthermore, for students the actual use of language to write, and learning to write, is a "live" interactional process involving subject content-based tasks, and their writings are subject to expert opinions and judgments. So template-driven guidance is of limited utility, and wholesale reproduction of expert sample texts is often neither appropriate nor possible. For these reasons academic language remains a somewhat elusive and hard-to-pin-down phenomenon, particularly when interpreting theory and research findings for pedagogic application. The National Academies of Sciences (2017, p. 5) recently stated that "while of critical importance, 'academic language' has been difficult to define, and is variously characterized in functional, grammatical, lexical, rhetorical, and pragmatic terms. As a result, efforts to support its development in classrooms have been inconsistent, just as efforts to assess its development have been problematic." There is little doubt that, given the work-in-progress nature of our understanding of academic language and literacy, the teaching and learning of using language for academic purposes is only partially supported by text-focused research. And because much of the research is focused on expert texts (with some notable exceptions such as Nesi & Garder, 2012 and Tribble & Wingate, 2013), an additional challenge for teachers of academic writing is that novices may have difficulty engaging with such texts; indeed they may even be seen to be irrelevant by students. Wingate (2016, p. 6) makes this observation: "when we used expert texts in academic writing classes in the past, we often heard from students that they found these texts not only intimidating but also irrelevant to the assignments they had to write."

It seems that there is an unbridged gap between research-linked conceptualization and pedagogic application. Perhaps we can throw some light on this conundrum by referring to Street's (1984, 2012, among others; Leung & Street, 2012, 2014, 2017) work on literacy, with particular reference to the contradistinction between autonomous and ideological models of literacy in education and in society more generally. Street's (2012) conceptual analysis identifies two models of literacy: the autonomous model of literacy "works with the assumption that it is, in itself, independent and will consequently have effects on other social and cognitive practices" (p. 28). This model of literacy, once embedded in curriculum specifications and introduced into teaching programs, will claim universal applicability and usability. For instance, in recent years the National Curriculum in England has adopted a phonics-based reading program for the school subject English in the early stages of primary (elementary) education. The policy claim is that phonics skills, once acquired, will equip students to decode and make sense of the reading materials they encounter, irrespective of the topic, domain, and context involved. Recontextualizing this view for academic writing, the autonomous model would suggest that once we have identified the textual features of representative writings (however defined), we can use them as a template for teaching and learning. By learning these textual features successfully, we would be able to tackle all kinds of academic writing effectively. This is a totalizing claim. The ideological model, by contrast, is premised on a more situated, culturally sensitive and pluralistic view of what counts as reading and writing in context. Street (2012) argues that "literacy is a social practice, not simply a technical and neutral skill...it is embedded in socially constructed epistemological principles" (p. 29). There are two conceptual components in this view: literacy as manifestation and reflection of epistemological diversity, and literacy as social practice. These components are fundamentally connected to the ways in which we understand academic literacy as situated practice.

The ideological model of literacy suggests that reading and writing do not just involve the use of seemingly neutral language knowledge such as vocabulary and grammar: "The ways in which people address reading and writing are themselves rooted in conceptions of knowledge, identity and being" (Street, 2012, p. 29). I will first address the issues related to knowledge, or more broadly epistemological principles. Reading and writing can be understood from a variety of perspectives. The phonics-based method to decoding text adopted in the current English National Curriculum is but one of the many approaches to teaching reading. In this approach, to know and use language for reading and writing is, first and foremost, to know features of lexical level phonation and (linguistic) morphology. There are other approaches such as "Whole Language" which prioritizes understanding of whole text meaning for personal appreciation and cultivation of individuality (rather than technically oriented word level decoding and spelling with reference to standardized conventions). Seen in this light the adoption of the phonics approach in the English National Curriculum is a policy choice in that it favors a technical and standards-based view of reading over a more personal development orientation associated with liberal democratic sentiments. (The contestations over the validity and effectiveness of different reading approaches are often referred to as the Reading Wars; for a summary, see Anderson, 2000.) From this perspective all literacy approaches and practices are ideological, even when they claim to be context-independent and content-neutral.

Linked to the idea of models of literacy are the concepts of literacy event and literacy practice. These are related to "identity and being" in Street's formulation. Heath (1983, p. 93) refers to a literacy event as "any occasion in which a piece of writing is integral to the nature of the participants' interactions and their interpretative processes." The concept of literacy event forms the basis of literacy practice which takes account of the activities around literacy events and connect them to cultural and social ways of seeing and doing things. Just as there are different ways of doing and using reading and writing for different purposes and contexts, there are different literacy practices. "Literacy practices…refer to both the activities of reading and/or writing in which people are involved in specific contexts and also to the idea that such people have of literacy, involving the particular ways of thinking and doing reading and writing in cultural contexts" (Street, 2012, p. 37). So the concept of literacy practice locates literacy events within a nexus of beliefs, knowledges, and values among participants of a particular community in a particular setting; such participants' beliefs, knowledges, and values give particular meaning to their reading and writing, and in turn the meanings they give to their reading and writing reflect, in full or in part, their actual or aspirant membership of a particular community. Therefore, the literacy practice of a church gospel group in, say, a particular part of New York should, *inter alia*, be seen as embodying and reflecting the group's collective way of doing things in that context. A cautionary ontological point is that individual members of a particular literacy practice community are not assumed to be totally homogeneous in their beliefs and values, but that their engagement with literacy activities are informed by their particular community's beliefs and values.

Perhaps it should be noted that while literacy events can be observed, literacy practice has to be inferred from observation of actual conduct. Street (2000) comments thus: "we cannot get at [literacy practices] simply by sitting on the wall with a video and watching what is happening: you can photograph literacy events but you cannot photograph literacy practices." The concept of literacy practice is an attempt "to handle the events and the patterns of activity around literacy but to link them to something broader of a cultural and social kind" (p. 22). The extracts of student assignments discussed later in this chapter are therefore part of literacy events; the analytic comments on them represent an effort to tap into the participants' enactments of underlying literacy practice. At this point I turn to a related discussion on academic literacy and try to identify the commonality between literacy practice and academic literacy with a view to exploring the demands and challenges faced by students in terms of academic writing.

Academic Literacy as Ideological Literacy Practice

The effective use of language for academic purpose is regarded as an essential capability for all members of the academic community. It is also one of the key challenges for students across all disciplines. Wingate (2016) offers a view of academic literacy that encompasses a wide-ranging communicative repertoire:

> Academic literacy is far more than academic writing, although the term is often used with reference to writing only. I understand academic literacy as the ability to communicate competently in an academic discourse community; this encompasses reading, evaluating information, as well as presenting, debating, and creating knowledge through both

> speaking and writing. These capabilities require knowledge of the community's epistemology, of the genres through which the community interacts, and of the conventions that regulate these interactions. This understanding of academic literacy has two main implications. First, academic literacy has to be acquired by ALL students...and second, it cannot be acquired outside the discourse community. (p. 2, emphasis in original)

The invocation of "the community's epistemology" and "the genres through which the community interacts" resonates with Street's idea of people and their "particular ways of thinking and doing reading and writing in cultural contexts."

The concept of genre, as it has been defined and interpreted in the field of academic literacy has undoubtedly been very influential. The term is so well-established that it is often invoked in research papers and pedagogic discussions by researchers without glossing (e.g., Hyland & Hyland, 2006; Trible, 2017, among others). Given the wide acceptance and use of this concept, it is worth revisiting how it has been defined in the field. In an early effort to define genre, Swales (1990, p. 58) puts it thus: "a class of communicative events, the members of which share some set of communicative purposes. These purposes are recognized by the expert members of the parent community and thereby constitute the rationale of the genre. This rationale shapes the schematic structure of the discourse and influences and constrains choice of content and style." Hyland (2007, p. 149) defines genre as:

> abstract, socially recognized ways of using language. It is based on the idea that members of a community usually have little difficulty in recognizing similarities in the texts they use frequently and are able to draw on their repeated experiences with such texts to read, understand, and perhaps write them relatively easily. This is, in part, because writing is a practice based on expectations: the reader's chances of interpreting the writer's purpose are increased if the writer takes the trouble to anticipate what the reader might be expecting based on previous texts they have read of the same kind.

Genre then is a way of describing and understanding the communicative activities in which members of a particular academic disciplinary community interact with one another, and of special interest to this discussion, the particular ways in which spoken and written language and other semiotic resources are deployed in communally recognizable ways. In many ways genre is an inclusive term to represent the agreed models for conducting and enacting communicative activities such as attending lectures, and reading and writing research papers. That said, models are abstractions of established ideals or standards, they do not always ensure effectiveness in actual communication. As Swales (1990) points out, genre is a framing device, and "the frame is a starting place, an initial orientation, with no consequent guarantee that effective rhetorical action will actually be accomplished" (p. 61). From the point of view of academic literacy education, this comment on "no guarantee" is both conceptually and pedagogically salient. One of the reasons for "no guarantees" is that the communicative practices can vary in different institutional and teaching–learning contexts, in addition to the variations across the range of academic disciplines. Bhatia (1993) adds a further observation that

> [most] often [genre] is highly structured and conventionalized with constraints on allowable contributions in terms of their intent, positioning, form and functional value. These constraints, however, are often exploited by the expert members of the discourse community to achieve private intentions within the framework of socially recognized purpose(s). (p. 13)

In other words, authorial communicative intent or purpose should be taken into account when we try to understand what a genre comprises in context (Askehave & Swales, 2001). As Paltridge, Starfield, and Tardy (2016) observe:

> The link between text and context...is often indirect and depends on how language users themselves view the context in which the communication is taking place. Contexts, then, are not objective conditions but rather (inter)subjective conditions that are as much created by participants in their interactions with each other (and with others' texts) as by members of particular groups or communities. (p. 23)

The inter-subjective aspect of context is particularly relevant for this discussion. From the teaching and learning point of view, academic literacy can be seen as part of the process of learning and practicing to be part of a scholarly community (e.g. university students) with a specific disciplinary membership (e.g., as a student of Biology). University teachers are generally entrusted to act as experts in their disciplines within their institutions. They are expected to set benchmarks for how things are done and what counts as effective communication. Seen in this light, analytically student academic writing that has been marked and commented on by teachers can reveal explicitly and vividly what students are expected to appropriate and (re-)produce in terms of expert knowledge and practice.

University Student Writing in Academic Disciplinary Practice

University-level academic literacy is widely recognized as discipline-related and institutionally variable (e.g. Lea & Street, 1998; Lillis, 1999; also see university academic support materials, e.g. https://awelu.srv.lu.se/genres-and-text-types/writing-in-academic-genres/research-articles-ras/examples-of-specificity-within-disciplines/). The disciplinary treatment of historical data in, say, History may partially overlap with that in Philosophy in terms of concepts and theories, accepted facts and propositions, and prevailing methods of enquiries. From a student's point of view though, being inducted into an academic discipline such as History would mean, *inter alia*, attending lectures, seminars, and workshops (actual and/or virtual) to get acquainted with content information and producing spoken and written texts for learning and assessment purposes in particular academic contexts. While the use of both spoken and written modes of language is part of this lived process of acquisition, discipline-based written formal language (even if delivered in an oral presentation) has been and remains a key mode of display of acquired knowledge and learning. Echoing Wingate's (2016, p. 4) observation that "writing is the end product of a complex literacy process," we can see the academic written assignment (in a variety of formats of presentations, either individually or as a group) comes at the end of a chain of intellectual and scholarly activities within particular disciplinary contexts:

- the student coming into contact with information in terms of disciplinary facts, concepts and idea, methods and approaches to enquiry,
- identifying and developing discipline-relevant perspectives and sources of information,
- choosing and evaluating relevant information for the task at hand,
- synthesizing selected and assembled information,
- presenting this assemblage in the form of a logical and coherent argumentation.

The everyday activities of attending classes and tutorials, discussing ideas with classmates outside the classroom, working in the library, and studying by oneself are all part of this chain of activities that, in one way or another, contribute to the student's developing disciplinary knowledge and capacity to display such knowledge in discipline-preferred formats (e.g., written essays, laboratory reports) embedding community-acknowledged qualities of argumentation. These qualities turn on notions of logic and coherence.

What counts as logical and coherent is in part discipline-specific and in part academic community-wide within a broader sociocultural milieu. The conceptual distinction between discipline-specific and community-wide logic and coherence is not a zero-sum phenomenon. Rather, disciplinary logic and coherence are Janus-like in that discipline specificity and community-wide commonality manifest themselves at the same time.

Discipline-specific Logic and Coherence

The discipline-specific part is related to the particular perspective or school of thought adopted by the practitioners involved. For instance, in the field of teacher education for the subject English (the subject for school and university, not English as an Additional/Second Language) there is a school of thought associated with the work of Eisner (2003, among others), who championed the notion of connoisseurship which can be deployed to critically appraise actual education practice. So connoisseurship in English teaching is underpinned by a complex body of disciplinary knowledge and professional values concerning pedagogy and classroom experience. A teacher's classroom teaching has to be seen in terms of contingent decision-making regarding what to prioritize—for example, content coverage or student engagement—in context. This perspective can be extended to all subject areas. In contrast, Alexander's (2008, among others) view of dialogic teaching would suggest that the focus of attention is on the ways in which classroom talk between teachers and students are tied to the task at hand (or not, as the case may be). In any study and appraisal of classroom teaching the evidential base should be premised on how far the interactional talk between the teacher and students is contributing to the continuance and development of the topic/subject at hand. The perspectives of Eisner and Alexander are clearly very different. So what counts as logical and coherent in discussing the merits (or otherwise) of any classroom practice would be based on the recourse to the particular perspectives and/or the school of thought involved. It follows that, at a high level of abstraction, the components of the interiority of a discipline—for example, accepted and discredited "facts," concepts, and theories (both current and out of favor ones), qualitative and quantitative characteristics of "admissible" data, levels and use of references—are combined to form the bedrock of disciplinary logic and coherence. This is not to suggest that we should overlook that there may well be different schools of thought in terms of disciplinary logic and coherence amongst the experts in any field; the point here is that each school of thought would have their own configuration of disciplinary logic and coherence.

Community-wide Logic and Coherence

The academic community-wide part of what counts as logical and coherent can be seen to be related to a set of established steps of reasoning. In this respect Toulmin's (1958/2003) seminal work on informal logical structure of argument has been very influential in shaping the ways in which reasoning is construed in academic work generally. More particularly in the field of language education, especially with reference to additional/second language, the analysis of cross-curricular knowledge structures and semantic features underlying subject contents is also directly relevant (e.g., Chamot & O'Mally, 1987; Crandall et al., 1987; Mohan, 1986, 1990, 2001; Mohan, Leung, and Slater, 2010; Tang, 1992). I will first turn to Toulmin's work to provide an account of the structure of argument.

Toulmin's work (1958/2003, 2004; Toulmin, Rieki, & Janik, 1984) is widely recognized to be a major influence on the ways in which argument has been analyzed (see, for example, Andrews, 2001; Andrews & Mitchell, 2001; Bachman, 2005; Boller, Swasy, & Munch, 1990; Chapelle, Enright, & Jamieson, 2008; Hitchcock & Verhej, 2006; Simon, 2008). In his work the terms reasoning, argument, and argumentation appear to be used interchangeably. For this discussion, I will adopt the elaborations made by Andrews (2009) and Andrews and Mitchell (2001) where argumentation is understood in relation to the process and activities that give rise to the "product" of argumentation, that is the argument. In this sense, argument is a manifestation of a thinking process showing "revealed reasoning," in other words argumentation, or the presentation of the steps by which a position can be reached or supported (Mitchell, 2001, p. 22). Seen in this light, argument in academic discussions can be regarded as an end-product of reasoning, and argumentation is the steps in the thinking process involved. The analytic usefulness of this view of reasoning will be shown in the discussion on student writings and tutor comments.

Toulmin's work is relevant to academic literacy because he made a significant shift in argument theory from the abstract and formal criteria drawn from mathematical logic and from formal syllogistic argument to a concern for substantive reasoning in real-world contexts, for example in a study of empirical and/or theoretical issues in Business Studies. The abstract and formal orientation, Toulmin argued, was not helpful in practical arguments dealing with real-world matters. This led to his call for a richer empirically minded format for analysis beyond the traditional formal logic in which only premises and conclusions are of interest. To take account of the complexities material to practical reasoning, his model expands the traditional concerns for premise–conclusion by including four additional distinctive elements of warrant, backing, qualifiers, and rebuttal. Another significant feature of Toulmin's model of argument is its relevance to "trans-disciplinarity" by being both field-invariant and field-dependent at the same time (for the term "field" read "academic discipline" in this discussion, see Toulmin, 1958/2003, Ch. 4, for a discussion). The idea of field invariance is based on the claim that the broad steps in the structure of an argument represented by the six elements in argumentation—namely claim (premise–conclusion), data (grounds), warrant, backing, qualifiers, and rebuttal—would apply across different fields (and academic disciplines). However, the nature and use of evidence used in support of claims or conclusions, and the way in which such evidence is used to support the conclusion, will vary according to the field or academic discipline (Toulmin, 1958/2003):

> What has to be recognised is that validity is an intra-field not an inter-field notion. Argument within any field can be judged by standards appropriate in that field and some will fall short; but it must be expected that the standards will be field-dependent, and that the merits to be demanded of an argument in one field will be found to be absent from entirely meritorious arguments in another. (p. 235)

It seems clear that our earlier discussion on discipline-specific logic and coherence resonates with the notions of intra-field-dependence and inter-field validity. Toulmin's model of argument has been taken up by subject specialists in a range of fields in the humanities, sciences, and social sciences, from jurisprudence to medicine, from artificial intelligence to zoology.

As indicated above, Toulmin's model of argument consists of six elements, operationalized as moves: claim (or conclusion), data (also labelled as "grounds" for the claim in Toulmin et al., 1984), warrant, qualifier, rebuttal, and backing. The function of each element will be described briefly in turn, leading to an illustrative example of the argument structure "in action."

The basis of any argument is a Claim (or conclusion, C) for which supporting Data (D—grounds, evidence, information, facts) is provided, giving the following move:

The move from D to C constitutes a step which gives rise to the question: how do you get from D to C? The answer to this question is Warrant (W). It acts as a bridge from D to C, in other words, it "warrants" authorizing this step or registers the legitimacy of the step involved. The warrant generally consists of general rules and principles rather than additional factual information or data (D). In arguments the warrant may be implicit, whereas the data is always explicit.

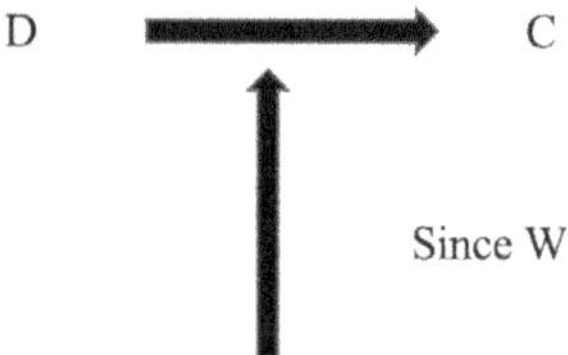

Warrants may vary in the strength or force they confer on the claim they justify and support, from the unequivocal to degrees of qualification, expressed through the use of modal qualifiers (Q), such as "possibly," "probably," "presumably," and so on.

An additional element to include is that of Backing (B) which is used to answer the question arising from the warrant: Why you would think that this warrant is appropriate or relevant? In other words, backing is used to establish the authority of warrants in particular fields or disciplines, which, in all probability, will be field- or discipline-dependent.

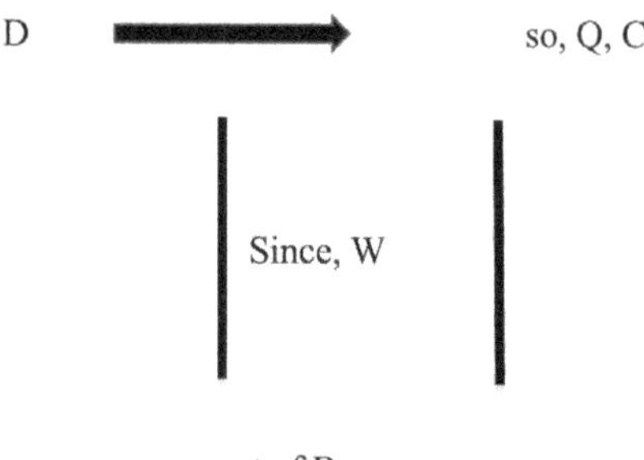

The warrant may only justify the claim or conclusion if subject to certain conditions, which, if not met would lead the warrant to be set aside. This is known as the rebuttal (R). As such, we now have the process and structure:

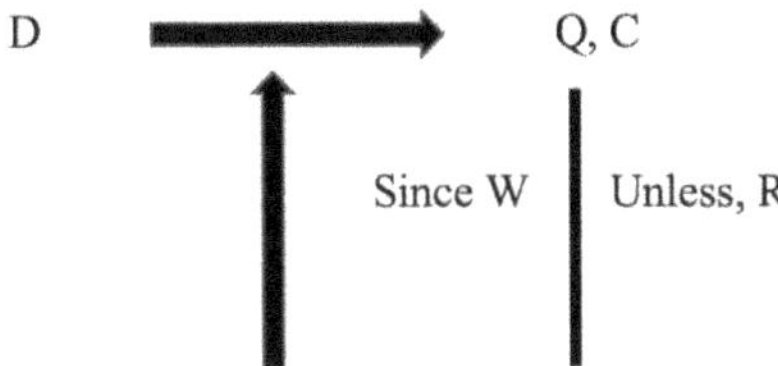

To illustrate the model and its elements, we draw on the example often cited in relation to the Toulmin model (1958/2003) of Harry from Bermuda.

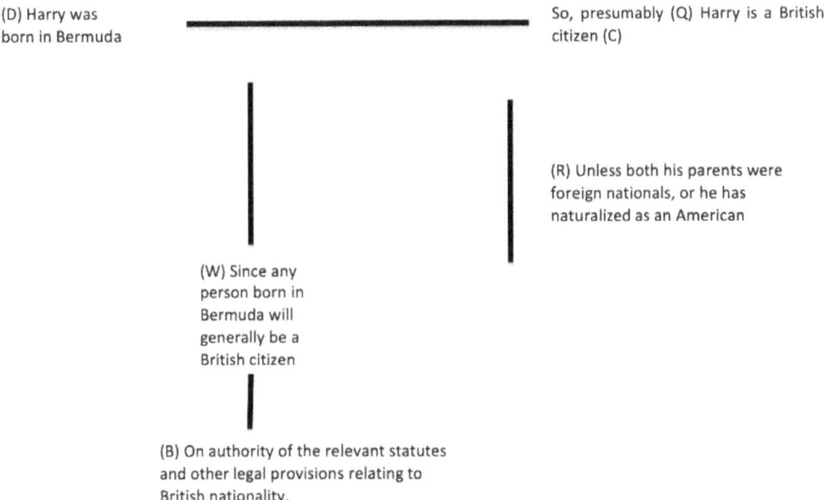

Perhaps it should be pointed out that it is assumed that Toulmin's schema of informal logic is not always straightforward in application. As Crammond (1998) remarks:

> Toulmin's (1958) schematic was developed in response to a concern with formal argument as it was related to epistemology. Whereas his treatment of the issue represented a definite advance in the conceptualization of everyday, naturally occurring arguments, it provided little information as how such arguments might be presented or identified in extended discourse. (p. 233)

That said, the Toulmin model will be invoked here as part of the commentary on student writing presently; "local" discourse complications alluded to by Crammond will be readily addressed. To complete the discussion on community-wide logic and coherence, I will draw on Mohan and his colleagues' work on knowledge structures, as this body of work is articulated very closely to actual curriculum content.

Academic literacy can be seen in terms of curriculum content and tasks as expressed through spoken and written discourse. A curriculum is essentially a set of specifications of content knowledge and activities to be included in teaching and learning with reference to a disciplinary area, for example, History. For heuristic purposes Mohan (1986, 1990) conceptualizes the teaching and learning as curriculum activities which comprise practical hands-on tasks accompanied by conceptual and theoretical engagement. Drawing on aspects of schema theory and ethnographic semantics, he further suggests that curricular tasks across different subject areas can be analyzed into identifiable knowledge structures within a knowledge framework:

> There are three pairs of related structures: a description of a particular object or person involves a classification or set of general concepts; a particular temporal sequence of states, events or actions often involves general principles (social rules or cause-effect relations) which relate one state to another; a particular choice or decision often involves general values. (Mohan, 1990, p. 17; see Chapter 1 this volume for further details.)

Knowledge structures thus characterized are abstractions. But they can be related to classroom activities quite readily

The three pairs of related knowledge structures of DESCRIPTION and CLASSIFICATION, SEQUENCE and PRINCIPLES, and CHOICE and EVALUATION are intended to represent a set of general patterns of information organization found in a broad range of cultural and institutional contexts, including classrooms at different levels of education. The broken lines in the middle of Table 3.1 signal that thinking and enacting are not regarded as separate and compartmentalized activities; indeed they are meant to be "leaky" and intertwined in teaching and learning. Likewise, the knowledge structures are not stand-alone entities; in many if not all lesson activities, they are composites within a framework. For instance, in History the study of the political events leading up to, say, the decolonization of India in the 1950s (associated principle: cause and effect) is likely to include descriptions of incidents (associated classification: peaceful, violent) and key players such as Lord Mountbatten, Nehru, and Gandhi (associated classification: British colonists, Indian nationalists), and choosing a historical perspective on outcomes (associated evaluation: failure of empire, moral redemption in

Table 3.1 Key knowledge structures across curricula

Conceptual/ theoretical level	**CLASSIFICATION**	**PRINCIPLES**	**EVALUATION**
Thinking	• classifying • categorising • defining…	• experimenting • explaining • generalising (cause, effects, rules…) • interpreting & concluding…	• assessing • judging • criticising • justifying (opinions and preferences)…
Enacting	• comparing • contrasting • describing • observing…	• noting and working with time and chronology (e.g. creating a narrative of unfolding events) • observing change over time • plan and execute procedures (e.g. experiments)…	• identifying answers and solutions • making decisions • problem solving • recommending…
Classroom activity level	**DESCRIPTION**	**SEQUENCE**	**CHOICE**

the mid-20th century). Knowledge structures can be seen as serving a framing device for content selection and discourse articulation in curriculum tasks, which are connected to the notion of meaning coherence (Carrell, 1982; Carrell & Eisterhold, 1987; Nassaji, 2007).

From the point of view of this discussion, while it is not claimed that these knowledge structures cover all possible curricular knowledge and activities, they are heuristically useful for analyzing curriculum-based literacy activities. Across the curriculum at all levels of education it is quite easy to see that DESCRIPTION is just as much a part of studying literature (describing characters) as studying biology (describing a plant); SEQUENCE is an indispensable part of a narrative in stories as it is in the steps involved a science experiment; CHOICE is as much part of a town planning exercise in Social Studies or Geography involving locating a municipal car park as it is in choosing a particular technology or style in Product Design.

Knowledge structures, as they are presented in work of Mohan and his colleagues, are both discipline-specific and community-wide. They are discipline-specific in that they manifest themselves in the content of the subject matter: For example, the description of the character of Lenny in Steinbeck's novel *Of Mice and Men* is part of the study of that particular work in the discipline of English Studies. At the same time, DESCRIPTION is community-wide in that, as already indicated above, they are part of the teaching and learning activities in practically all disciplinary areas, from Engineering to Religious Studies. It is this dual discipline-specific and community-wide character of knowledge structures, formulated abstractly, that lends itself to the main concern of this discussion, the interiority of academic literacy, as the discussion in the next section will elaborate and exemplify.

Looking into Academic Writing

By bringing together the triumvirate of concepts of genre, argument, and knowledge structure, we are now in a position to tap into the interiority of academic writing with an analytic lens. I will use a set of samples of student writing and their tutors' to-the-point comments to make visible the key features or qualities in academic writing, as construed and enacted by the key players. The sample texts are drawn from a corpus of written university student assignments from a variety of disciplines collected by Wingate and Tribble (2012; also Wingate, 2016). The student text extracts will be accompanied by tutor comments, to be followed by my comments in respect of genre, argument, and/or knowledge structure as appropriate. I will provide contextual information where appropriate to assist understanding of the student discourse. The extracts of student writing are selected as samples to illustrate how student academic writing is construed by tutors, who serve simultaneously as expert practitioners and judges of academic quality in their own disciplines. Although the analytical remarks respond specifically to the substantive issues in the texts involved, many if not all of them are motivated by the trans-disciplinary analytic issues discussed earlier. It should also be said that the tutors' comments are treated as situated expressions of their disciplinary and scholarly sensibilities for heuristic purposes; they are not seen as some kind of reified and immutable manifestations of disciplinary authority. In the interest of clarity my analytic comments on tutor remarks related to the triumvirate of concepts discussed earlier will be tagged as follows:

G—Italicized *G* in Genre/Generic
T—Informal logic of argument (Toulmin)
M—Knowledge structure (Mohan)

Sample Assignment 1

- Discipline: Business Studies
- Assignment title: Use Hackley's Typology to develop and structure a critical review of a marketing idea/theory/concept: Service-Dominant Logic (SDL)

Student text 1a	**Tutor comment**
As explained by Vargo & Lusch, (2004), the reasoning behind the SDL dates back several decades, when resources started to include intangible components such as knowledge and skills. Although abstract, these "*new*" resources have been viewed as increasingly significant to the development of marketing (Brown, 2007).	Which resources? Product? Marketplace?

NB: The acronym "SDL" stands for Service-Dominant Logic. It is glossed elsewhere in the assignment as "an ideology that '*emphasizes the centrality of firm-consumer cooperation in innovative and productive efforts*'."

Analytic comments
The tutor's questions point to inadequate M DESCRIPTION of knowledge and skills involved in the development of SDL. The three questions of "resources, product and marketplace" signal specific disciplinary and Genre sensibility in that they can be seen as reflecting what should be included in the M DESCRIPTION on this topic within the discipline. These questions can also be seen as indicating a problem with T Data and T Claim. The T Claim made on behalf of SDL is not supported by adequate Data.

Student text 1b	Tutor comment
As Ballantyne & Varey (2008) argue, the reason for which the SDL is aptly coherent is that it takes into account important and relevant historical factors of marketing that have inevitably led to the birth of this paradigm. That being said, the consistency behind this ideology has led to the co-creation of value between firms and consumers, whereby both entities become contributors to the overall value of a good or service (Vargo & Lusch, 2004).	This phrase suggests that you are going to say something contradictory, when in fact what follows is consistent with what comes before.

Analytic comments

The linguistic signposting "That being said" is seen to have triggered a particular reader anticipation of contrast in the M DESCRIPTION. The ensuing information, however, is in fact an affirmation and elaboration of the preceding statement. This can be seen as a problem of M DESCRIPTION informed by disciplinary knowledge and sensibility. If the phrase "that being said" were removed, the second statement could be seen as a form of T Data for the T Claim made in the preceding statement.

In addition, the tutor offers this opinion in the "summary feedback":

> The review is very well constructed and quite convincing in its critiques. I would however raise concerns about the way some source material is used. Even if the quote seems to say what you want it to say, you need to think about the author intent, e.g. Zwick et al. are quite "critical" of the notion of co-creation, so to use their words in support of the range of positive attributes of SDL is probably inappropriate, and would jar with any reader who has read their paper …

The first comment is about the *Generic* structure. The concern expressed by the tutor seems to reflect a problem with T Data-T Claim at the cross-text level, that is, the support for Zwick et al. as presented by the student is not "safe" from a disciplinary perspective. More specifically, the tutor's comment on this point suggests that there is no T Warrant for T Claim made. Again this comment is informed by the tutor's disciplinary knowledge and Genre sensibility, and it can be seen as an instance of the complexity of interpreting the meaning of extended discourse raised by Crammond (1998).

Sample Assignment 2

- Discipline: History
- Assignment title: The movement fell apart from within. Is that an adequate explanation for the decline of Chartism?

Student text 2a	Tutor comment
From 1832[9] the Chartist movement grew and grew, delivering petitions to Parliament with over 1 million signatures, and holding mass rallies and national conventions where attendance was large enough on occasion to require 8,000 troops to be deployed along with the enlistment of thousands of special constables.[10]	[Referring to footnote 9 which states: "The start-point of the movement that Stedman Jones ascribed".] I don't think you need to footnote this. [Referring to the 8000 troops] Could these troops be an overreaction by the State in response to the perceived threat?

Analytic comments

The tutor's comment on footnote 9 suggests that it is an unnecessary detail. This comment reflects a sensibility based on discipline-based knowledge; implicitly it tells the student that "everyone knows this." Adequacy of M DESCRIPTION can therefore be seen as contingent on what is being talked about and what counts as commonplace or new information. Some T Claims may not need to be accompanied by T Data, T Warrant, and T Backing, if they are already widely accepted or known. The comment on the deployment of the 8000 troops is related to the M PRINCIPLES of cause-effect and interpretation. The M SEQUENCE of events—large rally and deployment of troops—is seen to be in need of an alternative explanation.

Student text 2b	Tutor comment
Brown concisely identifies the problem: "to Lancashire cotton-workers, for example, Chartism held out the prospect of economic improvement and factory reform; to the London artisans, it pointed the way to political equality."[20] While this multi-faceted appeal would usually be a strength of a political movement, in this case it was coupled with the Chartist leaders chasing different goals.	Good Could you suggest an example?

Analytic comments

The comment "Good" indicates the tutor's approval in terms of M DESCRIPTION, signaling that the information provided in text on the different aspirations of the Chartist movements in different parts of the country is accurate. The request for an example (of a strength of a political movement) suggests a need for (more) T Data to support the T Claim.

In the summary feedback the tutor says:

> This is a good essay and a useful platform on which to build improvements. You have done some good extra reading and demonstrated a good understanding of the material. I suppose the answer to this question depends on how you view Chartism, as you suggest. Some historians such as Asa Briggs have focussed on materialist explanations, while Gareth Stedman Jones has left such explanations behind, to focus on issues of political representation. You might want to consider Miles Taylor and what he says about State resistance to Chartism and how oppression oscillated between heavy handed intervention and quieter legislative efforts. Structurally, perhaps you might want to think about spending less time on who Chartists were and what they were about and instead focus on the main debates of historians of Chartism. You also might want to ask yourself whether the historians you are dealing with are really convincing.
>
> Structurally, the essay is quite clear, though you might want to try and make paragraphs of a more consistent length.

The first eight lines of this summary feedback are informed by disciplinary knowledge and sensibility. The tutor is offering advice as to how to dissect the issues, more specifically, how to discuss and examine the different T Arguments presented by different historians. At the same time this advice is related to M CLASSIFICATION, that different perspectives on history should be understood, described, and compared. The recommendation "…asking yourself whether the historians you are dealing with are really convincing" can be seen as advice on critically assessing the quality of the T Arguments: Are the claims well supported by T Data, what are the T Warrants and T Backings, are there grounds for T Rebuttal? The comments on the structuring of the assignment are related to Genre conventions, as understood by the tutor: content selection and inclusion with respect to the title of the assignment, and proportionate treatment of key content in terms of word length.

Sample Assignment 3

- Discipline: History
- Assignment title: How did Early Modern Culture Shape Ideas about Civility and Manners?

Student text 3a	**Tutor comment**
From the language found in Fanny Burney's diary, written in the late 18th Century, it is clear that manners and civility in the presences of the King had developed from a code of strength and virility to one of politeness and presentation	It would be nice to hear what it is that Burney had to say.

Analytic comments

This remark by the tutor suggests the T Claim that "manners and civility in the presences of the King had developed from a code of strength and virility to one of politeness and presentation" is in need of (more) T Data support. Given that the source of this T Data is to be drawn from Burney's account, an exposition of this account may trigger considerations of T Warrant, T Backing, T Qualification, and T Rebuttal. This tutor remark can also be seen as indicating inadequate M DESCRIPTION from a disciplinary point of view: One should not simply make an assertion on the authority of one unexplicated reference, which in itself is informed by Genre sensibility regarding "good" scholarly practice.

Student text 3b	**Tutor comment**
Whilst Burney provides strong evidence that courtiers had begun to embrace the rules set down by Castiglione,[1] such as being "well spoken and faire in language" and avoiding being "a babbler, brauler, or	What is this evidence?
chatter,[2]" Elias' argument is inherently flawed. In order to make his conclusions, he has made a key presumption: that the works of Castiglione, Erasmus and even Machiavelli were designed to be achieved.	I'm not sure that this is the case—Elias describes in great detail the ways in which nobles failed to live up to courtly ideals.
[1] Burney [2] Baldassare Castiglione, "A breef rehersall of the chiefe conditions and qualities in a courtier" in Castiglione, The Courtier, trans. Sir Thomas Hoby (translation 1561)	

Analytic comments

The tutor's question "What is this evidence?" suggests that the support for the T Claim (Burney providing some evidence) is unclear; more T Data is required. The second comment contradicts what the student has asserted ("Elias' argument is inherently flawed"); the tutor points out that Elias's work provides details of un-courtly use of language by nobles. This represents the tutor's T Rebuttal of the student's argument on grounds of the T Data is inadequate.

Sample Assignment 4

- Discipline: Philosophy
- Assignment title: Could an agent sincerely accept that she is morally obliged to do something and yet have no inclination at all to do it? And what does this tell us about the relationship between moral reasons and motivation?

Student text 4a	Tutor comment
Moral judgments are distinct from moral rules which lay outside an agent's belief system. A person makes an additional effort to internalize a moral rule. When someone calls something right, he puts it in his *motivational set*, a term used by Williams.	It doesn't seem entirely clear that merely sincerely calling something "right" involves placing it within the motivational set—presumably, in defending an externalist position, you may want to deny this. Perhaps you will say that in calling something right, he *may* put it into his motivational set, if he has other desires that support doing this...

Analytic remarks

The comment by the tutor points out that it is not enough to assert a self-evident truth (calling X right—X becoming motivation). The M SEQUENCE of the movement from calling X to be right and X becoming a person's motivation (or part of it) is an inadequate explanation of the imputed cause-effect, therefore the M PRINCIPLE of causation cannot be sustained. The comment offers an alternative formulation of the M SEQUENCE. From an T Argument point of view the self-evident truth of "calling X and X becoming motivation" is probably not admissible because the validity of a T Claim without T Data is dubious. The alternative suggestion reflects a disciplinary and Genre sensibility as to what may be possible and acceptable as T Argument.

Student text 4b	Tutor comment
We need desires or another non-moral internal reason to internalize these *cold* moral facts. One line of objection would be following Plato's reasoning who asserts that there is no need to internalize moral facts. Moral facts carry within the motivational force and necessarily overrides other reasons. The knowledge of these forms will guarantee motivation by itself.	It may be worth clarifying things a little here. The idea of "cold moral facts" seems somewhat ambiguous. You could mean facts *entirely* external to the agent (as in the sheer wrongness of murder say, which the agent may or may not *judge* to be wrong), or you may mean to refer to what the agent *judges* to be cold facts, but which remain *external* to the agent's *motivations*. It seems it is the latter that would be most effective for your argument, but it would be good to make clear.

Analytic comments

The student text asserts that cold moral facts need to be internalized by a person through some other desire (a T Claim and an on-going point of discussion in this assignment); it is immediately followed by a counter argument (Plato's reasoning reflecting an immanent entelechy). The comments made by the tutor comprise a suggestion to provide a more adequate M DESCRIPTION, and a piece of advice on how to take the T Argument forward. The suggestion is to provide a fuller M DESCRIPTION of cold moral facts that lends itself to M CLASSIFICATION. The advice picks up on the line of reasoning that cold moral facts are judged to be so by an individual and they remain external to an individual's motivations, which can then be seen as T Warrant for the T Claim. All of this is informed by disciplinary knowledge and Genre sensibility.

Concluding Remarks

Academic writing continues to be a complex phenomenon that evades easy characterization. Drawing on Street's ideological model of academic literacy, this discussion explored the disciplinary and rhetorical interiority of academic writing by taking account of the ideas associated with the concepts of genre, argument, and knowledge structure. The concept of genre provides some purchase on the disciplinary content selection and text organization; knowledge structure offers a semantic framework to adjudge content adequacy; argument lays down a structure for analyzing what counts as accepted and acceptable reasoning. The analytic affordances of these concepts are seen through the discussion on the samples of student writing and their tutors' comments. The three-pronged analytic approach, paying particular attention to genre sensibilities, Toulmin's informal logic of argument and Mohan's knowledge structures, has shown its discipline-relevant heuristic value. One can begin to see the merits and the inadequacies (as adjudged by subject tutors) in academic writing more clearly. By paying attention to tutors' comments it is possible to see dynamic and agentive aspects of academic literacy practice related to considerations of genre, informal logic, and knowledge structure. From this point view it is clear that academic literacy is not static and template-driven; what counts as "good" or "poor" student writing, for example, is contingent on tutors' (as situated experts) disciplinary sensibilities and practices. As a corollary, this perspective suggests that academic literacy has to be studied and understood as situated and context-embedded enactments of a nexus of complex ideas and concepts within particular disciplinary communities (for a further discussion see Prior, 2005). It is unlikely that text-oriented characterizations of academic writing, indeed academic literacy more generally, arising from a specific locale and time, would have universal currency. This approach to analyzing student writing and tutor comments also suggests itself to be potentially fruitful in identifying where teaching intervention and support may be needed in specific contexts. In other words, it can be used as an evaluative frame for formative assessment that would focus on individual students' strengths and weaknesses in academic language use in a discipline- and content-relevant way.

References

Alexander, R. (2008). *Towards dialogic teaching: Rethinking classroom* talk (4th edition). Diaogas.

Anderson, K. (2000). The Reading Wars: Understanding the debate over how best to teach children to read (Review article). *Los Angeles Times*. Retrieved from https://papers.ssrn.com/sol3/papers.cfm?abstract_id=935776

Andrews, R. (2001). Reconceiving argument. In R. Andrews & S. Mitchell (Eds.), *Essays in Argument* (pp. 34–44). Middlesex University Press.

Andrews, R, (2009). *The importance of argument in education*. London Institute of Education, University of London.

Andrews, R., & Mitchell, S. (2001). *Essays in argument*. Middlesex University Press.

Askehave, I., & Swales, J.M. (2001). Genre identification and communicative purpose: A problem and a possible solution. *Applied Linguistics, 22*(2), 195–212.

Bachman, L. (2005). Building and supporting a case for test use. *Language Assessment Quarterly, 2*(1), 1–34.

Bazerman, C., Bonini, A., & Figueiredo, D. (Eds.). (2009, August 7). *Genre in a changing world (electronic version).*

Bhatia, V.K. (1993). *Analysing genres: Language use in professional settings.* Longman.

Boller, G., Swasy, J., & Munch, J. (1990). Conceptualizing argument quality from argument structure. [2018-04-13]. Retrieved from http://acrwebsite.org/volumes/9831/v17/NA-17

Carrell, P.L. (1982). Cohesion is not coherence. *TESOL Quarterly, 16*(4), 479–488.

Carrell, P.L., & Eisterhold, J.C. (1987). Schema theory and ESL reading pedagogy, In M.H. Long & J.C. Richards (Eds.), *Methodology in TESOL: A book of readings* (pp. 218–232). Heinle and Heinle.

Chamot, A.U., & O'Malley, J.M. (1987). The cognitive academic learning approach: A bridge to the mainstream. *TESOL Quarterly, 21*(2), 227–249.

Chapelle, C.A., Enright, M.K., & Jamieson, J.M. (2008). Test score interpretation and use. In C.A. Chapelle, M.K. Enright, & J.M. Jamieson (Eds.), *Building a validity argument for the test of English as a foreign language* (pp. 1–25). Routledge.

Crammond, J.G. (1998). The uses and complexity of argument structures in expert and student persuasive writing. *Written Communication, 15*(2), 230–268.

Crandall, J., Spanos, G., Christian, D., Simich-Dedgeon, C., & Willetts, K. (1987). *Integrating language and content instruction for language minority students.* National Clearing for Bilingual Education.

Cummins, J. (1992). Language proficiency, bilingualism, and academic achievement. In P.A. Richard-Amato & M.A. Snow (Eds.), *The multicultural classroom: Readings for content-area teachers* (pp. 16–26). Longman.

Cummins, J. (2008). BICS and CALP: Empirical and theoretical status of the distinction. In B.V. Street & N.H. Hornberger (Eds.), *Encyclopedia of language and education (2nd ed.)*(pp. 71–83). Springer.

Eisner, E. (2003). Educational connoisseurship and educational criticism: An arts-based approach to educational evaluation. In T. Kellaghan & D. L. Stuffebeam (Eds.), *International handbook of educational evaluation* (pp. 153–166). Kluwer Academic Publishers.

Heath, S.B. (1983). *Ways with words: Language, life and work in communities and classrooms.* Cambridge University Press.

Hitchcock, D., & Verheji, B. (2006). *Arguing on the Toulmin model: New essays in argument analysis and evaluation.* Springer.

Hyland, F. (2007). Genre pedagogy: Language, literacy and L2 writing instruction. *Journal of Second Language Writing, 16*, 148–164.

Hyland, K. (1999). Disciplinary discourses: Writing stance in research articles. In C. Candlin & K. Hyland (Eds.), *Writing texts processes and practices* (pp. 99–121). Longman.

Hyland, K. (2004). *Disciplinary discourses: Social interactions in academic writing.* Michigan University Press.

Hyland, K., & Hyland, F. (2006). Feedback on second language students' writing. *Language Teaching, 39*(2), 83–101.

Ivanič, R. (1998). *Writing and identity: The discoursal construction of identity in academic writing.* John Benjamins.

Ivanič, R. (2004). Discourses of writing and learning to write. *Language and Education, 18*(3), 220–245.

Lea, M.R., & Street, B.V. (1998). Student writing in higher education: An academic literacies approach. *Studies in Higher Education, 23*(2), 157–172.

Leung, C., & Street, B. (2012). English in the curriculum: Norms and practices. In C. Leung & B. Street (Eds.), *English: A changing medium for education* (pp. 1–21). Multilingual Matters.

Leung, C., & Street, B. (2014). Classroom constructions of language and literacy activity. In M. Prinsloo & C. Stroud (Eds.), *Educating for language and literacy diversity* (pp. 23–44). Palgrave.

Leung, C., & Street, B. (2017). Negotiating the relationship between theory and practice in the fields of literacy and language. In J. McKinley & H. Rose (Eds.), *Doing research in Applied Linguistics* (pp. 192–200). Routledge.

Lillis, T.M. (1999). Whose common sense? Essayist literacy and the institutional practice of mystery. In C. Jones, J. Turner, and & B. Street (Eds.), *Student writing in university: Cultural and epistemological issues* (pp. 127–147). John Benjamins.

Lillis, T., & Scott, M. (2007). Defining academic literacies research: Issues of epistemology, ideology and strategy. *Journal of Applied Linguistics, 4*(1), 5–32.

Martin, J.R., & Rose, D. (2008). *Genre relations. Mapping culture.* Equinox.

Mitchell, S. (2001). What is this thing called argument? In R. Andrews & S. Mitchell (Eds.), *Essays in argument* (pp. 22–33). Middlesex University Press.

Mohan, B. (1986). *Language and content.* Addison-Wesley.

Mohan, B. (1990). LEP students and the integration of language and content: Knowledge structures and tasks. In C. Simich-Dedgeon (Ed.), *Proceedings of the first research symposium on limited English proficient students' issues* (pp. 113–160). Office of Bilingual Education and Minority Languages Affairs.

Mohan, B. (2001). The second language as a medium of learning. In B. Mohan, C. Leung, & C. Davison (Eds.), *English as a second language in the mainstream: Teaching, learning and identity* (pp. 107–126). Longman.

Mohan, B., Leung, C., & Slater, T. (2010). Assessing language and content: A functional perspective. In A. Paran & L. Sercu (Eds.), *Testing the untestable in language and education* (pp. 217–240). Multilingual Matters.

Nassaji, H. (2007). Schema theory and knowledge-based processes in second language reading comprehension: A need for alternative perspectives. *Language Learning, 57* (Supplement s1), 79–113.

National Academies of Sciences. (2017). *Promoting the educational success of children and youth learning English: Promising futures.* The National Academics Press.

Nesi, H., & Gardner, S. (2012). *Genres across the disciplines: Student writing in higher education.* Cambridge University Press.

Paltridge, B., Starfield S., & Tardy, C.M. (2016). *Ethnographic perspectives on academic writing.* Oxford University Press.

Prior, P. (2005). Toward the ethnography of argumentation: A response to Richard Andrew's models of argumentation in educational discourse. *Text, 25*(1), 129–144.

Simon, S. (2008). Toulmin's argument pattern in the evaluation of argumentation in school science. *International Journal of Research and Method in Education, 32*(3), 277–289.

Street, B. (1984). *Literacy in theory and practice.* Cambridge University Press.

Street, B. (2000). Literacy events and literacy practices. In M. Martin-Jones & K. Jones (Eds.), *Multilingual literacies: Comparative perspectives on research and practice* (pp. 17–29). John Benjamins.

Street, B. (2012). New literacy studies. In M. Grenfell, D. Bloome, C. Hardy, K. Pahl, J. Rowsell, and B. Street (Eds.), *Language, ethnography and education* (pp. 27–49). Routledge.

Swales, J. (1990). *Genre analysis: English in academic and research settings.* Cambridge University Press.

Swales, J. (2004). *Research genres: Exploration and applications.* Cambridge University Press.

Tang, G. (1992). The effect of graphic representation of knowledge structures on ESL reading comprehension. *Studies in Second Language Acquisition, 14*(2), 177–195.

Toulmin, S. (1958/2003). *The uses of argument.* Cambridge University Press.

Toulmin, S. (2004). Reasoning in theory and practice. *Informal Logic, 24*(2), 111–114.

Toulmin, S., Rieke, R., & Janik, A. (1984). *An introduction to reasoning.* Macmillan Publishing Company, Inc.

Tribble, C. (2017). ELFA vs. genre: A new paradigm war in EAP writing instruction? *Journal of English for Academic Purposes, 25,* 30–44.

Tribble, C., & Wingate, U. (2013). From text to corpus: A genre-based approach to academic literacy instruction. *System, 41*(2), 307–321.

Wingate, U. (2016). Academic literacy across the curriculum: Towards a collaborative instrumental approach. *Language Teaching, First View.* https://doi.org/10.1017/S0261444816000264

Wingate, U., & Tribble, C. (2012). The best of both worlds? Towards an EAL/academic literacies writing pedagogy. *Studies in Higher Education, 37*(4), 481–495.

About the Author

Constant Leung is Professor of Educational Linguistics at King's College London. His research interests include additional/second language curriculum development and language assessment. He is Editor of Research Issues for *TESOL Quarterly* and Co-Editor for *Language Assessment Quarterly*. He is a Fellow of the Academy of Social Sciences (UK).

4 Perceived Effectiveness of AWE for Focus on Forms, Focus on Meaning, and Interactional Modifications

Aysel Saricaoglu, Evgeny Chukharev-Hudilainen, and Hui-Hsien Feng

Abstract

This study investigates the effectiveness of automated feedback on causal language based on student perceptions at a higher education level. The target automated writing evaluation tool was developed based on the PRINCIPLES semantic text pattern of Mohan's Knowledge Framework. Analyzing learners' perceptions provides an opportunity to identify problems stemming from the pedagogical features of the tool and to determine the adjustments needed for better learning outcomes. To this end, in this qualitative study, we evaluated automated feedback on causal language from the perceptions of 27 undergraduate ESL students who used the tool for two cause-and-effect assignments in an academic writing class. Data were collected through semi-structured interviews in which students were asked questions regarding the capacity of the automated feedback features of the tool to help students focus on causal forms and causal meaning and to create opportunities for interactional modifications. Findings showed that the text-level feedback was more positively perceived by the students for focus on causal forms than the sentence-level feedback. On the other hand, the sentence-level feedback was more positively perceived for focus on causal meaning than the text-level feedback. Timing of the automated feedback appeared to be a source of negative perceptions regarding interactional modifications.

Keywords: written explanations; automated feedback; Knowledge Framework; focus on forms and meaning; interactional modifications

It is not only a scientist "who has a 'why' question" (Shireman, 2009, p. 6). Academic literacy, in general, is characterized by "why" questions and the expressions of cause-and-effect relationships (Mohan & Slater, 2004; Slater, 2004). In a survey of eight US universities about assignment requirements, Hale et al. (1996) found cause/effect to be the most frequent among types of essays (including argument, process, classification, exemplification, comparison/contrast, definition, and analysis). As a key element of academic discourse, causal explanations fall in Mohan's Knowledge Framework (KF), specifically the PRINCIPLES Knowledge Structures (KSs). The KF has served not only as an instructional framework for English as a second language (ESL) teaching and learning but also as a central theoretical foundation for linguistic and educational research over the past 20 years, including the present study. This study is concerned with the PRINCIPLES KS that links causal meaning to causal language form within the social practices of academic disciplines.

For academic success, students' constructions of explanations need to be supported, which requires explicit teaching, repeated practice, and continuous formative feedback. While this is an energy-, time-, and ability-demanding process, its burden on teachers can be lessened with computer technologies. Automated writing evaluation (AWE) systems can effectively evaluate grammar and mechanics; however, evaluating the *meanings* constructed through the various knowledge structures is still a challenge for natural language processing despite a few successful efforts (e.g., Cotos, 2011; Feng, 2015). One such effort has been on the automated evaluation of explanations (Chukharev-Hudilainen & Saricaoglu, 2016).

AWE has become a widespread educational technology in writing pedagogy and has generated much research directed towards error detection accuracy (e.g., Chen, Chiu, & Liao, 2009; Lavolette, Polio, & Kahng, 2015), different classroom practices (e.g., Chen & Cheng, 2008; Link et al., 2014), and improvement in mechanical and grammatical aspects of written language (e.g., Li, Feng, & Saricaoglu, 2017; Wang, Shang, & Brody, 2013). In the majority of the existing AWE studies, students' perceptions have been a major focus in understanding how effective AWE tools are in improving students' written language. As Cotos and Huffman (2013) accentuate, it is important, especially in the early stages of tool development, to involve learners' perspectives in the evaluations of AWE effectiveness in order to gain the instructional outcomes expected. This study thus attempts to build on the value of established work on the discourse of the knowledge structure of PRINCIPLES by exploring undergraduate ESL students' perceptions of an AWE tool that evaluates the use of causal language. It does so after the first classroom implementation with the goal of refining the tool. We seek to examine students' perceptions of the effectiveness of the AWE tool for its (a) focus on causal forms, (b) focus on causal meaning, and (c) interactional modifications (i.e., learners' interruptions of their interaction with the AWE tool in order to receive feedback to improve their causal language).

Causal Language and Assessment

When making explanations in writing, students need to use certain linguistic patterns because "particular language forms perform certain communicative functions and that students can be taught the functions most relevant to their needs. Functions are the means for achieving the ends (or purposes) of writing" (Hyland, 2003, p. 6). This relationship between meaning and form is well illustrated by Mohan (1989) in his Knowledge Framework (KF), which contains six semantic text patterns, or knowledge structures. The focus of this study is the knowledge structure of PRINCIPLES. The PRINCIPLES thinking skills are to explain, draw conclusions, and apply causes and effects, among others. Mohan believes that when learners write in a semantic pattern (cause and effect in this study) in a particular context (discussing the causes and effects of a natural disaster or an economic event in this study), they should be taught the linguistic features that are related to that semantic pattern, which in this study is causal language (see Mohan & van Naerssen, 1997 for a detailed illustration of how causal meaning and causal language are related). Information about the linguistic features of a causal text with the communicative purpose of explaining appears in Table 4.1.

Table 4.1 Mohan's principles of semantic pattern (adapted from Slater and Gleason, 2011, p. 10)

Semantic Pattern of Text	Communicative Purpose	Linguistic Features	Language Examples
PRINCIPLES	To explain, draw conclusions, apply causes & effects	Action verbs Consequential conjunctions and adverbials Cause-effect lexis: verbs and nouns Passive	since, because, consequently, if- clauses effect, produce, bring about is caused by

As children develop, they expand their resources for creating meaning and grow the capacity for using grammatical metaphor, which means that their causal language moves from more to less congruent (Halliday, 2003). This change in wording is accomplished by "a substitution of one grammatical class, or one grammatical structure, by another (Halliday & Martin, 1993). In other words, as Halliday and Martin's example in italics below shows, grammatical metaphor allows language users to reconstrue meaning by changing what is connected by reality (e.g., a verb as an action in a clause such as *She spoke recently*) to one that is not (e.g., a noun or "thing" as an action such as *Her recent speech*). The focus shifts from the *doer* as the subject of the clause to the *doing* with the *doing* becoming a noun. The meaning is expressed with different words, and different wording results in being able to express things differently. This move from the more congruent to the more grammatically metaphoric signifies a major development in linguistic sophistication.

The developmental path of causal language from a more congruent form (conjunctions) to a less (nominalizations) was observed in both oral and written language (Mohan et al., 2002; Slater, 2004). Slater and Mohan (2010) argued that this developmental path of cause can be a basis for successful assessment of causal explanations in instructional settings: "this developmental path of cause allows teachers to create a formative assessment-for-learning cycle" (p. 268). ACDET (Automated Causal Discourse Evaluation Tool), a newly developed tool that analyzes causal language, provides this suggested formative assessment in an automated way and thus has been employed in this study.

Perception-based Evaluation of Automated Feedback

Student perceptions have had an important role in AWE research. As pointed out by Roscoe and McNamara (2013), "[s]uccessful deployment of writing technologies may depend upon whether teachers and students view the tools as valid, useful, and usable" (p. 1011). Existing studies on students' perceptions of AWE have concentrated primarily on learner motivation or confidence, satisfaction, ease of use, revision behaviors, and usefulness/helpfulness for improvement in writing quality, in particular grammatical and mechanical (e.g., Chen & Cheng, 2008; Ebyary & Windeatt, 2010; Grimes & Warschauer, 2010; Lai, 2010; Li, Link, & Hegelheimer, 2015; Roscoe & McNamara, 2013; Roscoe et al., 2017; Warschauer & Grimes, 2008). In one study, Wang et al. (2013) interviewed 15 EFL freshmen students who used *CorrectEnglish* in their English writing and explored students' perceptions of the AWE tool for accuracy, learner autonomy, and interaction. Students' perceptions were found to be positive in that the AWE tool improved their accuracy and increased their learner autonomy awareness; however, the majority of students reported that their interaction with the AWE tool was not meaningful. In another study, Dikli and Bleyle (2014) measured 14 advanced-level students' perceptions of *Criterion* through a survey for each feedback category (i.e., grammar, usage, mechanics, style, and organization and development), and overall strengths and weaknesses. One major weakness that students reported was that *Criterion* either failed to identify some errors or incorrectly identified some language features as errors. *Criterion*'s strength, as perceived by the students, was its ability to detect grammatical, mechanical, and usage errors, as compared to its inability to address problems of content and organization in student writing.

The studies mentioned above add to our understanding of the perceived strengths and weaknesses of AWE systems; however, these systems were not designed around an evaluation framework that specifically addresses the qualities of computer-assisted language learning (CALL). A major flaw in AWE studies has been limiting the perspective-based investigation to AWE tools' error detection capacity and the level of increase in the correctness of students' language production and excluding the important conditions in the language learning process (i.e., focus on forms, focus on meaning, interactions between the AWE tool and the students) from the investigation. Cotos and Huffman (2013) refer to such reported perceptions as "decontextualized perceptions" (p. 79) since they rely on the language products rather than the learning processes, or both. The effectiveness of an AWE tool in enhancing language development can only be understood by gathering students' perceptions specifically on the necessary conditions for learning (i.e., focus on forms, focus on meaning, interactional modifications) rather than simply asking whether students find AWE feedback useful or not.

Applying concepts and perspectives from second language acquisition research to the CALL research, Chapelle (2001) proposed six criteria for evaluating the interactions between learners and a computerized program: language learning potential, learner fit, meaning focus, impact, authenticity, and practicality. Evidence of each criterion in students' interactions with an AWE tool can show how effective the tool is in interacting with learners and enhancing their language development. In their study, Cotos and Huffman (2013) examined the learner fit quality of the Research Writing Tutor (RWT) by analyzing the effectiveness of the tool in terms of its difficulty level and usefulness based on nine graduate students' interactional modifications and their perceptions of its feedback. They found that RWT created several interactive opportunities for learners at an appropriate difficulty level and was perceived by the students to be useful.

The current study investigates the perceived effectiveness of an AWE tool by addressing two CALL qualities: the language learning potential and meaning focus. In this study, language learning potential refers to the capacity of the AWE tool to draw learners' attention to *causal* forms and to create opportunities for interactional modifications. Meaning focus refers to the capacity of the AWE tool to draw learners' attention to *causal* meaning. More specifically, this study attempts to find out how students perceive the effectiveness of ACDET (a) for focus on causal forms; (b) for focus on causal meaning; and (c) for opportunities for interactional modifications. We define focus on causal forms as *reported noticing by students of the target linguistic forms used to express causal meaning,* especially through metalinguistic terminology, such as verbs or adjectives. We define focus on causal meaning as *reported noticing of meaning by students,* especially reason/result or the relationship between them that is expressed by the target linguistic forms. We define interactional modifications as *the interruptions students make during their interactions with the AWE tool to receive sentence-level and text-level feedback.*

Methodology

Participants

The participants in this study were 27 undergraduate students taking an academic writing class at a Midwestern university in the US. They were all ESL students majoring in different disciplines (e.g., Agricultural Biochemistry, Business, Civil Engineering, Computer Science, and Supply Chain Management) and were between 18–25 years of age.

Materials

Students used ACDET to revise two cause-and-effect essays. They wrote their essays out of class and received feedback from ACDET in class. They were given a full class meeting (i.e., 50 minutes) for each essay to improve their causal language. ACDET was developed based on an analysis module that detects causal forms expressing causal meaning (see Chukharev-Hudilainen & Saricaoglu, 2016 for a detailed description of the analyzer) and a feedback module that generates sentence-level and text-level feedback based on the developmental path of causal language (see Slater & Mohan, 2010).

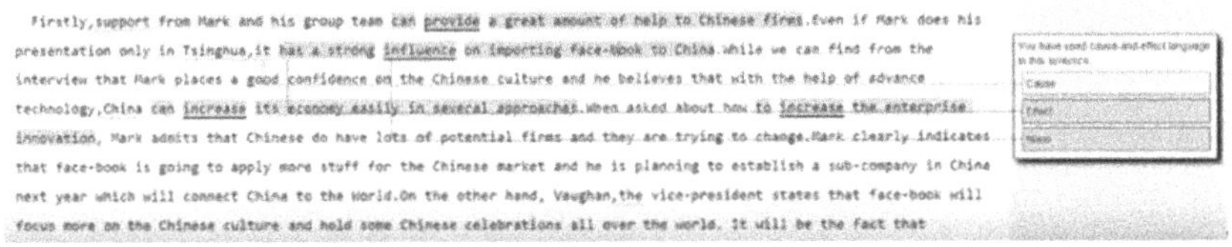

Figure 4.1 ACDET's sentence-level feedback

Sentence-level Feedback. ACDET's sentence-level feedback, as displayed in Figure 4.1, on the screen has color-coding and underlining features. In the student's sentence "it has a strong influence on importing face-book to China," ACDET highlights *it* in green (the cause) (light gray in Figure 4.1) and the rest of the sentence in blue (the effect) (dark gray in Figure 4.1) as well as underlining the word *influence* (the causal word). When the student clicks on the underlined word, they can read in a pop-up box what the color-coded and underlined parts of the sentence belong to.

Text-level Feedback. Based on the frequencies of causal language features that ACDET's analyzer detects (i.e., the number of conjunctions, verbs, nouns, etc.), it generates text-level feedback. The text-level feedback provides a summary of the causal language features used in the text (both numerical and linguistic) and offers suggestions for improvement. For example, the following feedback is given for repeated use of a conjunction: "You have used the causal conjunction *because* repeatedly. because=3 times." Moreover, because the sophistication of causal discourse in no way depends on the quantity of discourse features used, examples of how to express the causal meaning in a less congruent (i.e., a more grammatically metaphoric) way is also provided, as shown in an authentic example by one student:

> Student writing:
> Work place maternity harassment happens in Japan because Japanese men tried to reassert control on Japanese women.
>
> ACDET suggestion:
> Work place maternity harassment happens in Japan due to the attempt of Japanese men to reassert control on Japanese women.

Interviews

The perceived effectiveness of automated feedback on explanations was explored qualitatively by conducting semi-structured face-to-face interviews with the 27 students who used ACDET in two cause-and-effect assignments in two academic writing classes. They were asked three main guiding questions: if the automated feedback helped them focus on cause-and-effect forms; if the automated feedback helped them focus on cause-and-effect meaning; and if they were able to interact with the tool. For each question, they were asked which specific features of the automated feedback helped them or did not help them with focus on forms, focus on meaning, and interactions. The interviews were recorded with a digital audio-recorder. The length of the interviews ranged from five to 14 minutes. Student responses to interview questions were coded and analyzed using the qualitative data analysis software *NVivo 10.*

Coding

A coding scheme was created based on the three questions asked: focus on forms, focus on meaning, and interactions with the tool. For each, coding categories were created around automated feedback features as text-level feedback, sentence-level feedback, color-coding feedback feature, and underlining feedback feature. Student responses for each coding category were coded as negative or positive. Coding categories for focus on forms and examples for each coding category are presented in Table 4.2.

Findings

Perceived Effectiveness of Focus on Causal Forms

The analysis of 27 learners' perceptions revealed both positive and negative comments about the effectiveness of automated feedback to help students focus on causal forms.

The analysis of participants' responses to the question of ACDET's feedback to help them focus on causal discourse forms indicated negative evaluation by two students (7%). One said, "No 'cause it's not helping anything it just leave me, uh, it just tell me this is a cause-effect sentence and, uh, and how many times, the, uh, the verb you use that's, that's all" (S5). On the other hand, 35 (67%) comments from 18 students contained positive evaluations of ACDET overall indicating that ACDET's feedback helped them focus on causal discourse forms in a general way without referring specifically to text-level or sentence-level feedback, color-coding or underlining features, as exemplified by the following student remarks:

Table 4.2 Coding categories for focus on forms and examples

Coding Categories	Examples for Positive Perceptions	Examples for Negative Perceptions
Overall	Yes like since it shows you know the specific word, like it's a specific adjective or maybe it's a conjunction (S13)	No. it just tell me this is a cause-effect sentence and how many times the verb you use that's all (S5)
Text-level feedback	Yeah because I when I wrote my article, I didn't realize I have so many repeated words, and when I see the feedback and I can find the words and then change it to another word (S31)	No examples
Sentence-level feedback	For example you can search what like the inter relation cause and effect on a word like the key word for that relationship and which part is the relation which part is the cause and which part is the effect (S21)	No examples
Color-coding feature	Yeah …the blue one and the green one can indicate both the cause or effect, and while I'm writing the sentence, I can restructure, I can form my structure of my sentence (S12)	No examples
Underlining feature	When I see the underline I know it's the verb or something (S17)	No examples

Table 4.3 Frequencies of negative and positive comments on focus on causal form

	# negative comments	# students (n = 27)	# positive comments	#students (n = 27)
Overall	3	2 (7%)	35	18 (67%)
Text-level feedback	0	0	39	25 (93%)
Sentence-level feedback	0	0	5	5 (19%)
Color-coding feature	0	0	11	9 (33%)
Underlining feature	0	0	12	11 (41%)

> I think the only thing that helped me was yeah the forms (S14)

> I think so um sometimes when I use the word to connect the cause and effect, I only use the word that I feel very comfortable for me, but sometimes maybe it can express some other uh, meanings when I choose to use another word, that it also works, that I never thought of before (S17)

> Try to put like a little bit of different like actual causal verbs or adjectival verbs I can put that into the everything in the essay (S21)

> I think so because you can use all kinds of forms not like only conjunction (S30)

Table 4.3 indicates 39 positive comments about the ACDET's text-level feedback with regards to helping learners focus on causal forms as illustrated by students remarks: "I feel like the charts summarize, the summarize charts, so here it's uh more it's very uh directly tell you uh what did you did in this, in this essay so, it it it is more like a summarize here so it's more, it it's easier to find a program, uhh, something I should do or I can improve in this essay" (Student 9) or "It mentioned what features I need to uh improve or add, and like there's some more suggestions down here to give me a idea of how to change them" (Student 14).

The analysis also yielded five comments from five students that showed positive perceptions that ACDET's sentence-level feedback helped them focus on causal forms: "Umm for example you can you can search what like the inter relation cause and effect on a word like the key word for that relationship and which part is the relation which part is the cause and which part is the effect, the effect" (Student 21).

Eleven comments from nine participants (33%) indicated positive perceptions that the color-coding feature of the automated feedback was helpful for them to focus on causal forms: "Yeah I I really focus on that because you know it's highlighted" (Student 18) or "The color yeah it's the repeat word so I can I can find another word to use instead of that" (Student 31).

There were also 12 comments in which learners (n = 11, 41%) expressed positive perceptions of the underlining feature of the automated feedback in that it helped them focus on causal discourse forms: "Uh the underline tell you that like, that what this part exactly be like is cause or effect or cause or verb or something like that" (Student 16) or "I like the underlining, that one thing that show it's like the how to um, its show you like the what cause and effect words that we use in the sentence" (Student 23).

Table 4.4 Frequencies of negative and positive comments on focus on causal meaning

	# negative comments	**# students (n = 27)**	**# positive comments**	**#students (n = 27)**
Overall	16	14 (52%)	25	16 (59%)
Text-level feedback	0	0	0	0
Sentence-level feedback	0	0	18	10 (37%)
Color-coding feature	0	0	20	12 (44%)
Underlining feature	0	0	5	4 (15%)

Perceived Effectiveness of Focus on Causal Meaning

Table 4.4 presents the number of negative and positive comments on the effectiveness of ACDET's feedback to draw attention to causal meaning and the number of students who commented.

Regarding the overall effectiveness of ACDET to help students focus on causal meaning, 14 students (52%) evaluated ACDET negatively and made 16 comments that ACDET was not helpful for drawing their attention to causal meaning, as represented by the following remarks by students:

> I don't know, I didn't focus on meanings (S8)

> Sometimes like I didn't think it was, it's helpful, but it's not much because sometimes I was like it's not even cause and effect, it's like sentence, but then it showed the cause and effect (S23)

> Not really. it's just like I write the sentence, I don't really think about the meaning (S26)

Regarding positive evaluation overall, 25 comments appeared from 16 students (59%), remarking that ACDET was helpful for bringing their focus on causal meaning without referring to any specific ACDET features such as the text-level feedback, the color-coding or underlining features of the sentence-level feedback:

> Yeah, I. first of all, I think I cannot get the point about cause and effect at the first because I don't know which is the cause and which is effect.

> And after use this, I think it is clearly to show that, umm, which one is which (S2)
>
> It can, the contrast, and it give me the reason and the result of every sentence and phenomena (S12)
>
> It can, cause, when I wrote the article I don't know which sentence I use cause and effect and this can help me to to know, how can I improve my sentence and which sentence, I use cause and effect (S31)

Twenty positive comments on the color-coding feature of the sentence-level feedback indicated that it was helpful to focus on causal meaning, such as:

> When I see the colors differences, I can know which is a cause and if we lost something, I can add them to my passage (S11)
>
> That as soon as I see the green color then I know this is a cause when I see the underline I know it's the verb or something (S17)
>
> The different color and it can tell me the cause and the effects so I can understand about my article (S24)

Referring to the underlining feature, five positive comments from four students (15%) showed that these learners perceived ACDET's underlining feature as helpful for focusing on causal meaning. For example, one student commented, "It's underline, cause it can show, the relationship between the sentence that has cause and effects it show the relationship. Maybe I write it, include the both elements but if don't have this underline feature, it may takes me more time to find out what I wrote, why I wrote, what I wrote in this essay, If I, so this feature can save much time" (S9).

Perceived Effectiveness of Interactional Modifications

Table 4.5 presents the number of negative and positive comments on the effectiveness of ACDET to create opportunities for interactions and the number of students who commented.

The majority of responses regarding the overall effectiveness of ACDET to create opportunities for interactional modifications were positive while there were also 13 negative comments from 13 (48%) students. While most of the participants expressed their perceptions with a short answer such as "no"

Table 4.5 Frequencies of negative and positive comments on interactional modifications

	# negative comments	# students (n = 27)	# positive comments	#students (n = 27)
Overall	13	13 (48%)	45	22 (81%)
Text-level feedback	11	8 (30%)	32	22 (81%)
Sentence-level feedback	0	0	0	0
Color-coding feature	7	5 (19%)	34	20 (74%)
Underlining feature	0	0	13	11 (41%)

(S16) or "not really" (S14), a few participants offered explanations as to why they perceived their interactions with ACDET negatively. Eight students reported that they were not able to interact with ACDET feedback, mostly because the text-level feedback did not update with students' changes in the text:

> That the effect doesn't sometime show up. Sometime it doesn't show up (S6)

> But sometimes I find it fun to go back to like when we receive the feedback it couldn't refresh it, so… (S7)

> Sometimes like I didn't think it was, it's helpful, but it's not much because sometimes I was like it's not even cause and effect, it's like sentence, but then it showed the cause and effect (S23)

> Yeah, but it still has a some mistakes because when you make some change to the, article, on so you change it, but the way you, you open the feedback, it is still not changed (S4)

> The real time doesn't update thing for the text level feedback (S6).

Regarding the specific features of ACDET feedback, 32 comments from 22 (81%) students that showed learners' positive perceptions that they were able to interact with the text-level feedback:

> Yeah, I can see which kind of vocabulary I use the most and which kind I use the least so, it can improve at least one (S2)

> You can see how many times you use a word a conjunction and then you can stop like and it gives you a way just repeat that again and you can change (S30)

> When I wrote my article, I didn't realize I have so many repeated words, and when I see the feedback and I can find the words and then change it to another word (S31)

The color-coding feature of ACDET feedback was also perceived by students to be both negative (11 comments from five students) and positive (34 comments from 20 students). A negative comment by one student suggested that the color-coding might be distractive: "Sometimes it might distract the reader because of the green and the blue linings everywhere, all over the place" (S7). Another student comment referred to the timing of the feedback: "because we usually only do it like half the colors after we finish our assignments so I'm not sure if it really helps like we can't really like finish it and then we see it only shows like white and until usually I go to class and then I'll see the color" (S13). Such negative perceptions were due to the fact that ACDET feedback was activated only in class. Even though students could write their essays on the tool outside class, they did not receive feedback. The student's comment "it only shows like white and until usually I go to class and then I'll see the color" refers to the white background of ACDET's text box when students typed in their essays outside class time. Their causal language was color-coded only during class use.

Compared to those negative perceptions, several positive comments showed how the colors helped students understand the cause and the effect in a sentence:

> It can find which is the cause and which is the effect, and the verb I use (S2)

> Actually it can, the blue one and the green one can indicate the cause or effect, and while I'm writing the sentence, I can restructure, I can form my structure of my sentence (S12)

> As soon as I see the green color then I know this is a cause (S17)

The underlining feature of ACDET did not receive any negative comments from the students. Eleven (41%) students perceived the underlining feedback as helpful for interactions. One student commented, "underlined words can help me pay more attention about my language form, like, this is verb this is adjective, and so I can use different word form to improve my article" (S24). Another student referred to the time-saving effect of the underlining feature of ACDET feedback: "Also I like the underline the picture, it's underline, cause it can show, the relationship between the sentence that has cause and effects it show the relationship. Maybe I write it, include the both elements but if don't have this underline feature, it may takes me more time to find out what I wrote, why I wrote, what I wrote in this essay. So this feature can save much time" (S9).

Discussion and Conclusions

According to Mohan's functional perspective of academic discourse as a socially constructed practice, language serves the function of making meaning in specific contexts, and academic discourse can only be understood within the context of its social practice (Mohan & Slater, 2005, 2006). This perspective is well illustrated in Mohan's KF. The KF has helped establish research not only on how meaning is constructed through language form in different types of discourses (i.e., DESCRIPTION, CLASSIFICATION, SEQUENCE, PRINCIPLES, CHOICE, and EVALUATION) but also on how the link between meaning and form can be assessed using a functional approach (Mohan et al., 2010), highlighting the need for automated formative assessment of different KSs as well. Responding to this need, our study explored the effectiveness of automated evaluation of written causal language—the PRINCIPLES KS—from the perceptions of students.

Although automated writing evaluation (AWE) has already gained popularity in writing classrooms, efforts continue with the intent to maximize its effectiveness. Findings from classroom research have served to identify accuracy and reliability issues with AWE tools so as to inform their further development and have assessed any improvement in any aspects of writing so as to inform pedagogical implementations. Several studies have involved student perceptions in exploring the effectiveness of automated feedback. However, these investigations are limited by the lack of a CALL-quality oriented design (see Chapelle, 2001 for the qualities to measure in CALL evaluation). Obtaining students' opinions about whether they find automated feedback, or certain features of automated feedback, "useful" is not enough to understand whether the target AWE tool creates the necessary conditions for acquisition. It is necessary, on the other hand, to find out how students perceive the effectiveness of automated feedback to provide these conditions, which is what we attempted to do in this study. In order to find out the perceived effectiveness of ACDET, this study examined how students perceived ACDET's capacity to help them focus on causal forms, to focus on causal meaning, and to create opportunities for interactional modifications.

Overall, ACDET's effectiveness to help students focus on causal discourse forms was more positively perceived by students than its effectiveness for focus on causal meaning and interactional modifications. Focus on linguistic form is important for learning the target language structures (Robinson, 1995). Making meaning and key linguistic features salient through highlighting them in colors and underlines might be helpful for drawing learners' attention to them, as suggested by Chapelle (1998). The findings illustrated more positive perceptions of ACDET's text-level feedback than its sentence-level feedback, which is not surprising. The sentence-level feedback made causal discourse forms and meaning salient and elaborated on them while the text-level feedback was negative, pointing out learners' weaknesses in causal language. This is in line with the theoretical perspectives of second language acquisition; learners' attention to form is triggered by problems with production (Long & Robinson, 1998). Sentence-level feedback did not inform learners about weaknesses in their causal language or about how to improve their written explanations. Moreover, given that *forms* construct *meaning*, some students may have found it difficult during the interviews to separate the two in ways that may have better informed the data analysis. Still, findings on learners' perceptions in this study support that attention is drawn to form by providing feedback on the problematic areas in the language.

ACDET's focus on causal meaning was not as positively perceived as focus on causal forms by the students. The sentence-level feedback received more positive perceptions than the text-level feedback in terms of its capacity to draw attention to causal meaning. The purpose of ACDET's color-coding feature was to help learners to notice causal meaning by highlighting the causes and/or effects in their sentences using colors, which was achieved for about the half of students in this study. Our findings support the potential of the KF approach to help ESL learners connect causal meaning to causal forms in the PRINCIPLES KSs, which can be applied to making form/meaning relations in various KSs. The fact that ACDET was designed with the KF approach to help with formative assessment and the development of causal discourse confirms that tool developers will benefit from this functional perspective for the automated evaluation of different types of academic discourses.

Negative comments from some students indicating that sometimes a cause or an effect would inaccurately be color-coded bring attention to an accuracy issue of ACDET. While ACDET's accuracy was previously found to be sufficient (see Chukharev-Hudilainen & Saricaoglu, 2016), analyzing meaning still appears to be a challenge for automated systems, and students' perceptions about meaning vs. forms certainly call for a revisit, as noted above.

While it was understood from students' comments that ACDET created several opportunities for interactional modifications, some students held negative perceptions of that the text-level feedback was not real time. ACDET's text-level feedback was delayed, unlike the sentence-level feedback that was provided instantaneously to students. This means that learners were not able to receive real-time text-level feedback every time they made causal language modifications. They received text-level feedback on a cause-and-effect essay once in class and made modifications based on that throughout their use of ACDET in class. The inability to update the text-level feedback every time students made a causal modification resulted in negative perceptions, as timing of the feedback is one of the most important characteristics of AWE (Shute, 2007).

This study has demonstrated that the effectiveness of feedback from an AWE tool designed with the KF approach receives positive perceptions from ESL learners in terms of focus on forms, focus on meaning, and interactional modifications. Our findings raise important implications for the automated formative assessment of learners' causal language. With the KF approach, it is possible to expand the capabilities of automated systems from analyzing form to analyzing meaning and allow students to focus on form/meaning relations in specific types of academic discourses, such as cause-effect in this study. The importance of taking a functional perspective to focusing on form/meaning relations must not be overlooked in AWE implementations and research.

References

Chapelle, C.A. (1998). Multimedia CALL: Lessons to be learned from research on instructed SLA. *Language Learning, 2*(1), 22–34.

Chapelle, C.A. (2001). *Computer applications in second language acquisition: Foundations for teaching, testing and research.* Cambridge University Press.

Chen, C.F., & Cheng, W.Y. (2008). Beyond the design of automated writing evaluation: Pedagogical practices and perceived learning effectiveness in EFL writing classes. *Language Learning and Technology, 12*(2), 94–112.

Chen, H.J., Chiu, T.L., & Liao, P. (2009). Analyzing the grammar feedback of two automated writing evaluation systems: My Access and Criterion. *English Teaching and Learning, 33*(2), 1–43.

Chukharev-Hudilainen, E., & Saricaoglu, A. (2016). Causal discourse analyzer: Improving automated feedback on academic ESL writing. *Computer Assisted Language Learning*, 29(3), 494–516. https://doi.org/10.1080/09588221.2014.991795

Cotos, E. (2011). Potential of automated writing evaluation feedback. *CALICO Journal, 28*(2), 420–459.

Cotos, E., & Huffman, S. (2013). Learner fit in scaling up automated writing evaluation. *International Journal of Computer-Assisted Language Learning and Teaching, 3*(3), 77–98.

Dikli, S., & Bleyle, S. (2014). Automated essay scoring feedback for second language writers: How does it compare to instructor feedback? *Assessing Writing, 22*, 1–17.

Ebyary, K.E., & Windeatt, S. (2010). The impact of computer-based feedback on students' written work. *International Journal of English Studies, 10*(2), 121–142.

Feng, H-H. (2015). *Designing, implementing, and evaluating an automated writing evaluation tool for improving EFL graduate students' abstract writing: a case in Taiwan.* (Unpublished doctoral dissertation.) Iowa State University, Ames, USA.

Grimes, D., & Warschauer, M. (2010). Utility in a fallible took: A multi-site case study of automated writing evaluation. *Journal of Technology, Learning, and Assessment, 8*, 4–43.

Hale, G., Taylor, C., Bridgeman, B., Carson, J., Kroll, B., & Kantor, R. (1996). *A study of writing tasks assigned in academic degree programs.* (ETS Research Report No. RR-95-44). Educational Testing Service.

Halliday, M.A.K. (2003). *On language and linguistics.* Continuum.

Halliday, M.A.K., & Martin, J. (1993). *Writing science.* Falmer Press.

Hyland, K. (2003). *Second language writing.* Cambridge University Press.

Lai, Y.-H. (2010). Which do students prefer to evaluate their essays: Peers or computer program. *British Journal of Educational Technology, 41*(3), 432–454.

Lavolette, E., Polio, C. and Kahng, J. (2015) The accuracy of computer-assisted feedback and students' responses to it. *Language Learning & Technology, 19*(2), 50–68.

Li, Z., Feng, H.-H., & Saricaoglu, A. (2017). The short-term and long-term effects of AWE feedback on ESL learners' grammatical accuracy. *CALICO Journal, 34*(3), 355–375.

Li, Z., Link, S., & Hegelheimer, V. (2015). Rethinking the role of automated writing evaluation (AWE) feedback in ESL writing instruction. *Journal of Second Language Writing, 27*, 18.

Link, S., Dursun, A., Karakaya, K., & Hegelheimer, V. (2014). Towards best ESL practices for implementing automated writing evaluation. *CALICO Journal, 31*(3), 323–344.

Long, M., & Robinson, P. (1998). Focus on form: Theory, research, and practice. In C. Doughty & J. Williams (Eds.), *Focus on form in classroom second language acquisition* (pp. 15–63). Cambridge University Press.

Mohan, B.A. (1989). Knowledge structures and academic discourse. *Word, 40* (1–2), 99–115.

Mohan, B., Leung, C., & Slater, T. (2010). Assessing language and content: A functional perspective. In A. Paran & L. Sercu (Eds.), *Testing the untestable in language education* (pp. 217–240). Multilingual Matters.

Mohan, B.A., & van Naerssen, M. (1997). Understanding cause-effect: Learning through language. *English Teaching Forum, 35*(4), 22–29.

Mohan, B., & Slater, T. (2004). The evaluation of causal discourse and language as a resource for meaning. In J.A. Foley (Ed.), *Language, education and discourse: Functional approaches* (pp. 255–269). Continuum.

Mohan, B., & Slater, T. (2005). A functional perspective on the critical "theory/practice" relation in teaching language and science. *Linguistics and Education, 16*, 151–172.

Mohan, B., & Slater, T. (2006). Examining the theory/practice relation in a high school science register: A functional linguistic perspective. *Journal of English for Academic Purposes, 5*, 302–316.

Mohan, B., Slater, T., Luo, L. and Jaipal, K. (2002) *Developmental lexicogrammar of causal explanations in science.* Paper presented at the International Systemic Functional Linguistics Congress (ISFC29), Liverpool, UK.

Robinson, P. (1995). Attention, memory, and the noticing hypothesis. *Language Learning, 45*, 283–331.

Roscoe, R.D., & McNamara, D.S. (2013). Writing Pal: Feasibility of an intelligent writing strategy tutor in the high school classroom. *Journal of Educational Psychology, 105*(4), 1010–1025.

Roscoe, R.D., Wilson, J., Johnson, A.C., & Mayra, C.R. (2017). Presentation, expectations, and experience: Sources of student perceptions of automated writing evaluation. *Computers in Human Behavior, 70*, 207–221.

Shireman, M. (2009). *Developing science writing skills.* Mark Twain Media.

Shute, V.J. (2007). *Focus on formative feedback.* (ETS Research Report No. RR-07-11). Educational Testing Service.

Slater, T. (2004). *The discourse of causal explanations in school science.* Unpublished doctoral dissertation, University of British Columbia, Vancouver, Canada. DOI:10.14288/1.0078228

Slater, T. & Gleason, J. (2011). Integrating language and content: The Knowledge Framework. In J. Morrison (Ed.), *Conference proceedings of MidTESOL: Gateway to global citizenship* (pp. 5–20). University of Saint Louis. Retrieved from http://www.midtesol.org/docs/MIDTESOLProceedings_2011.pdf

Slater, T., & Mohan, B. (2010). Towards systematic and sustained formative assessment of causal explanations in oral interactions. In A. Paran & L Sercu (Eds.), *Testing the untestable in language education* (pp. 259–272). Multilingual Matters.

Wang, Y.-J., Shang, H.-F., & Briody, P. (2013). Exploring the impact of using automated writing evaluation in English as a foreign language university students' writing. *Computer Assisted Language Learning, 26*(3), 234–257.

Warschauer, M., & Grimes, D. (2008). Automated writing assessment in the classroom. *Pedagogies, 3*(1), 22–36

About the Authors

Aysel Saricaoglu (PhD, Applied Linguistics and Technology, Iowa State University) is an associate professor in the English Language and Literature department at Social Sciences University of Ankara. She investigates academic writing, automated formative assessment, L2 written complexity, and telecollaborative learning. Her work has appeared in journals such as *ReCALL*, *CALL*, and *CALICO*.

Evgeny Chukharev-Hudilainen is an associate professor in the Applied Linguistics and Technology program at Iowa State University. His research addresses the urgent societal need of improving language learning, teaching, and assessment practices by taking advantage of new technological opportunities. Specifically, he uses his background in psycholinguistics, computer science, and natural language processing to design, build, and evaluate technologies for second language learning and assessment.

Hui-Hsien Feng is an assistant professor in the English department at National Kaohsiung University of Science and Technology, Taiwan. She holds a Ph.D. in Applied Linguistics and Technology at Iowa State University. Her research interests include computer-assisted language learning, second language writing, corpus linguistics, and computational linguistics.

5 Coaching as Activity/Social Practice

Carolyn Kristjánsson and Bernard A. Mohan

Abstract

This chapter draws on Mohan's Knowledge Framework to facilitate the analysis of a coaching session in higher education as an activity/social practice. In the study, a coach interacts with a student who is making a *choice* or *decision* about a PhD program and *evaluating* possible options. The analysis draws on Dewey's theory of emotion and process of inquiry as well as a Systemic Functional Linguistics (SFL) perspective on language, with attention to reflective discourse and appraisal analysis, to shed light on the integration of emotion, inwardness, ethics, and cognition in decision-making. It considers implications for coaching research as well as research on activity/social practice and points to the possibility of productive dialogue between Deweyan philosophers and functional linguists.

Keywords: coaching; decision-making; emotion; cognition; activity/social practice

Decision-making (CHOICE) is a central element in the Knowledge Framework heuristic, where it is linked with Valuing (EVALUATION), an important basis for deliberating and making decisions. This chapter will undertake a decision-making analysis of a coaching session where the coach interacts with a physics student who is completing a master's degree at a small university and contemplating choosing a PhD program at a large university. Recent research (see below) has questioned the bias of decision-making research towards a sole concentration on cognition, and indeed the session contains important emotional elements which sets the problem of going beyond a cognitive analysis of decision-making. For this we will draw on the functional theory of emotion, ethics, and aesthetics in situation, context, and activity developed by John Dewey and elaborated by contemporary Deweyan philosophers. Dewey's theory does more than include emotion; it sees decision-making as central to the growth of a self.

For Dewey, the person "is not an empty vessel or a wax tablet, impressed by discrete and external stimuli, but an agent actively engaged with her environment and *growing insofar as she frames and uses events in experience* [emphasis added]" (Hildebrand, 2008, p. 18). Dewey's psychological model is "an ecological model—mind, body and world are mutually created by their ongoing interaction. A mind is like a friendship: it only exists through ongoing conversation and activity" (Hildebrand, 2008, p. 21).

In its turn, this sets the problem of an appropriate analysis of discourse data. We will use the Systemic Functional Linguistics (SFL) approach to the language and discourse of evaluation with particular reference to the analysis of appraisal (Martin & White, 2005). We will consider implications for coaching research. We will also consider implications for research on activity/social practice that includes the functional analysis of elements other than cognitive, and the possibility of a productive dialogue between Deweyan philosophers and functional linguists.

In the past two decades, coaching, adapted from models grounded in business, life coaching, and executive coaching, has emerged as a growing and effective source of student support in higher education (Bettinger & Baker, 2014; Kristjánsson et al., 2018; Robinson, 2015). Nevertheless, a recent survey of representatives from 160 American colleges and universities with active coaching programs found that only 35% of these programs ground their work in conceptual or theoretical frameworks (Robinson, 2015, p.78). This finding is arguably reflective of the fact that coaching is itself an emerging discipline with a fledgling scholarly knowledge base (Cox & Ledgerwood, 2003).

From our perspective, coaching can be helpfully understood as a dynamic activity or social practice, a relational view of persons, their actions, and the world in which "objective forms and systems of activity, on the one hand, and agents' subjective and intersubjective understandings of them on the other, mutually constitute both the world and its experienced forms" (Lave & Wenger, 1991, pp. 50–51). Our analysis draws upon John Dewey's theory of emotion in context (Garrison, 2003), ethical theory, and process of inquiry (Hildebrand, 2008) and uses an SFL approach to language (Halliday, 1994) with attention to the reflective discourse of EVALUATION (Mohan, 2011) combined with an analysis of appraisal (Martin & Rose, 2007) to illuminate the integration of emotion, ethics, and cognition in decision-making.

What are our aims in this chapter? The Knowledge Framework heuristic facilitates an analysis of the coaching session as a dynamic activity or social practice, where the student, John (a pseudonym), is making a *choice or decision* about a PhD program and is *evaluating* possible PhD programs. Our model for activity or social practice builds on Dewey's model of activity. However, we wish to go beyond a cognitive approach and incorporate emotion in the functional analysis of coaching discourse. For our model of emotion, we follow Dewey's theory of emotion interacting in the context of activity. This theory of emotion will be explained in detail below.

Hildebrand (2008, p. 27) comments that "Dewey's account of emotion diverges deeply from those where a subject 'has' this incredibly private, subjective mental event called 'emotion'. For Dewey, emotion emerges from the fluid boundary connecting organism and event, 'called out by objects, physical and personal' as an intentional 'response to an objective situation' (Dewey, 1925/1981, p. 292)." Taking a somewhat related position, contemporary philosopher Martha Nussbaum views emotion as an intelligent response to the perception of value. Nussbaum's compact definition of emotions is very helpful for gaining a sense of the issues involved. For her, emotions "all involve intentional thought or perception directed at an object and some type of evaluative appraisal of that object made from the agent's own viewpoint. This appraisal ascribes significance to the object in terms of the agent's scheme of goals and ends" (Nussbaum, 2013, pp. 399–400). Dewey's view of emotion is also intentional and also connects emotion with evaluative appraisal involving ethics/morals but it is much more holistic, since it considers the role of emotion in situations, contexts, and activities. Emotion is thus "situated" in activity bound to social, cultural, and physical contexts. Emotion interacts with the activity in which it is situated.

To investigate this and accomplish our aim of exploring how emotion interacts with activity, we will conduct two analyses of the coaching session. The first, operating at the macrolevel, aims to trace the general shape of the coaching session, considered as an activity. We will examine it using Dewey's pattern of inquiry. In what sense is it an activity that corresponds to Dewey's definition of activity? How far does it develop following Dewey's ecological concept of experience as an interaction between an organism and its environment? How do the student's emotions relate to his situation and his wider environment, to his deliberations with his coach and his final decision? The macrolevel analysis will be dynamic. For example, it will not only consider choices/decisions, it will also note whether choices/decisions are made or abandoned. Furthermore, it will draw on the affordance of the Knowledge Framework to facilitate identification and analysis of linguistic expressions of reflective thought in the student's deliberations with his coach. Reflection discourse can be seen to fall on a continuum ranging from specific to general, the former addressing specific activities or events, and the latter providing insights into the broader values and beliefs that give them meaning. How might John's engagement in the dynamic process of general and specific reflection during coaching come to bear on the decision at hand?

The second analysis will operate at the micro level. As noted above, it will make a functional linguistic analysis of appraisal (Martin & White, 2005) in the coaching session to illuminate the role of emotion in the context of the activity and its dynamics. Is there linguistic evidence to indicate whether or not emotion is significantly related to the decision-making and valuing process? Our analysis of appraisal includes affect, judgement, and appreciation, and we consider affect as an indication of emotion. We therefore have the opportunity to compare affect with other types of appraisal, which may throw light on the integration of emotion, ethics, and cognition in decision-making as mentioned above.

We now turn to reasons for the importance of research on emotions in coaching, particularly qualitative work. Recent research in a variety of areas has led to a strong current interest in work on emotions. The importance of this research is succinctly summarized by Asma (2018) who states that:

> According to prominent neuroscientists like Jaak Panksepp, Antonio Damasio and Kent Berridge, as well as neuropsychoanalysts like Mark Solms, our minds are motivated primarily by ancient emotional systems, like fear, rage, lust, love and grief. These forces are adaptive and help us survive if they are managed properly—that is if they are made strong enough to accomplish goals of survival, but not so strong as to overpower us and lead to neuroses and maladaptive behavior. (para. 9)

Simply put, identifying and understanding the presence and role of emotions in human experience has the potential to provide valuable insights for flourishing on many levels.

Nevertheless, there are varying degrees of appreciation for the insights to be gained. In the field of coaching, the stance on emotions can be classified into three primary positions: (1) they are to be ignored given an assumption that coaches are to facilitate rationality, (2) they are significant but inconvenient, thus requiring careful management and control, and (3) they have the potential to be a valuable source of information, an understanding that is gaining prominence (Duffell & Lawton-Smith, 2015, p. 32). This is not unlike the stance taken towards emotion in decision-making.

Human decision-making or choice has often been understood as a form of information processing, commonly represented by models grounded in an overarching cognitive paradigm, with limited attention to affect (Lehto,

Nah, & Yi, 2012). However, a recent review of research on emotions and decision-making shows a marked increase in publications in this area, with the number of scholarly papers doubling annually from 2004 to 2011 and many researchers now viewing emotions as having significant influence in most meaningful decisions (Lerner, Li, & Valdesolo, 2015, pp. 800–801). Nevertheless, the great majority of this work has been quantitative. Much less qualitative work has been done (Lerner, et al., 2015). Furthermore, to the best of our knowledge no qualitative work has occurred at the intersection of coaching, emotion, decision-making/choice, and language in the context of higher education.

Some of the issues arising in the coaching session reflect recent trends in universities. *The Economist* (May 19th 2018, pp. 51–53), in an article entitled "Higher and higher education," notes that there is an ongoing international race between countries to establish "world-class universities," and that there are now around 20 global league tables, such as the Times Higher Education (THE), ranking the world's universities. The article draws attention to biases in this process, noting that "League tables lead universities to favor research over teaching and hard sciences over the humanities" (p. 51). Students choosing a university and accessing this widely available institutional information need to be aware of these biases. In our view, an area of difficulty for them may concern the adequacy of provision of research supervision, and particularly students' awareness and judgment of their personal needs for support for learning, as this requires a sophisticated degree of "inwardness" and insight into one's own depth of thought and feeling about learning.

The philosopher Charles Taylor (1989, 1991) draws attention to the significance of "inwardness." For Taylor, to be a self (to be a person, have an identity) is to "know where you are coming from when it comes to questions of value, or issues of importance" (1991, pp. 305–306). His development of this understanding in "The sources of the self" (1989) points to a number of distinctive aspects of the modern western self or identity culture, one of which is "inwardness," an idea of the person as a being with inner depths that, while mysterious, can be explored (pp. 173–183). This entails an understanding of selfhood as having a moral dimension, in which "to ascertain the right things to do, be or *feel* (our italics), the self should turn inward, not outward to the opinions of others" (Abbey, 2000, p. 85) even though these inner depths might not be easily available to discovery or self-interpretation. In our present case study, we find that the student initially tends to emphasize the opinions of others, but later turns inward to address more adequately this aspect of awareness and the role inwardness plays in his decision process. The dynamic is well represented in an outstanding poetic articulation of the struggle between outwardness and inwardness written by the 16th-century English poet Sir Phillip Sydney (1554–1586) in "Astrophil and Stella 1":

> I sought fit words to paint the blackest face of woe;
> Studying inventions fine, her wits to entertain,
> Oft turning others' leaves, to see if thence would flow
> Some fresh and fruitful showers upon my sunburn'd brain.
> But words came halting forth, wanting Invention's stay;
> Invention, Nature's child, fled step-dame Study's blows;
> And others' feet still seem'd but strangers in my way.
> Thus great with child to speak, and helpless in my throes,
> Biting my truant pen, beating myself for spite,
> "Fool," said my Muse to me, "look in thy heart, and write."
> (Ringler, 1962, p. 165)

Theoretical Framework

Activity

In this study, our concept of activity follows the tradition of Dewey's 1911 encyclopedia entry "Activity: Logical Theory and Educational Implication of" where he writes:

> For educational purposes this concept may be defined as a series of changes definitely adapted to accomplishing an end... By way of emphasizing the conscious share of the individual in the initiation and execution of a series of changes directed to an end, activity generally appears in educational literature as self-activity...owing to the influence of Aristotle, pure activity was identified with the operation of pure reason, a process beginning and ending exclusively in the mind and expressed wholly in logical terms...and had to be conceived quite independently of any changes effected among objects or through the body. ...this dualistic and exclusively intellectualistic philosophy...has had great historic influence, much of which still survives. Embodied in the scholastic theory of the superiority of the contemplative to the practical life, it finds an echo to-day in the assumption that all professional and even useful education must be illiberal and noncultural. (p. 33)

However, he concludes that "by relieving it of its excessive intellectual associations" the notion of activity "is losing its purely philosophical meaning, and is becoming identified with all types of directed action in which the purpose, choice, and reflection of the individual take a part" (p. 34).

We note that the purpose, choice, and reflection of the individual are major elements of activity. They inclusively extend beyond the dualistic and exclusively intellectualistic philosophy. They include more than cognition. They bring in ethical judgments by the moral self and valuing as a practical and emotional act. In Dewey's view, "choice is the most characteristic activity of a self…" (Dewey & Tufts, 1932, p. 316). Furthermore, "only deliberate action, conduct into which reflective choice enters, is distinctively moral, for only then does there enter the question of better and worse" (Dewey 1922/1983, p.193). As such, "conduct as moral may thus be defined as activity called forth and directed by ideas of value or worth, where the values concerned are so mutually incompatible as to require consideration and selection before an overt action is entered upon" (Dewey & Tufts, 1908/1978, p.194). We will summarize this moral process as "choice and moral deliberation of values."

As a philosopher, Dewey analyses the elements of activity from his philosophical standpoint of "logical theory." As linguists, we analyze the components of activity from the linguistic standpoint of semantic structures of meaning. This is not an opposition but a complementarity, because linguistic evidence of the components of activity is of value to both philosophers and linguists. Mohan's Knowledge Framework is a heuristic account of semantic structures of activity: DESCRIPTION and CLASSIFICATION, SEQUENCE and PRINCIPLES, CHOICE and EVALUATION/values. Our aim for the "activity theme" of this chapter is to try to build a bridge between Deweyan "choice and values" and semantic "choice and evaluation/values" so that one side of the bridge offers linguistic evidence, and the other side leads to a rich theory of ethics/morality.

Philosophers and Emotion: Dewey's Holistic View of Emotion

For centuries, the relationship between emotion and cognition has captured the attention of thinkers, such as Aristotle, who typically privileged cognition over emotion, yet not without debate. Hildebrand (2008) notes that the philosophers of ancient Greece not only elevated cognition over emotion, but "developed an exaggerated disrespect for emotion" and that "moderns such as Descartes and Spinoza go so far as to argue that emotion is merely a species of confused thought" (p. 26). In contrast, as early as the 1890s,

Dewey recognized the importance of emotion in "The Theory of Emotion" (1895/1971, p. 174) and thereafter contested the cognitive bias against it in the philosophical tradition.

Dewey and Emotion in Decision-making/Choice and Action

Hildebrand (2008) provides an example which offers insights into Dewey's situational view of emotion in decision-making and action:

> As I stride confidently across the street, my eye catches sight of a strange dog in my way. My predictable situation is suddenly precarious and the emotion seizing me indicates that my habit (striding quickly) must be inhibited so a readjustment (avoidance, perhaps) can follow.
>
> Note that it is *the inhibition of habit*—rooted in my perplexity over how to adjust to this event—*that excites emotion.* Were I to encounter a familiar and friendly dog, I might pause and pet him, but that would not excite great emotion because my usual habits would lead frictionlessly to response. Again, in the case of a strange dog, it is the flood of *incompatible* responses (should I run? call for the owner? walk slowly?) that creates the tension that interrupts and inhibits habits, and this is experienced as emotion. In Dewey's rendering, emotion arises within the field of action. (p. 28)

More broadly, the example illustrates the unity of thought and emotion in action.

Unity of thought and emotion in action is of foundational importance in Deweyan thinking. The extent of its significance is highlighted by Garrison (2003), who observes that "[i]n completing his reconstruction of the theory of emotion, Dewey relies on what may be his most fundamental idea, the unity of thought and emotion in naturalistic functional 'co-ordination' of action (behaviour)" (p. 406). This is a model of intentional human agency, not a model of automatic stimulus-response: "Dewey flatly denies that a living behavior-agent requires anything to prompt it" (Garrison, 2003, p. 425). To extend Hildebrand's example, if I decide that the dog is dangerous and therefore to be feared, I need to draw on my cognitive knowledge about dogs to make a plan and to act on it, deciding, perhaps, not to turn around and run away (which responds to my fear but encourages attack) but to back away slowly and calmly, avoiding eye contact. In other words, I need a process which coordinates emotion, relevant contextual knowledge, and decisions to build thoughtful and appropriate sequences of action that I hope will be functional in the local environment. Suppose that I have backed away from the dog calmly and found that the dog has not attacked me. Then I have taken a precarious and problematic situation, thought reflectively in order to "stimulate deliberate readjustment to meet the surprises of a moving world" (Fesmire, 2015, p. 255), executed my plan to readjust matters, and observed the results. In this way I hope I have established a more stable and predictable situation, for the present.

What does Dewey mean by "situation"? "Situation refers to any experience at hand, from its brilliant focus—conspicuous and apparent –to its horizontal field or background, the obscured, concealed, enveloping, and felt context" (Dewey 1916/1980, p. 323). In our data, the coach and the student discuss part of the situation focus and part of the wider context at the beginning of their session.

Dewey and Emotion, Ethics/Morality, and Aesthetics

Dewey offers a perspective on ethics/morals that challenges traditional views. "Moral philosophers have consistently sought to prove that there exist, independently of the 'phenomenal' changes that occur in the world, special moral precepts that are universal, fixed, certain, and unchanging. But in Dewey's view, change, conflict, contingency, uncertainty and struggle are at the very heart of moral experience" (Pappas, 1998, p. 107). His view draws attention to the importance of people working towards a deeper understanding of problematic situations: "*This is the heart of Dewey's ethics*: the starting point of deliberation is a problematic situation. We reach for our toolbox of principles and ideals not to deduce the right thing to do, but to help us attend more perceptively and responsively to situational factors" (Fesmire, 2015, p. 137). Simply put, Dewey's moral theory highlights ordinary situations: "[it] begins from the practical starting point of everyday life.... what characterizes morality *per se,* is the existence of a *situation* saturated by conflicting elements which *demands* that engaged agents determine *reflectively* what to value and what ends to pursue" (Hildebrand, 2008, pp. 66–67).

Choice and moral deliberation of values are thus significant components of moral inquiry, which in Dewey's model consists of three predominant phases: "First, the agent finds herself in a morally problematic situation. Second, the agent engages in a process of moral deliberation. Finally, she arrives at a judgment that results in a choice" (Pappas, 1998, p. 108). Choice and values are also significant components of Mohan's Knowledge Framework, as noted above, so this forms a potential bridge between linguistic analysis and Dewey's model of moral inquiry. As we will see in our data, the student is in a problematic situation where he must choose between universities, and in the coaching session he and his coach reflectively discuss his alternative choices and morally deliberate about what to value and what ends to pursue.

This brings us to the experiential quality of this process and points us to Dewey's view of aesthetics, which has implications for his theory of ethics/morals. In his work on aesthetics, Dewey extends the application of aesthetic assessment to the everyday processes of living. He rejects the assumption that regards art as separate and distinct from everyday experience and argues strongly for "the continuity of esthetic experience with normal processes of living" (Dewey, 1934/1987, p.16), having reflected on activities and their contribution to the quality of life and experience (Dewey, 1925/1925, pp. 271–72). In Dewey's view, one can clearly distinguish between an activity which does not provide a meaningful experience (e.g., work that is drudgery) and an activity that does (e.g., work that is fulfilling). His name for an experience of an activity that does is a "consummatory" experience. An activity that provides a consummatory experience has immediate enjoyed intrinsic meaning.

Why does this matter? Dewey considers the quality of moral deliberation to be important for the moral progress of people: "Moral progress, for Dewey, really comes down to process—the degree to which we habitually inquire in nuanced and scrupulous ways" (Hildebrand, 2008, p. 72). We will use Dewey's pattern of inquiry to examine the process of moral deliberation between coach and student in the coaching session.

To sum up, to this point we have discussed evaluative appraisal based on emotion, evaluative appraisal based on morality/ethics, and evaluative appraisal based on aesthetics. Below we will discuss SFL work on the language of evaluative appraisal based on emotion, evaluative appraisal based on morality/ethics, and evaluative appraisal based on aesthetics. The similarity between these two sets of categories is notable, and it offers a potential bridge between Dewey's theory and linguistic analysis. We do not claim the two sets are identical, but we believe there is enough similarity to support a fruitful discussion.

Dewey's Pattern of Inquiry

What does it mean to think reflectively? How does it work? Dewey offers a "pattern of inquiry" composed of phases in human experience (see Hildebrand, 2008, pp. 53ff).

Phase 1 (P1): An indeterminate situation in which a difficulty is felt
Phase 2 (P2): The institution of a problem; its location and definition

Phase 3 (P3): Hypothesis of a possible solution (or resolution)
Phase 4 (P4): Reasoning out the bearings of a solution (or the implications of a (re)solution)
Phase 5 (P5): Active experimental or observational testing of the hypothesis

The broad outlines of the pattern of inquiry are that a problem is identified and a solution is developed and tested out. In the simple example above, the walker identifies the dog as dangerous and finds a quiet way to exit the scene safely. The example is a case of unified thought and emotion in the naturalistic "functional co-ordination" of action on its environment.

One of the things we will explore in what follows is whether there are similarities between the pattern of inquiry and the process in the data of the co-constructed coaching session that we will be analyzing. Consider Hildebrand's (2008) explanation about Phase 1, the beginning of the process:

> Inquiry that may become reflective typically does not begin that way; rather it begins by having a feeling that something is wrong (for example, a strange noise wakes me up in the middle of the night and I feel a vague doubt that something is amiss) [We should not try to dismiss the doubtful quality as just a subjective feeling—it is the entire situation which is doubtful, unsettled, or disturbed]. (p. 54)

Applied to the coaching session, at the beginning, does any participant feel that something is wrong, doubtful, unsettled, or disturbed? If so, this emotion may be the beginning of an extended inquiry.

What about the conclusion? Phase 5 is active experimental or observational testing of the hypothesis. A crucial point here is that "only meanings *tested in action* (only either observation or experiment) can justify a conclusion of inquiry" (Hildebrand, 2008, p. 56). On the face of it, we cannot provide this. If the hypothesis is: "John should go to City 1 University," future testing could mean seeing if he succeeds in his first year in the City 1 program. But this is beyond the scope of the coaching session. However, observation can include self-observation, and the coach makes strategic use of this in hypothesis testing, with important consequences in coaching. When John rejects City 1 because of his earlier bad experience in the hospital, which amounts to the hypothesis: "John should not go to City 1 University," the coach asks him how his current view of skill development is similar to or different from his understanding at the time of the bad experience in the hospital. *He reflects on his life experience, his personal history,* and has the significant insight that he is now different, being a graduate student doing his own research to develop his skills, and therefore he rejects the hypothesis "John should not go to City 1 University." Historical observation of the past can provide empirical testing.

Why is it important to see the relation between the coaching session and the pattern of inquiry? An inquiry that follows the pattern can be understood to be a large, coordinated unit of action on its environment. If the process of the coaching session follows the broad outlines of the pattern of inquiry, then the coaching session is also likely to be a large, coordinated unit of action on its environment. In that sense it is "functional."

SFL Attitudinal Meaning Analysis

Above, we have discussed Dewey's categories of evaluative appraisal based on emotion, evaluative appraisal based on morality/ethics, and evaluative appraisal based on aesthetics. We now discuss similar categories in SFL attitudinal meanings analysis. We believe that the similarity, though not identical, is close enough that the SFL categories can provide linguistic evidence relevant to the Dewey categories.

White (2015) offers a concise description of attitudinal meanings in SFL text analysis:

> Within the appraisal literature, the term "attitude" is used to reference the subsystem of evaluative meanings by which addressees are positioned to adopt a positive or negative view… A taxonomy of these positively or negatively attitudinal meanings is provided which is sensitive to such issues as the basis for the attitudinal assessment, the nature of what is being assessed, what is at stake socially, and whether the attitude is conveyed explicitly or implicitly. (p.2)

More specifically, drawing on White (2015, p. 2), attitudinal meanings of appraisal can be divided into the following three broad subcategories:

(1) Affect: "positive/negative assessment presented as emotional reactions,"
(2) Judgment: "positive/negative assessments of human behavior and character by reference to ethics/morality and other systems of conventionalized or institutionalized norms,"
(3) Appreciation: "assessments of objects, artifacts, texts, states of affairs, and processes in terms of how they are assigned value socially…that

is, in terms of aesthetic qualities, their potential for harm or benefit, their social salience, and so on."

We will give examples below of the analysis of attitudinal meanings in our data. We turn now to a closer look at our sample coaching session.

Sample Case

The coaching interaction under consideration in this chapter is the first of three sessions that occurred at irregular intervals between the coach and John during a six-week period in which he was contemplating future directions in academia. The session lasted just over 60 minutes, was recorded with permission, transcribed in full, anonymized, a pseudonym chosen, and the transcript reviewed by John prior to being released by him for use in the present discussion. Due to the length and richness of the transcript data, to facilitate analysis, we initially divided it into "moves" at naturally occurring points in the development of the interaction such as where a new aspect was introduced and examined. For the purposes of this chapter, we will focus on excerpts from select moves to illustrate functional patterns at three levels, including (1) fit between the process of coaching and Dewey's phases of inquiry, (2) the interaction between specific and general reflection leading to personally meaningful insights for the coachee, and (3) evaluative language used in the coaching interaction that illustrates the presence and role of emotion in the process of decision-making.

Our strategy for case analysis uses Dewey's pattern of inquiry at the macrolevel to give a sense of the flow of decision-making over the whole coaching session. Our strategy also uses an SFL appraisal analysis of attitude at the microlevel to show how it gives a detailed sense of shifts in attitude at an important part of the coaching session. Our SFL appraisal of attitude shows how our distinctions between affect, judgment (moral norms), and aesthetics are based on the evidence of linguistic analysis. As we pointed out above, Dewey's view of ethics/morals and aesthetics makes similar distinctions, so the SFL appraisal of attitudes holds out future promise for exploring linguistic evidence of Dewey's view.

Coaching and Patterns of Meaning

An examination of the coaching session suggests that Dewey's pattern of inquiry, broadly applied, can be seen to occur in three iterations, each iteration adding depth to John's quest for clarity. Figure 5.1 is a heuristic outline of these complex processes in the interview data, with general movement indicated in a simplified way by a line with arrows. Problems and solutions are not initially given, but are constructed, examined, and reworked throughout the interview. This is an iterative process, not a simple fixed procedure. Figure 5.1 also shows increasing depth and increasing clarity in a simplified way by

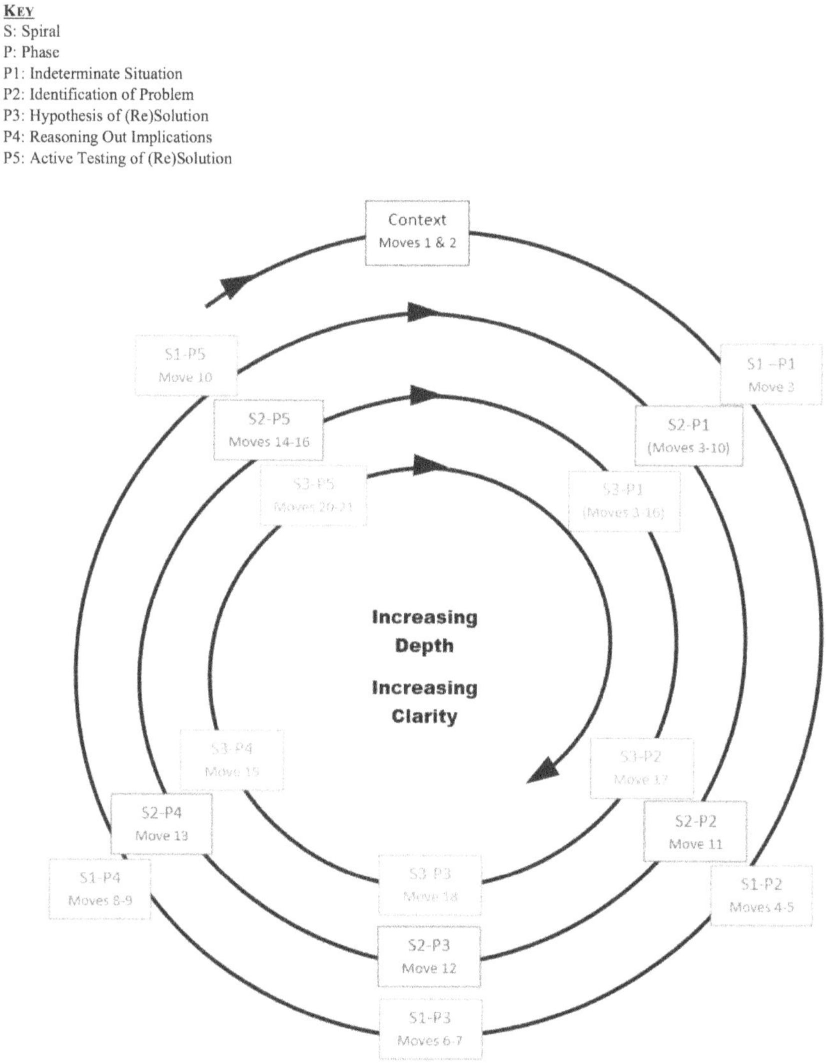

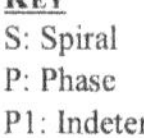

Figure 5.1 Coaching process and patterns of inquiry

a spiral that increasingly moves inward. This too is an iterative process, not a simple fixed procedure. With each iteration, the presence and role of affect as it comes to bear on the decision-making process also become increasingly clear, ultimately yielding the insight needed by John for his decision (see Table 5.1 for a synopsis). The interaction illustrates the dynamics of intersecting past experiences, present circumstances, and future possibilities in the emergent co-constructed coaching activity. This process also demonstrates that John's specific reflection on emotionally charged experiences and subsequent re-appraisal of them in light of other considerations at the level of general reflection leads him to new perspectives and possibilities for action.

In education, Jerome Bruner "proposed the spiral curriculum as a teaching approach in which each subject or skill area is revisited at intervals, at a more sophisticated level each time. First, there is a basic knowledge of a subject, then more sophistication is added, reinforcing principles that were first discussed" (Spiral Approach, 2022). Bruner's approach has been developed further in recent work (e.g., Murray, 2016; Woodward, 2019); however, while his use of spirals deals with the relation between principles and cases, our use of spirals deals with the relation between Dewey's pattern of inquiry and our coaching data.

Table 5.1 Synopsis

Context		Moves	Synopsis
		1	The coach explains the process and principles of coaching
		2	The coach and John set the interpersonal tone and John introduces the general topic—a big decision.
Spiral 1	Phase 1	3	John states his desire to consider pros and cons of three universities, notes anxiety associated with the decision, narrows his focus to a desire to understand why he wants a large university and raises a concern about his capability of handling PhD work.
	Phase 2	4	John observes that City1 is actually his preferred choice but wants to clarify why given the perceived problem of limited opportunity for interaction with his potential City1 supervisor.
		5	John highlights the importance of making the right decision in order to avoid being stuck in a punishing academic experience.

(*Continued*)

Table 5.1 (*Continued*)

Context		Moves	Synopsis
	Phase 3	6	John explores the desired features of academic experience with attention to interpersonal relationships and potential for close connections in City1, a big university, and City2, a small university
		7	John notes his choice of MA university was based on quality of relationship with his MA supervisor which outweighed the difficulty of his research focus, considers his developing abilities due in part to that relationship, and a resulting forthcoming publication with his supervisor.
	Phase 4	8	John considers the possibility for ongoing research on his current topic in City1 and City2 universities and recounts his ability to help a visiting scholar, leading to his own recognition of his expert knowledge.
		9	John weighs the importance he attaches to interpersonal relationships versus knowledge and skill development with regard to the decision at hand, concluding that the latter is priority in light of his life goals.
	Phase 5	10	John considers how City1 lines up with his priorities, naming various considerations, concluding with the observation that there are many reasons in favor of City1, reasons he has already thought about.
Spiral 2	Phase 1	(3–10)	[In spite of the above, the quest for clarity appears unresolved]
	Phase 2	11	The coach asks John what's holding him back which leads to the acknowledgement and account of a core affective concern rooted in a difficult relationship between John and a supervisor in his first research experience.
	Phase 3	12	The coach asks John how his current view of skill development is similar to or different from his understanding at the time of the difficult experience. He observes that he is pursuing his dream. If he has a bad experience, he'll think positively because he's doing this for himself.
	Phase 4	13	John has a pivotal insight when he realizes that he is now doing his own research in contrast to assisting in someone else's research.

(*Continued*)

Table 5.1 (*Continued*)

Context		Moves	Synopsis
	Phase 5	14	The coach invites John to apply this insight to his considerations of City1; in the process John gains awareness of his ability to design strategies to manage undesirable situations.
		15	The coach asks John to reflect on progress so far towards his desired outcome from the coaching session. John compares it to adding bricks to the building of his dreams. He adds that he is seeing more pros than cons.
		16	John elaborates on some of the pros, including the positive reframing of aspects of City1 that had been negatively perceived earlier. This leads to a positive memory of his first professional conference and a series of emphatic declarations of what he wants, potentially available via City1.
Spiral 3	Phase 1	(3–16)	[In spite of the above, the quest for clarity appears incomplete]
	Phase 2	17	John observes that going to City1 would mean leaving his comfort zone and expresses his fear of making a decision that would favour comfort over new experiences and potential growth. At the coach's request he reviews when he has stepped out of his comfort zone in the past decade.
	Phase 3	18	The coach asks what insights he can apply to the present situation. John positions City1 as one more challenge and adventure, another opportunity to prove himself. He also realizes he has already succeeded in life but doesn't want to stop yet.
	Phase 4	19	The coach notes John's courage, vision, and resilience. John observes that his awareness of this is sometimes obscured by anxiety and stress, as with City1. Yet he sees he has managed and overcome these affective elements all his life.
	Phase 5	20	The coach asks John what he has gained from the coaching conversation to which he emphatically replies he sees he is truly capable of going to City1 University. He states that the conversation has helped him put the pieces together and he wants to go.
		21	John comments on the value of his insight and his unqualified desire to go forward with the decision, identifying initial next steps and even more hope for the future.

Coaching and Dewey's Phases of Inquiry

Context. Dewey states that a situation of inquiry has a focus and emerges in a context. In the case at hand, we see evidence of this in Moves 1–2. In Move 1, the coach sets the stage with reference to a focus along with an explanation of the general sequence of the session, which aims to establish one aspect of the immediate context.

> Coach: I'm going to ask you what it is that you want to focus on today and then we'll work with that idea... And then part way through, I'll probably ask you how we're doing...the goal is to get to some place by the end of that conversation.

The coach then describes "the way coaching goes," referring to the roles of coach and coachee, another aspect of immediate context.

> Coach: Basically, the way coaching goes is that as the coach, I'm going to be asking you questions. So it's kind of like I steer the car. ... But this is your car...and all of the content, that's yours...

In Move 2, the coach articulates her affective disposition towards the coaching interaction with John and the situation that has given rise to the coaching encounter, explicitly attending to the interpersonal dynamics of context. John responds with positive appraisal of the situation and introduces the topic, thus establishing the general topical parameters of the interaction.

> Coach: I am delighted to be able to work with you. ...you've got some great opportunities ahead.
> John: Yeah, it's very cool and I have to make a big decision.

Thus, within the first moments of interaction, the coach and John make explicit select procedural, interpersonal, and topical dimensions that come to bear on the dynamics and general focus of the immediate coaching context.

Spiral 1 (S1)—External Considerations. As noted in the theoretical discussion above, Dewey's pattern of inquiry encompasses five phases.

S1-P1. Phase 1 is an indeterminate situation in which difficulty is felt. An examination of the interaction in our sample case shows this to be a reasonable characterization of Move 3. As John works to narrow and clarify what he would like to gain from the conversation, it becomes apparent that his initial statement of focus is in fact not the focus of primary significance to him.

John: ...I want to make the decision where I should go for my PhD... So if it's a big university, or a small university and see the pros and cons...umm on both sides. Like checking both sides and seeing which one would be the best for me and for [my wife] Mary. And [one-second pause] and yeah, and for my future too because [one-second pause] sometimes a big university means a better diploma, but sometimes it's the opposite, so that's why it's a tricky uh situation for me... And that makes me very anxious and [one-second pause] and uh and pretty stressed sometimes also.

Coach: I hear...a lot of things riding on your decision. ...what do you want to have by the end of our conversation...?

John: Well I really wish I could have a better idea [one-second pause] why I want to go to a big university...there are two big universities and a small one...not only that but [one-second pause] if I'm capable to go...that's one of my concerns. If I'm capable to go and handle four years of [one-second pause] of intense PhD.

At the start of Move 3, John describes the topic focus, functionally setting the specific agenda for the session. He also chooses to articulate the affective implications. In Dewey's terms we could say that he is experiencing unsettledness or a disturbance because he cannot be sure that the potential outcomes of any one choice of university will be in his favor. Yet when the coach asks for additional clarification, he states that he wants a large university, but does not understand why. In Dewey's terms, this might be seen as a second disturbance; he recognizes a preference but not the underlying reasons. He then adds one more element, a question about his capability. This can be understood as a third disturbance. As noted above, Dewey mentions inner and outer aspects of the person. We consider the first disturbance to be an outer one, possibly tackled with pros and cons about universities. In contrast, we see the second and third to be inner aspects. In the remainder of Spiral 1, John follows through with a closer examination of pros and cons, yet without broaching inner concerns.

S1-P2. Phase 2 of Dewey's pattern encompasses the identification of a problem in terms of its location and definition. We see this in Moves 4 and 5, where John acknowledges that not only does he want to go to a large university, City1 University is his preference. Nevertheless, in spite of several obvious benefits, John is also perplexed by this awareness given his potentially limited opportunity for interaction with the City1 supervisor:

John: ...my supervisor [there] he's all over the world...travelling and seeing people, making new connections, and publishing papers. ...that's the problem right there because the guy in City1 he travels a lot...he wouldn't be there for me when I need [him] most of the time...[yet] in my mind City1 is the first. It's my big shot...and I just want to make sure why...because I know already that it will be a problem that I have to work alone...but that's the university I want.

Limited access to a supervisor is, to John's mind, a significant problem and thus he does not understand his own desire. Much is at stake since the wrong decision could result in "punishment for four years" in his view.

S1-P3. The conversation takes a turn that can be represented by Phase 3 of Dewey's Pattern, a hypothesis of solution or resolution. John explores desirable features of his present academic experience, turning to reflect on the pros and cons of City1 and City2 in terms of size and opportunities for building friendships. The coach then makes an observation about what seems to matter and John concurs, supporting his position with an anecdote underscoring the benefits and mutual appreciation that characterize the interaction with his MA supervisor.

Coach: ...what I've been noticing in our conversation is that it seems to be the relationships...that are really of most importance. I heard you say that you chose your MA university because it was smaller and you could have a good relationship with your professor.

John: Yeah. That's true... The topic's very hard and technical, so [two-second pause]...uh, I can see myself doing something else actually.... It's hard [one-second pause] but it's something that [one-second pause] that I can do, I see that I can do, and it's not so many people who do it....so [one-second pause] someone needs to do it.... And I've got this training. When I started it, it was very complicated for me... It was too complicated. ... It was like, keep moving forward and learning more... I started studying it for real, uh, three months ago. ... And we are about to publish because I proved almost all the equations right.

Coach: That's quite an accomplishment!

John: Yeah...he's very impressed...

Here John expresses his sense of growth as he develops his ability to work with a very difficult topic, the value of his training, and anticipation of fulfillment in knowing that this will result in joint publication. In our view, following Dewey, these are aesthetic aspects of experiences which culminate in a "consummatory experience" or "*an* experience." For John, this accomplishment is the academic outcome of an enjoyable interpersonal relationship.

S1-P4. What might be the implications of this insight? Phase 4 of Dewey's pattern of inquiry encompasses reflection on the implications of a potential solution. The coach invites John to evaluate the meaning of what he has just described, and he considers the pros and cons of carrying on research in his area of specialty at City1 and City2. In Move 9 the coach asks John to weigh the importance of relationships versus knowledge or skill development

John: I know if I go to any university… I wouldn't treat my supervisor as a boss. I would try very hard to treat the person as a friend…and then this would make me like the research even more because it would be helping a friend. So, uh, developing my skills is very important, I think I would say even more important than umm helping a friend because I'm helping myself first. …because if I help myself first, I know in the future when I go back to my home country…to teach other people, I'll be able to use all those skills that I got to help other people too, so in one way or another I will help people.

Coach: So I just heard you say that even though relationships are important, as with your supervisor, the most important thing for you right now is to develop your own skills.

John: Yes because when I started here, I didn't know [one-second pause] which direction I should take. Now sometimes if I'm stuck with something, I can try something new…check, have ideas why it's not working…that's very important. Because I want to be a researcher, so going and having these experiences, learning how to do research, walking with my own feet, it's very important to me… Because I will have to apply for grants, I will have to supervise people, so that will be my life. And that's what's important…. I need that.

In the process of this exchange of general reflection, John not only identifies the most important of two key priorities, he also provides a window on his "moral self" and the moral framework which guides his choices and actions. He wants to learn how to research, to develop his skills, and ultimately use them to teach, supervise, and help people in his home country. He wants to be a scientific researcher, and these skills will help him and build on his natural endowment of mathematical ability. In this way he is expanding, harmonizing, and organizing his social self. This is a moral commitment (to help others in his home country). It is also a major, all-encompassing commitment ("that will be my life") and he has already given years of study to it, arriving at the masters' level. The evidence of John's account shows that he is able to self-interpret to a great degree his commitment and its progress. However, as will be seen, there are aspects of his inner self which he has not yet accessed.

S1-P5. Phase 5 of Dewey's process is an active (experimental or observational) testing of hypothesis. In Move 10, when invited to now apply the awareness he has gained to the decision at hand, John lists multiple pros for City1 and ends by noting that there are many reasons in favor of City1, reasons to which he has already given considerable thought. Yet despite this process and related anecdotes that highlight pleasurable academic experiences and underscore his academic capabilities, his awareness of connections to significant values and many reasons why City1 would be a preferred choice, John's deliberation is incomplete.

Spiral 2 (S2)—Inner Perspective I. This leads to another iteration of inquiry that we have identified as Spiral 2, where the incomplete resolution of the deliberation in Spiral 1 represents Phase 1 of Spiral 2.

S2-P2. Move 11 corresponds again to the institution of a problem, its location and definition. In response to the coach's inquiry at this point, John moves from external considerations to an inner focus which brings to light a significant concern which adds perspective to his focus in Spiral 1.

Coach: So you've thought about this already. What's holding you back?

John: What's holding me back? It's that, um. [one-second pause] if my supervisor is not a good person at all, so I would have the same experience I had here before, that I fell into a big depression and I couldn't work anymore... So [two-second pause], I don't know if it's because of my, I would say, heart that's very warm, and so then when I see someone very cold, so... [one-second pause] you lose all your heat [passion]...and just get mad like the other people.... Or [two-second pause], or just like I wouldn't see myself helping someone that doesn't appreciate me because that's what happened before. So, [sigh] I worked in the, at the hospital, and I wasn't appreciated, and it was very hard in the workplace. It was hard and I couldn't learn from that... Actually, I just ran away. ... I changed my whole research because of that.

In this move, faced with a very direct question, John becomes aware that his wish to choose City1 is blocked by a deep emotional concern rooted in the trauma of a negative early research experience. Whereas John's earlier comments of the City1 supervisor speak to the problem of him being busy and having little time for appointments, here the problem is different. It concerns the possibility of the supervisor disliking him, not appreciating him. John muses about the explanation for what happened before in emotional terms of inner life, speaking of his own "very warm" heart and another that is very cold. It has taken until now in the coaching session for him to begin to "look into his heart" and speak about it, but the disclosure adds perspective to his earlier remarks about his MA supervisor being "impressed" with him.

The problem that has been identified in this specific reflection is not something that can be resolved by more consideration of the "pros and cons" of City1. John's negative early research experience was also clearly not "an experience" in Dewey's sense of the word; in fact it was quite the opposite in that it contributed to a negative quality of life and was ultimately left incomplete when John "ran away." Instead, it calls for John to engage in deeper inner reflection to resolve this emotional conflict. He needs to answer his own questions: why he wants to go to a big university and whether he is capable to go, answers that require he look inward.

S2-P3. To expand John's exploration of this line of inquiry, in Move 12 the coach asks John how his current view of skill development is similar to or different from his understanding at the time of the difficult research experience. In this response, his specific reflection gives way to general reflection ("But...now...") from which emerges a significant insight.

John: Umm [three-second pause] at the hospital, I worked there while trying to develop my skills and I got a few bad experiences out of that. ... I could have had my first article published there. I left when they asked me to keep working so I couldn't have my article published even though I made all the graphs and everything. [two-second pause] But I left because I tried to solve the situation. I tried to solve the problem with the bad influence, with the person that wasn't so good with me. ... But instead of that [solving the problem], the person just acted like a child, and he didn't want to talk to me anymore. So I just spent a whole month like that [two-second pause] uh,

> so yes, I got skills from there. [two-second pause] Uh that was good for me. But I didn't get recognized by that. But...now my skill's a bit different. I'm older now and have more experience. That was my first bad experience in my life. And I know I will have like many, many more. But I know that now...I'm not an undergrad anymore... So, I have my skills. I know what my dream is. I want to become a professor and [two-second pause] and I know the way. ... So I need to, I need to find a place to go. Because I don't want to go back to my country now. ... I'm very homesick sometimes...but I don't want to go now. I want to keep going and developing my skills and getting the best education as much as I can. ... When I go back I'll go ready. ...So I just think that [one-second pause] even if I have a bad experience now, but I just think good now in my mind, I'm doing something that's for me. I'm not an undergrad now. I'm different, I'm at another level.

Although John's negative early research experience was not a fulfilling experience and was in fact aborted when John "ran away" in spite of being close to achieving a joint publication, in this exchange we see something different. John's general reflection from the vantage point of his present circumstances leads to affective-cognitive integration as he gains understanding of significant differences related both to his capabilities and the "why" of his life goal. He is now in pursuit of his dream, becoming a professor, and in spite of being in another country and feeling homesick, he is not ready to stop yet; he must continue to develop his skills so that he returns prepared. In light of this awareness, he considers a new course of action. Even if he has a bad experience going forward, he can "just think good now in my mind" because this situation is different. It is linked to his dream, his life goal. He is now focusing on his personal resources.

Spiral 3 (S3)—Inner Perspective II. In Spiral 3 of the coaching session, the coach and John take the assessment of his personal resources one step further in a final round of exploration. This time, his deepening awareness of how the present decision fits within the broader context of his life journey thus far, as well as his dreams for the future, lead him to a summary realization of the functional interaction of thought and emotion on action in his lived experience and achievements:

John: Sometimes I get anxious and stressed and everything gets blurry. That's why I have fears to go somewhere. I just need to have strategies to make it better.

In effect, his engagement in the coaching session has served as one of these strategies. When invited by the coach to reflect on insights related to the goals he set for the session, John returns to address, once and for all, that nagging question regarding the sum total of his personal resources. He makes an emphatic declaration and then elaborates on how the coaching processes has facilitated this insight along with the overall impact on his decision:

John: ...from our conversation I see that I'm capable to go. Seriously. ... I'm capable to go. ... [chuckle]. Yeah [chuckle]. ... So that's myself talking more, when I say things and when I put the pieces together, when I say that all my skills and all my capabilities of making new friends, learning new research, and growing as a person. So when I don't have all that together like we put everything together here...it's hard for me to think that I'm capable. But when you see that, and put all pieces together...it makes me want to go.

It is a realization that will now become a focal point of his thoughts going forward, and the springboard for stepping out on a course of appropriate action.

John: It's very valuable!... It's something that I will think about.... When I leave... I can go and say, "Oh, I want to do this..." and try to arrange something. So it gives me even more hope.

In short, we argue that the coaching activity, for John, has been a meaningful "consummatory experience" in the Deweyan sense of the term, encompassing dynamic integrated processes of thought and emotion. This is illustrated not only by his verbal expressions, but also the punctuation of those expressions with silence while he thinks, as well as use of paralinguistic resources such as sighing and chuckling, as evidenced in various excerpts.

Coaching and Appraisal

At this point we turn our attention to a closer look at the language of the coaching session to gain insight into the linguistic construction of attitude. A review of Moves 10, 11, and 12 indicates that there are striking major shifts in John's attitude, which combine to construct a pivotal turning point in the session. Does our SFL analysis of appraisal capture significant difference between these shifts? To answer this question, we need to see whether affect appraisals are evident in decision-making and valuing.

Initially, John approaches the choice of a university essentially in terms of the features of universities but does not include his personal resources, skills, and emotions. In Move 3 John says "I want to make the decision where I should go for my PhD. … So if it is a big university or a small university and *see the pros and cons on both sides* [emphasis added]."

In Move 10 the coach asks: "How would City1 [University] help you in the light of [your wish to develop your skills]?" In response, John appraises City1 University, mentioning a number of "pros" of City1 University that would help to develop his skills and also City1 itself. Table 5.2 shows these "pro" features as "judgments." The only negative "con" relates to "if my supervisor's not there all the time" along with related initial assessment of implications. Thus John appears to positively endorse City1 University using recognizable criteria for universities and Table 5.2 of the appraisal analysis reflects this.

Here it is helpful to note that in appraisal analysis, attitudinal meaning can be inscribed explicitly or invoked implicitly. Whereas inscribed Judgement explicitly encodes attitudinal meaning targeting people and/or their behavior, other constructions can be employed to invoke Judgement and construe it implicitly in light of a wider context of meaning (Martin & White, 2005). Such is the case here where the coach's question personifies City1 University as potentially "helping" John. In our analysis of John's response, we see instances where the appraised target is a non-conscious participant, identified as *City1University* (City1UNIV), which John also, in effect, personifies as affording him opportunities for academic and scholarly development (or not). This is likewise the case where *the city of City1 University* (the city of City1) is identified as the appraised target, which John construes as creating conditions and affording valued opportunities important to his quality of life, which in turn has direct implications for his well-being and academic work (a focus considered earlier in Moves 5 and 6).

In Move 11, when the coach asks John "What's holding you back [from choosing City1 University]," John's extended response is very largely negative, in striking contrast to the positive view he expressed in Move 10. It seems that his intense "subjective" narrative exposes deep "inward" emotions, fears arising from his earlier traumatic negative experience working at the hospital. The strong contrast between positive and negative views is mirrored in the contrast between positive judgment appraisals of a university in Table 5.2 and negative affect appraisals of a bad experience in Table 5.3.

Table 5.2 Move 10 appraisal analysis

Question: "How would it help you in light of these things (in light of [your wish to develop your skills]?)"			
Appraised	**Appraisal**	**Appraisal Category**	
There (At City1UNIV)	I would take more courses there than I took here	Judgement – POS.	Implicit
(At City1UNIV)	SO my general knowledge… would grow	Judgement – POS.	Implicit
It (City1UNIV)	By talking to more people such as grad students it would help me	Judgement – POS.	Implicit
(At City1UNIV)	I would have them as colleagues for the future	Judgement – POS.	Implicit
I	SO I would grow as well	Judgement – POS.	Explicit
I	If I have a good relationship with my supervisor	Judgement – POS.	Explicit
I	I would uh help him or her as a good friend	Judgement – POS.	Explicit
(At City1UNIV)	We would always work together	Judgement – POS.	Implicit
(At City1UNIV)	if my supervisor's not there all the time	Judgement – NEG.	Implicit
I	would have to learn how to walk with my own feet,*	Judgement – NEG.	Implicit
It (to walk with my own feet)	even though it's very complicated	Judgement – NEG.	Implicit
I	if I learn how to do that, I would grow as well	Judgement – POS.	Explicit
it *(the city of* ***City1)***	uh maybe it would be good for me	Judgement - POS.	Implicit
(the city of ***City1)***	because there are more places to go	Judgement - POS.	Implicit
(the city of ***City1)***	there are more things to do than we have here	Judgement - POS.	Implicit
it *(the city of* ***City1)***	it would be close to Mary's family	Judgement - POS.	Implicit
([From] the city of ***City1)***	so it would be easier to go there.	Judgement - POS.	Implicit

In Move 11, John's response shows that negative emotions are "what is holding him back" from choosing City1. *Thus emotions guide his decision.* In Nussbaum's (2013) terms, these emotions contribute to an evaluative appraisal of City1 made from John's own viewpoint in terms of his "scheme of

Table 5.3 Move 11 appraisal analysis

Question: "What's holding you back [from choosing City1 University]?"			
Appraised	**Appraisal**	**Appraisal Category**	
My supervisor	If… is not a good person at all	Judgement – NEG.	Explicit
I	(would have) the same experience as before	Affect –NEG.	Implicit
(*experience before*)	I fell into a big depression [was depressed]	Affect – NEG.	Explicit
(*experience before*)	I couldn't work anymore	Affect – NEG.	Implicit
my heart	My heart is very warm	Affect – POS.	Explicit
someone	When I see someone very cold	Affect – NEG.	Explicit
You [coachee]	You lose all your heat	Affect – NEG.	Explicit
[you]	You just get mad	Affect – NEG.	Explicit
I	I wouldn't see myself helping	Judgement – NEG.	Implicit
someone	someone who doesn't appreciate me	Affect – NEG.	Explicit
(*experience before*)	I worked at the hospital	Affect – NEG.	Implicit
(*experience before*)	I wasn't appreciated	Affect – NEG.	Explicit
in the workplace	It was very hard in the workplace	Affect – NEG.	Explicit
(*experience before*)	It was hard	Affect – NEG.	Explicit
(*experience before*)	I couldn't learn	Affect – NEG.	Implicit
(*experience before*)	actually I ran away	Affect – NEG.	Implicit
(*experience before*)	I changed my whole research because of that	Affect – NEG.	Implicit

goals and ends." John has decided on that appraisal not to go to City1 University as seen in Table 5.3. On this evidence, emotion is significantly related to the decision-making and valuing process (CHOICE and EVALUATION).

In Move 12, the coach asks John to compare his present skills with his skills when he was at the hospital. Firstly, John continues discussing his hospital experience and then, secondly, he reports on his positive current view of going to City1 University to develop his skills. Table 5.4 deals with the second, and we will discuss the second. Clearly, his positive Move 12 view is a complete reversal from his negative view in Move 11, but it is not a return to his positive appraisal of City1 University in Move 10. In his discussion of wishing to go to City1, he is not appraising City1 University, he is appraising *himself, his resources and emotions*. Table 5.4 is largely positive judgement appraisals of his personal resources for sustained academic work on a PhD.

Table 5.4. Move 12 appraisal analysis

Appraised	Appraisal	Appraisal Category	
Question: "So how is that view of doing it to develop your skills…similar to or different to the view you had at the hospital?"			
my skill (now)*	Now my skill's a bit different	Judgement – POS.	Implicit
I	I'm older now	Judgement – POS.	Implicit
I	and have more experience	Judgement – POS.	Implicit
I	I'm not an undergrad anymore	Judgement – POS.	Implicit
I	I have my skills now	Judgement – POS.	Implicit
I	I know what my dream is	Judgement – POS.	Explicit
I	I want [desire] to be a professor	Affect – POS.	Explicit
I	I know the way	Judgement – POS.	Implicit
I	So I need to find a place to go……	Judgement – POS.	Implicit
I	I want [desire] to keep going and developing my skills and getting the best education as much as I can.	Affect – POS.	Explicit
I	even if I have a bad experience now	Affect – NEG.	Explicit
I	I just think good now in my mind	Affect – POS.	Explicit
something	[because] I'm doing something that's for me	Appreciation – POS. [of activity]	Implicit

To sum up, we believe this analysis of appraisal captures significant differences between these shifts of John's attitudes and shows how his decision-making process in Move 12 develops to bring together his assessment of City1 University and his assessment of his personal resources and achievement in an integrative decision.

Conclusion

Our macrolevel analysis of this coaching case in light of Dewey's phases of inquiry has identified three iterations of the phases, which may suggest that the prospect of closure can bring to light new problems, new layers of complexity. We relate this to the theme we mentioned earlier of the unification of thought and emotion in the naturalistic functional coordination of action on the environment. In the final phase of the first two iterations, John expresses anxiety, leaving the current iteration without closure and starting a new iteration, since he is still doubtful, feeling that something is wrong, or as yet unresolved. As noted above by Asma (2018), emotions can be maladaptive, or can be adaptive if they are managed properly. Each time, John's coach encourages him to reflect on the anxiety in context of his life experience; this seems to help him develop deeper awareness of his resources and appropriate strategies. As John says, "Sometimes I get anxious and stressed and everything gets blurry. That's why I have fears to go somewhere. I just need to have strategies to make it better." In this way, with the coach's help, he appears to functionally coordinate thought and emotion and choose a course of appropriate action on his environment. Ultimately, he expands his perspective of himself to include both his early unfortunate experiences and his later achievements, and to see himself as a strong student capable of coping with the more demanding university. This is seen in the last phase of the final iteration. As John addresses the third concern regarding his capability of sustained PhD work at the university of choice, he concludes by observing, "From our conversation I see that I'm capable to go." The statement is underscored with laughter, arguably an expression of pleasure at the thought. It combines with his final reflective statements on the value of the coaching experience to present concluding evidence that the coaching session has been a meaningful activity for him.

At the macrolevel of analysis, John's movement through the various phases and iterations of inquiry is helpfully illuminated by the affordance of the Knowledge Framework to facilitate an understanding of coaching activity with reference to reflection discourse. As noted earlier, reflection discourse can be seen to fall on a continuum ranging from specific to general reflection, the former addressing specific events and activities and the latter providing insight into the values and beliefs that give them meaning. In the case examined here, for example, identifying John's specific reflection on particular events and activities such as his MA level research and his co-publication with his MA supervisor, in contrast to specific reflection on his first research experience and the aborted publication, provides a simple way of tracing some of the thought and emotion underlying more general reflection and evaluation that come to bear on his decision-making process. The coaching activity, while removed in time and space from these events and activities, is not removed from the influence of the emotions they continue to evoke in John. However, by engaging in the reflective process of coaching, including moving back and forth between general and specific reflection, John is able to revisit and reframe his perceptions. This gives rise to new insights regarding events of the past as well as new awareness and beliefs that have implications for the decision at hand. It also encompasses noteworthy shifts in attitude exemplified by the sample microlevel SFL appraisal analysis showing a turnaround to positive emotions. The combination may offer insight into the process by which attitudinal shifts can occur in coaching activity.

In sum, with respect to implications for the analysis of activities, our study of the coaching session aimed to illustrate ways to go beyond the analysis of an activity as cognitive elements only. Our macrolevel analysis gets at the general flow of the coaching activity while the microlevel analysis provides linguistic examples of places where the flow gives rise to emotion. We also set out to illustrate the possibility of relating Deweyan and SFL perspectives. SFL and Dewey both share a recognition of the importance of emotions and of *situation* and *context/environment*. Dewey's ecological conception of experience sees John's *situation* as precarious (as John does) and his *emotions* of anxiety and stress as guiding him to reflect and act as a purposive organism on his wider educational *context/environment*. John sees that he needs to make a *choice* between universities and that he must *evaluate* the various alternatives. Our use of Dewey's *pattern of inquiry* shows the way in which the macrolevel of interaction is a functional unity of the above elements which moves towards a final decision. It is a dynamic process of *deliberation* to which John and the coach mutually contribute, and the coach guides John to see his anxieties in the context of his life experience, bringing together emotion and cognition. The Inquiry analysis has an ethical/moral dimension which is made explicit at various points, but perhaps most clearly in Move 9 where John says that he is developing his skills so that he can help people when he goes back to his home country. The ethical/moral dimension is also a major focus of our microlevel appraisal analysis of attitude, where the distinction between affect, judgment, and aesthetics runs parallel to Dewey's work, offering a bridge for future exploration. At the same time, we wish to stress that this is a preliminary study, and that a number of areas that we have not covered in any detail continue to exist, such as the vital question of the coach's contribution, which are beyond the scope of this paper but await future research.

Acknowledgments

We wish to thank Alex Martins and Paul Meighan for their assistance in the preparation of this chapter.

References

Abbey, R. (2000). *Charles Taylor.* Princeton University Press.

Asma, S. (2018, June 3). What religion gives us (that science can't). *New York Times.* Retrieved from: https://www.nytimes.com/2018/06/03/opinion/why-we-need-religion.html

Bettinger, E. & Baker, R. (2014). The effects of student coaching: An evaluation of a randomized experiment in student advising. *Educational Evaluation and Policy Analysis, 36*(1), 3–19. Retrieved from: http://journals.sagepub.com/doi/abs/10.3102/0162373713500523

Cox, E. & Ledgerwood, G. (2003). Editorial: The new profession. *International Journal of Evidenced Based Coaching and Mentoring, 1*(1), 3–5. Retrieved from: https://radar.brookes.ac.uk/radar/file/ce783bb6-e49e-478c-aee8-b9a1c1bdd466/1/vol01issue1-editorial.pdf

Dewey, J. (1895/1971). The theory of emotion. In J.A. Boydston (Ed.), *John Dewey: The Early Works* (Vol. 4, pp. 169–188). Southern Illinois University Press.

Dewey, J. (1911). Activity, logical theory and educational implications of. In P. Monroe (Ed.), *A cyclopedia of education* (pp. 33–34). The Macmillan Company

Dewey, J. (1916/1980). Introduction to essays in experimental logic. In J.A. Boydston (Ed.), *John Dewey: The middle works* (Vol. 10, pp. 320–365). Southern Illinois University Press.

Dewey, J. (1922/1983). Human nature and conduct. In J.A. Boydston (Ed.). *John Dewey: The middle works* (Vol. 10). Southern Illinois University Press.

Dewey, J. (1925/1981). Experience and Nature. In J.A. Boydston (Ed.), *John Dewey: The later works* (Vol. 1). Southern Illinois University Press.

Dewey, J. (1934/1987). Art as experience. In J.A. Boydston (Ed.), *John Dewey: The later works* (Vol. 10). Southern Illinois University Press.

Dewey, J. & Tufts, J. (1908/1978). Ethics. In J.A. Boydston (Ed.), *John Dewey: The early works,* (Vol. 1). Southern Illinois University Press.

Dewey, J. & Tufts, J. (1932). *Ethics.* Henry Holt and Company. Retrieved from: https://archive.org/details/ethics02tuftgoog

Duffell, P., & Lawton-Smith, C. (2015). The challenges of working with emotion in coaching. *The Coaching Psychologist, II*(1), 32–41.

Fesmire, S. (2015). *Dewey.* Routledge.

Garrison, J. (2003). Dewey's theory of emotions: The unity of thought and emotion in naturalistic functional "co-ordination" of behavior. *Transactions of the Charles S. Peirce Society, Vol. 39*(3), 405–443.

Halliday, M.A.K. (1994). *An introduction to functional grammar* (2nd ed.). Arnold.

Higher and higher education. (2018, May 19). *The Economist,* pp. 51–53.

Hildebrand, D. (2008). *Dewey: A beginners guide.* Oneworld.

Kristjánsson, C., Dissen, M., Goertzen Martins, M., Klassen, G., Rotchford, S. (2018). Coaching in TESOL. *Contact Magazine, 44*(1), 35–43.

Lave, J., & Wenger E. (1991). *Situated learning: Legitimate peripheral participation.* Cambridge University Press.

Lehto, M., Nah, F., & Yi, J. (2012). Decision-making models, decisions support, and problem solving. In G. Salendy (Ed.), *Handbook of human factors and ergonomics* (4th ed.) (pp. 192–242). John Wiley & Sons.

Lerner, J., Li, Y., Valdesolo, P., & Kassam, K. (2015). Emotion and decision making. *The Annual Review of Psychology, 66*, 799–823.

Martin , J. & Rose, D. (2007). *Working with discourse* (2nd ed.). Continuum.

Martin, J. & White, P. (2005). *The language of evaluation: Appraisal in English.* Palgrave Macmillan.

Mohan, B. (2011). Social practice and register: Language as a means of learning. In E. Hinkel (Ed.), *Handbook of Research in Second Language Teaching and Learning* (pp. 57–74). Routledge.

Murray, J. (2016). Skills development, habits of mind, and the spiral curriculum: A dialectical approach to undergraduate general education curriculum mapping. *Cogent Education, 3*(1), 1–19.

Nussbaum, M.C. (2013). *Political emotions: Why love matters for justice.* Harvard University Press.

Pappas, G. (1998). Dewey's ethics: Morality as experience. In L. Hickman (Ed.), *Reading Dewey: Interpretations for a postmodern generation* (pp. 100–123). Indiana University Press.

Ringler, W. (Ed). (1962). *The poems of Sir Philip Sidney.* Oxford University Press. Retrieved from https://archive.org/

Robinson, C.E. (2015). *Academic/success in coaching: A description of an emerging field in higher education.* (Doctoral dissertation). Retrieved from http://scholarcommons.sc.edu/etd/3148

Spiral approach. (2022, May 11). In *Wikipedia.* https://en.wikipedia.org/w/index.php?title=Spiral_approach&oldid=1067298037

Taylor, C. (1989). *Sources of the self: The making of the modern identity.* Harvard University Press.

Taylor, C. (1991). The dialogical self. In J. Bohman, D. Hiley, R. Schusterman (Eds.), *The interpretive turn: Philosophy, science, culture* (pp. 304–314). Cornell University Press.

White, P.R.R. (2015). Appraisal theory. In Tracy, K., Ilie, C., & Sandel, T. (Eds.), *International encyclopedia of language and social interaction.* Wiley-Blackwell.

Woodward, R. (2019). The spiral curriculum in higher education: Analysis in pedagogic context and a business studies application. *E-Journal of Business Education & Scholarship of Teaching, 13* (3), 14–26.

About the Authors

Carolyn Kristjánsson has a PhD in Language Education and is an associate professor of applied linguistics at Trinity Western University (TWU) in Canada where she teaches in the online and resident tracks of the MA TESOL program. She is also a Certified Executive Coach (CEC) and has developed and leads an in-house coaching program for MA TESOL students at TWU.

Bernard A. Mohan was Chair of Linguistics at the University of Milwaukee Wisconsin, then professor in Language Education at the University of British Columbia, Canada, working with immigrant learners in Vancouver's schools. Now emeritus at UBC, he is a Research Fellow at King's College, London who participated in an eight-nation study that recommended changes in teacher education across the European Union to benefit immigrant language learners. Known for his pioneering work on integrated language and content learning, he is a functional linguist who sees language as a resource for learning about the world in dynamic interaction with its cultural context.

6 Voting as a Social Activity: Voter Suppression, the Common Good, and Evidence

Bernard A. Mohan

Abstract

Students in higher education are typically eligible to vote. Voter suppression is an unethical removal of the right to vote and is often part of a wider attack on democratic rights and activities. Respected authorities have emphasized the importance of developing strong democratic norms for the survival of democracy. Can these norms be enhanced by an understanding of the traditional (e.g., Aristotle) and contemporary (e.g., Habermas) ethics of politics and a critical engagement with their application to political activities and discourses? In this chapter, taking a functional linguistics perspective, I focus on a Knowledge Framework approach to the linguistic analysis of political discourses and activities that students in higher education may find helpful to work with in order to respond to current political problems and to engage more intensively with their role as informed voters. This chapter takes a *political* linguistics approach, by contrast with other chapters in this volume that aim at an *educational* linguistics approach. Important ethical themes that will be examined include concern for the common good, and for "practical reasoning" (Aristotle) and respect for evidence-based reasoning, and for sincerity (Habermas).

Keywords: voting; ethics; discourse; human activity; voter suppression; democracy

This chapter deals with the issue of voter suppression within the activity of democratic political elections. According to Wikipedia, voter suppression is a strategy used to influence the outcome of an election by discouraging or preventing specific groups of people from voting. This is a matter of great current concern. The analysis in this chapter employs the KF heuristic to illustrate how electoral systems have a theory–practice relation just as in the KF. The chapter will argue that popular sovereignty is a concept that is central to the *theory* of democratic systems, but it does not necessarily describe the reality of what is happening in *practice*. The connections between the related knowledge structures of theory and practice will be illuminated through a discussion of informed choices (EVALUATION and CHOICE), the debate of who can and who cannot vote (CLASSIFICATION), and the rules and reasoning of the Voting Rights Act of 1965 (PRINCIPLES).

There is surprising general agreement between citizens internationally on the top priorities for political action. Climate change and the spread of infectious disease are seen as the top threats by the majority of people in fourteen economically advanced nations recently surveyed by the Pew Research Center (Fagan & Huang, 2020). These are issues that require politicians to make major changes to deal with them adequately. Major changes threaten vested interests and public-spirited politicians need massive support by public-spirited voters, old and young, to carry out these changes. Young people require these changes most, for they will live with them and be most disadvantaged if no changes are made. But many young people do not vote:

> Fewer than half of Americans 18 to 29 voted in the 2016 presidential election ... This is not unique to the United States. Our new analysis of turnout for the most recent national general elections for heads of government in two dozen countries revealed that the general population's voting rate exceeds the voting rate for young people in every single one of them. (Symonds, 2020, paras. 1–2)

> Why don't young people vote? … It's not apathy, it's voter suppression. That includes not just the active efforts by some Republican officials to reduce turnout by closing polling places, limiting hours and kicking people prematurely off the voter rolls, but also the specific challenges that the voting system poses for young people. (Hu, 2020, para. 2)

It is imperative that many more young voters overcome voter suppression and vote, for theirs is the future.

Democracy Under Siege

In America, Britain, and elsewhere, it is widely recognized that democracy is under siege. In their 2012 book *It's Even Worse Than It Looks: How the American Constitutional System Collided with the New Politics of Extremism*, the political analysts Thomas Mann of the Brookings Institution and Norman Ornstein of the American Enterprise Institute, noted for their bi-partisanship, describe the Republican party during the Obama presidency as an "insurgent outlier—ideologically extreme, contemptuous of the inherited social and economic policy regime; scornful of compromise; unpersuaded by conventional understanding of facts, evidence and science and dismissive of the legitimacy of its political opposition" (Mann & Ornstein, 2012, p. xxii). There is a rejection of ethical standards and democratic values and a concomitant rejection of science. This description raises general concerns for the survival of democracy. In their book *How Democracies Die* (2018), Stephen Levitsky and Daniel Ziblatt describe how democracies can die in piecemeal steps with the election of an autocratic leader, the abuse of governmental power, and the complete repression of opposition. Levitsky and Ziblatt point to the importance of the development of strong democratic norms, unwritten rules which "serve as the 'soft guardrails of democracy', preventing day-to-day political competition from devolving into a no-holds-barred conflict" (p. 101). To counter "a rejection of ethical standards and democratic values and a concomitant rejection of science," I suggest that two of the "soft guardrails of democracy" should be "aiming at the common good of the society being governed" and "being guided in this by the best available knowledge and evidence."

Voter Suppression in the United States and the United Kingdom

Voter suppression is an action against the common good, against the individual's right to vote and against democracy in general. We will discuss the case of voter suppression by voter identification.

Democratic Senator Dick Durbin (2018), former Chair of the United States Senate Judiciary Committee's Subcommittee on the Constitution, Civil Rights, and Human Rights, gives a summary of voter suppression in the US by the use of voter identification (ID) laws. He asserts that, under the auspices of combatting "voter fraud," the Republican Party has used a range of strategies, including gerrymandering, reducing voting opportunities, and the creation of voter identification laws to ensure their electoral success. Voter identification laws, he argues, discourage voting among demographics unlikely to vote Republican: minorities, the elderly, the young, and those living in poverty. At the same time, he points out that the supposed rationales for these laws put forward by Republican lawmakers have been repeatedly refuted, noting that the actual number of cases of proven voter fraud is negligible, and that federal appeals court judges reviewing such laws have noted the precision with which they have been designed to disproportionately target African Americans. As Durbin states, "Republicans clearly believe their future success depends more on constricting rather than convincing the electorate" (p. x).

In *Democracy and Its Crisis*, A. C. Grayling (2018), the well-known British philosopher and academic, raises concerns about the health of democracy in Britain. Grayling examines politics in Britain to consider the failure of the democratic system and how to put it right. In his opinion, one failure of the British system was to fail to equip the electorate to play their part in the democratic process, to fail to provide the civic education required to make democracy work. I will first outline Grayling's analysis of Brexit and the failure of democracy, and then discuss the current situation in Britain with respect to voter suppression. Grayling states:

> A House of Commons Briefing Paper 07212, published on 3 June 2015, pointed out to MPs, members of the House of Lords and other readers that the referendum was *advisory only, and would not be binding on Parliament or Government* [emphasis added]. This point was reiterated *viva voce* by the Minister for Europe in the debate in the House of Commons later that month. *This was the reason given for not including a threshold and for not extending the franchise appropriately* [emphasis added]. (2018, p. 190)

In fact, the franchise was reduced. Excluded were expatriate British citizens who had lived abroad for more than fifteen years (many of whom were living in Europe), and tax-paying European Union (EU) citizens resident in the UK and paying taxes there. Both groups should have been included as having a major interest in the outcome of the vote, and representing the active relations between the EU and Britain.

No voting threshold for winning was given. The final outcome was that 37% of the registered electorate given the franchise for the referendum voted to leave the EU. Grayling comments:

> This outcome is by any standards insufficient to justify a constitutional change so significant as the UK's exiting the EU. There is scarcely any civilised state in the world where a simple majority, let alone a small

> one, would permit this: for such a change, a supermajority would be required, of 60% or 66% either of votes cast or of the entire electorate. (Grayling, 2018, p. 190)

The "leave" voters won by a margin of 1,269,501 votes. That year (2016), according to the BBC, there were 2.9 million EU citizens resident in the UK, more than double that margin. In addition, 1.22 million British citizens were living in the EU prior to 2017, according to UK Office for National Statistics (O'Reilly, 2018). Thus 4.12 million possible voters were excluded, more than three times the leave margin, all of them committed to the EU by their choice of residence. Had the government not prevented these groups from voting, the result might have been very different.

We now turn to the situation in Britain with respect to voter suppression. On 19 December 2019, *The Independent* newspaper (Kentish, 2019) reported that Boris Johnson, the British Prime Minister, had confirmed that his government would push ahead with controversial laws to require voters to show identification at polling stations:

> The proposals were included in the Queen's Speech this week, meaning they are likely to be implemented in law in the coming months. The government insists that the changes are necessary to tackle electoral fraud, but critics say they are unnecessary and will disenfranchise tens of thousands of people. (paras. 1–3)

This is despite the fact that the British Electoral Reform Society (ERS) showed that out of millions of votes cast in the United Kingdom last year, there were just eight allegations of personation fraud. The ERS pointed out that 3.5 million United Kingdom citizens did not have access to photo identification, and in 2013–14 about 11 million did not have a passport or driving license (Davies, 2019). With good reason, Grayling (2018) believes that no form of democracy can defend itself from "being hijacked by a hidden oligarchy… unless the franchised are informed and reflective" (p. 161). In his opinion, one failure of the British system was to fail to equip the electorate to play their part in the democratic process, to fail to provide the civic education required to make democracy work. Grayling recommends that "voting should be compulsory for all citizens, and the voting age should be sixteen. Civic education on the political and government system should be obligatory in schools for pupils aged fourteen and above" (p. 187). In my view, education on the political and government system needs to be given a much more important place in higher education as well.

Aristotle: Activities, Practical Wisdom, and the Common Good

Commenting on the suppression of democracy in Belarus, the international journalist Simon Tisdall (2020) reflects upon how democracy is under siege across the world:

> The thwarting of Belarus's revolution comes during an increasingly intense, global battle for democratic rights. In one camp, broadly speaking, sit all the forces of reaction—autocrats, authoritarian nationalists, populists and racists who rule by division, violence and fear. In the opposing camp, liberals and progressives adhere to ideas of universal, law-based human rights and values. (p. 18)

Since democracy is under siege, should democratic states deliberately cultivate among their citizens the democratic ideas and activities on which a good democratic society depends, as the best way to live? Or should the law be neutral towards ideas of democracy?

In *Justice: What's the Right Thing to Do?* (Sandel, 2009), the political philosopher Michael Sandel argues that standard political theories (utilitarianism or libertarianism) are in effect neutral towards democracy and he recommends that we follow Aristotle who strongly valued it. Sandel points out that these theories do not question

> the moral worth of the ends we pursue, the meaning and significance of the lives we lead, and the quality and character of the common life we share… To achieve a just society we have to reason together about the meaning of the good life, and to create a public culture hospitable to the disagreements that will inevitably arise. For Aristotle,…the purpose of politics is nothing less than to enable people to develop their distinctive human capacities and virtues—to deliberate about the common good, to acquire practical judgment, to share in self-government, to care for the fate of the community as a whole. (pp. 260–261)

For Aristotle, activities are purposeful. Each activity has a purpose or end (*telos*). The Nicomachean Ethics (Ostwald, 1962) opens with Aristotle's strong statement about (human) activities and the ends, goals, or purposes that they aim at: "Every art or applied science and every systematic investigation, and similarly every action and choice, seem to aim at some good; the good therefore has been well defined as that at which all things aim" (p. 3). Thus, all of these activities have aims or ends. His examples of the many activities and their ends include medicine (end: health), of shipbuilding (end: a vessel), and of strategy (end: victory). These are comprehensive activities involving large numbers of people over long periods of time and can be called "macrolevel" activities. But it is clear that Aristotle also includes microlevel activities when he states, "and similarly every action and choice." Large or small, all of these activities are purposive, they have an aim or end. Voting is an activity. Its main purpose is to register a vote for a candidate. Voter suppression disables this purpose. Blackburn states:

> Aristotle's political tradition is an ethical approach. We live in an ethical environment...the surrounding climate of ideas about how to live. It determines what we find acceptable or unacceptable, admirable or contemptible...it gives us our standards of behaviour...[however] the workings of the ethical environment can be strangely invisible. (2001, pp. 1–2)

How can we make the ethical environment more visible to ourselves? One way is to examine the purposeful activities we do in our everyday lives. Why do we do them and how do we prioritize them? If we apply this perspective to our everyday lives it is not difficult to find many frequent activities and purposes that are important to us and raise ethical questions. To take an obvious example, we sleep at night to refresh ourselves, but research indicates that many people do not get enough sleep, perhaps being overworked or prioritizing other activities, and thus endanger their own health, violating their ethic of self-care. According to the National Heart Lung and Blood Institute (n.d.), about 7–19 percent of adults in the United States reported not getting enough rest or sleep every day, and sleep deficiency is linked to many chronic health problems, including heart disease, kidney disease, high blood pressure, diabetes, stroke, obesity, and depression. We thus live and continually interact in a complex ethical environment of the activities and purposes of ourselves and others. This theme is developed systematically and in depth in Sadler (n.d.), an online course on Aristotle's Nicomachean Ethics that shows effectively how purposeful virtuous human activities are at the center of Aristotle's philosophy and of our lives.

Practical wisdom (Greek: *phronesis*), is the ability to choose the right course of action or decision in a given situation by bringing together knowledge of the specifics of the particular situation and knowledge of general principles or laws, rather than simply following laws. It results in action or decision. Aristotle considered practical wisdom as the most important virtue. Aristotle deemed the learner as needing to learn it practically and experientially by participation in the political community. Aristotle recognized that political and ethical knowledge is broad and general, and decisions do not have the certainty of mathematics (Ostwald, 1962).

Practical knowledge may be expressed in a *practical syllogism*, which brings together universals and particulars, as in the following example:

> Reasoning on matters of conduct involves two premises, one major, one minor. The major premise is always universal, e.g., "to remove by stealth another person's property is stealing." and the minor premise is particular e.g., "this horse is another person's property," so that the conclusion would be: "To remove this horse by stealth is stealing." (Ostwald, 1962, p. 55)

To talk about the relation between general laws and particular situations or between universals and particulars, I will use the convenient terms "theory" and "practice." To do so, I must make it clear that "theory" has its modern sense, as in scientific theory, and not the sense of Aristotle's "theoria."

Aristotle certainly established a rich tradition of thought about human activities but Aristotle did not see theory and practice as related in this way.

> The Aristotelian tradition…held that one could work out all the laws that govern the universe by pure thought: it was not necessary to check by observation. So no one until Galileo bothered to see whether bodies of different weight did in fact fall at different speeds. (Hawking, 1998, p. 15)

The concept of theory and practice has changed considerably from Aristotle to Marx (see Lobkowicz, 1967). Aristotle's "common good" view of ethics and politics is part of the European political tradition. It was very influential in politics in the Middle Ages in Europe. For example, the "Allegory of Good and Bad Government" is a series of three frescos painted on the walls of the Council Room by Ambrogio Lorenzetti in 1339 for the City Council of the Republic of Siena. The Virtues of Good Government are represented by six stately female figures: Peace, Fortitude, Prudence, Magnanimity, Temperance, and Justice. On the lower border of the first fresco there is a text which says that the citizens in unity make the Common Good (*ben commune*) their lord (see "Ambrogio Lorenzetti" in Wikipedia).

Albert the Great and his pupil Thomas Aquinas synthesized Aristotle's philosophy with Christian theology, and Thomas Aquinas wrote a book-length commentary on Aristotle's Nicomachean Ethics. Aquinas's conception of the common good became standard in Roman Catholic moral theology. Contemporary Catholic social teaching on the common good is summarized in the *Compendium of the Social Doctrine of the Church* (Libreria Editrice Vaticana, 2004). It is useful to consider with the broad definition of the common good given in *Wikipedia*:

> In philosophy, economics, and political science, the common good refers to either what is shared and beneficial for all or most members of a given community, or alternatively, what is achieved by citizenship, collective action, and active participation in the realm of politics and public service. ("Common good", n.d.)

In effect, common good can be viewed as a still picture or as a changing picture.

The classical definition of common good, formulated in the Middle Ages on the basis of Aristotelian principles, referred to "a good proper to, and attainable only by, the community, yet individually shared by its members" (Dupré, 2009, p. 687). To modern readers, this might seem to overemphasize community, but Aristotle's emphasis on community is shared by communitarianism, the contemporary philosophy that examines the connection between the individual and the community. Communitarian thinkers insist on the importance of communal or collective forces in explaining such things as social life and individual identity:

> Instead of seeing society as an aggregate of cooperating and competing individuals...communitarians point to the shared elements that make social life possible, that cannot be reduced to individual choices, desires, intentions or possessions... [F]or many communitarians, invigorating a sense of solidarity is as difficult as it is urgent in a world where economic forces, like the movements of global capital, privatisation, multiculturalism and the changed nature of work threaten any immediate sense of community. (Abbey, 2000, pp. 102–103)

A general concern of communitarianism is with the bonds of community—their importance, creation, maintenance, and reproduction. This suggests that there is an important role for younger members of a community to work to maintain the political bonds of their community and in particular to reinvent them.

Voter Suppression from an Aristotelian Perspective

It is helpful to interpret voting from an Aristotelian perspective as a social activity with a *telos*, a theory and a practice viewed by practical wisdom and a potential for common good. Some forms of voter suppression can be seen as a manipulation of these aspects of the activity and a violation of Aristotelian ethics. To define what I mean by theory and practice I will rely on the definition by John Dewey (1913), in which theory (thought) "is used to denote any intellectual principle; that is, any conception which is employed to explain and organize a body of facts" (p. 606), and is not seen as oppositional to practice (action), but rather, "appears as the chief instrumentality in the emancipation and enrichment of action. The antithesis is no longer between theory and practice but between idle and unverifiable thinking and thinking to a purpose, between blind and enlightened practice" (p. 607). To explicitly include the human sciences and the legal system, I will expand this definition to include any intellectual principle which is employed to explain and organize the practices of a community. Dewey was particularly critical of how Descartes' dichotomy of mind and body separated what was integral.

I will discuss two examples of voter suppression described by Carol Anderson (2018). I will interpret these cases of voter suppression as claiming that their theory and practice are appropriately connected while in fact intentionally disabling the connection: the theory promises justice but the practice is aimed at suppressing it. It is a deliberate separation of knowledge and practice, the reverse of Dewey's position, in order to deny the common good and unjustly favor a segment of the community.

Anderson (2018) explains how, in the American South, legislators passed the Mississippi Plan which included "a dizzying array of poll taxes, literacy tests, understanding clauses, newfangled voter registration rules, and 'good character' clauses—all intentionally racially discriminatory but dressed up in the genteel garb of bringing 'integrity' to the voter booth" (p. 3). Particularly effective were literacy tests to register to vote where African Americans were given difficult sections of the Constitution to interpret to "prove" their literacy, while whites were presented with a simple sentence. In one case, shortly after World War II, a black coal miner tried to register to vote in Alabama. After deliberately ignoring him, the registrar gave him an official form which contained the test. The miner went through the literacy test and wrote out his answer in considerable detail. The voter registrar took his paper without reviewing it, balled it up, and threw it in the wastebasket, saying "You disqualified. You didn't answer the question" (pp. 6–7).

I suggest that examples of voter suppression like this rely for perceived legitimacy on community knowledge of the body of understandings of a well-established social activity. In this case the social activity is the use of tests of literacy. These were familiar enough to legislators for them to accept that literacy might be chosen as a requirement to allow a citizen to vote. Such tasks were altered to serve partisan purposes of voter suppression for racial discrimination, being made easy for whites and very hard for blacks. But to alter them meant to disable their original *telos* or purpose of being a test of writing. They were no longer honest tests of writing, even in intention, but were simply being used as a means of racial discrimination to pass whites and fail blacks. The theory of what the tests were for remained the same. It was pretended that their original *telos* or purpose remained the same. It was a useful "cover" to deal with objections and challenges. It was sheep's clothing for the wolf within. But the uses to which the tests were put in practice had changed; the "theory–practice" relations of the original social activity had been altered to discriminate. The registrar had now to engage in the pretense of administering the "test" and reporting the "result": "You disqualified. You didn't answer the question." He had to pretend it was a test, but he failed to perform a test because he did not review the paper at all. However, the miner could not raise this as an objection because he was not allowed right of appeal. In fact, all partisans of this voter suppression had to pretend, to be dishonest, and honesty is one of the Aristotelian virtues. To pretend is to lack sincerity, and sincerity is an element in Habermas's theory of communicative action, as we will see below.

In another case discussed by Anderson (2018), a Navy veteran, returning home in 2015 after serving overseas, found that his valid Illinois driver's license was not recognized as a form of voter identification in his new home state of Wisconsin. Due to a combination of factors, including the Republican governor's efforts to close or limit the opening hours of Department of Motor Vehicles offices in traditionally Democratic areas such as Milwaukee, the veteran was unable to secure a new driver's license in time, and was ultimately denied the right to vote. The veteran assumed that the normal processes of voting were in operation. But he received a "rude awakening." The voting administration was not supporting all voters but was trying to discourage urban African Americans from voting by removing access to the vehicle licensing centers. This change was part of a larger pattern of legislative alterations. After the 2010 election the Republicans had introduced a process of partisan gerrymandering and redistricting that guaranteed them large legislative majorities even with a minority of the state-wide vote.

These two cases of voter suppression are broadly similar in Aristotelian terms. In both cases the *telos* or aim of the activity was blocked; the test was automatically a failure, and the voting process was not completed. Normal expectations of what would happen in practice were not fulfilled; there was no genuine assessment of writing, and there was a deliberate closing of licensing centers. Finally, there was the pretense of normal legitimacy and "voter fraud" to cover the real discrimination against minority voters and the violation of the common good. The Aristotelian perspective helps to account for what is unethical about voter suppression.

I now turn to the question of linguistic analysis of the relation between theory and practice in political social activities such as those under discussion. The theory of these social activities is created by legislation. As stipulated in the 1901 Alabama constitution, "the following persons, and no others…shall be qualified to register as electors… First. Those who can read and write any article of the Constitution of the United States in the English language" (Alabama Constitution, art. VIII, § 181., 1901, repealed 1965). The 2011 Wisconsin Act 23 states under "Voter fraud Penalties for Violations" that "Whoever swears falsely to any absent elector affidavit under this section may be fined not more than $1,000 or imprisoned for not more than 6 months or both" (Wisconsin Constitution, Act 23, § 19, 2011). Each one of these rules functions as an intellectual principle which is employed to organize the activities of a community. They are the "rules" which control "play" in the "games" of the community, general rules which apply to particular "cases," such as the miner and the veteran. When the registrar says, "You disqualified. You didn't answer the question," he is maintaining that he is following literacy test requirements and ultimately the Alabama law. He is connecting theory and practice.

Dewey applied his concept of theory and practice to education where is it is often termed "experiential learning." Following Dewey, David Kolb designed a model of the experiential learning cycle (see Smith, 2001/2010) which includes abstract conceptualization and concrete experience. In Mohan et al. (2015), we showed how linguistic analysis could trace the experiential learning cycle to capitalize on linguistic evidence and illuminate development of language as a means of experiential learning. We look forward to exploring the possibilities of future work on experiential learning of practical wisdom in purposeful activities.

Habermas's Theory of Discourse Ethics

Jürgen Habermas's Theory of Discourse Ethics is widely respected. I will briefly outline Habermas's approach, draw upon a short description of how it analyzes discourse, and then apply it in a basic way to texts. A short description of discourse ethics from encyclopedia.com is "Discourse Ethics has two aims: to specify the ideal conditions for discourse, and to ground ethics in the agreements reached through the exercise of such discourse. Discourse Ethics thus instantiates the intuition that if people discuss issues in fair and open ways, the resulting conclusions will be morally binding for those appropriately involved in the conversation" ("Discourse ethics," n.d.). A related concept is the "public sphere." A helpful definition of the public sphere is provided by Wikipedia: "The public sphere is an area in social life where individuals can come together to freely discuss and identify societal problems, and through that discussion influence political action. Such a discussion is called public debate and is defined as the expression of views on matters that are of concern to the public—often, but not always, with opposing or diverging views being expressed by participants in the discussion" ("Public sphere," n.d.).

Habermas's book, *The Structural Transformation of the Public Sphere* (1989), conveys a sense of some of his central concerns. It is a social history of the formation of the bourgeois "public sphere" in 18th and 19th century Europe. Habermas "gives an account of the way in which newspapers, coffee shops, pubs...and other public forums facilitated the emergence of powerful new social norms of discourse and debate that mediated between private interests and the public good...and helped freely form the public political will needed for collective self-determination" (Cherem, n.d.). The bourgeois public sphere was influential in the breakdown of the ancient regime in the French Revolution. The public sphere raises theoretical issues: "Habermas's theoretical system is devoted to revealing the possibility of reason, emancipation, and rational-critical communication latent in modern institutions and in the human capacity to deliberate and pursue rational interests" ("Jürgen Habermas," n.d.). A number of these issues are brought together in his important work *Theory of Communicative Action* (Habermas, 1984, 1987). As Bohman and Rehg (2014) write, for Habermas, in *communicative action* "speakers coordinate their action and pursuit of individual (or joint) goals on the basis of a shared understanding that the goals are inherently reasonable or merit-worthy" (para. 23)... Many speech acts involve a set of tacit validity claims: the claim that the speech act is sincere (non-deceptive), is socially appropriate or right, and is factually true (or more broadly, representationally adequate). Conversely, speech acts can be criticized for failing on one or more of these scores. Thus, fully successful speech acts, insofar as they involve these three world relations, must satisfy the demands connected with these three basic validity claims (sincerity, rightness, and truth) in order to be acceptable" (para. 26). In addition, Habermas (1998) adds the question of reasons:

> We understand a speech act when we know the kinds of reasons that a speaker could provide in order to convince a hearer that he is entitled in the given circumstances to claim validity for his utterance—in short, when we know *what makes it acceptable*. (p. 232)

In my interpretation of this, reasons include evidence.

Communicative action is contrasted with *strategic action*. In strategic action, actors are interested in their individual goals rather than mutual understanding. For example, actor A might play upon actor B's desires and fears in order to get actor B to do what A wants.

Above, Durbin (2018) mentioned the 2013 North Carolina voting law. The law illustrates the violation of Habermas's criteria of truth, rightness, and sincerity. According to the judges, it was not *true* that the law was aimed at voter fraud, it was really aimed at voter suppression. As voter suppression, the law *ethically violated* African American voters' right to vote. Any legislator who argued that the law was aimed at voter fraud but knew that it was aimed at segregation was *being insincere*.

We will now relate Habermas's approach in a very basic way to two texts which appeared together in *US News & World Report*, one by Hans A. Von Spakovsky (2012), Senior Legal Fellow at the Heritage Foundation, which takes the Republican standpoint outlined by Durbin, and the other, which takes the opposite point of view, by Wendy Weiser (2012), Director of the Democracy Program at the Brennan Center for Justice, New York University.

We will briefly explore the illocutionary aspect of speech acts of the two texts and ask, Does the author of the text satisfy the three basic validity claims (sincerity, rightness, and truth)? Sincerity and rightness in particular can be expected to be central to the pursuit of the common good.

It is not difficult to see differences between the Von Spakovsky and Weiser texts in speech act terms. Von Spakovsky's (2012) title, "Voter ID Laws Protect the Integrity of Our Democracy," is an implicit recommendation in favor of voter identification laws. Weiser's (2012) title, "Voter ID Laws Are Designed to Keep People From Voting," is an implicit recommendation against voter identification laws. They each support these recommendations with further auxiliary speech acts. Both authors refer to "ID laws" in their title, but they elaborate the characterization of voter identification in very different ways.

Weiser (2012) is very careful to distinguish between different kinds of voter identification laws and to identify and describe the strict ones:

> Some (like the one in federal law) are flexible, to try to make sure that every eligible citizen can be identified and can vote. Others are stricter, designed in a way that will keep large swaths of the population from voting. … More than 20 million Americans—one in 10 eligible voters—do not have the kinds of photo ID required by strict new state voter ID laws. (para. 1)

Weiser cites "Citizens Without Proof" (Brennan Center for Justice, 2006), an accessible 2006 survey of Americans' possession of documentary proof of citizenship and photo identification which can provide further descriptive details, such as the requirement to have your current address and current name (as opposed to a maiden name) on the photo identification.

Von Spakovsky (2012) does *not* distinguish between different kinds of voter identification laws. On the contrary, he treats "voter ID" and "photo ID" as freely interchangeable and equivalent, which of course they are not. This needs to be explained in detail, and in the following analysis I format these terms in bold to help readers keep track of this. He begins with "photo ID": "All states should require **photo ID** [emphasis added] both to vote in person and to vote by absentee ballot" (para. 1). He then changes to "**voter ID**": "**Voter ID** [emphasis added] can significantly defeat and deter impersonation fraud" (para. 2). He continues with "**Voter ID**" in three more instances, but then changes back in two significant claims: "Americans of every background overwhelmingly have **photo ID** [emphasis added]. And the few who do not can easily obtain **a free one** [emphasis added] in the states that have implemented such laws" (para. 4) and "Americans have to use **photo ID** [emphasis added] constantly in everyday life" (para. 5). Here "**a free one**" must mean a valid voter ID. But the terms are not interchangeable. If we switch them, we find that "Americans of every background overwhelmingly have **a valid voter ID**" is simply untrue: "Citizens Without Proof" (Brennan Center for Justice, 2006) clearly demonstrates that 25% of African Americans do not have these kinds of voter identification, as Weiser (2012) says. Conversely, we find that "Americans of every background overwhelmingly have **photo ID** *(in the sense of a picture of themselves)*" is simply irrelevant to his argument. It seems that Von Spakovsky's (2012) strategy is to normalize the voter suppression of strict new state voter identification laws by equivocating about their strictness.

In another article available at https://www.washingtonpost.com/opinions/voter-id-laws-are-good-protection-against-fraud/2011/07/08/

gIQAGnURBI_story.html), Kris Kobach (2011) makes the same equivocation, misrepresenting the Brennan Center's claim:

> The editorial also cited a questionable 2006 survey from the Brennan Center, using the claim that 11 percent of the U.S. population lacks a **photo ID** as a basis for concluding that hundreds of thousands of citizens lack **photo IDs**… It is simply incorrect to assert that there are tens of thousands of voters in Kansas, or any state, without photo identification. **Photo IDs** have become ubiquitous and unavoidable. You can't cash a check, board a plane or drive without one. That is why it's not unreasonable to require picture identification to protect our most important privilege of citizenship. And just in case a voter lacks a **photo ID**, Kansas's legislation requires that he or she be given one free of charge. (paras. 10–12)

Von Spakovsky (2012) thus does three things: he makes an important factual claim that is simply untrue, he unethically attempts to disguise the role of voter identification laws in producing voter suppression, and he uses the tactic of equivocation rather than straightforwardly communicating with his readers sincerely. He therefore violates Habermas's three criteria.

By contrast, Weiser (2012) is consistent with Habermas's criteria. She bases her factual claims on a publicly available, independently conducted, and relevant study which enables her truthfulness to be assessed. She is straightforward rather than deceitful to her readers. She explains very clearly and explicitly the ethical position she is taking, referring to the intrinsic value of democratic voting. She begins by quoting the Declaration of Independence that all men are created equal and finishes saying: "denying people the right to vote should not just be an acceptable political tactic. It's the one time we are all equal—when we cast our vote" (para. 7). This is a well-known intrinsic value of democratic voting. As the political philosopher Jonathan Wolff (2016) says, commenting on women's suffrage: "it is insulting and demeaning to give men the vote while denying it to women. Universal suffrage is a way of expressing the idea that we believe women, just as much as men, are owed respect as citizens" (p. 102). The same can be said of denying the vote to minority voters.

Being Guided by Facts, Evidence and Science When Seeking the Common Good: The Analysis of Evidence

In the second analysis of the two texts, we will concentrate on truth validity claims (the claim that a speech act is factually true) from the standpoint of Habermas's *theory of truth and knowledge*. In this way we will pursue the theme of best available evidence. We will enquire whether a claim is supported by evidence or is assumed to be unproblematically true. Habermas's theory of truth and knowledge posits that

> as we take propositional contents as unproblematically true in our daily practical engagement with reality, we act confidently on the basis of well-corroborated beliefs about objects in the world. What Habermas [(2001, p. 94; 1984, p. 23)] calls "theoretico-empirical" or "theoretical" discourse becomes necessary when beliefs lose their unproblematic status as the result of practical difficulties, or when novel circumstances pose questions about the natural world. Such cases call for an empirical inquiry in which truth claims about the world are submitted to critical testing…as we see in scientific inquiry…field studies and laboratory experimentation." (Bohman & Regh, 2014, para. 49)

In our texts of political argumentation, I suggest that the contrast between "unproblematic" versus "theoretico-empirical" claims takes the form of the contrast between "common-sense" claims versus "evidence-based" claims. A common-sense claim is immortalized in the song line, "You don't need a weatherman to tell you how the wind blows." An example of an evidence-based claim is Weiser's (2012) claim that more than 20 million Americans do not have the kinds of photo identification required by strict new state voter identification laws, a claim that is based on survey evidence. Von Spakovsky's (2012) attempt to move it from a claim about official voter identification to a claim about everyday photo identification is an attempt to change it to a claim that can be contradicted as false on the basis of unproblematic, everyday, common-sense knowledge. This comes out most clearly in the language of his claim: "Americans have to use photo ID constantly in everyday life—to drive a car, board a plane, buy a beer, check into a hotel, get into many government buildings, or see a doctor." This is an appeal to what is "unproblematically true in our daily practical engagement with reality." But it is an illegitimate appeal.

There is a need to be aware of the boundary between the appropriate use and inappropriate use of common-sense claims. Legitimate uses of common-sense assumptions are part of everyday interactions; we assume more common-sense understanding when we talk to adults than when we talk to young children. However, the term *common sense* has become part of political rhetoric. "The phrase Common Sense Revolution…has been used as a political slogan to describe conservative platforms with a main goal of reducing taxes while balancing the budget by reducing the size and role of government" ("Common Sense Revolution", n.d.). So there is a need to recognize illegitimate cases where the appeal to common sense may be an appeal for agreement to a claim that avoids the need to provide necessary evidence.

Our aim at this point is to explore a way of identifying the role of evidence in political discourse and offering a basic analysis of it that does not assume a detailed knowledge of linguistics. An analysis of evidence in texts is provided by Rhetorical Structure Theory (RST, for more information, see Mann & Taboada, n.d.). RST describes coherence patterns in text. "The most frequent structural pattern is that two spans of text (virtually always adjacent, but exceptions can be found) are related such that one of them has a specific role relative to the other. A paradigm case is a claim followed by evidence for the claim" (Mann & Taboada, n.d.). RST posits an "evidence" relation between the two spans and provides a definition of the relation of evidence, defined as "information intended to increase the reader's belief in the claim" (Mann & Taboada, n.d.). Here is an example, where Sentence 1 makes a factual claim and Sentence 2 provides evidence for the claim:

For our purposes, we will elaborate the evidence relation further. We will describe two kinds of claim in our texts: factual claim and value claim. We will describe three kinds of evidence: research evidence, legal evidence, and "public knowledge." We note that evidence usually appears as a statement, but may also appear as a *case*, described in several statements. Finally, we note that an evidence statement may be followed by further "support," for example, another research study. Where a claim has no evidence to back it up, it will be labelled UNSUPPORTED.

Since we are aiming at a basic analysis that does not assume a detailed knowledge of linguistics, we will not draw on other parts of RST. So for our

Table 6.1 Example RST analysis

Sentence	Text
1	[CLAIM 1:] But not all voter ID laws are equal.
2	[EVIDENCE for CLAIM 1:] Some (like the one in federal law) are flexible, to try to make sure that every eligible citizen can be identified and can vote.

purposes we will not use the RST convention of graphic representations of the relation between spans, but use comments based on a sentence numbering system instead. Where a sentence contains more than one claim, we will identify the claims with letters (e.g., CLAIM 1A, CLAIM 1B). Finally, to keep things straightforward for non-linguists, in our analysis, we will refer explicitly to sentences (graphological constituency) but only implicitly to clauses (lexicogrammatical constituency).

It should be said that more detailed RST analysis is highly relevant to the kind of persuasive political texts we are working with. For example, see Christian Matthiessen's (Halliday & Matthiesen, 2014) RST analysis of a persuasive text, which shows "the general schema of persuasive texts where the key unit is a proposal ('vote against…!'): Motivation [Claim Evidence] Appeal" (p. 657).

Table 6.2 RST analysis of "Voter ID Laws Are Designed to Keep People From Voting" (Weiser, 2012)

Sentence	Text
1	[CLAIM 1:] Voter ID Laws Are Designed to Keep People From Voting
2	[CLAIM 2:] All men are created equal, [LEGAL EVIDENCE for CLAIM 2:] says the Declaration of Independence.
3	[CLAIM 3:] But not all voter ID laws.
4	[EVIDENCE for CLAIM 3:] Some (like the one in federal law) are flexible, to try to make sure that every eligible citizen can be identified and can vote.
5	[EVIDENCE for CLAIMS 1 & 3:] Others are stricter, [CLAIM 5:] designed in a way that will keep large swaths of the population from voting.
6	[CLAIM 6A] Unfortunately, there has been a concerted effort to push strict voter ID laws this past year—an effort that has resulted in eight new laws [EVIDENCE for CLAIMS 5 & 6A] requiring voters to show forms of ID [CLAIM 6B:] that many Americans don't have.
7	[EVIDENCE for CLAIM 6B:] More than 20 million Americans—one in 10 eligible voters—do not have the kinds of photo ID required by strict new state voter ID laws, [RESEARCH EVIDENCE:] according to research by the Brennan Center and others.
8	[CLAIM 8:] Some are even harder hit: [RESEARCH EVIDENCE (same as in Sentence 7) for CLAIM 8:] Eighteen percent of older Americans, 18 percent of citizens aged 18 to 24, and 25 percent of African-Americans don't have these kinds of photo IDs.

(Continued)

Table 6.2 (*Continued*)

Sentence	Text
9	[CLAIM 9:] It is wrong to pass laws that block some Americans from voting and to deny them the opportunity to participate equally in our democracy. [LEGAL EVIDENCE for CLAIM 9: Declaration of Independence as in Sentence 2]
10	[CLAIM 10:] These ID laws affect real people.
11	[CASE EVIDENCE for CLAIM 10:] Viviette Applewhite is 92 years old and uses a wheelchair.
12	[CASE EVIDENCE for CLAIM 10:] She was a wartime welder ...
13	[CASE EVIDENCE for CLAIM 10:] But she does not have a driver's license or other state photo ID to vote.
14	[CASE EVIDENCE for CLAIM 10:] So far, state officials have been unable to find her birth certificate, which she needs to get a new state ID.
15	[EVIDENCE for CASE presented in Sentences 11–14] She is currently part of a lawsuit challenging Pennsylvania's voter ID law, which would prevent her from voting this year.
16	[EVIDENCE for CLAIM 10:] The list goes on and on. [Text hyperlinked to now removed page on www.lawyerscommittee.org, presumably listing similar lawsuits to Applewhite's]
17	[CLAIM 17:] These laws also affect elections.
18	[CLAIM 18:] Indeed, that appears to be their main point.
19	[EVIDENCE for CLAIMS 1, 5, 17 & 18] The leader of the Pennsylvania legislature recently said [PUBLIC EVIDENCE:] new voter ID laws would "win the election" for Mitt Romney.
20	[RESEARCH EVIDENCE for CLAIM 19:] A recent government report shows 758,000 registered Pennsylvania voters don't have the ID they now need to vote.
21	[CLAIM 21:] All told, millions of eligible voters [RESEARCH EVIDENCE:] could find it harder to vote this year because of strict new ID laws and other voting changes.
22	[VALUE JUDGMENT:] Politics is one thing, but denying people the right to vote should not just be an acceptable political tactic.
23	[CLAIM 23:] It's the one time we are all equal—when we cast our vote. [LEGAL EVIDENCE for CLAIM 23: Declaration of Independence (as in Sentence 2)]
24	[VALUE JUDGMENT:] And no one should mess with that.

Table 6.3 RST analysis of "Voter ID Laws Protect the Integrity of Our Democracy" (Von Spakovsky, 2012)

Sentence	Text
1	[CLAIM 1:] Voter ID Laws Protect the Integrity of Our Democracy. [UNSUPPORTED]
2	[VALUE CLAIM:] All states should require photo ID both to vote in person and to vote by absentee ballot (by providing a copy of the ID).
3	[CLAIM 3:] This is a basic requirement to help ensure the integrity of elections. [UNSUPPORTED]
4	[VALUE CLAIM:] All Americans who are eligible should have the opportunity to vote, but their ballots should not be stolen or diluted by fraudulent votes.
5	[CLAIM 5:] The vast majority of Americans of all racial and ethnic backgrounds support such common-sense election reform. [UNSUPPORTED]
6	[CLAIM 6:] Voter ID can significantly defeat and deter impersonation fraud at the polls, voting under fictitious names or in the names of dead voters, double-voting by individuals registered in more than one state, and voting by individuals who are in the United States illegally. [UNSUPPORTED]
7	[CLAIM 7:] The Supreme Court has upheld voter ID [Supreme Court's LEGAL EVIDENCE for CLAIM 7:] since "flagrant examples of voter fraud… have been documented throughout this nation's history."
8	[CLAIM 8 (of no claim!):] No one claims that there is voter fraud in every election.
9	But, as the Supreme Court said, [Supreme Court's LEGAL EVIDENCE for CLAIM 7:] "not only is the risk of voter fraud real," but "it could affect the outcome of a close election."
10	[CLAIM 10:] And it wasn't too long ago that we had a presidential election decided by only about 500 votes. [PUBLIC EVIDENCE for CLAIM 10]
11	[CLAIM 11:] Voter ID also increases the public's confidence in election results, an essential element in a stable democracy. [UNSUPPORTED]
12	[CLAIM 12:] Opponents are wrong that voter ID will depress turnout or prevent large number of individuals from voting.
13	[EVIDENCE for CLAIM 12:] ID laws have been in place in Georgia and Indiana for more than five years, and there has been no decrease in the turnout of minority, poor, and elderly voters.
14	[CLAIM 14:] That is because Americans of every background overwhelmingly have photo ID. [UNSUPPORTED]

(*Continued*)

Table 6.3 (*Continued*)

Sentence	Text
15	[CLAIM 15:] And the few who do not can easily obtain a free one in the states that have implemented such laws. [UNSUPPORTED]
16	[PUBLIC EVIDENCE for CLAIM 14:] Americans have to use photo ID constantly in everyday life—to drive a car, board a plane, buy a beer, check into a hotel, get into many government buildings, or see a doctor.
17	[CLAIM 17:] They even need one to get into the Justice Department in Washington where Eric Holder is unjustly and unfairly fighting election integrity by trying to stop voter ID laws. [PUBLIC EVIDENCE for CLAIM 17]
18	[CLAIM 18:] Voter ID is a perfectly reasonable and easily met requirement that protects the integrity of our democracy. [UNSUPPORTED]
19	[CLAIM 19 (paraphrase of CLAIM 5):] That is why the American people support it. [UNSUPPORTED]

My analysis of evidence in the two texts finds that Weiser (2012) makes thirteen factual claims and two value claims. In Weiser's text, all thirteen of her factual claims are supported. Von Spakovsky (2012) makes fourteen factual claims and two value claims. In Von Spakovsky's text, nine of his factual claims are not supported. My aim with this analysis was to see if it could capture differences between writers in their use of evidence, and it seems to have made a beginning at this. Recall that Habermas holds that speech acts inherently involve claims that are in need of reasons—claims that are open to both criticism and justification. I would judge that Weiser (2012) has justified her claims well with her supporting evidence, and that Von Spakovsky (2012) has not, but other analysts might make a different judgment. Are there arguments for Von Spakovsky's more implicit approach?

The idea of evidence is further explored in many different fields. For our purposes, books which guide the examination of evidence for evaluating social science research are particularly relevant because they raise further questions about the use of evidence which need to be applied to political texts. Stern (1979) provides an example of such a question:

> Are any relevant abstractions in the factual assertion concretized by observable specific examples or operational definitions? If not, it is an untestable assertion. For observations to be scientifically useful, their abstractions must be concretized. This is the only way we can know exactly what the author is talking about. (p. 11)

The title of Von Spakovsky's text contains an abstraction, "Integrity," that raises this problem: "Voter ID Laws Protect the Integrity of Our Democracy." Is this an untestable assertion?

Continuing on the issue of evidential support for claims, I have so far particularly focused on evidential support inside the text itself, so I need to discuss how hyperlinks are being used to provide evidential support outside the text for or against a claim. Weiser's (2012) link "according to research by the Brennan Center" is a clear example of providing support for a claim; it references a supportive research study, and it also mentions "others," which is an expired link to a resource on research on voter identification. Her link "part of a lawsuit" connects to newspaper information that gives further detail about the case of Viviette Applewhite. All in all, she has seven hyperlinks that fulfill the evidential support function. Von Spakovsky (2012) follows a very different policy; his sole hyperlink directs to a collection of political cartoons on the 2012 Campaign. Kobach asserts evidence of claims of voter fraud in the J.J. Rizzo and Will Royster case (*alleged* fraud by a group of Somalis) and the Minnesota Minority case (*alleged* fraud by felons). The American Civil Liberties Union (2017) document, *Fact Sheet on Voter ID Laws* (https://www.aclu.org/other/oppose-voter-id-legislation-fact-sheet?redirect=oppose-voter-id-legislation-fact-sheet), is the prime example of the use of hyperlinks for the evidential support function. It has twelve footnotes and corresponding hyperlinks that relate the claims discussed in the body of the text to the research literature.

Conclusion: Relations Between Aristotle's Approach and Habermas's Approach?

Aristotle's approach and Habermas's approach are very different. Aristotle's approach is based on action and activity, Habermas's approach is based on discourse. Can these two approaches support each other? Can their results be complementary? Aristotle's work on actions stimulated early work on speech acts, and speech acts are a feature of Habermas's approach. We can use the case of the early development of speech act theory to show a relationship between action and discourse in the two approaches.

In the Nicomachean Ethics, Aristotle explores the question of an agent's moral responsibility for actions. Aristotle argues that when we make voluntary actions, we receive praise or blame, but when we make involuntary actions, this does not happen. Thus, people are held morally responsible for the voluntary actions they make (like winking) but not for the involuntary ones (like blinking). J. L. Austin took up Aristotle's question of an agent's moral responsibility for actions. Austin was the major figure of the movement known as linguistic philosophy or ordinary language philosophy (Blackburn, 1996, p. 30), and the major figure in the development of speech act theory. Austin studied and discussed the Nicomachean Ethics with his students for many years (see Akrill, 1981, p. 8). Austin's seminal article "A Plea for Excuses" (Austin, 1968) discusses how an agent can disclaim responsibility for a blameworthy act by using speech acts of excuse, for example: "I'm sorry I drank your coffee, *but I mistook it for my tea.*" Using the data of everyday discourse and the discourse of court cases as linguistic evidence, Austin's study throws light on different aspects of excuses, conveys a richer and more subtle understanding of moral responsibility, and illustrates how ethical questions about action and responsibility identified by Aristotle can be fruitfully explored using linguistic speech act categories and language data. Here the relationship is between blameworthy acts and speech acts of excuse.

In a somewhat similar way, Austin drew on legal concepts for linguistic distinctions: "Jurisprudents reduce all description of acts to three classes, namely 'acts proper' (the basic physical movement of the agent, such as pulling the trigger of a gun), 'acts and circumstances' (trespass, perjury, bigamy), and 'acts and consequences' (assault, battery, homicide). In a parallel way, Austin classed all speech acts as either locutions…illocutions…or perlocutions" (White, 1968, p. 9). Here the relationship is between types of actions in law and types of speech acts in discourse.

Is it possible that there are also relations between activity and discourse in the two approaches? It was mentioned above that Aristotle considered that the purpose of politics was to enable people to develop their distinctive human capacities to deliberate about the common good. This was taken up in the current movement for deliberative democracy, which promotes authentic deliberation in a reason-giving process. Are there actions and activities which provide supportive conditions for deliberative democracy?

The current times are a difficult period for many working people, and they may find little hope in politics. In *Deaths of Despair and the Future of Capitalism*, Anne Case and Angus Deaton (2020) report that working-class life in the United States is more difficult than it is in any other high-income country. They show that working-class life expectancy has fallen, inequality has risen, and incomes have stagnated more than any other wealthy nation. In the past two decades, deaths of despair from suicide, drug overdose, and alcoholism for working-class people have risen to 150,000 per year.

What does this mean for working-class life at the local level? *We're Still Here: Pain and Politics in the Heart of America*, Jennifer Silva's (2019) intensive study of working-class people in a small town in the coal country of eastern Pennsylvania, found that the trauma of the decline of a secure economy and the rise of inequality evoked pain and self-isolation. The collapse of social institutions that once supported collective struggle has led to self-defeating political alienation and cynicism and civic disengagement. Those who have most to gain from political action are estranged from it.

What can be done about this? Silva references a body of research that indicates how building robust public forums that counter self-insulation, and where pain and solutions can be shared openly, could provide a vehicle for collective mobilization among those who are suffering. One of the relevant research studies is Mazelis (2017), where poor people who joined a welfare rights union created lasting ties with each other that allowed them to build networks of mutual reciprocity, share resources, build skills, and mobilize against injustice quickly.

Silva (2019) recommends that "a network of trustworthy community organizers, from civic, political and religious organizations could help working-class people tie the pain and inequalities that they experience within their own families to the experiences of others, building a compassionate bridge between the individual and the community" (p. 173).

Silva's recommended activities fostering supportive friendships and group membership are vital for addressing the present alienation and estrangement. If these are not reversed, there is no political participation. These activities with community organizers and organizations speak to the fundamentals of social engagement needed for participation in political discourse. They are activities which provide supportive conditions for deliberative democracy. There is a parallel between "building a compassionate bridge between the individual and the community" and Aristotle's concept of the activity of friendship, or *philia* (Aristotle distinguishes between friendship as a characteristic and as an activity). *Philia* has a much broader meaning than individual friendship and covers the bond between the members of any association, whether it is the family, a community, or social and political associations in the state. Promoting the activity of friendship is given more space in the Nicomachean Ethics (two of the ten chapters, Ostwald, 1962) than any other political problem. Aristotle regards friendship as a virtue that concerns emotion and actions aimed at living well together. It is most indispensable for life. In the Rhetoric, Aristotle offers a list of common occasions for tragic compassion. It includes friendlessness; having few friends; being separated from one's friends and relatives. In her book *Political Emotions*, Martha Nussbaum (2013) discusses the political importance of compassion extensively and acknowledges her debt to Aristotle. To sum up, could Aristotle's activity of friendship build a basis for Habermas's communicative action? Could it help speakers coordinate their actions? Could it help them increase their shared understanding of their communicative goals? Could it add to their trust to engage in rational-critical communication? Could it promote more young voters to become involved in their futures?

References

Abbey, R. (2000). *Charles Taylor.* Princeton University Press

Akrill, J.L. (1981). *Aristotle the philosopher.* Clarendon.

Alabama Constitution art. VII, § 181, (1901 repealed 1965). Retrieved from https://alabama200.org/uploads/files/1901_voting.pdf

American Civil Liberties Union. (2017, May). *Fact sheet on Voter ID Laws.* Retrieved from https://www.aclu.org/other/oppose-voter-id-legislation-fact-sheet?redirect=oppose-voter-id-legislation-fact-sheet

Anderson, C. (2018). *One person, no vote: How voter suppression is destroying our democracy.* Bloomsbury.

Austin, J.L. (1968). A plea for excuses. In A.R. White (Ed.), *The philosophy of action* (pp. 19–42). Oxford University Press.

Blackburn, S. (1996). *Dictionary of philosophy.* Oxford University Press.

Blackburn, S. (2001). *Being good: A short introduction to ethics.* Oxford University Press.

Bohman, J., & Rehg, W. (2014). Jürgen Habermas. In E.N. Zalta (Ed.), *The Stanford Encyclopedia of Philosophy. Retrieved from* https://plato.stanford.edu/archives/fall2017/entries/habermas/

Brennan Center for Justice. (2006). *Citizens without proof.* Retrieved from https://www.brennancenter.org/our-work/research-reports/citizens-without-proof

Case, A., & Deaton, A. (2020). *Deaths of despair and the future of capitalism.* Princeton University Press.

Cherem, M. (n.d.). Jürgen Habermas (1929–). *Internet encyclopedia of philosophy.* Retrieved from https://www.iep.utm.edu/habermas/

Common good. (n.d.). In *Wikipedia.* Retrieved January 9, 2021 from https://en.wikipedia.org/wiki/Common_good

Common Sense Revolution. (n.d.). In *Wikipedia.* Retrieved April 9, 2020 from https://en.wikipedia.org/wiki/Common_Sense_Revolution

Davies, C. (2019, October 13). Conservatives accused of suppressing voters' rights over leaked photo ID plans. *The Guardian.* Retrieved from https://www.theguardian.com/politics/2019/oct/13/conservatives-accused-of-election-rigging-leaked-id-plans-voter-fraud

Dewey, J. (1913). Theory and practice. In P. Monroe (Ed.), *A cyclopedia of education* (pp. 606–607). The Macmillan Company.

Discourse ethics. (n.d.). In *Encyclopedia.com*. Retrieved January 10, 2021 from https://www.encyclopedia.com/science/encyclopedias-almanacs-transcripts-and-maps/discourse-ethics

Dupré, L. (2009). The common good and the open society. *The Review of Politics*, *55*(4), 687–712.

Durbin, D. (2018). Foreword. In C. Anderson, *One person, no vote: How voter suppression is destroying our democracy* (pp ix–xi). Bloomsbury.

Fagan, M., & Huang, C. (2020, October 16). Many globally are as concerned about climate change as about the spread of infectious diseases. *Pew Research Center*. Retrieved from https://www.pewresearch.org/fact-tank/2020/10/16/many-globally-are-as-concerned-about-climate-change-as-about-the-spread-of-infectious-diseases/

Grayling, A.C. (2018). *Democracy and its crisis*. Oneworld.

Habermas, J. (1984). *The theory of communicative action. Vol. I: Reason and the rationalization of society* (T. McCarthy, Trans.). Beacon.

Habermas, J. (1987). *The theory of communicative action. Vol. II: Lifeworld and system* (T. McCarthy, Trans.). Beacon.

Habermas, J. (1989). *The structural transformation of the public sphere* (T. Burger and F. Lawrence, Trans.). MIT Press.

Habermas, J. (1998). *On the pragmatics of communication* (M. Cooke, Ed.). MIT Press.

Habermas, J. (2001). *On the pragmatics of social interaction* (B. Fultner, Trans.). MIT Press.

Halliday, M.A.K., & Matthiessen, C.M.I.M. (2014). *Halliday's introduction to functional grammar* (4th ed.). Routledge.

Hawking, S. (1998). *A brief history of time*. Bantam Books.

Hu, K. (2020, July 31). Young people could decide the 2020 election. *Los Angeles Times*, Retrieved from https://www.latimes.com/opinion/story/2020-07-31/young-voters-suppression-2020-election-pandemic

Jürgen Habermas. (n.d.). In *Wikipedia*. Retrieved February 7, 2020 from https://en.wikipedia.org/wiki/J%C3%BCrgen_Habermas

Kentish, B. (2019, December 19). What is Boris Johnson's voter ID policy and why is it so controversial? *The Independent*, Retrieved from https://www.independent.co.uk/news/uk/politics/voter-id-policy-boris-johnson-election-polling-stations-queens-speech-a9254641.html

Kobach, K. (2011, July 13). Voter ID laws are good protection against fraud. *The Washington Post*, Retrieved from https://www.washingtonpost.com/opinions/voter-id-laws-are-good-protection-against-fraud/2011/07/08/gIQAGnURBI_story.html

Levitsky, S., & Ziblatt, D. (2018). *How democracies die*. Crown.

Libreria Editrice Vaticana. (2004). Compendium of the social doctrine of the church. Retrieved from http://www.vatican.va/roman_curia/pontifical_councils/justpeace/documents/rc_pc_justpeace_doc_20060526_compendio-dott-soc_en.html#Meaning%20and%20primary%20implications

Lobkowicz, N. (1967). *Theory and practice: History of a concept from Aristotle to Marx*. University of Notre Dame Press.

Mann, T.E., & Ornstein, N.J. (2012). *It's even worse than it looks: How the American constitutional system collided with the new politics of extremism*. Basic Books.

Mann, W.C., & Taboada, M. (n.d.). Relation definitions. Retrieved from http://www.sfu.ca/rst/01intro/definitions.html

Mazelis, J.M. (2017) *Surviving Poverty: Creating Sustainable Ties Among the Poor.* NYU Press.

Mohan, B., Slater, T., Beckett, G., & Tong, E. (2015). Tasks, experiential learning, and meaning-making activities: A functional approach. In M. Bygate (Ed.), *Domains and directions in the development of TBLT* (pp. 157–192). John Benjamins.

National Heart Lung and Blood Institute. (n.d.). Sleep deprivation and deficiency. Retrieved September 20, 2020 from https://www.nhlbi.nih.gov/health-topics/sleep-deprivation-and-deficiency

Nussbaum, M. (2013). *Political Emotions*. Harvard University Press.

O'Reilly, K. (2018, May 7). Far more British citizens live in EU than government statistics suggest. *The Independent*. Retrieved from https://www.independent.co.uk/travel/british-citizens-europe-residents-eu-brexit-a8332986.html

Ostwald, M. (1962). *Aristotle: The Nichomachean Ethics*. MacMillan.

Public sphere. (n.d.). *Wikipedia*. Retrieved January 10, 2021 from https://en.wikipedia.org/wiki/Public_sphere

Sadler, G. (n.d.) Aristotle's Nicomachean Ethics (1) bk 1–5: Happiness and the Virtues [Online course]. *Study With Sadler!* https://reasonio.teachable.com/p/aristotle-s-nicomachean-ethics-books-1-5

Sandel, M.J. (2009). *Justice: What's the right thing to do?* Farrar, Straus and Giroux.

Silva, J. (2019). *We're still here: Pain and politics in the heart of America*. Oxford University Press.

Smith, M.K. (2001/2010). "David A. Kolb on experiential learning", *The encyclopedia of pedagogy and informal education.* Retrieved from https://infed.org/mobi/david-a-kolb-on-experiential-learning/

Stern, P.C. (1979). *Evaluating social science research*. Oxford University Press.

Symonds, A. (2020, October 8). Why don't young people vote, and what can be done about it? *The New York Times*, Retrieved from https://www.nytimes.com/2020/10/08/upshot/youth-voting-2020-election.html

Tisdall, S. (2020, August 23). From Washington to Minsk, democracy is under siege ... and losing the battle. *The Guardian*. Retrieved from https://www.theguardian.com/commentisfree/2020/aug/23/from-washington-to-minsk-democracy-is-under-siege-and-losing-the-battle

Von Spakovsky, H.A. (2012, July 13). Voter ID laws protect the integrity of our democracy. *U.S. News & World Report*. Retrieved from https://www.usnews.com/debate-club/should-photo-id-be-required-to-vote/voter-id-laws-protect-the-integrity-of-our-democracy

Weiser, W. (2012, July 13). Voted ID laws are design to keep people from voting. *U.S. News & World Report*. Retrieved from https://www.usnews.com/debate-club/should-photo-id-be-required-to-vote/voter-id-laws-are-designed-to-keep-people-from-voting

White, A.R. (1968). Introduction. In A.R. White (Ed.), *The philosophy of action* (pp. 1–18). Oxford University Press.

Wisconsin. Constitution, Act 23, § 19 (2011). Retrieved from https://docs.legis.wisconsin.gov/2011/related/acts/23

Wolff, J. (2016). *An introduction to political philosophy*. Oxford University Press.

About the Author

Bernard A. Mohan was Chair of Linguistics at the University of Milwaukee Wisconsin, then professor in Language Education at the University of British Columbia, Canada, working with immigrant learners in Vancouver's schools. Now emeritus at UBC, he is a Research Fellow at King's College, London who participated in an eight-nation study that recommended changes in teacher education across the European Union to benefit immigrant language learners. Known for his pioneering work on integrated language and content learning, he is a functional linguist who sees language as a resource for learning about the world in dynamic interaction with its cultural context.

7 Disciplinary Differences in the Knowledge Structures in University Lecture Slides

Zhi Li

Abstract

Lecture slides, as a common companion to academic discourse, can play important roles in students' academic listening comprehension partly because subject content or knowledge structures in Mohan's terms can be constructed through both language and visuals on the slides. Previous studies have recognized some disciplinary differences in both written and oral academic discourse which may impose challenges on academic listening. Despite the prevalence of lecture slides in classroom contexts, the slides are still under-researched as a part of academic genre and even fewer, if any, studies have paid attention to the potential differences in the knowledge structures between slides used in different disciplines. This exploratory study aims to fill in this gap with a comparative analysis of the knowledge structures in the lecture slides from six undergraduate courses in two broad disciplines, namely, Engineering and Social Sciences. The slide contents were manually coded for both text-based and visual-based knowledge structures. Descriptive statistics indicate that while there were some noticeable differences in the frequencies of occurrence of the six knowledge structures within each discipline, these two disciplines also saw similarities in the general distribution of the knowledge structures. The implications of the findings for EAP pedagogy and assessment are discussed.

Keywords: academic discourses; PowerPoint slides; Knowledge Framework; multimodality; cross-disciplinary differences

Academic success is closely tied to students' listening skills, and particularly the ability to comprehend lectures or academic listening. This is especially true for non-native English-speaking students in an English-medium university in that many are still in the process of academic discourse socialization but must face lectures full of complex content and linguistic features (Biber, 2006). In these contexts, academic English or lecturing discourse is usually mediated with lecture slides, whose functions include presenting key information, structuring lectures, and managing classroom activities. It becomes beneficial to study the lecture slides from a functional linguistic perspective to better understand the relationship between language forms and the content or knowledge construction delivered through them.

Literature Review

Lecture Slides as a Genre of Academic Discourse

Lecture slides, created in presentation software such as PowerPoint, have become a popular pedagogical aid in course delivery. In university classes, lecture slides are also frequently made available to students before or after class, thus making them a valuable resource for students to preview or review the course content. Lecture slides have generally been perceived in a positive light (Apperson, Laws, & Scepansky, 2008; Lynch, 2011). For example, Apperson et al. (2008), in their survey of 275 students studying psychology, reported that students found positive benefits of using lecture slides in classes. For example, well-prepared slides can make the teaching "more organized, clear, and interesting" (p. 148). This positive view may be related to the multimodal features and structuring functions of lecture slides, which are believed to be conducive to English language learners' listening comprehension of subject content (Lynch, 2011). With multimodal information presented in a linear fashion, lecture slides serve both as scaffolding devices (display of headings and keywords) and carriers of class content. In addition, visuals and other multimedia content on lecture slides can attract students' attention and facilitate their understanding of complex concepts (Lynch, 2011). Linguistically, while slides' messages are usually used to highlight the key information lecture, they may vary in terms of sentence structures and textual density. Therefore, paying attention to the text in the slides is undoubtedly rewarding.

Design features of lecture slides have been widely discussed, and general guidelines for creating effective lecture slides have been proposed in the literature (Alley, 2013). For example, the results of the survey by Apperson et al. (2008) suggest that the following features are favorably perceived by the students: inclusion of visual elements and multimedia in the presentations, completeness of information about key terms, slides with an appropriate amount of text, and use of full sentences as opposed to fragments. While the first few features are easy to incorporate in slide design, fragments are far more common than complete sentences in lecture slides. This is due to the nature of the templates in the presentation software. It is customary to use bullet formats in presenting text information, which appears neat with shorter structures (Adams, 2006). Admittedly, fragments can be ambiguous for students to interpret. The missing elements can cause issues in identifying the knowledge structures associated with these units in this study (see Chapter 2 in this volume for related observations).

Compared with the large body of literature on the styles and effectiveness of lecture slides, some studies have explored the multimodality features of presentation slides (Zhao, Djonov, & van Leeuwen, 2014; Zhao & van Leeuwen, 2014) while very few studies have examined the linguistic features of the slide texts (Li, Jones, & Lodge, 2017). What is even rarer is research that explores the ideational functions or knowledge construction in the language and visuals of slides which form the backbone of a lecture and require attention from students.

Disciplinary Differences in Academic Discourse

Lecture slides are seen in various disciplines. Given the fact that there are disciplinary differences in academic discourse, one would expect that there may also be variations found in lecture slides. Hyland (2006), for example, presented an overview of the findings on disciplinary differences, primarily in academic written discourse, in the following aspects: development of argument, rhetorical structure, expression of stance, and levels of engagement. While these differences may not be immediately relevant to classroom teaching, they do highlight the perceivable differences in academic discourse communities.

Disciplinary differences in classroom-based academic discourse have been studied by Biber (2006) and Dudley-Evans (1994). In his corpus-based study of academic discourse, Biber (2006) included both textbook data and classroom teaching scripts from six disciplines (Education, Humanities, Social Science, Engineering, Business, and Natural Science) collected from multiple universities in North America. A multidimensional analysis or factor analysis of a diversity of linguistic features in the corpus data was conducted in Biber (2006) to reveal linguistic variations across these disciplines. The resultant dimensions reflected the co-occurring tendencies of relevant linguistic features and were capable of capturing possible cross-disciplinary variations in academic discourses. Biber's study yielded four dimensions (Dimension 1: Oral vs. literate discourse, Dimension 2: Procedural vs. content-focused discourse, Dimension 3: Reconstructed account of events; and Dimension 4: Teacher-centered stance). Noticeable disciplinary differences were reported on two out of the four dimensions for both textbooks and classroom teaching data. For example, Natural Science, Social Science, and Humanities differed from Business and Engineering on Dimension 2 Procedural vs. content-focused discourse in that the former group showed content-focused characteristics while the latter had features related to procedural knowledge. On Dimension 3 Reconstructed account of events, Humanities and Social Science contained more linguistic features related to narrativeness or reconstructed accounts of events, compared with Natural Science and Engineering. To account for these disciplinary differences on Dimensions 2 and 3, Biber (2006) made a distinction of "professional" disciplines (including Business and Engineering) and "academic" disciplines (including Humanities and Social Science) and argued that the linguistic variations reflected the differences in the emphasis of these disciplines.

Unlike Biber's study of large corpus data, Dudley-Evans (1994) focused on four lecture scripts from two courses, Plant Biology and International Highway Engineering, at the University of Birmingham. His qualitative analysis suggested that these lectures followed different structure patterns in content delivery. The Plant Biology lectures presented the content in a point-driven or information-driven fashion; in other words, facts were listed in a linear manner. The International Highway Engineering lectures, on the other hand, took a problem-solution approach to organizing the content to form an argument based on multiple sources of evidence.

The disciplinary differences discussed above are mainly related to sentence- or discourse-level linguistic features or overall rhetorical patterns. The linguistic aspects related to knowledge construction also merit some attention because learning subject matter is closely tied to language learning and comprehension. In this study, lecture slides from Engineering and Social Sciences were selected for two considerations. First, these two disciplines have attracted a large number of international students in North America, and the majority of these are English language learners (OECD, 2014). Second, previous studies on academic English indicate the existence of disciplinary differences in linguistic features across these two disciplines (Biber et al., 2002).

As discussed above, lecture slides play an important role in content teaching and serve as key resources of knowledge construction for students. Lecture slides, as a teaching artifact and special multimodal genre, engage instructors and learners alike in a variety of activities that require both theoretical and practical knowledge. In this sense, teaching with lecture slides can be treated as a social practice and be analyzed using Mohan's Knowledge Framework (Mohan, 1986). Because of a lack of research on the connection between language and content presented through lecture slides, this study focuses on the knowledge structures used in the lecture slides in Engineering and Social Sciences to address the following question: How do the lecture slides in Engineering and Social Sciences differ in their use of text-based and visual-based knowledge structures? Such a comparative study of lecture slides is meaningful for pedagogical practices related to academic listening. It has been argued that awareness of disciplinary differences can help learners familiarize themselves with the features of disciplinary discourse and have the potential to improve their lecture comprehension (Dudley-Evans, 1994; Tauroza & Allison, 1994). Furthermore, learning to follow and utilize these disciplinary conventions in academic discourses is an important part of academic socialization (Hyland, 2006).

Methodology

Data Collection

Lecture slides from six undergraduate-level courses (three in Engineering and three in Social Sciences) were collected from North American universities through a comprehensive search on Google. Written permission to use the slides was obtained from the instructors of the selected courses. To make sure the lectures slides represent authentic university teaching practices, the following exclusion criteria were applied at the data preparation stage. The lecture slides needed to contain sufficient course information such as course title and number to be identified as an actual undergraduate-level course; the lecture slides needed to be designed primarily for a single period of lecture with a focus on one topic; the lecture slides from the first meeting of a course were not included because they tended to have more information related to course orientation and management; instructor-made lecture slides were preferred in the data collection because it was decided that these would better reflect authentic teaching experiences compared to publisher-provided lecture slides that accompany a textbook.

Table 7.1 presents an overview of the lecture slides used in this study. The topics in the collected lecture slides were sampled from a variety of sub-fields, including computer engineering and electrical engineering in Engineering; economics, sociology, and psychology in Social Sciences. The lecture slides

Table 7.1 Overview of the configuration of the lecture slides

Discipline	Lecture	# of target slides [a]	# of text-only slides	# of visual-only slides	# of mixture slides	Word count
Engineering	Control structures	18	9	4	5	999
	Intelligent agents	19	11	2	6	819
	Energy in transition	21	8	0	13	1530
Social Science	Market forces	52	18	22	12	1419
	Race in America	34	17	17	0	1064
	Measurement	30	15	1	14	1056

Note: a. The number does not include the following slides: title slides, slides with repeated content from preceding slides, slides with regulatory contents, and/or exercises/practices.

vary in the number of target slides, overall configurations (e.g., number of visual-only slides, number of text-only slides, and number of mixture slides), as well as word counts. The selected lectures in Engineering have fewer slides than those in Social Science (18–21 slides vs. 30–52 slides). In terms of slide configuration, all the lectures had a well-balanced use of visual-containing slides and text-only slides. In other words, about half of the lecture slides in each lecture contained visuals. For example, in the lecture on Control Structures, nine out of 18 slides contained visuals. The identification of visuals was carried out based on Rowley-Jolivet (2002)'s typology of the visuals which include four general types: graphical images (e.g., diagrams and graphs), figurative images (e.g., photos), scriptural visuals (e.g., screenshot of texts), and numerical visuals (e.g., mathematical formulae and programming script). On average, the lecture slides in Engineering have slightly fewer words (1116 vs. 1179 words); however, calculations show that the Engineering lecture slides have a higher textual density than those in the Social Science lectures (64 words vs. 47 words per text-containing slide).

Annotation for Knowledge Structures

Building on Systemic Functional Linguistics, Mohan's Knowledge Framework provides an appropriate perspective to study the ideational functions of the content and multimodal features of lecture slides. Drawing on the connection between language and content, Mohan (1986, 1989) proposed the Knowledge Framework to capture the major semantic relations constructed through language. Six knowledge structures are included in the framework to form three theory–practice pairs, with CLASSIFICATION, PRINCIPLES, and EVALUATION on the theory knowledge side and DESCRIPTION, SEQUENCE, and CHOICE on the practical knowledge side. Knowledge Framework-based studies have primarily focused on the oral language used in the classrooms at primary and secondary schools in North America. As a heuristic model, the Knowledge Framework has been applied to shed light on how language and content can be integrated into a number of content areas (Gleason, Berg, & Huang, 2017; Huang, Normandia, & Greer, 2005; Mohan & Slater, 2006; Slater & Butler, 2015).

UAM ImageTool 2.1, an image annotation tool developed by Mick O'Donnell (2011), was used to annotate the lecture slides manually for knowledge structures in an iterative manner. The counts of knowledge structures were tabulated, and queries for examples of specific knowledge structure were made using the same software.

Previous Knowledge Framework-based studies on classroom talk used social practice as a unit of analysis (e.g., Mohan & Slater, 2006) partly due to the interactive nature of classroom discourse, which consists of multiple rounds of conversation and/or question-answering turns. In this study of written language and visuals on lecture slides, individual slides were treated as a macrolevel unit of analysis because lecture slides usually contain one major concept or idea per display. While some slides are connected thematically or logically in a lecture, an analysis of inter-slide relations is beyond the scope of this study. On individual slides, the T-unit was used as a microlevel unit of analysis. A T-unit includes an independent or main clause and the subordinate clauses or other structures attached. The reason for choosing T-unit as the unit of analysis instead of the clause is that the focus of this study is on the major functions fulfilled by bigger idea groups, rather than the function of each clause, which can be easily embedded into larger units. It is noteworthy that lecture slides tend to contain a variety of syntactic structures, from single words and phrases to clauses and complete sentences. When bullet point structures are used, the slide is more likely to contain fragments such as verb phrases and/or noun phrases. For example, on Slide 16 in (Psychological) Measurement, "set of categories," as a lower-level point, follows "Categorical variables" without any verb. For the fragments with missing verbs in the lecture slides, plausible verbs were inserted to re-construct corresponding clauses or sentences. In the slide of "categorical variables," for example, it was natural to insert "have" so that the text then read as "categorical variables have (a) set of categories."

A series of factors were considered for identifying knowledge structures. The three types of transitivity, or three processes, were distinguished at the T-unit level, namely processes of being (typically relational and existential processes), doing (typically material and behavioral processes), and sensing (typically verbal and mental processes). As Mohan (1986) explained, knowledge structures are closely connected with the ideational meta-function in Systemic Functional Linguistics. Through the lens of the transitivity system, initial distinctions were made with regard to the six knowledge structures. In addition, lexicogrammatical features of the texts were examined to help the annotation decisions. For example, evaluative lexis plays a key role in enabling the knowledge structure of EVALUATION, whose functions include evaluating, ranking, judging, and criticizing. Visuals and visual representation of the textual contents on a slide were also taken into account. Typical graphic organizers discussed in Tang (2001) and Mohan (2007) were used as a key resource for annotating knowledge structures.

The annotated slides were checked multiple times to ensure an acceptable intra-coder consistency or reliability. Conflicting annotations from different rounds were resolved by consulting other Knowledge Framework studies on academic language.

Data Analysis

Given the small sample size in this study, only descriptive statistics are reported. Excerpts of texts and visuals from the lecture slides are analyzed qualitatively. Considering the fact that lecture slides contain both text-based and visual-based knowledge structures, it is reasonable to normalize the counts of these knowledge structures against different types of slides, namely, text-containing slides and visual-containing slides. For example, in the lecture on Control Structures, nine text-based knowledge structures of CLASSIFICATION were identified out of a total of 14 text-containing slides (total number of slides 18 minus visual-only slides 4). The normalized average frequency of occurrence for CLASSIFICATION was thus 0.64, meaning that for every ten text-containing slides there are about six cases of text-based CLASSIFICATION used in the lecture slides. The averages obtained through this calculation method have the same references, text-containing slides in this case, and hence are comparable across lectures. In addition, this procedure of normalization helps control the impact of varying length of lecture slides and overall configuration of the lecture slides.

Results

In this section, an overview of the normalized counts of text-based and visual-based knowledge structures is presented first. Then, analyses of examples of each knowledge structure are structured in theory–practice pairs of knowledge structures.

Tables 7.2 and 7.3 show both the raw counts and normalized counts of knowledge structures in the selected lectures and by the discipline for text-based knowledge structures and visual-based knowledge structures, respectively. Overall, a large variability exists in both text-based and visual-based knowledge structures among these six lectures (also see Figures 7.1 and 7.2 for a lecture-level distribution of knowledge structures in percentage). For example, In the lecture on (Psychological) Measurement, text-based CLASSIFICATION is the dominant knowledge structure, taking up over 50% of the total number of knowledge structures in that lecture, whereas the lecture on

Table 7.2 Raw counts and normalized counts (in parenthesis) of text-based knowledge structures

Topics	CLASSIFICATION	DESCRIPTION	PRINCIPLES	SEQUENCE	EVALUATION	CHOICE	Total raw counts	Normalized Average
Control Structures	9 (0.64)	0 (0)	9 (0.64)	16 (1.14)	13 (0.93)	1 (0.07)	48	3.4
Intelligent Agents	22 (1.29)	4 (0.24)	11 (0.65)	0 (0)	14 (0.82)	1 (0.06)	52	3.1
Energy in Transition	36(1.71)	4 (0.19)	17 (0.81)	1 (0.05)	21 (1.00)	0 (0)	79	3.8
Normalized average (Engineering)	1.22	0.14	0.70	0.40	0.92	0.04		
Market Forces	31 (0.89)	2 (0.06)	16 (0.46)	3 (0.09)	8 (0.23)	0 (0)	60	1.7
Race in America	27 (1.59)	0 (0)	7 (0.41)	7 (0.41)	7 (0.41)	1 (0.06)	49	2.9
Measurement	45 (1.55)	5 (0.17)	3 (0.10)	3 (0.10)	22 (0.76)	1 (0.03)	79	2.7
Normalized average (Social Sciences)	1.34	0.08	0.32	0.20	0.47	0.03		

Table 7.3 Raw counts and normalized counts (in parenthesis) of visual-based knowledge structures

Topics	CLASSIFICATION	DESCRIPTION	PRINCIPLES	SEQUENCE	EVALUATION	CHOICE	Total raw counts	Normalized average
Control Structures	3 (0.33)	0 (0)	0 (0)	5 (0.56)	0 (0)	1 (0.11)	9	1
Intelligent Agents	2 (0.35)	0 (0)	0 (0)	7 (0.88)	2 (0.25)	0 (0)	11	1.4
Energy in Transition	9 (0.69)	0 (0)	1 (0.08)	1 (0.08)	0 (0)	0 (0)	11	0.8
Normalized average (Engineering)	0.43	0	0.03	0.50	0.08	0.04		
Market Forces	27 (0.79)	0 (0)	9 (0.26)	5 (0.15)	2 (0.06)	0 (0)	43	1.2
Race in America	14 (0.82)	1 (0.06)	0 (0)	2 (0.12)	0 (0)	0 (0)	17	1
Measurement	5 (0.33)	5 (0.33)	0 (0)	0 (0)	5 (0.33)	0 (0)	15	1
Normalized average (Social Sciences)	0.65	0.13	0.09	0.09	0.13	0		

Control Structures had about 20% of the knowledge structures as text-based CLASSIFICATION. As for visual-based knowledge structure, the normalized counts of CLASSIFICATION ranged from 0.33 to 0.82 among the six lectures. A similar variability in the genre of academic discourse has been reported in Thompson (1994) with regard to the rhetorical functions in the introduction part of lectures, as instructors tend to have somewhat different teaching styles.

Despite the variability, both disciplines shared the same set of top three text-based knowledge structures based on the average of normalized counts, including CLASSIFICATION, PRINCIPLES, and EVALUATION. It is noteworthy that these top three text-based knowledge structures are all on the theoretical side of the Knowledge Framework, suggesting the prevalence of higher-level thinking skills involved in the lectures. CLASSIFICATION was the most frequently used knowledge structure (1.22 in Engineering vs. 1.34 in Social Sciences), highlighting the common practices of defining concepts and showcasing part-whole relationships in classroom teaching. The Engineering lectures contained about twice as many PRINCIPLES (0.70 vs. 0.32) and EVALUATION (0.92 vs. 0.47) as used in the Social Sciences lectures (see Figure 7.1).

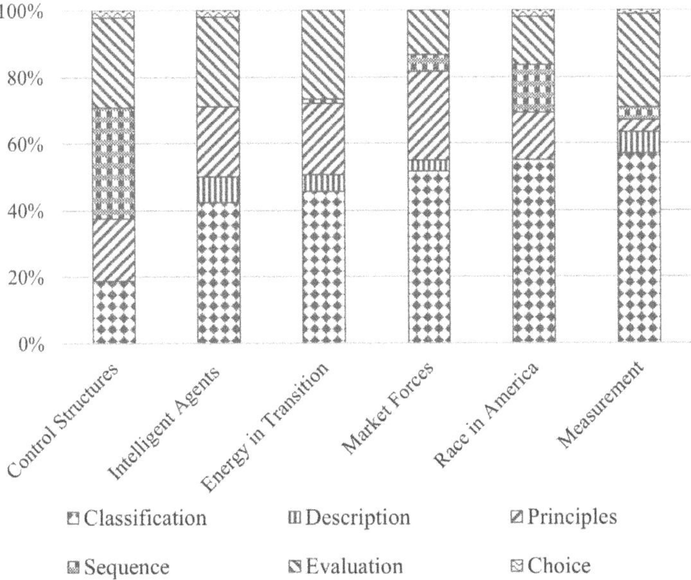

Figure 7.1 Lecture-level distribution of text-based knowledge structures

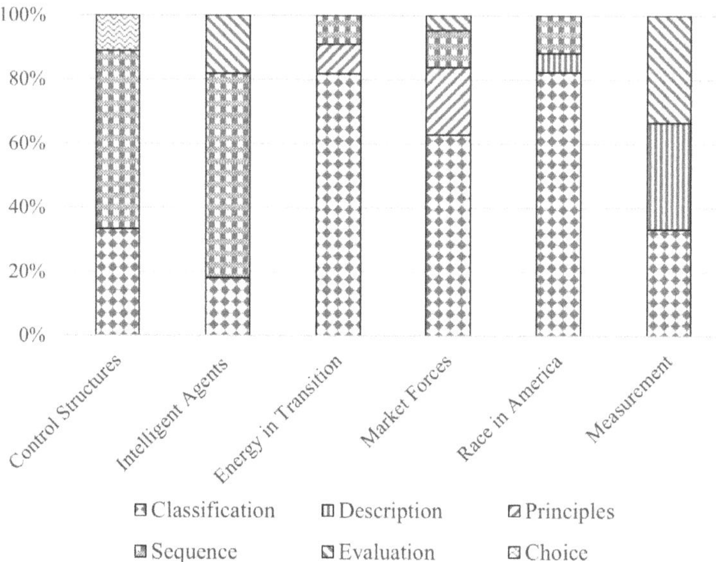

Figure 7.2 Lecture-level distribution of visual-based knowledge structures

In contrast to the theory-level knowledge structures, the practical or action-related ones were much less frequently used in the lectures (see Table 7.2 and Figure 7.1). For instance, the knowledge structure of CHOICE was absent in the lecture on Energy in Transition and the one on Market Forces; this knowledge structure was used only once in other lectures. Likewise, the knowledge structure of DESCRIPTION was absent in the lecture sides of Race in America and Control Structures. This pattern may be dictated by the nature of the lecture topics. Although the knowledge structure of CHOICE may be common in classroom discourse as instructors can interact with students by asking questions which tend to elicit CHOICE knowledge structure, the presentation of the knowledge structure may not appear on slides, as was apparent in this study's data.

In comparison to the text-based knowledge structures, different profiles of visual-based knowledge structures were observed among the lectures. Five out of six sets of slides used only three types of visual-based knowledge structures (see Figure 7.2). The visual-based knowledge structures in the lecture on Intelligent Agents were CLASSIFICATION, SEQUENCE, and EVALUATION, while the visual-based knowledge structures in the lecture on Race in America included CLASSIFICATION, DESCRIPTION, and SEQUENCE. In other words, different sets of top three visual-based knowledge structures were used in the two disciplines. The Engineering lectures used visual-based

SEQUENCE (0.50), CLASSIFICATION (0.43), and EVAUATION (0.08), whereas the lectures in Social Sciences had more frequent use of visual-based CLASSIFICATION (0.65), DESCRIPTION (0.13), and EVALUATION (0.13). This difference may be attributable to the types of visuals typically employed in these disciplines. For example, to illustrate procedural information, the lectures in Engineering contained more flowcharts, which represent the knowledge structure of SEQUENCE.

In the following subsections, specific examples of both text-based and visual-based knowledge structure are analyzed with special attention to the lexicogrammatical structures and visual types.

CLASSIFICATION and DESCRIPTION

In subject content courses, CLASSIFICATION associates or defines a concept with reference to related concepts or ideas and presents it under a taxonomy, if applicable. The CLASSIFICATION knowledge structure embodies the thinking skills of *classifying, grouping, defining,* and discussing *part/whole relationship*. As previously mentioned, relatively speaking, there are more examples of text-based and visual-based CLASSIFICATION in the lecture slides compared to the other two theory-based knowledge structures, namely PRINCIPLES and EVALUATION. The two disciplines seem to be similar in the total occurrences of text-based and visual-based CLASSIFICATION. As discussed above, many lecture slides contain a large proportion of fragments or incomplete clauses, presented in the format of bullet points. Likewise, the knowledge structure of CLASSIFICATION in lecture slides is typically realized through bullet points as shown below.

Example 1: Slide 12 in (Psychological) Measurement
Two properties of measurement

- Unit of measurement—minimum sized unit
- Scale of measurement—correspondence between properties of numbers & variables measured

When bullet points are used, it is common to observe additional information presented as DESCRIPTION, PRINCIPLES, or CHOICE, depending on the disciplines. In the example above, each property of measurement is further described with noun phrases that can be categorized as DESCRIPTION with omitted verbs (being). The example below is from the lecture on Control Structures in the discipline of Engineering. In this example, each control structure is explained by specific procedures which can be categorized as CHOICE. The CLASSIFICATION knowledge structure is realized with a general statement ("all programs can be written in terms of three control structures") followed by specific types of control structures in the format of bullet points. In this example, PRINCIPLES (*is executed*) and CHOICE (*select between one statement or another*) are used to supplement the knowledge structure of CLASSIFICATION.

Example 2: Slide 4 in Control Structures
All programs can be written *in terms of* three control structures (like building blocks)

- Sequence
  - o "Built-in" to C
    - § Unless otherwise directed, one statement after the next is executed
- Selection (three types)
  - o Depending on a condition, select between one statement or another
    - § *If* Var1 is greater than 10, do this ..., else do that ...
- Repetition (three types)
  - o Depending on a condition, execute one or more statements repeated

Alternatively, the similar part-whole relations are expressed with the lexis related to CLASSIFICATION such as "encompass," "consists of," and "is divided into" in clauses (see Example 3).

Example 3: Slide 20 in Measurement
Ordinal Scale: Consists of *a set of* categories that are organized in an ordered sequence.

Two main types of visuals are employed in the lectures slides to represent CLASSIFICATION: bar graphs and tree diagrams (see Figure 7.3). The bar graph by design shows the numerical values in several categories of interest, thus displaying the similarities or differences among them. In Figure 7.3, the bar graph from the lecture on Race in America shows the spending per pupil in four districts. The tree diagram used in the lecture on Market Forces illustrates four types of market structures (i.e., monopoly, oligopoly, monopolistic competition, and perfect competition), based on two criteria: the number of firms and type of products. These two examples of visual-based

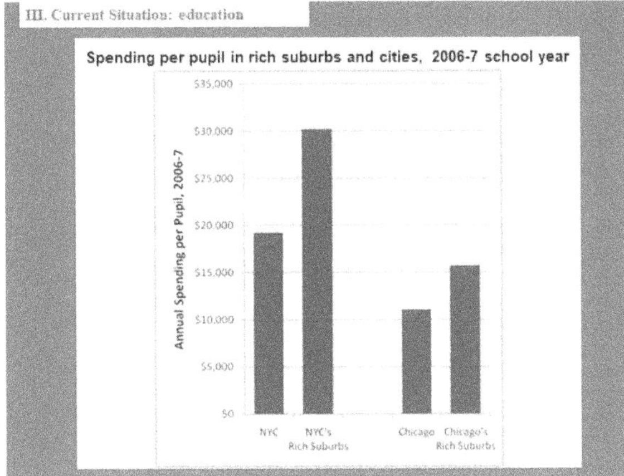

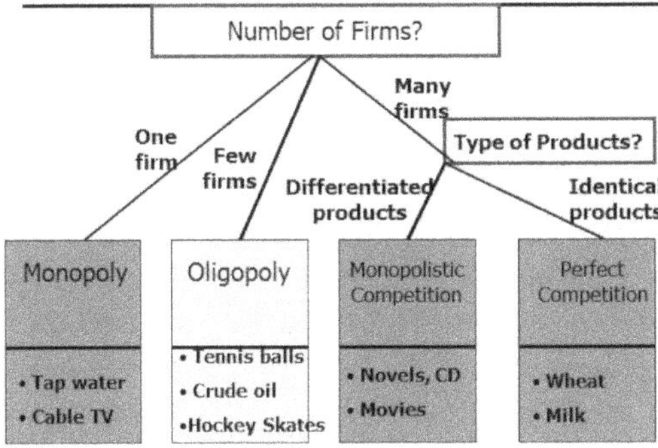

Figure 7.3 Example visual-based CLASSIFICATION on Slide 27 in Race in America (left) and Slide 9 in the Market Forces Lecture (right)

CLASSIFICATION are self-explanatory and occupy the whole slide without using additional knowledge structures.

DESCRIPTION constitutes a small portion of the knowledge structures used in lecture slides. Two text-based examples are from Slide 13 in the lecture on Energy in Transition: "Motion is horizontal" and "the horizontal acceleration is constant." These examples of DESCRIPTION are characterized by being processes and attributive lexis.

Only two lectures had examples of visual-based DESCRIPTION as a knowledge structure: Race in America and Measurement. The visual in Figure 7.4 was employed as a description of a phenomenon in measurement. The corresponding text-based knowledge structure of DESCRIPTION reads "points are NOT all close together (dissimilar) & centered on the target."

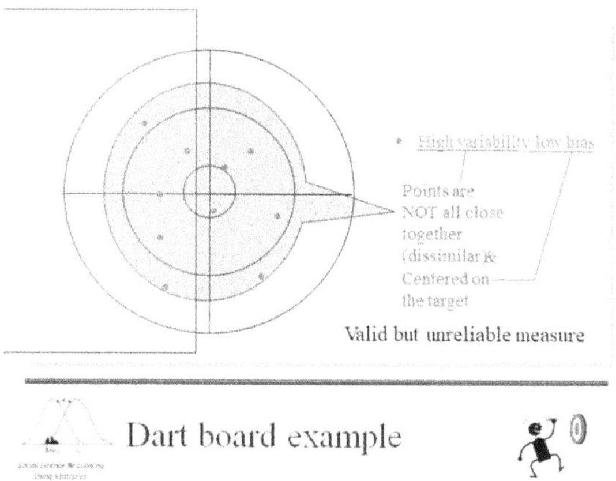

Figure 7.4 Example of visual-based DESCRIPTION on Slide 35 in Measurement

PRINCIPLES and SEQUENCE

Action verbs in the *doing* processes are one of the key indicators of PRINCIPLES in the sampled lecture slides, especially in the presence of general reference as opposed to specific reference. Examples 4 and 5 showcase some of the *doing* processes used in the knowledge structure of PRINCIPLES. Notice that two actions verbs "stacked" and "nested" are used in Example 4, along with a *to* + infinitive structure "to handle more sophisticated decision/action functionality" to construct a causative meaning. In Example 5, a causal circumstance ("by mechanical work") is connected to the action verb "transferred." Another salient feature associated with PRINCIPLES is the use of consequential or conditional conjunctions such as "if" in Example 5.

> Example 4. Slide 24 in Control Structures
> Selection structures can be stacked or nested to handle more sophisticated decision/action functionality.

> Example 5. Slides 10 and 18 in Energy in Transition
> Energy can be transferred to and from a system by mechanical work
> *If* gas volume increases, work is done by the gas on the piston and hence on the connecting rod and the crank shaft etc.

In this pool of lecture slides, text-based knowledge structures of PRINCIPLES appeared to be more prevalent in Engineering lectures, while only the

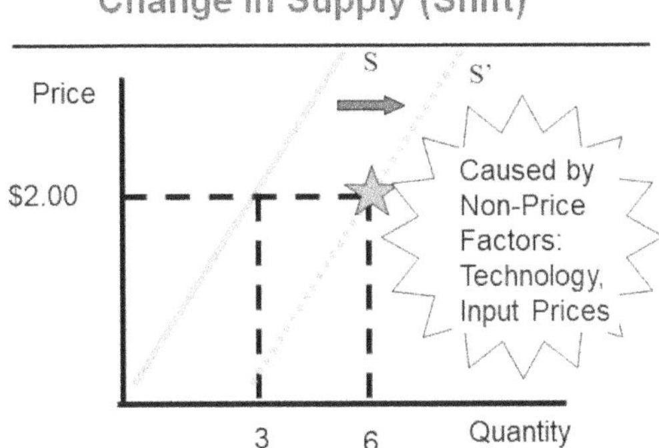

Figure 7.5 Example of visual-based PRINCIPLES on Slide 43 Market Forces

lecture on Market Forces in Social Sciences showed comparable raw counts of PRINCIPLES.

A small number of visual-based PRINCIPLES were found but only in Energy in Transition and Market Forces. Figure 7.5 is an example of this; note the use of text to help construct causal meaning in the visual.

The knowledge structure of SEQUENCE is closely connected to PRINCIPLES. Since Engineering courses tend to have content related to procedures used in experiments and other operations, it is not surprising to see more examples of both text-based and visual-based SEQUENCE in Engineering lecture slides than in those of Social Sciences. Similar to the linguistic features used in PRINCIPLES, action verbs (e.g., "skipped"), particularly those that construct sequential meaning (e.g., "continues"), and temporal conjunctions such as "then" are commonly used to show sequences of events (see Example 6). SEQUENCE in the Social Science slides was typically realized through signposting with temporal conjunctions or other time-related references (see Example 7).

Example 6. Slide 12 in Control Structures
If expression is non-zero, statement1 is executed, then the program continues with the statement after statement 2, i.e., statement 2 is skipped.

Example 7. Slide 5 in Race in America
Full citizenship for blacks was not enacted *until 1964*, less than half a century ago.

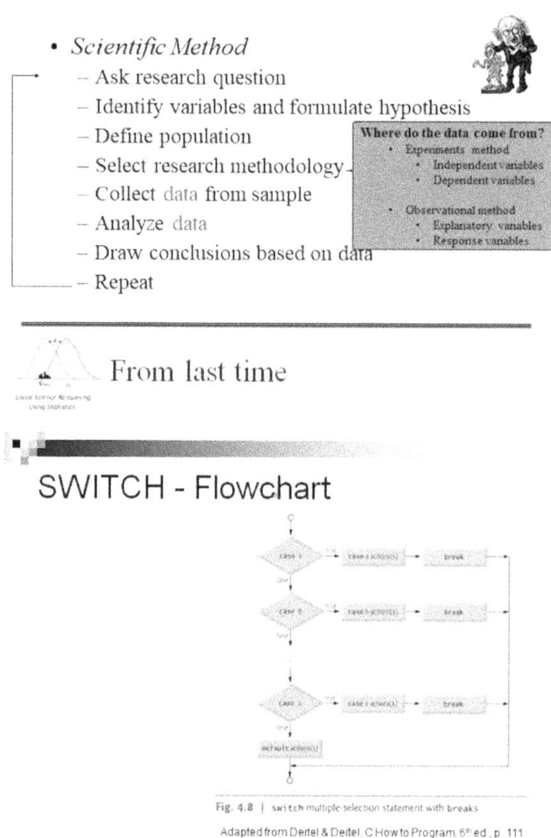

Figure 7.6 Example SEQUENCE on Slide 3 in Measurement (left) and Slide 9 in Control Structures (right)

The visuals for SEQUENCE were primarily flowcharts (see Figure 7.6). The example at the top of Figure 7.6 is an example of SEQUENCE in the Social Sciences slides, which is a combination of both textual and visual messages. A series of steps as defined in the scientific method are ordered in the format of bullet points and linked with a line arrow connector. The example at the bottom of Figure 7.6 illustrates the working sequence of switch operation with arrows arranged in a sequential and logical manner.

EVALUATION and CHOICE

The knowledge structure of EVALUATION involves sensing processes or being processes as well as evaluative lexis. In the lecture slides, the knowledge structure of text-based EVALUATION is popular in both Engineering and Social Sciences. EVALUATION is commonly used to present instructors' judgment and/or critical analysis. EVALUATION is also frequently used in conjunction with other knowledge structures such as CLASSIFICATION and DESCRIPTION to add depth to the introduction of a concept or entity. Below are examples of EVALUATION in the lecture slides. For Example 9, one salient feature of EVALUATION is the use of evaluative adjectives to attach values, in this case, "illegal" and "widely tolerated."

> Example 8. Slide 12 in Race in America
> Rationality is *distinct* from omniscience (all knowing with infinite knowledge).

> Example 9. Slide 7 in Intelligent Agents
> This may be officially illegal, but widely tolerated in practice.

There are relatively fewer visuals employed to express EVALUATION compared to CLASSIFICATION, PRINCIPLES, and SEQUENCE in the sampled lecture slides. Three lectures contained visual-based EVALUATION. The visual in Figure 7.7 presents a working environment for an intelligent agent that receives signals from the environment and then acts on the signals and changes or provides feedback to the environment. Inside the visual, the word "Impractical" in its artistic form is used as an extra piece of information to suggest an evaluation of this type of agent. In other words, EVALUATION co-occurs with SEQUENCE in the same chart.

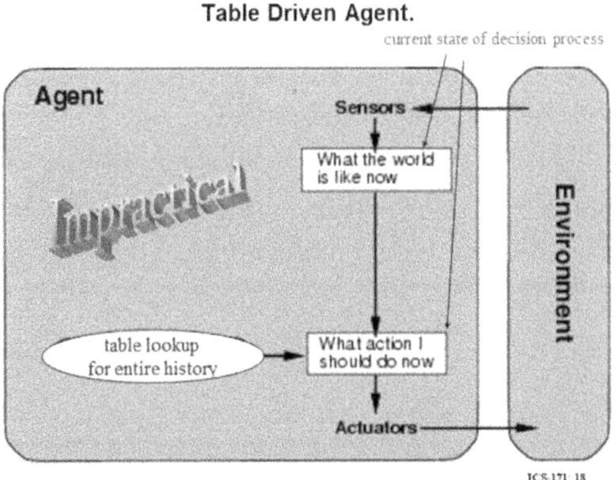

Figure 7.7 Example of visual-based EVALUATION on Slide 18 in Intelligent Agent

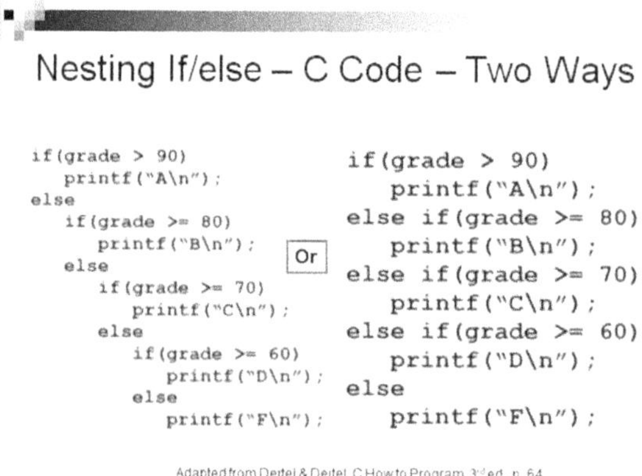

Figure 7.8 Example of visual-based CHOICE on Slide 17 in Control Structures

Comparatively speaking, the knowledge structure of CHOICE appears to be the least frequently used in both text-based and visual-based slides, and only one visual-based CHOICE was represented in the sampled lecture slides (see Figure 7.8).

This lack of CHOICE may be an inherent nature of lecture slides whose primary functions are to deliver course content in an organized way and do not necessarily aim to elicit choice responses. By contrast, four out of six lectures in Engineering contain text-based CHOICE with noticeable use of an alternative conjunction "or" and appositional choice lexis such as "select" (see Examples 14–15 below).

Example 14. Slide 4 in Control Structures
Depending on a condition, select *between* one statement *or* another.

Example. 15. Slide 6 in Intelligent Agents
For each possible percept sequence, a rational agent should select an action that is expected to maximize its performance measure, based on the evidence provided by the percept sequence and whatever built-in knowledge the agent has.

Discussion and Conclusion

This study focused on the knowledge structures expressed in six lecture PowerPoint files from six undergraduate-level courses. These lecture slides represent two broad disciplines taught at North American universities. The knowledge structure analysis indicates that while there is some noticeable variability in the frequencies of occurrence of the six knowledge structures within each discipline (e.g., Engineering and Social Sciences), these two disciplines also saw similarities in the general distribution of the text-based knowledge structures.

The text-based knowledge structures on the theoretical or reflection side (CLASSIFICATION, PRINCIPLES, and EVALUATION) seemed to be pervasive in the lecture slides across these two disciplines. This general pattern is somewhat unique compared to previous Knowledge Framework-based studies on oral discourse. This may reflect the nature of lecture slides as a specialized multimodal genre of academic discourse. Defining and contextualizing concepts appear to be one of the major tasks in classroom teaching. This is also shown in the use of CLASSIFICATION on the lecture slides, usually constructed with "being" processes. For such a condensed form of academic language, it could be argued that one of the key goals of lecture slides is to summarize concrete examples and present cause-effect relations through language and visuals. The content of the selected slides reflects this orientation with an abundance of linguistic features and visuals devoted to the "doing" processes. On the other hand, the knowledge structure of EVALUATION signifies teacher's judgment and values about the entity or concept. It also plays an important role in engaging students and eliciting their responses (Gleason et al., 2017).

The practice side of the Knowledge Framework seemed to be less utilized in the sampled lecture slides. SEQUENCE was the most frequently used knowledge structure. It is also the one that distinguished the two disciplines in that Engineering used it twice as many as the Social Sciences in both text and visual form. This observation is in line with the findings of a multidimensional analysis of a comprehensive university corpus in Biber (2006), which revealed that both textbooks and classroom discourses in Engineering are noticeably different from those in Social Sciences in Dimension 2 Procedural vs. content-focused discourse, with Engineering on the side of using more procedural discourse. In Biber (2006), procedural discourse is constructed through modal verbs, to-clauses, activity verbs, and so on, while content-focused discourse tends to have more adjectives. The other two practice-oriented knowledge structures, DESCRIPTION and CHOICE, were minimally represented in the slides. In previous examples of oral classroom discourse, CHOICE was found to be commonly used by students in response to teacher's questions (Gleason et al., 2017). This may help explain the sparsity of

CHOICE in the lecture slides sampled in this study given the register difference between oral classroom discourse and lecture slides.

Visual-based knowledge structures are equally noteworthy. The visuals are used in conjunction with text-based knowledge structures and exhibit some variation in both visual types and language-image interaction (Unsworth, 2006). This type of visual-text synergy has been touched on in the literature (Zhao et al., 2014).

Some limitations need to be acknowledged in this study. First, only a small number of PowerPoint slides were analyzed and thus their representativeness has to take into consideration the existence of idiosyncratic lesson preparation and teaching styles. Although the findings in this study may not be generalized beyond the samples collected, they gain strength when compared to corpus studies of academic discourse such as those of Biber (2006) and Biber et al. (2002). Future research would benefit from applying the same analytical approach to a larger collection of lecture slides. Second, this analysis treated slides as isolated pieces of information, rather than a part of a coherent development of course content with inter-slide relations (Adams, 2006; Zhao & van Leeuwen, 2014). In addition, the analysis was based on the content on the slides without the accompanying oral discourse from the teacher and students. Some slide content may be more difficult to interpret when de-contextualized. The relationship between PowerPoint content and spoken discourse may vary depending on presenters' speaking styles in slide-supported lectures (Rowley-Jolivet, 2012). Future studies could benefit from using richer datasets that include both lecture slides as pedagogical artifacts and recorded classroom talk.

Despite the limitations mentioned above, the findings of this study are particularly meaningful for practitioners in the field of teaching and assessing English for academic purposes (EAP). From a pedagogical perspective, the linguistic and visual features associated with specific knowledge structures should be incorporated in EAP classes to familiarize non-English native-speaking students with authentic materials. In this way, students can be better prepared for content learning while becoming aware of the linguistic and visual resources for meaning-making. This is in line with the lecturing in a second language (LSL) model proposed by Miller (2002), who stressed that "in order to develop the LSL model for academic listening we need to examine language features, language and pedagogical interaction, and pedagogical features themselves" (p. 150). With regard to the assessment of EAP, especially in assessing academic listening, lecture PowerPoint slides should be a part of the input materials if technology affordance is available. In this case, the knowledge structures on the lecture slides should be sufficiently represented to enhance situational authenticity of the assessment tasks.

References

Adams, C. (2006). PowerPoint, habits of mind, and classroom culture. *Journal of Curriculum Studies*, *38*(4), 389–411. http://doi.org/10.1080/00220270600579141

Alley, M. (2013). *The craft of scientific presentations*. Springer. https://doi.org/10.1007/978-1-4419-8279-7

Apperson, J.M., Laws, E.L., & Scepansky, J.A. (2008). An assessment of student preferences for PowerPoint presentation structure in undergraduate courses. *Computers & Education*, *50*(1), 148–153. http://doi.org/10.1016/j.compedu.2006.04.003

Biber, D. (2006). *University Language*: A corpus-based study of spoken and written registers. John Benjamin Publishing Company. http://doi.org/10.1075/scl.23

Biber, D., Conrad, S.M., Reppen, R., Byrd, P., & Helt, M. (2002). Speaking and writing in the university: A multidimensional comparison. *TESOL Quarterly*, 36(1), 9–48. http://doi.org/10.2307/3588359

Dudley-Evans, T. (1994). Variations in the discourse patterns favoured by different disciplines and their pedagogical implications. In J. Flowerdew (Ed.), *Academic Listening: Research Perspective* (pp. 146–158). Cambridge University Press. http://doi.org/10.1017/CBO9781139524612.012

Gleason, J., Berg, M., & Huang, J. (2017). Patterns of oral Choice and Evaluation across secondary content areas. *Language and Education*, 1–19. http://doi.org/10.1080/09500782.2017.1391279

Huang, J., Normandia, B., & Greer, S. (2005). Communicating mathematically: Comparison of knowledge structures in teacher and student discourse in a secondary math classroom. *Communication Education*, *54*(1), 34–51. https://doi.org/10.1080/14613190500077002

Hyland, K. (2006). Disciplinary differences: Language variation in academic discourses. In K. Hyland & M. Bondi (Eds.), *Academic discourse across disciplines* (pp. 17–45). Peter Lang.

Li, Z., Jones, J., & Lodge, S. (2017, May). Disciplinary differences in university lecture slides as a part of classroom discourse: Findings from corpus-based analysis and multimodal analysis. Paper presented at the 2017 Annual Conference of the Canadian Association of Applied Linguistics (CAAL). Toronto, Canada.

Lynch, T. (2011). Academic listening in the 21st century: Reviewing a decade of research. *Journal of English for Academic Purposes*, *10*(2), 79–88. http://doi.org/10.1016/j.jeap.2011.03.001

Miller, L. (2002). Towards a model for lecturing in a second language. *Journal of English for Academic Purposes*, *1*(2), 145–162. http://doi.org/10.1016/S1475-1585(02)00017-6

Mohan, B. (1986). *Language and content*. Addison-Wesley.

Mohan, B. (1989). Knowledge structures and academic discourse. *WORD*, *40*(1–2), 99–115. http://doi.org/10.1080/00437956.1989.11435799

Mohan, B. (2007). Knowledge structures in social practices. In J. Cummins & C. Davison (Eds.), *International handbook of English language teaching* (pp. 303–315). Kluwer Academic Publishers. http://doi.org/10.1007/978-0-387-46301-8_22

Mohan, B., & Slater, T. (2006). Examining the theory/practice relation in a high school science register: A functional linguistic perspective. *Journal of English for Academic Purposes*, 5, 302–316. http://doi.org/10.1016/j.jeap.2006.08.004

O'Donnell, M. (2011). UAM ImageTool 2.1. [Computer Software]. Retrieved from http://www.wagsoft.com/ImageTool/index.html

OECD. (2014). "Indicator C4: Who studies abroad and where?" In *Education at a Glance 2014: OECD Indicators*. OECD Publishing. https://doi.org//10.1787/888933118656

Rowley-Jolivet, E. (2002). Visual discourse in scientific conference papers A genre-based study. *English for Specific Purposes*, *21*(1), 19–40. https://doi.org/10.1016/S0889-4906(00)00024-7

Rowley-Jolivet, E. (2012). Oralising text slides in scientific conference presentations: A multimodal corpus analysis. In A. Boulton, S. Carter-Thomas, & E. Rowley-Jolivet (Eds.), *Corpus-Informed Research and Learning in ESP: Issues and applications* (pp. 137–166). John Benjamin Publishing Co.

Slater, T., & Butler, J.I. (2015). Examining connections between the physical and the mental in education: A systemic functional linguistic analysis of PE teaching and learning. *Linguistics and Education, 30,* 12–25.

Tang, G. (2001). Knowledge framework and classroom action. In C. Leung, C. Davison, & B. Mohan (Eds.), *English as a Second Language in the Mainstream: Teaching, Learning and Identity* (pp. 127–137). Routledge.

Tauroza, S., & Allison, D. (1994). Expectation-driven understanding in information systems lecture comprehension. In J. Flowerdew (Ed.), *Academic Listening: Research Perspective* (pp. 35–54). Cambridge University Press.

Thompson, S. (1994). Frameworks and contexts: A genre-based approach to analysing lecture introductions. *English for Specific Purposes*, 13(2), 171–186. https://doi.org/10.1016/0889-4906(94)90014-0

Unsworth, L. (2006). Towards a metalanguage for multiliteracies education: Describing the meaning-making resources of language-image interaction. *English Teaching: Practice and Critique*, *5*(1), 55–76.

Zhao, S., & van Leeuwen, T. (2014). Understanding semiotic technology in university classrooms: a social semiotic approach to PowerPoint-assisted cultural studies lectures. *Classroom Discourse*, *5*(1), 71–90. http://doi.org/10.1080/19463014.2013.859848

Zhao, S., Djonov, E., & van Leeuwen, T. (2014). Semiotic technology and practice: A multimodal social semiotic approach to PowerPoint. *Text & Talk*, *34*(3). http://doi.org/10.1515/text-2014-0005

About the Author

Zhi Li is an assistant professor in the Department of Linguistics at the University of Saskatchewan, Canada. His research interests include language assessment, technology-supported language teaching and learning, and corpus linguistics. His research papers have been published in *System*, *CALICO Journal*, and *Language Learning & Technology*.

8 Causal Explanations in Physics: A Functional Analysis of EFL Lectures and Textbook Excerpts

Kimberly Becker and Xiaoping Liang

Abstract

This paper reports on a case study of a Chinese physics professor at a university in Shanghai, China. The purpose of the study is to investigate how his classroom explanations of causal meanings are realized through lexicogrammatical features in English as a foreign language. Data consist of one 60-minute lecture purposefully selected from a series of 20 hours of video recording of physics lectures compared to language from an English-medium physics textbook associated with the course. Instances of grammatical metaphor in causal explanations in the physics lecture were identified and analyzed using a functional approach. Drawing on an up-down metaphor, this paper uses the term "upward" movement to refer to "functional recasts" from simpler towards more advanced (more grammatically metaphorical) wording, and "downward" movement to describe functional recasts from more advanced towards simpler wording. Employing that metaphor combined with the Knowledge Framework (KF) revealed results which demonstrated that the Chinese physics professor used a range of lexicogrammar such as conjunctions, verbs, and nominalizations to assemble causal explanations that showed downward functional recasts to address the meaning and wording relationship in causal explanations. The study proposes implications for teacher training, specifically the training of International Teaching Assistants (ITAs) with the use of the KF heuristic.

Keywords: functional analysis; academic EFL lectures; Knowledge Framework; causal language; science education

In recent years, education has become more internationalized (Altbach & Knight, 2007; Qiang, 2003). Within many countries, science is increasingly taught in English by non-native speaking instructors to non-native speaking students (Dearden, 2018). While the literature has examined content-based English-as-a-second-language (ESL) classes (e.g., Mohan & Beckett, 2003; Mohan & Slater, 2006; Slater, 2004), little has been discussed about science classes taught by English-as-a-foreign-language (EFL) science instructors to EFL students. One critical issue is discovering how science is explained (Leach & Scott, 2000) by EFL instructors. In this case study, we explore how an EFL science instructor explains concepts using EFL and how the students are initiated into the social practice of the science community through a language that is neither the teacher's nor the students'. We do this through a comparison of language resources in a science textbook and those of an EFL instructor's lectures.

Theoretical Framework

Much literature that examines second language acquisition (SLA) research based on "focus on form" analyzes instructional discourse reductively, meaning that classroom instruction is interpreted as vocabulary and grammar teaching. Vocabulary instruction in a second language (L2) usually involves an instructor providing a label in the L2 for an equivalent term in the first language (L1), whose meaning is assumed to be familiar to the students. However, science teaching involves teaching both new concepts and new meanings, and language is the medium of such teaching. Thus, we have chosen a framework that explains language resources as learning tools, for while explaining general academic vocabulary is helpful, it is insufficient to clarify the relevant scientific concepts as an interlinked system of meanings.

Systemic Functional Linguistics (SFL) provides a framework for language analysis that takes a functional approach to L2 vocabulary instruction. For that reason, this study takes an SFL approach to the exploration of language resources used as a means of teaching and learning the social practices of an EFL science class. Specifically, our study employs Mohan's register analysis of social practice (Mohan, 1989) to analyze lectures taught by a Chinese physics instructor using EFL to teach first-year Chinese university students in Shanghai. We also employ the Knowledge Framework (Mohan, 1986) to accomplish our purpose: To explore the problematics of this type of educational situation and to reveal how a Chinese professor uses language resources to respond to the challenge in such a context.

Underlying SFL Tenets

SFL sees language as meaning making in a social context. As Halliday and Martin (1993) explain, language in the SFL perspective is "a resource for meaning rather than as a system of rules," oriented to "speakers' meaning potential (what they can mean)," and concerned "with texts, rather than sentences, as the basic unit through which meaning is negotiated" (p. 22). This perspective approaches language as a system of relationships between text and context and considers text as a semantic choice in social contexts (Halliday, 2002).

The central way to understand the relationship between text and context is the concept of register. Halliday and Hasan (1985) define register as "variation according to use" (p. 89). Bloor and Bloor (2004) interpret register as "functional varieties" (p. 12) or "styles...(such as business English, legal English, and scientific English)" (p. 4). Thompson (2004) takes register to mean "certain recognizable configurations of linguistic resources" (p. 40) that language users typically employ in certain contexts. As a fundamental feature of functional grammar, register depicts the intimate link between language and context. For Halliday (1977), register functions to relate text to context and is "the necessary mediating concept that enables us to establish the continuity between a text and its socio-semiotic environment" (p. 58). It is this latter definition that this paper adopts because it situates scientific language resources within a specific register where causal realizations would be expected. Register is a way to view the language resources happening within the specific context of an EFL physics course.

The Knowledge Framework (KF)

One method of examining the connections between content (text) and its socio-semiotic environment is Mohan's (1986) Knowledge Framework (KF). This framework views language through the context of a social practice and relies on both knowledge (theory) and action (practice). In the present study, the social practice is a physics lecture. The activity is discussions of cause and effect in physics. Specifically, the case study relies on two aspects of the KF—PRINCIPLES and SEQUENCE—to compare excerpts from a physics textbook to language from the lecture.

In relation to the teaching and learning of science, Halliday and Martin (1993) point out that defining science terminology presents the problem of "interlocking definitions," which is the meaning of one term drawing upon other definitions in a circle of definitions. For beginning learners, it can be difficult to understand one meaning without understanding all the others in the circle, let alone in another language. Moreover, learners may need to operate not only with abstract definitions but also with prototypes. This means that science instructors cannot simply rely on defining key technical terms but must use other strategies to explain science meanings because "textbooks assume that the learner will create a model of the social practice" (Mohan, 2007, p. 308). The KF provides a way to examine the social practice of lecturing in an EFL physics course. With that in mind, this study uses the register concept of functional grammar to exemplify how a physics instructor responds to the challenge of defining science terminology and teaching physics concepts, thus providing a linguistic account of content-area instruction as a social practice. Two specific areas of the functional approach that inspire this study are how interlocking definitions are described. The instructor, as an expert in the content area (physics), scaffolds the cause/effect meaning potential of the textbook in a lecture by using language resources that explain concepts both theoretically and practically.

Science textbooks are content-oriented, concerned primarily with information transmission, and the wording of science textbooks often involves grammatical metaphor (Lakoff & Johnson, 1999). Halliday and Martin (1993) and Halliday and Matthiessen (2004) refer to grammatical metaphor as the process of non-objects becoming objectified by being realized as nouns. For example, processes such as events, actions, and states that are commonly realized by verbs come to be realized as nouns. Grammatical metaphor "involves a choice between a more straightforward and a more oblique realization of meaning. One key way that this is done is via grammatical rather than lexical options" (Bloor & Bloor, 2004, p. 127). In scientific language, a frequently used grammatical form is nominalization (Halliday & Martin, 1993), which refers to "the use of a nominal form to express a process meaning" (Thompson, 2004, p. 225). In other words, a process that is more congruently expressed as a verb (e.g., "to look") is instead expressed as a noun (e.g., "a look"). Table 8.1 presents a developmental trajectory of scientific causal language.

One important function of nominalization is the condensing of a clause into a noun so that it can be more efficiently used and recycled in the rest of the text. Thompson (2004) identifies two types of nominalized technical terms and their problems. One type refers to a clause established from previous sentences. The other type relates to the general concept which is the subject of the whole text. Nominalized technical terms are very economical in textbooks, but they pose serious problems for beginning learners, who need to "be able to identify the uncondensed wording that the nominalization relates to" (Thompson, 2004, p. 229). Unfortunately, it is not always

Table 8.1 Historical development of causal expressions (adapted from Halliday & Martin, 1993, p. 66)

Stages	Examples: Internal	Examples: External
Initial stage	• A happens, so we know X happens. • Because A happens, we know X happens.	• A happens, so X happens. • Because A happens, X happens.
Second stage	• That A happens proves X to happen. • Happening A proves happening X.	• That A happens causes X to happen. • Happening A causes happening X.
Final stage	• Happening A is the proof of happening X.	• Happening A is the cause of happening X.

immediately obvious what the relevant uncondensed wording is. The uncondensed wording is likely to occur when concepts are first introduced. The writer then assumes that readers are familiar with the concepts under discussion and therefore discusses them in their condensed form as technical terms. However, if readers miss the previous chapter or the beginning of the textbook in which a concept is introduced, they may have a hard time understanding the nominalization. From this point of view, Thompson (2004) sees education at every level "as largely a question of learning to handle condensed wordings" (p. 230).

In scientific disciplines, cause-effect and means-end concepts are considered central to the constitution of general knowledge (Lakoff & Johnson, 1999). In the KF, these concepts can be explained as specific "knowledge structures" (KSs). Cause/effect explanations would be classified under the KS called PRINCIPLES. These are marked by action verbs, consequential conjunctions and adverbials, cause-effect lexis, and passives (Mohan, 1986). PRINCIPLES can be enacted through activities that reflect the KS called SEQUENCE. SEQUENCE provides a specific reference, includes action verbs, emphasizes temporal conjunction and adverbials, and sequential lexis. Slater and Gleason (2011) explain:

> We create sequential order (practice) informed by our understandings (theory) of the principles behind the order. We may order certain things because we are aware of what we are attempting to achieve (means/

> ends)... We may also order actions in a particular sequence to discover cause and effect. (p. 9)

Several studies (e.g., Mohan & Slater, 2005, 2006; Slater & Mohan, 2010a, 2010b; Ma & Slater, 2015, 2016) have examined the construction of causal explanations from a KF perspective; others have explored how teachers have used recasts to teach and develop causal language. This latter group, which is most relevant to the current study, will be described next.

Related Studies

Many scholars exploring content-based language learning have analyzed classroom recasts from the perspective of SFL. Among these works, Mohan and Beckett's (2003) study is closely related to this chapter. It analyzes the grammatical scaffolding by a teacher to help second language learners develop their causal explanations. Their research reveals different aspects of the recast, including the lexicogrammar of causal meanings, the place of grammatical metaphor in the process of language development, and the nature of causal explanations as knowledge structures of "ideational meaning" in discourse. It offers an example of a functional approach to analysis of recasts in causal explanations.

Other related research includes Loewen and Philp's (2006) study on the characteristics, explicitness, and effectiveness of recasts in the adult English L2 classroom. Their research suggests that recasts vary in implicitness, which may have an impact on their effectiveness. It also indicates that the ambiguity of recasts is greatly reduced by the phrasal, prosodic, and discoursal cues that teachers provide. Egi's (2007) research reveals that the length and the number of changes between the original and the recasted language might in part determine the explicitness of recasts as feedback. These studies highlight the significance of teacher recasts to second language students. The studies also reveal the elements which influence the effectiveness of recasts and suggest how to achieve effective recasts. All these related studies have second language students as participants and thus serve as a reference for our study. One major difference, however, is that the participants in these studies are English majors while the participants in our study are science majors. Still, the methods of analysis of the effectiveness of recasts in these earlier investigations offered us insights.

Except for Unsworth (1999), who illustrated key differences between the language of talk and the language of writing from an SFL perspective, few studies have compared oral recasts from classroom interaction to textbook language. Moreover, few have addressed teacher explanations of causal discourse in science classes taught by EFL science instructors to EFL science students. Although we would expect differences in the written language of an English textbook versus the oral language of an EFL instructor, we can assume that both contain knowledge structures (KSs), but that these may be realized through different linguistic resource types. Thus, the present study focuses on making comparisons between the EFL instructor's spoken scientific language in physics lectures and the textbook's written language to examine how recasts are realized in the social practice of an EFL physics course. This study examines EFL physics lectures by using the KF and examining the language resources from two perspectives—meaning and wording. From the meaning point of view, the study explores physics lectures as cultural actions or social practices that are conveyed through language. From the wording point of view, it explores how physics lectures use register to construct a system of scientific meanings.

The significance of the study is to broaden an understanding of the two major language input resources for any content-based classroom: the written language of a textbook and the oral language of a lecture. Hence, the two research questions are:

1. What KSs does an EFL physics instructor use to teach causal physics concepts?
2. How does the instructor's oral causal language differ from the textbook language (i.e., how does the instructor mitigate the challenge of highly condensed textbook language)?

Research Methods

Participants and Data Sources

This paper reports on a case study of a Chinese physics professor at a university in Shanghai, China. The data consist of excerpts from one 60-minute lecture extracted from a series of 20 hours of video-recorded physics lectures. The lecture was purposefully selected because it includes rich examples of how the instructor taught causal physics concepts and mitigated the challenge of highly condensed textbook language. Other sources of data include excerpts from the English-language-medium physics textbook, *Physics for Scientists and Engineers* (Fishbane, Gasiorowicz, & Thornton, 1993).

Procedures

Instances of grammatical metaphor in causal explanations in the physics lecture and textbook were identified and analyzed using a functional analytic framework (Halliday, 1998; Halliday & Martin, 1993). The unit of analysis for identification of cause/effect language was a semantic unit (i.e., words, phrases, & clauses) that were lexical realizations of cause/effect. Those lexical realizations were concurrently coded using the stages in Table 8.1 and KSs.

Drawing on an up-down metaphor, this paper uses the term "upward" movement to refer to "functional recasts" (Mohan & Beckett, 2003) from simpler towards more advanced (more grammatically metaphorical and less congruent) wording, and "downward" movement to describe functional recasts from more advanced towards simpler wording (more literal and congruent). This upward and downward movement was captured in Slater and Mohan's (2010a) "Developmental Path of Cause," which empirically established a developmental trend along a grammatical axis based on Halliday's "general drift of grammatical metaphor" (Halliday, 1998) and along a semantic axis, from time to cause to proof. For example, a congruent causal statement is usually formed with conjunctions such as *because, so,* or *if.* Example one illustrates the use of such conjunctions:

1. **We know** that it gets cold in winter **because** water freezes.

This can be considered an example of what Halliday and Martin (1993) call the initial stage. As language becomes more sophisticated, it takes an upward turn toward a second stage, which uses language resources in a more metaphorical and incongruent way to realize this same causal principle. In this second stage, verbs such as *produce, arise from, depend on,* or *lead to* are used to demonstrate cause/effect, and could be formed as example two below:

2. That water freezes **proves** that it gets cold in winter.

Finally, the third stage of causal development in scientific English grammar is the use of nominalized forms (nouns formed from verbs). This is the most metaphorical and incongruent stage, as indicated in example three:

3. Water freezing is **proof of** cold weather in winter.

Beyond the progress from more to less congruent, Halliday and Martin (1993) point out that these stages can refer to external or internal relations.

Examples 1 through 3 above are internally referenced causal language, which focus on how humans observe causes and effects. External representations focus on the agents of cause and effect and are less easily understood by novices or L2 students. Using the examples above about temperatures and water freezing, examples four through six demonstrate the three stages of causal development with externally focused language in initial, second, and third stages, respectively:

4. It gets cold in winter, **so** water freezes.
5. Cold temperatures in winter **cause** water to freeze.
6. Cold temperatures are **the cause** of water freezing.

Halliday and Martin's (1993) framework, as shown in Table 8.1 above, was developed to explain historical changes in causal language; it can also be used to describe a developmental trajectory of scientific causal language. The developmental path of cause has been well documented in the SFL literature. Halliday and Martin (1993) created a chart to visualize the evolution that occurs as linguistic resources become increasingly sophisticated (Table 8.1 above is an adaptation of this chart). Slater and Mohan (2010a) also detail this causal development model, which notes both semantic and lexicogrammatical shifts as indicators of the growing sophistication of causal language, culminating in the realization of grammatical metaphor, usually via nominalization. This shift of linguistic resources is called agnation. *Agnate* is a term Halliday borrowed from Gleason (1965), who derived the term from the field of anthropology. In SFL, related language is said to be "agnate" if it is similar semantically but structurally different; for example, "He saw it" is agnate with "It was seen by him" (Matthiessen, Teruya, and Lam, 2010).

The results section below relies on the terms from Table 8.1 to demonstrate how the physics professor uses language resources from initial, second, and final stages as well as internal and external reference. The bulk of the analysis will focus on three main linguistic features: (1) conjunctions (indicative of initial stage), (2) verbs (indicative of second stage), and nouns (indicative of final stage). The analysis also focuses on how the professor uses internal relations to simplify the external relations used in the textbook, resulting in a "functional recast" (Mohan & Beckett, 2003) of sorts, and mimicking the metaphorical downward movement toward more sophisticated and ultimately advanced and grammatically metaphorical) wording.

This investigation has two broad aims. The first is to compare causal language features in a scientific textbook and an EFL lecture. We approach this from the perspective of systemic functional grammar, revealing the realization of more congruent forms and their ability to unfold grammatical metaphor in science instruction. The second aim is the use of the KF to differentiate oral and written language resources from both semantic and lexical perspectives.

Results

The transcribed data show the Chinese professor negotiating grammatical metaphor with the students in functional recasts, moving between more metaphorical and more congruent wording, depending on the pedagogical circumstances. The results will be presented as three examples, each of which have exemplary excerpts from both the textbook and the transcript. The analysis of the excerpts in each of the three examples demonstrates how the instructor scaffolds the language of the textbook by moving in a downward direction or making it more grammatically congruent. The first two examples are about the symmetric effect of time-dilation (the theory of relativity) and the third is about Newton's second law of motion. Each example starts with a textbook excerpt demonstrating salient features, offers an analysis of the language in the excerpt, and then compares the textbook language with the functional recasts provided orally by the professor in his lecture.

Example A Findings

Textbook Excerpt A. Excerpt A is a selection from the physics students' textbook that discusses the time-dilation effect:

> The time-dilation effect is symmetric. If there were a clock at rest in frame F' identical to the clock at rest in F, then the observer in F would see the clock in F' running slow, just as the observer in F' sees the clock in F running slow. Were it otherwise, the observers could use this asymmetry to decide who was moving and who was standing still, an explicit violation of the original premise that only relative motion has any meaning.

The discourse in Textbook Excerpt A includes several reasoning processes concerning both external and internal cause-proof relationship. The first is the expression of external causal relationship through the realization of positive causal-conditional linkages. The first causal relationship is contained in a clause introduced by the conjunction *if*. It is followed by two clauses functioning as the effect, "then the observer…just as the observer …" All the messages of causal conditions are within one clause which contains a semantically compact nominal group ("a clock at rest in frame F' identical to the clock at rest in F."). The postmodifier of this nominal group packs four conditions into one clause: (1) One clock is at rest; (2) This clock is in frame F'; (3) There is another identical clock at rest; (4) But the other clock stays in F.

The effect is presented in two clauses: (1) then the observer in F would see the clock in F' running slow, and (2) just as the observer in F' sees the clock in F running slow. There is also a nominal group in these two clauses, "clock in F' running slow." In this latter clause, the non-finite verb *running* is functioning as a postmodifier to replace the finite verb *runs*, which is a more congruent realization of the concept.

From the perspective of Mohan's (1986) KF, these cause/effect excerpts fall within the theoretical category of PRINCIPLES, relating closely to SEQUENCE in that the cause comes before the effect/result. The textbook takes for granted this relationship in its *if/then* statements, expecting students to picture in their mind the action sequence and understand the theory behind it. What we would hope to see in the professor's language would be a more explicit detailing of the connection to provide students with more explicit experiential learning.

Another point of interest in this textbook excerpt is the realization of negative causal-conditional relationship. The textbook presents the negative condition/alternative in a more congruent form starting with a copular verb: "were it otherwise." While the verb demonstrates a relatively straightforward second stage conditional *were*, the use of *otherwise* is highly metaphorical. It asks the reader (the learner, in this case) to "see" an opposite sequence because it is not stated directly; rather, it is *suggested* in the next sentence by only one word, *asymmetry*, leaving both condition and effect implicit and disconnected from any action.

Regarding internal and external reference in the textbook excerpt, the verb "decide," as in the clause "the observers could use this asymmetry to decide who was moving and who was standing still," shows an internally referenced causal relationship. The clause "decide who was moving and who was standing still" agnates to "determine the cause of the movement." Moreover, the understood processes (i.e., "one dilates, the other does not dilate") are represented by the noun "asymmetry." The expression "could use this asymmetry to decide who was moving and who was standing still" is agnate with the most advanced form (final stage) of causal relation, presented in Table 8.1: *Happening A is the proof/cause of happening X*. Again, the text requires the student reader to envision a sequence without an explicit action.

Finally, in Textbook Excerpt A, there are frequent nominalizations and nominal groups. In the nominal group "an explicit violation of the original premise that only relative motion has any meaning," *violation* is the nominalization of the verb *violate*, functioning as the head of the nominal group, and *motion* is the nominalization of *move*. The prepositional phrase *of the original premise* serves as a modifier that is embedded (a nominal group inside a prepositional phrase which is inside another nominal group). As prepositional phrases are already known to be difficult for learners (see Kao, 2001; Rastall, 1994), it follows that embedded prepositional phrases are even more difficult, and from the perspective of Mohan's social practice framework, it presents only part of the knowledge because it involves theory without action.

Lecture Excerpt A. The following excerpt comes from the part of the lecture related to the information in Textbook Excerpt A above.

> If you put these two clocks side by side, and you put them stationary with respect to you, they ticks the same rate. When they are in motion with respect to you, one dilate, the other one got not dilate. They tick in different rate. They go in different pace. That means you are violating the principle of relativity. Why? ... If these two clocks are stationary, they tick the same rate. And when they are in motion, they ticks a different rate. ... By watching that two clocks' rate ticking, you can tell you are in absolute motion or you are absolute stationary. Understand? That because when these two clocks ticks the same rate that means it's stationary. When they are in motion, they tick differently.

What is noticeable here are the several instances in which the instructor uses downward recasting to explain the concepts. For example, he uses an expression of internal causal relationship and realization of positive causal-conditional relationship to present the conditions in two clauses: (1) "If you put these two clock side by side," and (2) "and you put them stationary with respect to you." Compared with the nominal group used in the textbook, these spoken clauses indicate downward movement because their more congruent forms (conjunctions and verbs) are used to denote the cause/effect relationships. Furthermore, they ask learners to envision an action that they could undertake by using the second person "you" and the verb "put." Within the KF, this indicates a move from theory (PRINCIPLES) into action (SEQUENCE).

The effect under the stationary condition is expressed in a very brief way, "they ticks the same rate." However, the meaning of "the same rate" is less explicit than "running slow." So, the instructor proceeds to elaborate on the negative condition to unfold the hidden message. He does this by using the conjunction *when* and then spells out the contrast by repeating information in the form of four clauses: "… one dilate, the other one got not dilate. They tick in different rate. They go in different pace." The effect of this elaborated language is that semantic ambiguity is reduced. Also, the single, less congruent word *otherwise* is replaced by a full clause. Thus, in the lecture, both the positive and negative causal relationships are presented separately by more congruent and less grammatically metaphorical expression patterns from Halliday and Martin's (1993) framework (see Table 8.1): *If a, then X. If not a, then not X.* The use of this pattern renders both the positive and negative conditions more explicit.

When we look at the expression of internal causal relationship, we again see the instructor using downward recasting by utilizing more congruent forms than the textbook: "By watching…you can tell …" agnates to the initial stage of internal causal relation expression pattern, including transitive internal verbs. The clause "you can tell" uses a second person pronoun combined with a modal of ability ("can") to focus on the action of understanding ("telling" agnates to "understanding," both of which depict an action). Following this clause, the instructor uses another congruent form of expression by including conjunctions and internal verbs in the sentence: "That because when these two clock ticks the same rate, that means they are stationary," which agnates to *Because a happens, we know X happens*—the internal, initial stage listed in Table 8.1.

Another marker of downward recasting in the lecture is the less frequent use of nominalization or nominal groups. In the instructor's speech, processes are more frequently realized by verbs, for example, "you are violating the principle of relativity," rather than the agnate version from the textbook: "violation of the original premise." Further, the instructor replaces "A clock at rest in frame F'" from the textbook with "if you put them (clocks) stationary with respect to you" in the lecture, utilizing an initial stage conjunction ("if") and an external reference verb ("put"). By involving the students in the lecture ("you") and using action verbs, the instructor transforms theory into action.

For the first paired examples (Textbook Excerpt A and Lecture Excerpt A), a comparison of the written and oral discourse indicates the following major differences:

1. There are more conjunctions in oral representation rendering the causal-effect relationship explicit: The textbook uses only one conjunction ("if") while the lecture contains three conjunctions: "if," "because," and "when," which make the oral explanation more

congruent by providing language from both the PRINCIPLES and SEQUENCE layers of the KF.

2. There are enhanced explanations for technical terms in the lecture. For example, in the textbook, there is no explanation of the words *asymmetry* or *time-dilation*, both highly metaphorical terms. In the lecture, however, these are explained repetitively: "...the other doesn't dilate. They ticks in different rate. They go in different pace." These repetitive explanations use action verbs in both affirmative and negative ways to indicate the causal language more clearly.
3. In the textbook, the use of second or third stages of causal relation patterns are restored in the lecture to a more congruent form, namely from *happening a is the proof/cause of happening X* to *If a, then X*. This downward recast of causal relation expression patterns from the written version to oral presentation clarifies the meaning.
4. In the lecture, embedded meanings in grammatical metaphors (e.g., nominalizations) are unpacked with additional explanations or denominalization schemes, such as the representation of processes with verbs (*dilate, tick,* go) and the support of theories (PRINCIPLES, in KF terms) with actions (SEQUENCE).

Example B Findings

Textbook Excerpt B. The second pair of excerpts are related to the theory of relativity. As in the first example, the textbook will be analyzed first, followed by the lecture.

> The degree of change in a body's motion due to a given force depends on the mass of body. If any body accelerates more readily under the influence of a given force than a second body does, the first body is said to have smaller mass than the second. The mass of an object describes its inertia, or its resistance to a change in its motion. For a given force, there is an inverse relation between mass and acceleration. The mass of an object describes its inertia, or its resistance to a change in its motion.

An analysis of this excerpt reveals that grammatical metaphors abound. Nominalization permeates the passage, starting from the first sentence, where "The degree of change" has *degree* as the head of the nominal group. The word *degree* indicates an attribute of a process (adverb), which agnates to *how quickly*. Thus, the first example has an adverbial as the nominalized form.

The second occurrence of a nominal group is "change in body's motion," in which the word *change* is the name of an attribute resulting from a process (e.g., *the velocity changes*), as well as of the process itself. As a qualifier, the prepositional phrase "in body's motion," uses the nominal form of the verb "move." This nominalization transforms a process into a metaphorical participant of the process by using the possessive form *body's* to describe the noun *motion*.

Regarding internal versus external reference, Textbook Excerpt B realizes causal relation in a couple of ways. First, the finite verbal group *depends on* expresses the external causal relationship between not one but two processes, *a depends on x* (i.e., "the degree ...depends on ... mass."). So, while it is external in form, it has a complex meaning involving two agents. Second, the finite verb *describes* presents the internal causal relationship between the things, where *describe* agnates to the external verb, *determine*. These two examples make up the portion of the excerpt where the bulk of the explanation resides, thus making this section of the text particularly challenging and theory focused.

Additionally, Textbook Excerpt B features typical characteristics of written scientific language: Each clause consists of two or three elements only (e.g., nominal group + verbal group + nominal group / prepositional phrase), but the elements are highly compact, which increases the difficulty of comprehension. To illustrate, the first clause contains only three elements, "the degree + depends on + the mass." The difficulty lies in the complicated nominal group, especially the embedding in the nominal group: *degree [of [change [of [body's motion [due to [a given force]]]]]]*. The implied meaning needs to be unpacked and the intricate complexity deconstructed. In addition, embedding from a clause to a clause element is a frequent grammatical phenomenon in the textbook version. For example, the prepositional phrase "under the influence of a given force" from Textbook Excerpt B above agnates to "when a given force acts on a body." Another example is the nominal group, "an inverse relation between mass and acceleration," which agnates to "if mass is big, then acceleration is small, and if the mass is small, then acceleration is big."

Lecture Excerpt B. The excerpt below relates to the textbook excerpt discussed above, focusing on mass and velocity.

> The state of motion and final velocity of the object will be depended on some properties of these objects. We find mass of object. Massive object will be...more reluctant to change the state of motion. ... When something is massive, we'll find velocity will be less, because the more

> inertial, that means more resistance to the change of state. ... When... Vb is less or Va is great, we just use such kind of ratio of these two value to define the inertia.

In this excerpt, one obvious feature of downward recasting is the use of fewer metaphorical forms. The textbook uses the phrase/noun group, "an inverse relation between mass and acceleration," which is recast in the lecture as two separate clauses. The first is "When something is massive, we'll find velocity will be less," which is the more congruent and less grammatically metaphorical form of the noun phrase "inverse relation." Additionally, it involves the student listeners by using the plural first person "we" and using a verb to highlight a practice/action. In the lecture, the professor uses a grammatically simpler sentence, "The state of motion and final velocity of the object" as compared to "The degree of change in body's motion due to a given force" in the textbook. When contrasted with the embedded use of the nominal group, the use of paratactic (side-by-side or coordinating) conjunction is much less metaphorical and thus easier to understand. Moreover, the professor continues to involve the students by using "we" and focusing on a practice that they might complete in the form of a lab activity as well as using transitive verbs such as "find," "mean," and "use."

In these excerpts, however, there are some new strategies used to make the content easier to understand. First, the professor uses vocabulary not found in the textbook excerpt to scaffold background information. An example of this is the use of the word "properties" in the lecture to recycle information that would have been learned prior to this lesson on mass and velocity. "Properties" gives the students a concrete category under which to file the word "mass." This downward recast in effect reminds the students that they have heard about mass before. The textbook excerpt seems to assume the students know that mass is a property of physical objects. To simplify this, the professor uses "properties" first before introducing the word "mass" in his second sentence of this excerpt. He does this again in a later excerpt of the lecture (not analyzed in its entirety due to the scope of this chapter), but which demonstrates that the professor uses this word "property" as a reminder of a definition (CLASSIFICATION) that the students learned in previous class sessions. It is clear that this serves as a reminder (and thus that it is recycled background information) because of the question that ends this aside:

> We are talking about special **property** of inertia, a resistance. A **property** of resistance to the change of state of motion. But why we call this mass?...We try to define this quality, ... We need standard as a unit. Is

> right? For example, if you try to measure a length of something, you need a meter stake, or you need a ruler. All right? Every time you need such kind of things, such kind of standard, play a role as unit. **Still remember that?**

The second new strategy (not seen in the "A" excerpts) is the ordering of cause/effect information. One of the reasons hypotaxis is less congruent than parataxis is because in English, subordinate clauses in complex sentences do not have to be in temporally correct order. In other words, it is correct to say, "When water freezes, there is ice" and "There is ice when water freezes." This use of the subordinating conjunction "when" would agnate to, "First water freezes and then there is ice" in paratactic form. In the lecture, the professor restores the underlying theoretical cause/effect principles into their real-world (practical) sequential order (Slater & Gleason, 2011). This is accomplished by the presentation of the cause (the first event) in sentence initial position as opposed to presenting the effect followed by the cause (as in the textbook). This is illustrated in the examples below, where the italicized portion of the sentence is the cause (1st event) and the non-italicized part is the effect (2nd event):

> Textbook: The degree of change in a body's motion due to a given force *depends on the mass of body.* If any body accelerates more readily under the influence of a given force than a second body does, *the first body is said to have smaller mass than the second.*

> Lecture: *When something is massive,* we'll find velocity will be less, *because the more inertial,* that means more resistance to the change of state.

Presenting the real-world cause in sentence initial position highlights the temporal nature of the two events and is another way of unpacking metaphorical language into its more congruent form.

In sum, Pair B (Textbook Excerpt B and Lecture Excerpt B) demonstrates much of the same types of downward recasting as Pair A but also demonstrates two new strategies:

1. The scaffolding of background information with lexis (e.g., the addition of the word "properties"). This linguistic choice provides support for the underlying theoretical principles and recycles information that was covered in an earlier class session.

2. The reordering of causal information into its temporally correct position in the sentence with the use of the conjunction "when." Not only does the presence of the temporal conjunction enhance congruity, but also the sentence initial position of the cause and sentence-final position of the effect clarifies the sequence of events.

Example C Findings

The topic for Example C is Newton's second law of motion. Specifically, the discourse is about the reasoning of the observer's location in inertial or noninertial reference frames judged by Newton's second law of motion. As with the previous examples, the written and oral forms will be offered, but unlike the earlier examples, the current discussion will present the oral and written alternately to juxtapose closely the language usage.

> **Textbook Excerpt C.** Newton's second law: Forces, which behave as vectors, act on bodies and cause them to accelerate. For a given force, this acceleration is proportional to the mass of the body in question. … An observer who verifies that Newton's second law holds, with known or identifiable sources of forces, is said to be in an inertial frame. If a second observer moves with constant velocity relative to the first, the second observer is also in an inertial frame; if there is nonconstant relative motion, the second observer is in a noninertial frame. Those of you who have ever had the experience of sitting in a very slowly moving train leaving a station on a track adjacent to another train will recall a disorientation as to whether your own train or the other is moving.

This written excerpt contains typical features of written scientific language such as grammatical metaphor realized through nominalization (e.g., "acceleration," "motion," "disorientation"). However, there are also other features such as nouns surrounded by long attributive clauses: "An observer who verifies that Newton's second law holds, with known or identifiable sources of forces" is a case in point. This embedded language is "compressed" (as opposed to "elaborated") in form (Biber & Gray, 2010). The attributive (relative) clause "who verifies that Newton's second law holds") has an embedded complement clause ("that Newton's second law holds"). Moreover the prepositional phrase "with known or identifiable sources of forces" is exactly the kind of compressed, phrasal language that Biber and Gray (2010) found to be characteristic of academic writing. This compressed language can be juxtaposed against more elaborated forms as found in the lecture, where these long nominal groups are replaced by clauses, as demonstrated below in Lecture Excerpt C.

> **Lecture Excerpt C.** The inertial law offers a definition to discriminate between the inertial frame of reference and the noninertial one. If you find the motion of object satisfying the law of inertial, you can pretty sure that frame of reference must be inertial. If it experiences no force but it accelerate, and we can say as an observer you are sitting in a noninertial of reference frame. For example, when you are sitting in accelerating train, you find the building is accelerating backwards. But all these buildings suffer noninertial experience, or noninertial force, you cannot explain all these backwards acceleration with law of inertial. … So you can make decision that as an observer, you are sitting in the noninertial frame of reference because are sitting in accelerating train.

In the second sentence of Lecture Excerpt C, the professor's use of "If you find the motion of object satisfy the law of inertial," and "If it experiences no force" are clausal replacements (agnations) of the complicated nominal group highlighted in the excerpt from the textbook. In clauses, the language is more congruent because logical relationship and meaning are revealed in much clearer ways due to the elaboration and use of transitive verbs (e.g., "find," used twice).

Other differences between textbook and lecture discourse include the downward recast of a prepositional phrase in the textbook, "with known or identifiable sources of forces" to a full clause "If it experiences no force" in the oral presentation. These distinctions in oral and written language are examples of compressed (written) and elaborated (oral) language as described by Biber and Gray (2010):

> Conversation is more structurally elaborated than academic writing. In contrast, written academic discourse is actually much more "compressed" than elaborated. In particular, subordinate clauses—especially finite dependent clauses—are much more common in conversation than in academic writing. In contrast, phrasal (non-clausal) modifiers embedded in noun phrases are the major type of structural complexity found in academic writing. (p. 3)

Also evident in the comparison of excerpts in Example C is the difference in use of discourse-level features, such as the use of a topic sentence (see Lecture Excerpt C, sentence 1). This first sentence reveals the basis of reasoning, namely, the inertial law. In the textbook, there is no such introduction to the reasoning. A second discourse-level feature is the use of an example from everyday experience, which occurs within a temporal subordinate clause ("when you are sitting in accelerating train") provided by the professor in his lecture. The use of this type of example makes the abstract theoretical reasoning more vivid and specific by focusing on an action, thus pairing knowledge (explicit in the textbook excerpt) and practice (highly noticeable in the lecture excerpt). Through this anecdote, the teacher reminds students of their own relevant experiences that may help them interpret the principles they were studying. By encouraging students to imagine themselves in the familiar situation of sitting on a slow-moving train and then reminding them of what they probably perceived in that context, the professor can explicitly point out the factors inherent in that setting that link their common perceptions to the physics principles.

In the textbook, everyday examples are also offered, but they are presented in a compressed, scientific style despite the use of the personal pronoun:

> Those of you who have ever had the experience of sitting in a very slowly moving train leaving a station on a track adjacent to another train will recall a disorientation as to whether your own train or the other is moving.

This example from the textbook offers no conjunction, has long nominal groups, and includes complex nominalizations, such as "the experience of sitting" and "a disorientation as to whether your own train or the other is moving."

This final illustration (Example C) reveals two additional downward recast strategies:

1. Replacing long nominal groups with clauses, shifting from clausal element to full clauses. This shift allows for the explicit decompression of the clausal elements, rendering the language much more congruent.
2. The use of discoursal strategies such as a topic sentence and the differentiation between the introduction and exemplification of concepts. Thus, the explanations and examples provided in the textbook are taught via the use of language resources focused around sequential actions in the professor's lecture.

Summary of Results

Through the analysis of the three excerpts from the textbook and the corresponding elements within the lecture, it is clear that various downward recasting strategies take place. These strategies align not only with Mohan's (1986) KF but also with previous work on downward recasts (Mohan & Beckett, 2003), the developmental path of causal language (Halliday & Martin, 1993; Slater & Gleason, 2011), and corpus findings about linguistic complexity (Biber & Gray, 2010; Biber, Gray, & Poonpon, 2011) and include the following:

1. Lexical-focused recasts
   a. Enhanced use of conjunctions
   b. Increased explanations of technical language via repetition
   c. Scaffolding background information by providing additional and/or recycled terminology
2. Grammatical-focused recasts (i.e., restoration to more congruent forms)
   a. Unpacking of metaphorical meaning through denominalization schemes
   b. Use of internal relations (e.g., personal pronouns combined with verbs related to perception and experience)
   c. Replacement of nominal groups/phrases with clausal structures
   d. Employment of simple, transitive verbs such as "find" to clarify the constituents
3. Discourse-focused recasts
   a. Reordering information so that real-time sequences are favored (PRINCIPLES to SEQUENCE)
   b. Use of discourse structures such as topic sentences
   c. Use of everyday/common experiences and perceptions as a link to physics principles

While the textbook's language could mostly be classified as KF PRINCIPLES, which are theoretical, the language from the lecture is more activity/action focused. The professor's lecture provides the sequencing actions for the cause/effect principles presented in the textbook. The lecture creates a "sequential order (practice) informed by...understandings (theory) of the principles behind the order" (Slater & Gleason, 2011, p. 9).

Discussion

The above analysis reveals two primary findings with regard to the research questions. The first research question asked what KSs an EFL physics instructor uses to teach causal physics concepts. From the lecture, we can see that the instructor used more congruent forms of language, at times recasting PRINCIPLES as SEQUENCE. This is realized by certain grammatical features such as conjunctions, temporal dependent (hypotactic) clauses, and transitive verbs with internal references. The purpose of using such language is to render the theoretical causal relationships more explicit and more action focused. The functional downward recast schemes, such as replacing nominal groups with verbs or adjectives, denominalizing, and/or decoding messages embedded in grammatical metaphor by interpreting them from other perspectives, all contribute to making causal explanations in written scientific language more accessible to the EFL students. With regard to the second research question, how the instructor's oral causal language differs from the textbook language (i.e., how the instructor mitigates the challenge of highly condensed textbook language), it is clear that compared with textbook discourse, the oral presentation is more congruent and less grammatically metaphorical, employing SEQUENCE to explain the theoretical knowledge from the textbook. The findings demonstrate that the Chinese physics instructor used a range of lexicogrammar such as causal conjunctions, externally referenced transitive verbs, full clauses (as opposed to phrases with heavy embedding), and denominalizations to assemble causal explanations. It appears that he makes use of downward functional recasts to address the meaning and wording relationships in causal explanations. In such recasts, there are some lexical changes; however, what varies more commonly are the grammatical categories. In grammatical metaphor, the shift is not from one lexical item to another but from one grammatical category to another. Grammatical metaphor involves a "remapping" of the grammar underlying the semantics (Halliday & Matthiessen, 2004). Language presented in the metaphorical mode can deny access to the meaning potential that is associated with the congruent mode: there is a loss of ideational meaning. Thus, the metaphorical mode increases the difficulties of understanding because it separates theoretical knowledge from practical application of that knowledge.

From the study above, we propose the following implication: It is possible to remap scientific textbook language (Halliday, 1998, p. 191). The way to do this is to clarify the grammatical metaphor frequently presented in written scientific textbook by reversing the process of mapping language into metaphorical form—namely, return metaphorical language into its underlying

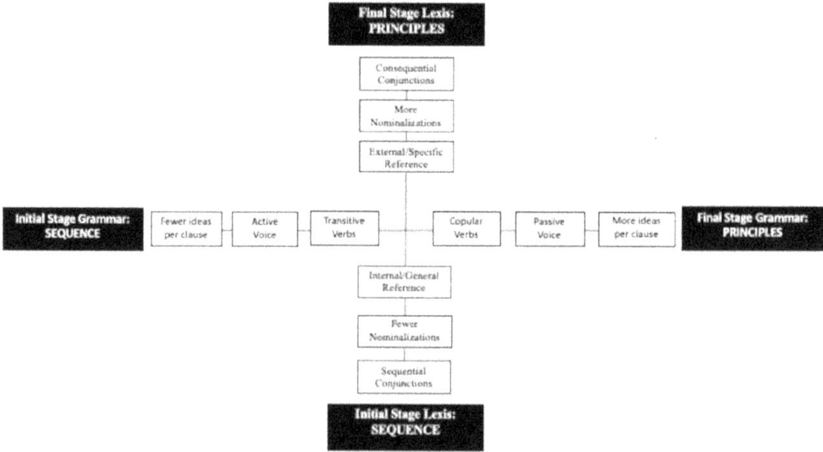

Figure 8.1 A proposed topology of linguistic agnation

congruent (nonmetaphorical) structures such as restoring a nominal group into a clause. To do this, we can envision a topology of agnation for situating linguistic forms. Figure 8.1 displays a graphic alternative for understanding the complexity of such linguistic evolution.

The Linguistic Agnation Topology (LAT) combines the work of both Feez and Joyce (1998) and Slater and Mohan (2010a). Feez and Joyce (1998) examine curriculum planning and show the movement from hands-on (speaking/listening focused) to minds-on (writing/reading focused). Slater and Mohan (2010a) discuss the developmental path of cause. Their model, which follows Halliday's (1998) notion of "drift" and Veel's (1997) work showing how the shift from congruent to metaphorical, can be applied to curriculum development. Both studies suggest that a semantic move happens with both lexical and grammatical resources. This move goes from external to internal cause and from relators (conjunctions) to metaphorical forms such as circumstances, processes, qualities, and entities.

Thus, the LAT provides a method for visualizing the complex linguistic changes (agnations) that language must go through to move from metaphorical to congruent. To demonstrate how this works, Figure 8.2 maps excerpts from the physics textbook and lecture onto the topology, showing the more complex and metaphorical textbook language in the upper right quadrant while the downward recasted language from the lecture appears in the bottom left.

Other paradigms of linguistic analysis have proposed such evolutionary processes for describing language complexity. Biber and Gray (2010) use

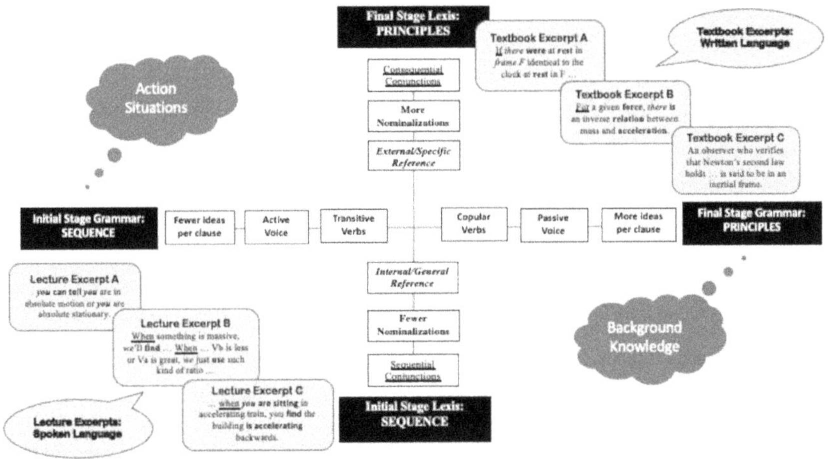

Figure 8.2 Textbook and lecture excerpts mapped onto the proposed topology

the phrase "structurally elaborated" to explain how academic writing differs from conversation, especially as it relates to clausal subordination. In Biber, Gray, and Poonpon (2011), the authors propose a sequence of developmental stages of student writing. More recently, Parkinson and Musgrave (2014) have shown that noun modification varies with proficiency level (i.e., more proficient students use more premodifiers and prepositional phrase while less proficient students utilize attributive adjectives). This finding aligns the more proficient writers with published academic writing.

This kind of specific characterization of linguistic resources could be helpful in a number of language- and/or content-teaching settings. If we know that students struggle with the language of textbooks, and we know that there is a way to simplify and recast that language, then it follows that learning the recasting strategies could be useful to a number of stakeholders. The next section will examine implications for practitioners.

Implications

Implications for Practitioners

Researchers agree that content-based language learning (CBLL) is most effective when it provides both meaningful communication about content and intentional language development (e.g., Pica, 2000). Teaching science in

English in ESL or EFL contexts is a means to both ends, the content learning and the language development. However, it can be a great challenge to both instructors and students. In teaching science to ESL students, there tends to be a common problem of the science textbook in English being difficult to understand. The difficulty lies in nominalized forms, technical terms, embedded nominal groups, grammatical metaphor at the phrasal level, and the typical scientific expression pattern of using externally referenced causal language to show the internal causal relation between two things or to demonstrate implicit causal relationships. The grammatical features of scientific discourse represented by these examples are far from rare and well documented in the literature (e.g., Maton & Muller, 2007; O'Halloran, 2007). Indeed, as Doran (2018) notes, physics has a reputation of being "the most 'sciencey' of the natural sciences" (p. 1). Furthermore, the discourse of physics, as it is presented in textbooks, is not only grammatically challenging, but also includes knowledge resources such as mathematics (e.g., equations) and images (e.g., graphs and other visual representations). These specialized disciplinary resources can pose challenges for both native and non-native speaking students alike. Doran also points out that before any multimodal set of resources can be examined, there is the need for "a common method for understanding them" (p. 4). The research traditions of SFL and others that focus on social semiotics have long acknowledged the need for ways to use linguistic resources for teaching, learning, and assessing knowledge in the disciplines. In the case of language resources, strategies such as recasting and the use of models such as the LAT can mitigate the difficulties of scientific language, thus providing more access to students, especially those who are studying unfamiliar language and content. Moreover, Mohans's Knowledge Framework can offer a useful heuristic for teaching students the types of language resources that help construct the thinking skills that are most characteristic of science. The LAT's visual representation of the linguistic features that differentiate the SEQUENCE and PRINCIPLES knowledge structures can provide a resource to help practitioners understand both how students learn about causal language and what language resources can be used to support them.

In the world of English for Specific Purposes (ESP), a model such as the LAT, in tandem with the Knowledge Framework, could provide a method for showing how language constructs content. It could also prove useful for teacher training, especially for International Teaching Assistants (ITAs) who often struggle to navigate the American academic culture (Subtirelu, 2018). Indeed, the intersection of language and content may be more obvious to an ITA than any other instructor in higher education. An examination of a course syllabus for ITAs at a large midwestern university revealed several objectives of the course which could likely be achieved more completely through the use of a model such as the LAT and the Knowledge Framework. Some examples of these objectives include but are not limited to the following:

- Developing the knowledge of academic English vocabulary (we might add grammar to this, based on the results of this study and others situated within SFL frameworks);
- Acquiring strategies for effective disciplinary communication (a well-rounded approach would include strategies based in both content and linguistic knowledge development which encompasses developing an understanding of the lexicogrammatical resources associated with both the SEQUENCE and PRINCIPLES knowledge structures);
- Strengthen effective teaching skills (recasting has long been touted as an effective instructional technique—perhaps solidifying this technique in a model such as the LAT could improve the performances of ITAs).

Beyond providing a specific strategy for teacher training and content-based instruction, the LAT model could also be tested and validated as an evaluation tool both for ITAs and for non-native speaking students of physics. The ability to use a flexible array of linguistic resources and knowledge structures to explain content-based principles can demonstrate a more thorough understanding of discipline-specific knowledge and pedagogy.

Implications for Further Research

Our study needs to be furthered on the following points. First, the recast of scientific text is a reversion to a certain stage of language use. In the case of causal discourse, for example, there are three stages of development of causal expressions. Which stages we should go back to depends on the students' level. Further research might attempt to match students' language proficiency and the degree of downward recast. Second, the effectiveness of the scientific text recast needs to be tested. For example, a comparative study of students' understanding of textbook content before lecture and after lecture could reveal to what degree the recast helps students understand the scientific discourse. Thirdly, because this study is confined to the Chinese traditional science education style, in a certain sense, the science class is more teacher-centered than in many other cultures. The instructor's one-way delivery of knowledge is dominant in science lectures within the Chinese education system. Therefore, researchers should consider gathering more data from contexts in which teachers and students interact. These data could be valuable to test the effectiveness of the recast strategies described in this research.

Our participants, as freshmen with low English proficiency, also indicate a limitation of the current study because of the extensive constraints on their oral communication. As a result, their class interaction is negatively affected by their English listening and speaking abilities. However, in a different context, where students' command of English may be at a higher level, further research is suggested to test the effectiveness of, for example, recasts by observing students' responses or utterances in class discussion and interaction. More quantitative research can be done in this way.

Finally, PowerPoint slides are a widely used media in science class presentations. PowerPoint slides are another form of written science, serving as a bridge between textbooks and oral presentations. In some contexts, especially for novice students or ESL/EFL science students whose English listening is relatively less developed, students might greatly depend on slides as a written resource. Two forms of recast, written form (language from slides), and oral form (recorded oral presentations/lectures) can be compared to investigate similarities and differences. Furthermore, the number and degree of changes from the original textbook version into these two forms of recasting language modes can be analyzed to determine what might be best practices within various academic circumstances. Multimodal analyses would be an integral extension to this research, following the work of Danielsson (2016). (See also Chapter 7 in this volume.)

Conclusions

This research analyzed the recasting of science textbook information in physics lectures and presented the following schemes employed by the instructor: (1) replacing or explaining the technical terms by using more practice-focused language, (2) adding background information to scaffold theoretical knowledge with actions, (3) paraphrasing from a different perspective thus moving from external to internal causal language, (4) bringing out the meaning of grammatical metaphor by nonmetaphorical expression mode, (5) denominalizing, namely, returning to the use of verbs to realize process or property, rather than the use of nominal groups or noun, and (6) converting the scientific expression pattern from the advanced stage to the original stage through the use of conjunctions and sentences with fewer ideas per clause. These categories of recasts summarized in our research can provide reference for science teaching instructors in EFL/ESL contexts to enhance the accessibility of science textbooks for EFL/ESL students. More research may uncover more categories of recasts applied by science instructors who use textbooks published in English in non-English speaking countries. Moreover, this research has the potential to test the effectiveness of recasts using SFL-based theories, such as Mohan's Knowledge Framework.

References

Altbach, P.G., and Knight, J. (2007). The internationalization of higher education: Motivations and realities. *Journal of Studies in International Education, 11*(3/4), 290–305.

Biber, D., & Gray, B. (2010). Challenging stereotypes about academic writing: Complexity, elaboration, explicitness. *Journal of English for Academic Purposes, 9*(1), 2–20.

Biber, D., Gray, B., & Poonpon, K. (2011). Should we use characteristics of conversation to measure grammatical complexity in L2 writing development? *TESOL Quarterly, 45*(1), 5–35.

Bloor, T., & Bloor, M. (2004). *The functional analysis of English* (2nd ed.). Hodder Education.

Danielsson, K. (2016). Modes and meaning in the classroom—the role of different semiotic resources to convey meaning in science classrooms. *Language and Education, 35*, 88–99.

Dearden J. (2018). The Changing Roles of EMI Academics and English Language Specialists. In: Kırkgöz Y., Dikilitaş K. (Eds.), *Key Issues in English for Specific Purposes in Higher Education* (pp. 323–338). English Language Education, vol. 11. Springer. DOI:10.1007/978-3-319-70214-8_18

Doran, Y.J., (2018). *The discourse of physics: Building knowledge through language, mathematics and image*. Routledge.

Egi, T. (2007). Interpreting recasts as linguistic evident: The roles of linguistic target, length, and degree of change. *Studies in Second Language Acquisition, 29*, 511–537.

Feez, S., & Joyce, H.D.S. (1998). *Text-based syllabus design*. National Centre for English Language Teaching and Research, Macquarie University.

Fishbane, P.M., Gasiorowicz, S.G., & Thornton, S.T. (1993). *Physics for scientists and engineers*. Prentice Hall.

Gleason, H.A. (1965). *Linguistics and English grammar*. Holt, Rinehart & Winston.

Halliday, M.A.K. (1977). Text as semantic choice in social contexts. In T.A. van Dijk and J. Petofi (Eds.), *Grammars and Descriptions* (pp. 176–225). de Gruyter.

Halliday, M.A.K. (1998). Things and relations: Regrammaticising experience as technical knowledge. In J.R. Martin & R. Veel (Eds.), *Reading science: Critical and functional perspectives on discourses of science* (pp. 185–235). Routledge.

Halliday, M.A.K. (2002). *On grammar* (Vol. 1). Bloomsbury Publishing.

Halliday, M.A.K., & Hasan, R. (1985). *Language, context and text.* Deakin University Press.

Halliday, M.A.K., & Martin, J.R. (1993). *Writing science: Literacy and discursive power.* University of Pittsburgh Press.

Halliday, M.A.K., & Matthiessen, C. (2004). *An introduction to functional grammar* (3rd ed.). Hodder Arnold Publication.

Kao, R.R. (2001). Where have the prepositions gone? A study of English prepositional verbs and input enhancement in instructed SLA. *IRAL, 39*(3), 195–216.

Lakoff, G., & Johnson, M. (1999). *Philosophy in the Flesh* (Vol. 4). Basic Books.

Leach, J., & Scott, P. (2000). Children's thinking, learning, teaching, and constructivism. In M. Monk & J. Osborne (Eds.), *Good practice in science teaching: What research has to say* (pp. 41–56). Open University Press.

Loewen, S., & Philp, J. (2006). Recasts in the adult English L2 classroom: Characteristics, explicitness, and effectiveness. *The Modern Language Journal, 90*(4), 536–556.

Ma, H., & Slater, T. (2015). Using the developmental path of cause to bridge the gap between AWE scores and writing teachers' evaluations. Special issue of *Writing and Pedagogy, 7*(2/3), 395–422.

Ma, H., & Slater, T. (2016). Connecting *Criterion* scores and classroom grading contexts: A systemic functional linguistic model for teaching and assessing causal language. *CALICO, 33* (1), 1–18.

Maton, K., & Muller, J. (2007). A sociology for the transmission of knowledges. In F. Christie and J.R. Martin (Eds.). *Language, knowledge and pedagogy: Functional linguistic and sociological perspectives.* Continuum, pp. 14–33.

Matthiessen, C., Teruya, K., and Lam, M. (2010). *Key terms in systemic functional linguistics.* Bloomsbury.

Mohan, B. (1986). *Language and content.* Addison Wesley.

Mohan, B. (1989). Knowledge structures and academic discourse. *Word, 40*(1–2), 99–115.

Mohan, B. (2007). Knowledge structures in social practices. In J. Cummins & C. Davison (Eds.), *International handbook of English language teaching, Vol. 15* (pp. 303–315). Springer.

Mohan, B., & Beckett, G.H. (2003). A functional approach to research on content-based language learning: Recasts in causal explanations. *The Modern Language Journal, 87*(3), 421–432.

Mohan, B., & Slater, T. (2005). A functional perspective on the critical "theory/practice" relation in teaching language and science. *Linguistics and Education, 16* (2), 151–172.

Mohan, B., & Slater, T. (2006). Examining the theory/practice relation in a high school science register: A functional linguistic perspective. *Journal of English for Academic Purposes, 5*(4), 302–316.

O'Halloran, K. (2007). Mathematical and scientific forms of knowledge: A systemic functional multimodal grammatical approach. In F. Christie and J.R. Martin (Eds.). *Language, knowledge and pedagogy: Functional linguistic and sociological perspectives* (pp. 205–236). Bloomsbury Publishing.

Parkinson, J., & Musgrave, J. (2014). Development of noun phrase complexity in the writing of English for Academic Purposes students. *Journal of English for Academic Purposes, 14*, 48–59.

Pica, T. (2000). Tradition and transition in English teaching methodology. *System, 28*, 1–18.

Qiang, Z. (2003). Internationalization of higher education: Towards a conceptual framework. *Policy Futures in Education, 1*(2), 248–270.

Rastall, P. (1994). The prepositional flux. *International Review of Applied Linguistics in Language Teaching, 32*, 229–231.

Slater, T.J.A. (2004). *The discourse of causal explanations in school science.* Doctoral dissertation, University of British Columbia.

Slater, T., & Gleason, J. (2011). Integrating language and content: The Knowledge Framework. In J. Morrison (Ed.), *Conference proceedings of MidTESOL: Gateway to global citizenship* (pp. 5–20). University of Saint Louis. Retrieved from http://www.midtesol.org/docs/MIDTESOLProceedings_2011.pdf.

Slater, T., & Mohan, B. (2010a). Towards systematic and sustained formative assessment of causal explanations in oral interactions. In A. Paran & L. Sercu (Eds.), *Testing the untestable in language education* (pp. 259–272). Bristol, UK: Multilingual Matters.

Slater, T., & Mohan, B. (2010b). Cooperation between science teachers and ESL teachers: A register perspective. *Theory into Practice, 49*(2), 91–98.

Subtirelu, N.C. (2018). Linguistic diversity and the politics of international inclusion: Challenges in integrating International Teaching Assistants at a university in the United States. In J.J. Crandall and K.M. Bailey (Eds.) *Global perspectives on language education policies* (pp. 119–129). Routledge.

Thompson, G. (2004). *Introducing functional grammar* (2nd ed.). Hodder Education.

Unsworth, L. (1999). Developing critical understanding of the specialized language of school science and history texts: A functional grammatical perspective. *Journal of Adolescent and Adult Literacy, 42*(7), 508–521.

Veel, R, (1997). Learning how to mean—scientifically speaking: Apprenticeship into scientific discourse in the secondary school. In F. Christie & J.R. Martin (Eds.), *Genre and institutions: Social processes in the workplace and school* (pp. 161–195). Continuum.

About the Authors

Kimberly Becker has a Ph.D. in Applied Linguistics and Technology from Iowa State University (ISU), where she was a lecturer in the English

Department. Currently Kim is the Managing Director of the Academic Insight Lab. Her research interests include disciplinary writing, corpus linguistics, CALL, and SFL.

Xiaoping Liang is a Professor Emerita in the Department of Linguistics at California State University, Long Beach. Her research interests include second language classroom discourse and socialization, academic discourse development in the first and second languages, bilingual classroom code-switching, and language attitudes and cultural identities.

9 The Role of Functional Recasts in EFL Undergraduate Students' Learning of Intercultural Communication

Masaki Kobayashi and Emi Kobayashi

Abstract

This chapter focuses on the role of functional recasts (FRs) in Japanese undergraduate students' linguistic construction of the knowledge structure of PRINCIPLES in their content-based EFL course in intercultural communication. While previous research has illustrated how FRs could be used to upgrade students' discourse, little is known about how students respond to such teacher assistance. Given that the goal of scaffolding is to help students perform tasks more independently, it follows that more attention should be paid to students' uptake of FRs.

This chapter reports on an action research project that involved two classes of EFL students who received FRs from their instructor. FRs in Class A took the form of oral feedback on student presentations while FRs in Class B were provided as written comments on drafts of student papers. In each case, all the instances were identified where the instructor functionally recast the presenter's or writer's utterances.

The analysis focuses on students successfully constructing causal knowledge structures by incorporating FRs from their instructor. However, the analysis revealed that only a few students in Class A acted upon the FRs in their write-ups while almost all the students in Class B incorporated their instructor's reformulations of their utterances into their writings. This difference is discussed with respect to time pressure involved in oral presentations, the appropriateness of the levels of FRs, and the use of key visuals. The pedagogical implications revolve around teacher roles: (1) teachers' scaffolding of students' use of FRs in subsequent tasks and (2) teachers' preparedness to respond to students' contributions.

Keywords: functional recast; causal knowledge structures; scaffolding; key visuals

In Japan, especially since the Ministry of Education, Culture, Sports, Science, and Technology (MEXT) launched an initiative in 2012 to promote the globalization in higher education, there has been a growing interest in English-medium instruction (EMI) (Rose & McKinley, 2017) as well as content-based instruction (CBI) and content and language integrated learning (CLIL) (Harada, 2017). Whichever approach is used, students need to cope with the language and content demands of their curriculum and teachers need to assist them in this process. However, only a few studies have examined how Japanese EFL students learn academic language and content simultaneously in their university courses. The present study therefore examines how undergraduate students used their instructor's functional recasts to construct knowledge structures linguistically in their content-based EFL course.

Previous Studies

Previous studies have demonstrated important contributions that interlocutors make in jointly constructing knowledge structures through oral discourse (Mohan, 1998; Mohan, Slater, Beckett, & Tong, 2015). For example, Mohan and Beckett (2003), drawing upon Halliday's theory of grammatical metaphor, addressed the notion of functional recasts (FR). Their analysis illustrated how a teacher recast her students' utterances during their presentations to model academically appropriate language. This type of recast contrasts with the type of recasts discussed in focus-on-form instruction in that the former aims to socialize students into the academic knowledge and discourse of the subject matter that they are expected to learn whereas the latter aims to help students correct their errors and to improve their grammatical accuracy. In their discussion of Mohan and Beckett's notion of FR, Linares, Morton, and Whittaker (2012) provided the following example identified in a CLIL history class for grade 8 students:

S1: Eh, yes because there was a lot of people in the countryside working and they have no place for everybody so they went to the cities and they went there.

T: ... so that is the, em, the **reason** of the **rebirth** of cities.

(adapted from Linares et al., 2012, p. 209, bold added)

Here, the student used two conjunctions *(because, so)* followed by two action verbs *(working, went)* to express a cause-and-effect relationship. The teacher then rephrased the same content in a more concise and metaphorical fashion. As Linares et al. put it, "the non-congruent and compact way in which the teacher expresses the content contrasts with the language used by the student" (pp. 209–210). These types of studies provide important insights into how teachers could model academic language in a meaningful context. In fact, as Mohan and Luo (2005) suggested, FRs can be considered a form of what is referred to as scaffolding by Vygotskian scholars (see, for example, Gibbons, 2015; van Lier, 1996; Walqui & van Lier, 2010; Wells, 1999), and thus a detailed analysis of their discourse features becomes vital to deepen our understanding of how scaffolding unfolds in teacher-student interactions.

However, only a little is known about how students respond to FRs within the same interaction or subsequently in writing. This is deemed to be an important topic for investigation given that researchers must provide "evidence of a learner's successfully completing the task with the teacher's help and evidence of the learner's having achieved a greater level of independent competence as a result of the experience" (Gibbons, 2003, p. 249). Of particular relevance here is Kobayashi and Kobayashi's (2018) study, which examined Japanese students' learning through repeated engagement in a poster presentation task in an undergraduate EFL course. The instructor reformulated a student presenter's utterances into more explicitly causal language in her second performance, introducing a nominalized phrase "global warming"; however, the analysis of their third performance showed that there was no evidence of uptake. A post-task interview revealed that although aware of the teacher question, she did not incorporate it into the subsequent performance because she thought that it would increase the chance of making grammatical errors and not being able to speak fluently if she had done so.

While the interaction contains what Mohan and Beckett (2003) called FR, a more explicit attempt to encourage use of academic language was made by teachers in Gibbon's (2003, 2006) study with young ESL students learning about magnetism in a science class. After doing hands-on group activities involving the manipulation of magnets, students were given opportunities to report their observations to the rest of the class. In this activity, the teacher helped students use a scientific register to talk about what they had found about magnets by explicitly prompting them to incorporate subject-specific terms (e.g., *attract*, *repel*). Students then wrote their observations in their journals. Importantly, the analysis of students' journal entries provided evidence of uptake from the teacher-guided reporting sessions. This finding seems to suggest that it was students' sustained engagement with the same content supported by their teacher that made this uptake possible.

In contrast to the above-cited studies, which focused on the upgrading function of FRs, other studies focused on the downgrading function. Building on Mohan and Beckett's (2003) work, Liu and Liang (2012) defined FR as "transformation between two expression modes namely, metaphorical mode and congruent mode" (p. 51). They compared the discourse of physics lectures given at a university in China and the discourse of the textbook on which they were based. Their quantitative analysis focusing on causal relations showed that the latter was more grammatically metaphorical than the former. Teachers in their study used a variety of strategies, such as de-nominalization and additional explanation, to present the highly academic content of the physics textbook in their lectures (see also Chapter 8, this volume). In the above-mentioned study by Kobayashi and Kobayashi (2018) on task repetition, two Japanese EFL students doing a group presentation made their discourse more audience friendly over three trials. In the question-and-answer session after their second trial, their teacher asked them to explain what they had said about heat island phenomenon, which led to the discussion of two other nominalized phrases (*concentrated development*, *massive energy consumption*) used in the definition of phenomenon. Seeing the presenters' struggle, the teacher helped them unpack the nominalized phrases and better understand the content. After this exchange, the students engaged in backstage talk which allowed them to confirm the meaning of the nominalized phrases in Japanese and to jointly construct a more audience friendly explanation in English. The analysis revealed how the presenters made use of the FR made by the instructor, thus providing evidence of their uptake. Given that "[p]rogress in academic discourse can be demonstrated through improvement in comprehension or improvement through production" (Mohan et al., 2015, p. 174), the ability to downgrade lexically dense texts should be evidence of such progress.

The present chapter aims to extend this body of literature by examining how EFL students respond to FRs made by their teacher on their oral and written L2 production. How do Japanese undergraduate students, enrolled in a content-based reading course, learn the principles of intercultural communication? How do they respond to FRs made by their teacher orally and in writing? These are the research questions that guided the present inquiry.

This chapter reports the findings of an action research project that consisted of two studies. In each of these studies, the first author used FRs to help his undergraduate students construct an explicitly causal line of meaning. However, the studies differed in that Study 1 took place in Class A and focused on

FRs that the students received on their spoken utterances during their oral presentations while Study 2 took place in Class B and focused on FRs that the students received on drafts of their term papers. Thus, these classes serve as contrasting cases to explore the role of FRs in students' learning of academic language and content.

Research Methodology

Participants and Context

The present project was carried out in an upper-division content-based reading course on intercultural communication offered at a private university in Japan. Participants included two classes of Japanese undergraduate students (37 in total) majoring in English. Seventeen students were labeled as being in Class A while 20 students were in Class B. All the students in each class were informed of the study's purpose and procedures and signed a form to indicate their consent. To reduce any possible risk of coercion on the part of the instructor as a researcher, we obtained a final consent from the students *after* their course grades were submitted. Their course instructor had roughly 20 years of teaching experience in Japan and had employed FRs as an instructional strategy in his previous courses. The focal course was taught in both English and Japanese, thus being a partial EMI. To register for the course, a student must have scored at least 480 on TOEFL ITP. Each class met once a week for 90 minutes over a 15-week period.

Data Collection

The larger project of which this is part included the following data: (1) audio- and video-recordings of classroom activities, (2) students' written products, including final papers and drafts, weekly written reflections, PowerPoint slides, and peer feedback, (3) email interviews with students, and (4) stimulated recall interviews with the instructor. The audio-recordings included not just students' presentations and teacher-fronted activities, but also small group interactions among students. However, we drew only on the former for the purpose of this chapter. Moreover, in order to reduce any possible risk of coercion on the part of the instructor as a researcher, we obtained a final consent from the students after their course grades were submitted.

Data Analysis

We transcribed all the video-recordings of eight student presentations given in Class A, using an adapted version of the conventions outlined by Duff (2002; see Appendix A). To examine how students draw connections between theoretical knowledge and particular experience, we conducted a social practice theory analysis (Mohan, 2007). Then, following Slater (2004), we transformed our data (i.e., transcripts of students' presentations and drafts of their term papers) into multi-column charts. While the chart for the oral data has four columns including the one named "Other," the chart for the written data has only two reflection columns (specific reflection and general reflection). The "Other" column is about what the presenter is doing (e.g., interacting with the audience, managing discourse) whereas the two reflection columns are the students' words (Kobayashi, 2006).

Speaker	Specific Reflection	General Reflection	Other

Instructor comments, both oral and written, were analyzed both deductively and inductively. The deductive analysis entailed identifying all instances of FRs in students' presentations and in the instructor's written feedback on students' essays, which were traced to subsequent write-ups (Class A) or drafts (Class B). In contrast, the inductive analysis involved constant comparison (Lincoln & Guba, 1985), which generated other categories, such as formal recasts, correction clues, specific questions, general questions, and suggested references. Also, comparisons of students' transcribed presentations and write-ups as well as comparisons of multiple drafts were conducted to identify changes that resulted from instructor feedback, especially FRs.

Findings

The findings of this project are presented below chronologically class by class. Before presenting the findings of each study, important background information about the focal assignment will be provided.

Study 1

Class A is a case in which FRs are made orally to upgrade presenters' utterances. Students worked together to give 20-minute oral presentations (including five minutes for the question-and-answer session), which was an integral part of a group project on non-verbal communication. After forming pairs or groups of three, the students first read the fifth chapter of Jackson (2014)—a chapter on the topic of non-verbal communication—and each pair/group chose a topic of interest. Students were expected not only to demonstrate their knowledge of non-verbal communication, but also to provide appropriate examples. One major requirement was for students to give a talk in English which answer these questions:

- Which type of non-verbal communication did you choose as your focus? Can you explain what it is and why you chose it?
- What are some of the key functions of the particular type of non-verbal communication that you chose? Give examples.
- What expectations do you have about this form of non-verbal communication? What happens if these expectations are violated? Discuss relevant experiences.

Thus, students were expected to construct the knowledge structures of CLASSIFICATION and PRINCIPLES. As such, the use of key visuals or "graphic representations of text/knowledge structures" (Early & Tang, 1991, p. 36) was strongly encouraged. In fact, the instructor introduced classification trees and cause-effects tables as tools to visually present academic content and to help students talk about it.

The audience for the students might not necessarily be familiar with the content of the material on which other groups' presentations were based although they were expected to have browsed through the chapter to decide their topic. Importantly, the students were required to write up their presentations within two weeks after their in-class performance. They were explicitly encouraged to see their presentations as opportunities to receive feedback from their audience and thus to include in this write-up not only what they talked about in their presentations, but also their responses to audience questions and comments—both oral and written.

Teacher Assistance for the Student Presentation

In the following two excerpts, the instructor is explaining two definitions of sociolinguistic competence (Texts 1 & 2) and as such, they concern the knowledge structure of CLASSIFICATION. In Excerpt 1.1, the instructor simplifies several nominalized phrases used in van Ek's (1986) definition by recasting them in more congruent form.

> Text 1:
> Sociolinguistic competence:
> The awareness of ways in which the choice of language forms…is determined by such conditions as setting, relationship between communication partners, communicative intention, etc. (van Ek, 1986, p. 41)
>
> Excerpt 1.1:
>
> Inst: so um—what this means is that sociolinguistic competence refers to:—whether you are aware how—people use language depending on—when and where you are, who you are talking to, what you want to do with language, or why you are saying what you're saying, and et cetera et cetera. for example—if you need to borrow one- ten yen from a good friend of yours, how would you ask? talk with your neighbors. and what about when you need to borrow ten yen from a total stranger.

The instructor's goal was thus to model the downgrading function of a functional recast as a strategy that student presenters could use not only to help their audience's understandings of densely packed academic texts, but also to demonstrate their own understandings.

Asked about this particular instance at the stimulated recall interview, the instructor said,

> I wanted to model how to make texts more accessible to audience members who read them for the first time. I've seen many students just read verbatim what's written in their textbooks and articles. In such presentations, I'm not sure how much their classmates can understand or how much the presenters themselves know the material. (originally in Japanese)

Another important feature of Excerpt 1.1 is exemplification. The instructor asked two hypothetical questions to illustrate the point that interlocutors are one important factor that influence our linguistic choices. Students did role plays first in small groups and then in a teacher-led whole-class session to share their ideas.

Excerpt 1.2 took place approximately four minutes after Excerpt 1.1. The instructor is now talking about another definition of sociolinguistic competence, which is cited in Jackson (2014).

Text 2:
Sociolinguistic competence: the ability to give to the language produced by an interlocutor—whether native speaker or not—meanings which are taken for granted by the interlocutor or which are negotiated and made explicit with the interlocutor. (Byram, 1997, p. 48)

Excerpt 1.2

1 Inst: so you'd all speak differently, depending on who your- **interlocutor is.**
do you remember this word? ((showing Quote 2)) **interlocutor**
2 (2.1)
3 ((most students nod))
4 S1 uh **person - you're communicating**
5 Inst: ye:s! a person you're communicating with is your interlocutor. great! thank you S1! so we decide how to express our meaning depending o:n—who our **interlocutor** is don't we.

In line 1, the instructor recaps what the students had said to answer his hypothetical questions posed in Excerpt 1.1. Notice his use of the pronoun *you* and the auxiliary verb *would* to refer to his students. Here they are unpacking the academic concept of *interlocutor*, which they have encountered in a previous lesson. The instructor then recast the content of his first utterance made in line 1 using more generic forms (i.e., we as participant and the present tense). Here it is important to note that the instructor is using the term interlocutor again, thus packing the information that he has previously unraveled with S1.

In the following excerpt, the instructor makes further use of the term *interlocutor* to construct the knowledge structure of PRINCIPLES with the class. His hypothetical question in line 1 elicited three answers (lines 2, 4, and 6).
Except 1.3

1 Inst: if you make a sociolinguistic error, say an inappropriate request, how would it impact how your interlocutors would see you?
2 S5: see negatively.
3 Inst: mm-hmm can you be more specific?
4 S5: they think you're rude
5 Inst: they think you're rude. anything else?

6 S6: you have no commo- common sense
7 Inst: no common sense. in other words **sociolinguistic errors might lead** to your interlocutors' negative evaluations of your—character?
8 Ss: ((nod))
9 Inst: I see.

The instructor's utterance in line 7 is important because it is an FR to recap their discussion in explicitly causal discourse. As these examples indicate, the instructor often went back and forth between congruent forms and grammatical metaphors by unpacking and packing relevant information. In addition, the class took the time to examine how nominalizations work in academic discourse, especially in causal discourse, as well as how classes and causality expressed in their required reading materials.

Functional Recasts in Student Presentations

Excerpt 2.1 illustrates how a student presenter and the instructor jointly constructed causal knowledge structures through discourse. In the first part of this excerpt, Mako talks about her third example and concludes by suggesting that emblems do not mean the same thing across cultures. In line 5, the instructor asks a *what-if* question to push her to think about the effect of using a culturally inappropriate gesture. Consequently, she comes up with a response, which is limited to the physical aspect of the consequence (line 6). This contribution is expanded by the instructor by introducing a psychological effect. In line 9, the instructor further upgrade the causal discourse by using the process of cause.

Excerpt 2.1

	Speaker	Specific Reflection	General Reflection	Other
1	Mako	and the last one is a good sign. In America, this ((thumb-up)) means- this meaning is really good, very simple, but in Iran, this is obscene.		

	Speaker	Specific Reflection	General Reflection	Other
2				so I don't wanna explain it in my words so please guess.
3			so emblems or some body language, gestures, have different meanings,	
4				so: if you use gesture, please—be careful.
5	Inst		so what happens if you use—((with a thumb-up)) this sign in some countries.	
6	Mako		you might get hurt.	
7	Inst		yeah or you might offend people and uh get yourself into trouble, right?	
8	Mako		((nods))	
9	Inst		yeah. so such **cross-cultural differences in- in gesture can cause misunderstandings and conflicts.**	
10	Mako		((nods))	

Our analysis indicated that Mako was one of the few presenters who responded to her teacher's oral feedback on their speech. The following example is an excerpt from her term paper. Although she did not discuss the thumb-up sign, she added a general statement that indicates her understanding of the principle related to cultural differences in gestures. Mako later commented that she thought that by adding her response to the instructor's question, she might be able to recap her point. She also said that she was too nervous to remember everything; she only remembered the instructor saying "cause." We would also like to emphasize here that although the assignment was for each student to write up his or her group's presentation, Mako took it as a place to discuss what she learned from other groups' presentations as well as her own experience doing the presentation. Thus, a gap existed between the *task* planned by the instructor and the *activity* in which Mako engaged (see Coughlan & Duff, 1994, for a relevant discussion).

Excerpt 2.2: Mako's term paper

	Specific Reflection	General Reflection
1		Through this presentation, I learned that gestures are very important to communicate and sometimes they have different meanings in different countries.
2	For example, OK sigh means OK in America and Japan. However, in Brazil and some parts of Europe, it has sexual meaning.	
3		**If we don't know meanings of gestures, we may cause some dangerous situations. So we need to know meanings of gestures.**

While reviewing the exchange in Excerpt 2.1, the instructor made the following comments:

> Maybe I should have used an *if*-conditional instead of saying something causes something else. So something like "if you assume all gestures mean the same thing to everyone, you may experience conflicts and misunderstandings." That way, she might have been able to get more out of my feedback. (originally in Japanese)

What this comment suggests is the challenge of providing level-appropriate feedback on the spot.

Excerpt 3 illustrates an episode in which the instructor provides a student presenter with an FR to move beyond specific reflection to construct the knowledge structure of PRINCIPLES. Yuya is discussing what happens if non-verbal expectations are violated. Notice how he moves from specific reflection to general reflection. In line 1, he starts to recount his own experience, thus constructing the knowledge structure of SEQUENCE. This is evidenced by the major features of Yuya's discourse: (1) specific participants (*I*, *an ex-classmate*), (2) a circumstance of time *(in the beginning of this semester*), (3) a circumstance of place *(at the university cafeteria*), (4) material processes in simple past tense *(met, passed, came, hugged)*, and (5) connectors of sequence *(after that)*.

Excerpt 3

	Speaker	Specific Reflection	General Reflection	Other
1	Yuya			and next is expectation and violation. I will umm talk a short story
2		and this is my experience, and **in the beginning of this semester**, uh at university cafeteria, I met an ex-classmate, umm the classmate is a lady, and— we met at cafeteria and we passed each other and **after that**, she came close to me and say—said hi Yuya or like that, and **after that**, she hugged me, and but it was surprise for me because we don't hug usually [so		
3	Inst	[hahaha		
4	Ss	[hahhh		
5	Yuya	it was strange,		
6			but I think this is an example of violation, because she invaded my personal space.	
7		Maybe she- I think she was so excited in that time, because I can understand by looking at her face, but this is violation and in that time, I felt umm not uneasy but strange.		

	Speaker	Specific Reflection	General Reflection	Other
8			so I think if these violations are happened, people feel uneasy or strange or sometime scary,	
9	Inst		**so invasion of—personal space—can cause uneasiness or anxiety, o:r even erm fear right?**	
10	Yuya		yes yes. ((laughing and nodding))	

Importantly, Yuya makes two important statements: a partially generalized statement labeling his friend's action as a violation (of personal space) (line 6) and a more generalized explanation involving an *if*-clause to denote a causal relationship. The instructor then recasts the latter statement to make it even more general. This FR is recognized by Yuya with two yeses accompanied by head nods and laughter (line 10). This is as far as most previous studies have reported. However, given the Vygotskian view that participation in social interactions with more capable others is essential to second language development (Gibbons, 2015; Walqui & van Lier, 2010), it becomes vital that we look beyond the confines of a single speech event to look for evidence of learning (Kobayashi & Kobayashi, 2018).

Unfortunately, neither Yuya nor his partner wrote about this example in their write-ups, but Yuya wrote the following comment in his post-class reflection: "Violation of personal space causes uneasy feelings and anxiety for me, but not for my friend. I'd like to know what makes this difference." Moreover, two classmates responded specifically to the above part of Yuya's talk in their post-class reflections in Japanese.

> Response 1
> I can understand well the idea that **if violation of personal space occurs, it leads to discomfort.** (e.g., someone taking a seat right in front of me or next to me when there is enough space).

> Response 2
> I have realized that the reason why I have sometimes felt awkward on a train or in a casual dining restaurant had to do with violation of personal space.

The writer of Response 1 constructed an explicitly causal line of meaning, using a Japanese equivalent of the nominalized phrase "violation of personal space" borrowing two English expressions from the textbook (i.e., violation, personal space). In contrast, the writer of Response 2 expressed the cause-and-effect relationship in a more personalized manner, attributing her own experience of feeling discomfort in a train or a restaurant to the academic concept of personal space intrusion. Although not written in English, these texts represent the knowledge structure of PRINCIPLES, thus demonstrating the writers' greater understanding of the subject matter.

Study 2

One major assignment for Class B was to write a reflective essay on boundary crossing. More specifically, students were instructed to write a narrative of critical incidents in which they experienced a misunderstanding, problem, or conflict in communicating with people from different cultural backgrounds. They were expected to relate their experiences to their readings and discuss the possible causes of their problems. As such, it was expected that successful final drafts would consist of both specific and general reflection. The instructor considered provision of FRs as an important way of helping students add causal explanations to temporal descriptions (SEQUENCE), rather than replacing the latter with the former. To this end, the instructor gave students blank copies of what is often referred to as a *fishbone diagram* (Ishikawa, 1984) and asked the class to list all the possible causes of culture shock in intercultural communication discussed by Jackson (2014) as well as the possible causes of problems in intercultural communication discussed by Barna (1994). Intended to help visually identify and display possible causes of a problem, the fishbone diagram can be considered as a key visual to construct the knowledge structure of PRINCIPLES. Also, students were often advised by the instructor to go back to the two fishbone diagrams created based on the readings so as to consider which factors might have caused their problems.

Excerpt 4 illustrates how the instructor assisted his students in talking about the causes of culture shock. Having filled out the fishbone diagram, the class starts to share information. After eliciting a cause from S1, the instructor constructs the knowledge structure of PRINCIPLES by using the conditional *if-then* (line 5). S2's contribution in line 7 is particularly noteworthy because it realizes causality in a non-congruent form.

Excerpt 4

1 Inst: what are some of the causes of culture shock discussed in the textbook.
2 S1: inadequate preparation.
3 Inst: yes—inadequate preparation. Do you all have it on your diagram?
4: ((Ss nod))
5 **Inst: okay—so if you are inadequately prepared for your life in a new cultural environment, you may experience culture shock.** ((writes this sentence on board)) so this ((referring to the if-clause)) is the cause, ((underlines and writes an E)) and this ((referring to the main clause)) is the effect ((underlines and writes a C)). any other ways of expressing the same meaning?
6 (8.6)
7 S2: **inadequate preparation causes culture shock.**
8 Inst: YES! **inadequate preparation causes culture shock.** ((writes this sentence on the board))
9 S3: ((raises her hand))
10 Inst: ((to S3)) yes?
11 S3: *ii kichatte daijoobu desu ka*? [Is it okay to categorically declare that?]
12 Inst: wow—that's what I was going to say next!
13 ((SS laugh))
14 Inst: we don't want to make claims that are umm too strong.—perhaps we should—use hedging language—like this, ((pointing at the board)) when we make a general statement like this. so you could say—for example, **inadequate preparation may—cause culture shock.**

Interestingly, S3 raises a question about the certainty of the claim being made, suggesting that a more cautious and tentative expression might be appropriate when making a generalization. This led the instructor to explain the use of the modal auxiliary *may* in line 14. The class later brainstormed other major processes of cause (e.g., *lead to, result in, result from, bring about*), and examined how they are used in texts, and discussed how to use them. This sequence of activities can be seen as part of pedagogical scaffolding (Walqui & van Lier, 2010) that was intended to help students move from comprehending academic texts to talking about them, and the fishbone diagram played a key role as a bridge in this process.

Functional Recasts Provided for Student Papers

The analysis of students' drafts showed that the instructor started to make FRs with the second or third draft and that many of his comments on the earlier drafts were questions (specific questions such as "Were there any rules for taking a shower? How did learn them?" and "What made you think so?" or general questions such as "What did you learn from this experience about intercultural communication?" and "Based on this experience, what can you say about intercultural communication?"). The analysis also revealed that all the students used the instructor's FRs more or less to improve their term papers. In this section, three students' cases are presented to illustrate how FRs contributed to student learning. Note that [RECAST] and [REFERENCE] indicate where the instructor made an FR and suggested a reference. The latter code is relevant to the present chapter, for, as primary sources of general theoretical knowledge, the textbook (i.e., Jackson, 2014) and Barna (1994) were often referred to by the instructor.

As can be seen, the following excerpt from Mika's second draft consists of specific reflection as it narrates her particular experience in the US. Although this excerpt contains some consequential conjunctions and adverbials (e.g., *because, due to, because of*), this text mostly realizes the knowledge structure of SEQUENCE. This is evidenced by specific referents (e.g., *I, my host family*), the past tense, and temporal expressions (e.g., temporal conjunctions, circumstance of time).

Excerpt 5.1 Mika's 2nd draft

Specific Reflection	General Reflection
When I met my host mother and my Chinese homemate at a meeting point and talked with them for the first time in their car to go to their house, I was very surprised and confused because they spoke very fast and I could not get what they said. [RECAST 1] At that time, I just thought that it was because of my tiredness and pain in my ears due to a long flight, but I realized it was because of my lack of English skill while a dinner time in the day. I had dinner with my host mother, father, and homemate, and they were enjoying talking a lot, but I could not understand what they were talking about or speak what I wanted to say. Therefore, I just kept listening carefully, smiling and pretending that I understood their whole conversation because I felt I was out of the loop. [RECAST 2]	

The instructor made two recasts to upgrade this text: one after the first sentence and the other after last sentence. The first one is a suggestion that the first sentence be made less congruent by replacing "because" with the causal process "lead to," "I was (very surprised and) confused" with the noun "confusion," "they spoke very fast and I could not get what they said" with the noun "language barriers." Likewise, the second recast involved such nominalizations (i.e., *language barriers, a feeling of isolation, a loss of confidence*). These changes were reflected in Mika's third draft. Importantly, she did not just take what was suggested by the instructor, but she combined the two recasts by using the not only…but also construction.

Excerpt 5.2 Instructor feedback

RECAST 1	Yes, language barriers can lead to confusion, can't they!
RECAST 2	Language barriers can also result in a feeling of isolation and a loss of confidence, right?

Excerpt 5.3 Mika's 3rd draft

Specific Reflection	General Reflection
After I met my American host mother and Chinese home-mate for the first time at a meeting point, I rode on my host mother's car to go to their house. In the car, they spoke to me and asked me some questions in English, but I was very confused and did not answer soon because they spoke very fast and I could not get what they said. At that time, I just thought that it was because of my tiredness and pain in my ears due to a long flight and did not care about it so much; however, I realized it was because of a lack of my English skill while dinner time in the day. That night, I had dinner with my host mother, father, and home-mate and had second language shock. Even though they were enjoying talking a lot, it was very uncomfortable for me because I could not understand what they were talking about or express what I wanted to say. The only thing that I could do was just keeping on listening carefully, smiling and pretending that I understood their whole conversation, for I felt like a fish out of the water and wanted to be in their loop. Then, I asked what they said again and replied simply only when I was asked something by them. Due to the language shock, I lost my self-confidence and missed everything in Japan.	
	In my opinion, **language barrier can result in not only confusion, but also a feeling of isolation and a loss of confidence.**

In his term paper, Takuto wrote not only about his experience at a fast-food Mexican restaurant in the US, but also about his experience playing Barnga in class. Barnga is a card game that is intended to simulate intercultural communication and to raise players' intercultural awareness (Sivasailam, 2006). The students of Classes 1 and 2 were given the chance to play this game and to reflect on their experience. This was because the instructor valued experiential learning highly and considered the game as an effective way of building a common ground to talk about abstract concepts and principles covered in the textbook.

As indicated by Excerpt 6.1, Takuto's 2nd draft was constituted mostly by specific reflection. In other words, he constructed the knowledge structure of SEQUENCE by using such resources as specific references, temporal conjunctions, and the past tense.

Excerpt 6.1 Takuto's 2nd draft

Specific Reflection	General Reflection
The same thing happened when we played Barnga. During the game, I was always in the second or first place in the group so I thought that I was good at the game but after moving to a totally different group of people with a full of confidence, I went on following my own rule, without knowing the rules were different in that group. When everyone looked at me after I put a "weird" card for them, I realized that I was the only one that the rule was different, then I took the card back and showed other cards one after another to check whether my understanding was correct or not. The situations, when I was so excited and wanted to order but did not have any idea about the names of foods, and when I moved to different group confidently but the rules were completely dissimilar, are comparable. I was shocked because everything what I thought "normal" was not. [RECAST & REFERENCE]	

The instructor recast Takuto's last sentence by replacing "everything I thought was normal" with the gerund "assuming similarity," "I was shocked" with intercultural problems, and because with the causal process "result in." Importantly, the instructor suggests that Takuto go back to the fishbone diagram (see Appendix B) that he created after reading Barna's (1994) article.

Excerpt 6.2 Instructor feedback

RECAST & REFERENCE	**So assuming similarity can result in intercultural problems, right? See the diagram based on the Barna article.**

Except 6.3 Takuto's 3rd draft

Specific Reflection	General Reflection
...I was shocked because everything what I thought "normal" was not.	
	This is one of an example of **"assumption of similarities" which can cause intercultural problems,** as Barna (1994: p. 337) explains.

Takuto's third draft demonstrates his creative use of the instructor's recast; he incorporated it into a relational clause by adding a relative pronoun "which." Although leaving some errors to be corrected, this text clearly indicates that Takuto is making progress toward a higher level of thinking and discourse.

While the first two cases are the illustrations of relatively smooth incorporation of FRs, the final case provides a more complex picture. Miyu chose to write about an intercultural problem that she had with some Russian girls. As the following table shows, most of her sentences in the selected excerpt are categorized as specific reflection because they exhibit many of the features that characterize SEQUENCE texts (e.g., specific references, temporal conjunctions and adverbs, the past tense). The only part that is categorized as general reflection is the last two sentences where she reported what she had previously learned from her Russian teacher. Miyu uses the present tense to make a generalization.

Excerpt 7.1 Miyu's 2nd draft

Specific Reflection	General Reflection
On that day, I had dinner with all of the members because I thought that was the last chance to talk with other volunteer members and local people. We talked about many things, such as school life, culture, and backgrounds. In the middle of the conversation, I realized that one Russian girl was staring at me, and she asked me that "Why are you laughing while I'm talking?" I was surprised to hear that because I did not laugh at her at all. Other Russian woman added that I always laugh even in serious conversations. I could not say anything at that time because I could not understand what they meant either. After that conversation, I remember what my Russian teacher told me in Japan.	
	In Russia, smiling and laughing are considered as same things. Therefore, Russian people only smile when they think it is funny or ridiculous. [RECAST] [REFERENCE]

To improve this text, the instructor made a recast to propose that the following paraphrases be included:

(1) "one Russian girl was staring at me, and she asked me that "Why are you laughing while I'm talking?" I was surprised to hear that because I did not laugh at her at all. Other Russian woman added that I always laugh even in serious conversations. I could not say anything at that time because I could not understand what they meant either." → intercultural problems

(2) "In Russia, smiling and laughing are considered as same things. Therefore, Russian people only smile when they think it is funny or ridiculous"→ different conceptions of smiling/laughing

To help the student make connections between her particular experience and the theoretical knowledge of the course, the instructor also made a suggestion for further reading by specifying what sections to read in the textbook.

Excerpt 7.2 Instructor feedback

RECAST	**So intercultural problems can arise from different conceptions of smiles and laughter, right?**
REFERENCE	Maybe you should read about kinesics (pp. 110–111) and variations in emotional display/nonverbal codes (p. 281).

Excerpt 7.3 Miyu's 3rd draft

Specific Reflection	General Reflection
(overlapping parts omitted) I almost forgot about that explanation because when I heard of it, I did not even think it could be a problem at all. Instead, I had worried about my linguistic skills, so I focused on studying Russian and English. Contrary to my expectation, the culture difference affected me significantly and I could not talk with that girl anymore because I was afraid of being a rude person at there. I suppose it was one of my biggest problems in intercultural communication.	
	In the context of body language communication, Jackson states that "Around the world, a smile usually signals happiness; however, in some cultural contexts it can also mask sadness or be used to conceal embarrassment" (p. 111). Therefore, body language including smiling can be varied in each culture. [RECAST]

In fact, the instructor made two formal recasts for this draft to help Miyu address her language problems ("can be varied in each culture" and "In the context of body language communication, Jackson states..."). One of these allowed her to solve the problem while the other inadvertently led to a bigger error in the fourth draft (i.e., misuse of the verbal process "refer to"). As a result, Miyu added general reflection, including a direct quotation from the textbook to support her claim that body language varies across cultures. However, the instructor's suggestion was only half-addressed because his FR was an explicit construction of the cause-and-effect relationship between different conceptions of smiling/laughing and intercultural issues. In other words, her writing does not discuss the effect of such variation in body language. Thus, to help Miyu notice this gap, the instructor made the following FR:

Excerpt 7.4 Instructor feedback

RECAST	And this can cause intercultural misunderstandings, right?

By making an anaphoric reference ("this"), the instructor is making it explicit what the actor of the causal process is. Miyu responds to this feedback in her fourth draft by adding it at the end. However, since she changed "this" to "it," it is now less clear what the actor of the causal process is. Nonetheless, Miyu has demonstrated her progress in academic discourse over multiple drafts under the guidance of the instructor.

Excerpt 7.5 Miyu's 4th draft

Specific Reflection	General Reflection
(overlapping parts omitted) I had almost forgotten about that explanation because when I heard of it, I did not even think it could be a problem at all. Instead, I had worried about my linguistic skills, so I focused on studying Russian and English. Contrary to my expectation, the cultural difference affected me significantly and I could not talk with that girl anymore because I was afraid of being a rude person there. I suppose it was one of my biggest problems in intercultural communication.	
	Jackson (2014) refers body language as "Around the world, a smile usually signals happiness; however, in some cultural contexts it can also mask sadness or be used to conceal embarrassment" (p. 111). Therefore, the meaning of body language including smiling can vary from culture to culture. **It can cause intercultural misunderstandings.**

Discussion

This chapter has reported the findings of an action research project that explored the role of FRs in undergraduate students' learning of academic language and content in two classrooms at a Japanese university. Because space is limited, we have only presented cases in which students succeeded in constructing causal knowledge structures by incorporating it into their writings. However, it is important to note here that the data collected for this project also included many instances where presenting students did not incorporate into their write-ups what the instructor functionally recast. In fact, Mako and Yuya were in the minority. In contrast, almost all students in Class B eventually succeeded in constructing causal knowledge structures in their drafts using FRs by the instructor. Incorporation of FRs was relatively smooth and immediate for some students (e.g., Mika, Takuto) while it took more drafts and efforts for others (e.g., Miyu). On the whole, the final drafts of their papers included narratives of specific events followed by causal explanations of the principles underlying them.

Here, one may wonder what made the outcomes of the two instructional approaches so different. One possible reason relates to the evanescence of spoken discourse. According to Wells (1999),

> Memory for the exact words spoken is extremely short and, without recourse to a definitive text of what is said, it is difficult work systematically to improve it and the understanding it embodies. (p. 115)

This is attested to by Mako's comment about being too nervous to remember everything. The effectiveness of oral FRs might be undermined by their ephemerality coupled with the pressure of public performance. However, Mako took up the word "cause," albeit in a different fashion, to write her final paper. This may be because the class had considerable time identifying and discussing causal language.

Another reason is that some of the FRs might have fallen out of what Vygotsky (1978) called the *zone of proximal development* (ZPD). Vygotsky claimed that individuals learn best when they were pushed through interactions with more skilled others to go beyond their current level of mastery to accomplish tasks that they could not accomplish by themselves. Recall Mako's case; although the instructor provided an FR involving a causal process, it was an *if-then* conditional that she ended up using to construct the knowledge structure of cause in her writing. This may be because the former construction is more complex than the latter as it entails nominalization—a process that requires speakers or writers to come up with nominal phrases that capture the essence of the topic under discussion. It takes more steps to construct causal knowledge structures because it requires not only to understand the cause-and-effect relationship, but also how each causal process works grammatically (e.g., *result in vs. result from*). In contrast to Mako, Yuya successfully incorporated the FR involving the causal process into his lesson reflection. Recall that he was able to construct the casual knowledge structure by using an *if-then* conditional on his own, and this was upgraded by the instructor to the less congruent form involving the process of cause. Arguably the *if-then* conditional was within Yuya's *actual developmental level* or part of his individual competence (Vygotsky, 1978) and the ZPD was created through the FR sequence.

A third possible reason for the huge differences between the two studies may have to do with the use of key visuals. Both classes were strongly encouraged to use key visuals for their assignments but differed in some important ways. Although all the pairs/groups in Class A used classification trees or concentric circles to talk about the types and function of non-verbal communication, none of them used key visuals to talk about the principles of non-verbal communication. In contrast, all students in Class B were required to complete the fishbone diagram and use it to think, write, and talk about the causes of their intercultural problems. According to Early and Tang (1991), key visuals "make visible the knowledge structure they represent, and in this way provide a schema which can be accessed again and again, thus facilitating comprehension" (p. 37). The fishbone diagram might have played an important role as a reminder of the connections between students' experiences and the principles of intercultural communication presented in their reading materials, helping them (and the instructor) stay focused on cause, within the knowledge structure of PRINCIPLES.

What was common to the findings of the two studies was that students were expected to connect the theory and practice of intercultural communication by applying theoretical knowledge to their personal experiences or using the latter to illustrate the former. Given this expectation, FRs were intended to help students make generalizations informed not only by their personal experiences, but also by the general principles of intercultural communication presented in the course readings. As discussed earlier, the fishbone diagram played a crucial role in reminding the students of the relevance of these principles. However, the instructor sometimes suggested materials not covered in his classes in order to provide individualized support for students. In such cases, the instructor often had to specify where to look for relevant information (e.g., Miyu's case) or give students relevant URLs. This kind of support should go hand in hand with FRs to assist students in learning to make informed generalizations in academic disciplines.

Pedagogical Implications & Conclusion

Based on the findings of the two studies, we can draw several implications for L2 pedagogy. One implication has to do with students' sustained engagement with the language features being targeted by FRs. Van Lier (1996) suggested that "language learning is the cumulative result of sustained effort and engagement over time, with continuity being central" (p. 43). Given this view, it becomes vital that students notice the target linguistic/discourse features being functionally recast and initiate and sustain their efforts to use them in meaningful contexts. One thing that teachers could do to promote such engagement would be to make available audio- or video-recordings of students' presentations. By listening to or watching their interactional performance multiple times, they might be able to notice more language features than they would otherwise. Also, they could stop the video to take notes of any audience feedback including FRs. It would not hurt to encourage presenters to take notes. However, as Mako's comments suggested, presenters are often put under huge pressure to speak in front of an audience, so they may find it difficult to take notes while interacting with their audience. Thus, audio- or video-recording their performance would be an ideal option. But if such recordings are not available, students could take turns taking notes of audience feedback. Members of a group can take notes for each other or audience members can take notes for the presenter(s).

Another implication concerns teacher preparedness to give FRs during student presentations. As reported in this chapter, the instructor of the course sometimes stopped the video to comment that he should have given more level-appropriate feedback or to identify missed opportunities to provide FRs. Considering all the mental work needed to come up with FRs in an accessible way and on the spot, we understand that it would be no easy task even for experienced teachers. One way to deal with this challenge would be to have students send their outlines or presentation materials, including keys visuals in particular, prior to their presentations. Another option would of course be to require them to prepare scripts and send them in advance, but the trade-off would be that some students might sound monotonous, trying to deliver their prepared speech without interacting with their audience. In either case, by familiarizing themselves with the content of upcoming presentations, teachers would be in a better position to provide on-the-spot feedback that is targeted at students at the appropriate level.

The present project focused almost exclusively on the role of FRs in students' construction of causality, or the knowledge structure of PRINCIPLES, but the instructor made other types of feedback in the two classes. Also, the project examined oral FRs and written FRs separately. Future research should examine how FRs and other types of feedback interact with each other and how two modes of FRs can be combined to help students' causal discourse production. Also, the project focused on meaning-making efforts within specific tasks (i.e., presentations and term paper writing) although it examined how the instructor guided his students for the focal tasks. However, as Mohan and Smith's (1992) study suggested, students' understanding of tasks may develop over time as they participate in other classroom activities. Thus, future studies should go beyond the examination of participants' engagement with FRs in individual tasks to detail how such engagement may constitute and be constituted by the *macroprocess processes* surrounding them (Mohan & Smith, 1992). This would require a longitudinal approach to trace individual students' development as academic readers and writers and how such development may contribute to the development of their class as a learning community. These future efforts would enrich our understanding of students' simultaneous learning of academic language and content in higher education in EFL contexts.

References

Barna, L.M. (1994). Stumbling blocks in intercultural communication. In L.A. Samovar & R.E. Porter (Eds.), *Intercultural communication: A reader* (4th ed.). Wadsworth Publishing.

Byram, M. (1997). *Teaching and assessing intercultural communicative competence.* Multilingual Matters.

Coughlan, P., & Duff, P. (1994). Same task, different activities: Analysis of an SLA task from an activity theory perspective. In J.P. Lantolf & G. Appel, (Eds.), *Vygotskian approaches to second language research* (pp. 173–193). Ablex.

Duff, P.A. (2002). The discursive co-construction of knowledge, identity, and difference: An ethnography of communication in the high school mainstream. *Applied Linguistics, 23*, 289–322.

Early, M., & Tang, G. (1991). Helping ESL students cope with content-based texts. *TESL Canada Journal, 8*(2), 34–44.

Gibbons, P. (2003). Mediating language learning: Teacher interactions with ESL students in a content-based classroom. *TESOL Quarterly, 37*, 247–273.

Gibbons, P. (2006). *Bridging discourses in ESL classrooms: Students, teachers, and researchers*. Continuum.

Gibbons, P. (2015). *Scaffolding language, scaffolding learning: Teaching English language learners in the mainstream classroom* (2nd ed.). Heinemann.

Harada, T. (2017). Developing a content-based English as a foreign language program: Needs analysis and curriculum design at the university level. In M.A. Snow & D.M. Brinton (Eds.), *The content-based classroom: New perspectives on integrating language and content* (2nd ed.) (pp. 37–52). The University of Michigan Press.

Ishikawa, K. (1984), *Nihonteki hinshitu kanri: TQC to wa nani ka* [Japanese quality management: What is TQC]. Nika Giren.

Jackson, J. (2014). *Introducing language and intercultural communication*. Routledge.

Kobayashi, E., & Kobayashi, M. (2018). Second language learning through repeated engagement in a poster presentation task. In M. Bygate (Ed.), *Language learning through task repetition* (pp. 223–254). John Benjamins.

Kobayashi, M. (2006). Second language socialization through an oral project presentation: Japanese university students' experience. In G.H. Beckett & P.C. Miller (Eds.), *Project-based second and foreign language education* (pp. 71–93). Information Age.

Linares, A., Morton, T., & Whittaker, R. (2012). *The roles of language in CLIL*. Cambridge University Press.

Lincoln, Y.S., & Guba, E.G. (1985). *Naturalistic inquiry*. Sage.

Liu, P., & Liang, X. (2012). Functional recasts of causal discourse: From textbook to lecture. In J.S. Knox (Ed.), *Papers from the 39th International Systemic Functional Congress* (pp. 51–56). The Organizing Committee of the 39th International Systemic Functional Congress.

Mohan, B.A. (1998). Knowledge structures in oral interviews for international teaching assistants. In R. Young & A.W. He (Eds.), *Talking and testing: Discourse approaches to the assessment of oral proficiency* (pp. 173–204). John Benjamins.

Mohan, B.A. (2007). Knowledge structures in social practices. In J. Cummins & C. Davison (Eds), *International handbook of English language teaching, Part I*, (pp. 303–315). Springer.

Mohan, B.A., & Beckett, G.H. (2003). A functional approach to research on content-based language learning: Recasts in causal explanations. *The Modern Language Journal, 87*(3), 421–432.

Mohan, B., & Luo, L. (2005). A systemic functional linguistics perspective on CALL. In J.L. Egbert & G.M. Petrie (Eds.), *CALL research perspectives* (pp. 88–96). Lawrence Erlbaum.

Mohan, B., Slater, T., Beckett, G., Tong, E. (2015). Tasks, experiential learning, and meaning making activities. In M. Bygate (Ed.), *Domains and directions in the development of TBLT* (pp. 157–192). John Benjamins.

Mohan, B., & Smith, S.M. (1992). Context and cooperation in academic tasks. In D. Nunan (Ed.), *Collaborative language learning and teaching* (pp. 81–99). Cambridge University Press.

Rose, H., & McKinley, J. (2017). Japan's English-medium instruction initiatives and the globalization of higher education. *Higher Education, 75*(1), 111–129.

Sivasailam, T. (2006). *Barnga: A simulation game on cultural clashes.* Intercultural Press.

Slater, T. (2004). *The discourse of causal explanations in school science.* Unpublished doctoral dissertation, University of British Columbia, Vancouver, Canada. DOI:10.14288/1.0078228

van Ek, J.A. (1986). *Objectives for foreign language teaching, Volume 1: Scope.* Councils of Europe.

van Lier, L. (1996). *Interaction in the language curriculum: Awareness, autonomy, and authenticity.* Longman.

Vygotsky, L.S. (1978). *Mind in society: The development of higher psychological processes* (M. Cole, V. John-Steiner, S. Scribner, & E. Souberman, Eds.). Harvard University Press.

Walqui, A., & van Lier, L. (2010). *Scaffolding the academic success of adolescent English language learners: A pedagogy of promise.* WestEd.

Wells, G. (1999). *Dialogic inquiry: Towards a sociocultural practice and theory of education.* Cambridge University Press.

Appendix A: Transcription Conventions

((comments))	comments or relevant details pertaining to interaction
<u>underlining</u>	spoken with emphasis
boldfaced	functionally recast utterances
:	unusually lengthened sound or syllable
.	terminal falling intonation
,	rising, continuing intonation
?	high rising intonation, not necessarily at the end of a sentence
!	an enthusiastic tone, not necessarily an exclamation
(numbers)	inter-turn pauses
-	(unattached) untimed intra-turn pauses
x-	(attached on one side) cutoff often accompanied by a glottal stop (e.g., a self-correction)
italics	L1 utterances
[utterances]	approximate translation

(adapted from Duff, 2002)

Appendix B: Instructor Diagram

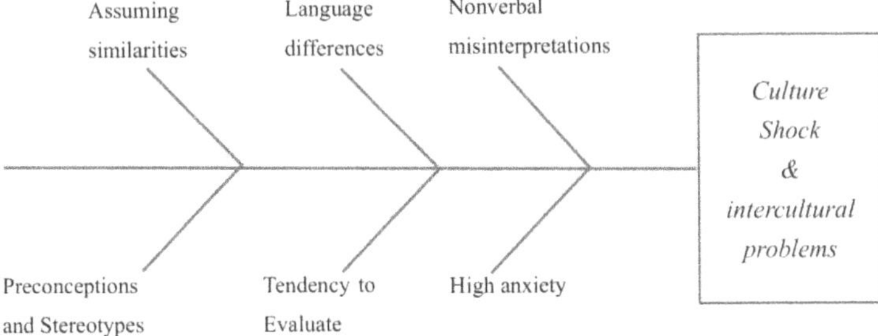

About the Authors

Masaki Kobayashi is a Professor and Deputy Chair of the English Department at Kanda University of International Studies with a cross-appointment to the MATESOL Program in the Graduate School of Language Sciences. His scholarly interests lie in the area of educational linguistics, ranging from academic discourse socialization and the integration of language and content instruction to task-based L2 research and teacher education. Masaki's work has appeared in international journals and edited volumes. He received his PhD from the University of British Columbia.

Emi Kobayashi is a Professor of TESOL and Program Chair of English Language Studies in the Department of International Social Studies at Kyoai Gakuen University. Her research interests include language teacher education, linguistic ethnography, task-based L2 learning, and the integration of language and content learning in higher education. Emi has published internationally on these topics. She holds a PhD in Education from the University of Stirling.

10 Online Teacher Training Using the Knowledge Framework and the Teaching–Learning Cycle for Literacy Development

Stephanie Link and Jesse Gleason

Abstract

While systemic functional approaches to literacy development have grown in popularity, there is still a lack of consensus on how to effectively build teachers' knowledge and how that knowledge then translates into practice. Access to materials is also a concern, sparking renewed interest in online and digital materials for teacher education. Thus, our study's purpose was twofold: First, it aimed to show how online materials development using the Knowledge Framework (KF) and the teaching–learning cycle (TLC) show promise for helping build teachers' understanding of form-function relationships. Second, it attempted to gauge to what extent these online professional development opportunities carried over into teachers' curricular planning. Informed by a socially motivated framework for the professional learning of teachers, we designed a situated, online training curriculum and evaluated the impact of the content on ten participants in a graduate-level literacy development course. Results showed that participants made a shift to a functional perspective after a two-week training involving pre-module activation, post-module reflection, and learning-to-teach activities. This functional shift was evident in their final assignment, an instructional case study/literacy plan, which served to connect learning-to-teach activities to the social practice of classroom teaching. Our research provides implications for supporting teachers' use and transfer of SFL theory into practice.

Keywords: literacy development; Knowledge Framework; teaching-learning cycle; online teacher training

Second language (L2) learners are known to struggle with constructing academic discourses (Gibbons, 2014; Schleppegrell, 2013), especially due to their limited knowledge about academic language use (Early, Mohan, & Hooper, 1988). Teachers' understanding of the distinct linguistic features that help to develop academic literacies can also be constrained, perhaps due to few opportunities for pertinent professional development. While traditional grammar provides sentence-level understanding, there is a need for teachers to teach beyond the sentence and develop learners' academic literacy in ways that makes them valued participants in the multitude of social practices in which they participate. Few studies, however, have focused on using a meaning-based approach to literacy development that can shift teachers' perspectives from traditional to functional understanding of language use (Gebhard, Chen, Graham, & Gunawan, 2013). And while functional approaches have been growing in popularity, there is still a lack of consensus on how to effectively build teachers' knowledge and how that knowledge then translates into practice, especially with ever-evolving educational reforms (Gebhard, 2010).

The Knowledge Framework (KF) and the teaching–learning cycle (TLC) are systemic functional heuristics that show promise for helping build teachers' understanding of form-function relationships across social practices. The KF (Mohan, 1986) provides practical insights for breaking down academic content from an SFL perspective into six manageable thinking structures that can be explicitly taught to express subject-matter knowledge. The TLC (Brisk, 2015; Rothery, 1996) provides suggestions for instructional activities centered around the types of writing that are valued in school contexts. Despite a growing number of academic articles using SFL, teacher-centered materials (e.g., professional development) in the US context in particular is more limited, perhaps due to the still emergent nature of SFL in the US.

This study's purpose was twofold: First, it aimed to show to what extent online material development using the KF and the TLC impacts graduate student teachers' conceptions of literacy development. Second, it attempted to gauge to what extent these online professional development opportunities carried over into their curricular planning. Informed by a socially motivated framework for the professional learning of teachers (Freeman, 2004; Freeman & Johnson, 1998), we designed a situated, online training curriculum and evaluated the impact of the content on ten participants in a graduate-level literacy development course. Results showed that participants made a shift to a functional perspective after a two-week training involving pre-module activation, post-module reflection, and learning-to-teach activities. This functional shift was evident in their final assignment, an instructional case study/literacy plan, which served to connect learning-to-teach activities to the social practice of classroom teaching. Our research provides implications for supporting teachers' use and transfer of SFL theory into practice.

The Knowledge Framework and the Teaching–Learning Cycle for Literacy Development

In literacy education across the globe, teachers often view language development from a first language, constructivist perspective. That is, the structure, grammar, and lexical forms of language activity are seen as fixed and unchangeable (Johns, 2011). SFL "considers language primarily as a resource for making meaning rather than as a set of rules" (Paltridge, 2007, p. 933). These semiotic resources are used to function in two kinds of social contexts. The context of culture is how people in a shared culture utilize language to achieve social purposes. The context of situation is the language used to talk or write about a topic (field), the relationship between participants (tenor), and the channel of communication—spoken or written (mode) (Halliday, 1985). These features correspond to a set of metafunctions, the ideational, interpersonal, and textual, respectively (Halliday, 1978).

Given the multidimensionality of SFL theory, researchers have noted language teachers' struggles with SFL metalanguage and the need for sustained support in using SFL to design curriculum (Gebhard et al., 2013). Despite these concerns, SFL also has demonstrated effectiveness for helping teachers analyze texts and describe how writers construct meaning even at the most basic, simple level of SFL (Slater & McCrocklin, 2016). More research is needed to provide implications for building on the strengths of this language-based approach and supporting teachers' use and transfer of SFL theory into practice. The Knowledge Framework (KF), developed by Bernard A. Mohan (1986), can be a starting point for developing curricula that address both language forms and academic content, potentially mediating the complexity of SFL metalanguage and supporting teachers in organizing their content-based units in a logical progression. The KF has been used in curricular design for beginning ESL students (e.g., Early, 1990; also see Chapter 1, this volume); however, teachers and teacher educators in other instructional contexts have only begun to acknowledge its significance, largely due to the lack of materials and training opportunities available. Such opportunities could expand the reach of the KF and provide more teachers with fundamental knowledge of how an explicit focus on functional language can be integrated into their content classrooms. Teachers' knowledge of form-function relationships can then allow their learners, in particular their English language learners, to reap the benefits of high-quality sheltered instruction.

SFL is perhaps the most "theoretically sophisticated and pedagogically developed approach" towards genre theory (Hyland, 2003, p. 22). Genre, from an SFL perspective, models texts through patterns of lexicogrammatical and rhetorical features that are systematically linked to context (Christie & Martin, 1997). The social context in which learners participate and the semiotic activities that provide input for language development define various genres that learners are likely to encounter in specific content areas and at different grade levels (Martin, 2009). Example genres include recounts, descriptions, or expositions (Butt, Fahey, Feez, Spinks, & Yallop, 2000; Rose, 2012), and SFL serves to describe and explain the variation of purpose and form that these genres represent in differing culturally and socially situated activities.

In SFL approaches to literacy instruction, teaching of genre-based discourse is typically seen as a cycle, as in the teaching–learning cycle (TLC) (Gebhard & Harman, 2011; Macken-Horarik, 2002; Martin, 2009). The TLC is an approach to writing instruction pioneered by literacy educators in Sydney, Australia (Martin, 2009; Rothery, 1996). At the core of this approach is the use of a model genre in order to explicitly teach students the characterizing elements of the most important types of texts found in school so that they can learn to interpret and produce these texts. Specifically, the cycle involves four stages of building a shared context of learning, modelling or deconstructing a mentor text to focus explicitly on structure and language, providing guided practice or jointly constructing a text, and then independently constructing an approximation of the genre (Derewianka & Jones, 2016; Humphrey & Feez, 2016).

While SFL in general has shifted teachers away from traditional grammar towards functional perspectives (Gebhard et al., 2013), research on the TLC has witnessed some challenges in this regard (Correa & Echeverri, 2017). Correa and Echeverri (2017) used the TLC in the Colombian EFL higher education context to explore what gains and challenges EFL pre-service teachers encounter in developing a situated view of academic writing. In their study, the TLC-based lessons assisted teachers in understanding writing as a situated social practice that varies according to context, purpose, and audience. However, teachers were still interested in explaining grammar points in isolation, arguing that general rules could apply to every text students encounter.

Together, frustrations towards the complexity of metalanguage and ambivalence towards shifting perspectives of grammar highlight concerns about the best practices for introducing SFL for effectively impacting teachers' approach to literacy development. Thus, there is a need for a reconceptualization of how SFL is presented in teacher education programs to allow for a more assessable and comprehensive understanding of its potential in curricular design. We argue that introducing both the KF and the TLC in teacher training programs has the potential to scaffold teachers' understanding of form-function relationships and motivate teachers to embrace a functional approach to instructional planning. Along with jointly introducing the Knowledge Framework and the teaching–learning cycle to achieve this aim, we explore the use of online materials development to address the evident lack of SFL-based training resources currently available for professional development programs. Specifically, we sought to answer the following questions: (1) To what extent do online learning-to-teach activities using function-based tools of the KF and TLC impact pre-service teachers' conceptions of literacy development? and (2) To what extent do teachers use their knowledge about the KF and the TLC for literacy planning?

Methodology

Participants and Context

The participants in our study included 10 graduate students in a Master of Science in Bilingual and Multicultural Education and TESOL program at a small public university in the northeastern United States. As shown in Table 10.1, nine of these participants were female in-service teachers with between one and 20 years of experience in the field, and one was a male student who was relatively new to the field, having recently changed careers from the business field, and was working in professional translation and interpretation.

Table 10.1 Participant profiles

Name[a]	Gender	Current Job Position
Aaron	Male	Translation and interpreting
Allison	Female	Elementary and special education
Ashley	Female	Elementary education
Cynthia	Female	ESL secondary education
Eloise	Female	Spanish middle and secondary education
Mandy	Female	Elementary education
Marilyn	Female	English secondary education
Raquel	Female	Elementary education
Olivia	Female	Adult ESL
Sylvia	Female	Bilingual elementary education

[a]All names used in this manuscript are pseudonyms and do not necessarily reflect the cultural or linguistic backgrounds of the participants.

Five of our participants were working in elementary educational contexts; four of which were in English-speaking or ESL classrooms, and one of which was working in a bilingual elementary classroom. Four of the participants were working with middle school, high school, or adult students, one of which was in English secondary education and another in Spanish secondary education.

Participants were all enrolled in one section of a graduate-level literacy development course, which was carried out using a hybrid/blended design with a mixture of face-to-face meetings and online asynchronous work during an intensive eight-week summer semester. The course aimed to survey multiple approaches to literacy development; as such it covered a broad range of topics involving literacy development for English learners, including traditional phonetic and contrastive analysis approaches to literacy development to more form-function approaches, such as the Knowledge Framework (KF) and genre-based pedagogy/teaching–learning cycle (TLC), critical and multiliteracies approaches, and multi-modality. The KF and genre-based units were taught over one week for each topic.

Design of Online Teacher Training and Development Activities

In order to calibrate the design of our teacher training and development with what we know about how teachers learn, we considered a socially motivated framework for the professional learning of teachers (Freeman, 2004). In this framework, teacher learning is framed as a social practice (SP). We acknowledged that students were immersed in the SP of learning to teach in preparation for the SP of real-world teaching in the classroom. We thus ensured our design provided tools that could shape activity in both practices. Figure 10.1 maps the cyclical and iterative process of how participant roles in our SFL-based design are shaped and defined by the two social practices, including the tools that mediate activities both in and over time to ensure transfer of knowledge from learning to teaching.

The training was designed to lead into a final instructional case study/literacy plan that served to bridge learning-to-teach activities with what participants anticipate for the classroom teaching context. For this project, participants were asked to incorporate their knowledge from the modules toward the creation of an instructional plan for an English language learner (ELL) they were assigned to on the first day. The rubric for this assignment can be observed in Appendix A. The assignment required them to (a) assess their English learner through an assessment battery which included reading, writing, and oral prompts, (b) analyze their assessment battery to ascertain

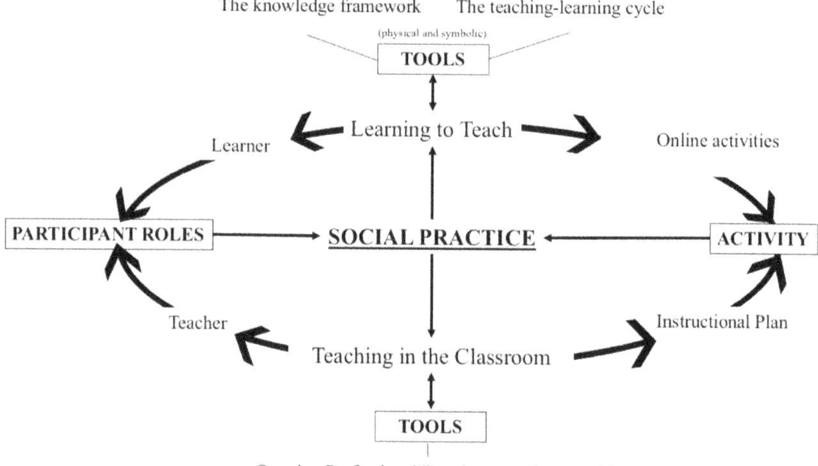

Figure 10.1 Map of social practices (including participant roles, tools, and activities) within a functional approach to designing language teacher training and development program (adapted from Freeman, 2004)

learner strengths as well as areas for improvement, and (c) create an instructional plan for literacy development, making suggestions based upon the course content in light of their observations and analysis.

Learning-to-teach activities for the KF and TLC units were employed using the Canvas learning management system (https://www.canvaslms.com/) and included a combination of videos, readings, and opportunities for asynchronous discussion and reflection. These activities were organized into four modules for each unit: (1) activating prior knowledge and experiences to provide a foundation for new knowledge, (2) introducing theoretical underpinnings, (3) providing theory-to-practice implications, and (4) reflecting on potential integration into real-world use.

A main objective of the online KF module was to help participants understand the thinking skills that their ELL used to compose written texts. In Module 1, students were asked to complete a pre-module analysis activity to practice examining the discourse they elicited from their English learner in the assessment battery for sentence-level language features. Along with activating prior knowledge, the activity served as a baseline for understanding their current approaches to analyzing form-function relationships. In Module 2, students were asked to watch a locally produced video that introduced the theoretical underpinnings of the KF and read two articles on the KF (Early, Mohan & Hooper, 1988; Slater & Gleason, 2011). Following the video and readings, participants were asked to take an online quiz designed to assess their knowledge of the concept of the KF. Module 3 was similar in organization to the previous module, but it was designed to help students apply the theoretical knowledge of the KF to their instructional planning. They first watched a recorded PowerPoint lecture based on Slater, Gleason, and Link (2012) about using the KF for form-function literacy development. They then read two articles that use the KF for instruction (Early, 1990; Tang, 1997) and completed a quiz to check for understanding. Finally, in Module 4, students were asked to respond to a series of questions in an online discussion forum geared toward understanding how they might be able to use the KF for their case study instructional plan. Specifically, participants had to identify which thinking skills/knowledge structures and sentence-level language features they would focus on explicitly in their plan.

The objectives of the second online (genre) module were to help participants (a) understand the systemic functional model of language upon which the KF is based, (b) identify the key components of such a model for literacy development, specifically genre-based pedagogy and the teaching–learning cycle (TLC), and (c) apply the model of literacy development to their own literacy planning and instruction. In Module 1, students completed a pre-module activation activity where they discussed through an online discussion forum what it means to teach language explicitly and if certain students might benefit more from an explicit approach (see Figure 10.2). In Module 2, they watched a video lecture about the theory behind systemic functional grammar, read three chapters about teaching language in context (Derewianka & Jones, 2016), and completed a quiz. In Module 3, they watched a video about the TLC and genre-based pedagogy, read three chapters about explicit language teaching (Gibbons, 2014), and watched a second video demonstrating the particular stages of the TLC (joint construction). In the final module, they reflected in an online discussion forum about the importance of explicit language teaching and a "visible curriculum" for the literacy development of historically underserved students.

Data Collection and Analysis

Data collected for the study came from the two, week-long online modules. To answer the first research question about the extent to which the modules influenced pre-service teachers' conceptions of literacy development, all learning-to-teach activities were collected, including pre-module activation and post-module reflection activities as well as quizzes and other course submissions. Pre-module activation activities were collected to explore initial

Why be explicit about language? A distinctive part of this approach is the idea that historically underserved students are best served when the literacy of schooling is treated in an explicit open manner. This explicit approach is known as "visible" pedagogy and has been developed as an alternative to many invisible pedagogies. This explicit pedagogy is based on the notion that language is a social phenomenon which allows meaningful communication between people.

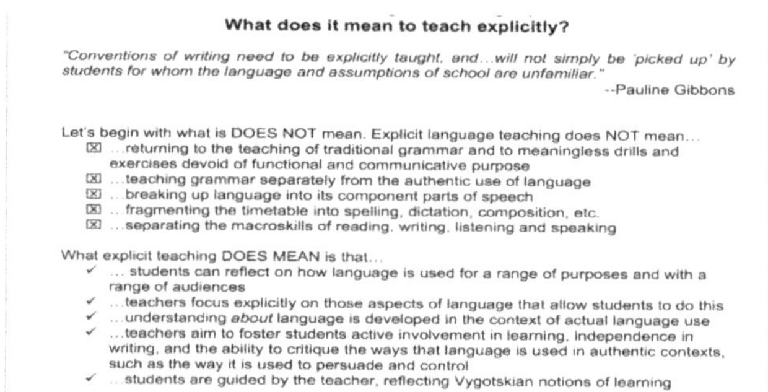

What does it mean to teach explicitly?

"Conventions of writing need to be explicitly taught, and...will not simply be 'picked up' by students for whom the language and assumptions of school are unfamiliar."

--Pauline Gibbons

Let's begin with what is DOES NOT mean. Explicit language teaching does NOT mean...

- ☒ ...returning to the teaching of traditional grammar and to meaningless drills and exercises devoid of functional and communicative purpose
- ☒ ...teaching grammar separately from the authentic use of language
- ☒ ...breaking up language into its component parts of speech
- ☒ ...fragmenting the timetable into spelling, dictation, composition, etc.
- ☒ ...separating the macroskills of reading, writing, listening and speaking

What explicit teaching DOES MEAN is that...

- ✓ ... students can reflect on how language is used for a range of purposes and with a range of audiences
- ✓ ...teachers focus explicitly on those aspects of language that allow students to do this
- ✓ ...understanding *about* language is developed in the context of actual language use
- ✓ ...teachers aim to foster students active involvement in learning, independence in writing, and the ability to critique the ways that language is used in authentic contexts, such as the way it is used to persuade and control
- ✓ ...students are guided by the teacher, reflecting Vygotskian notions of learning

Figure 10.2 A screenshot from the online module about the systemic functional model of language for literacy development

approaches towards analyzing form-function relationships and views towards explicit language teaching. Post-module reflection activities were collected to determine whether training transformed their understanding of how SFL may impact their language teaching. Participants' incorporation of literacy development strategies from the online units into their instructional plan for real-world application were documented through the final instructional case study/literacy plan.

For research question 1, content analysis (Saldaña, 2016) was employed to identify patterns indicating potential changes in conceptions of literacy development from pre- to post-module responses. To ensure credibility of the coding, one researcher coded the data and a second coder joined for a round of peer debriefing to clarify uncertainties and come to a consensus about data interpretation. Grounded analysis and coding (Charmaz, 2006) of participant data were utilized for research question 2. Specifically, end-of-course final instructional plans for the literacy development of English learners were examined and analyzed for emergent themes using a recursive approach to data analysis.

As Esterberg (2002) and others note, in qualitative research, it is important to explicitly state the role of the researchers. One of the researchers (Dr.

Gleason) was also the instructor of the hybrid, graduate-level literacy development course, thus her involvement in the study was both as an instructor, an online course module developer, and a researcher. We acknowledge that her participation as instructor likely influenced how students constructed their knowledge. Dr. Link served both as an online course module developer and as a researcher. All ethical guidelines were followed, and informed consent was obtained from participants according to the institutional review board of the university where the data were collected.

Results/Discussion

Impact of Online Professional Daevelopment on Conceptions of Literacy Development

The first research question sought to address, "To what extent do online learning-to-teach activities using function-based tools of the KF and TLC impact pre-service teachers' conceptions of literacy development?" Pre-module activation and post-module reflection activities were examined for each unit.

The KF Unit. Representative excerpts from students' responses within the KF online module are summarized in Table 10.2. As expected, students' pre-module activation activity, where they needed to analyze their ELL's proficiency using an assessment battery, showed that all students initially described their ELL's language in terms of a traditional view of sentence-level, form-function relationships. They referred frequency to the ELLs' use of nouns, verbs, and adjectives, and transitions without explicit reference to the functional context of use.

In the post-module reflection activity, five of the students (Allison, Mandy, Raquel, Olivia, Sylvia) showed strong indications of transforming their perspective towards form-function relationships by relating their analysis of their ELL's literacy development to functional uses of grammar. For example, Olivia described her ELL's writing in relation to each knowledge structure introduced in the learning-to-teach activities, and she is able to use this analysis to identify distinct areas of need. Here is an extended excerpt from her post-module reflection activity (underlines added for emphasis):

> [The ELL] uses the thinking skill of classification to categorize which foods are eaten at different meals in different countries. For example, she writes, "we have several kinds of cheeses..." She also gives examples of different foods by listing them in parentheses. She could make the writing more formal by writing, "for example" before she starts a list.

Table 10.2 Summary of representative excerpts of individual's conceptions of literacy development in Knowledge Framework online module

Name[a]	Pre-module Activation Activity	Post-module Reflection Activity	Transition
Allison	I would expect my student to use sentence-level language such as nouns, specifically ones that could replace "a person," descriptive language, verbs, and transition words.	I expected my student to utilize thinking skills…such as those of description, more specifically describing and identifying, … principles, including explaining, and choice, including making decisions.	Traditional towards Functional
Ashley	The sentence level features […] are the typical parts of speech required to compose full sentences consisting of a subject and predicate, as well as appropriate capitalization, punctuation, and conjunctions where necessary.	Because it is a decision making prompt, … I would have him use more descriptive words and provide a word bank full of descriptive adjectives and verbs. […] <u>I would also take the opportunity to reteach proper sentence structure</u>	Traditional towards <u>Traditional</u>/ Functional
Cynthia	The student used verbs, nouns, words, and phrases. […] the student used nouns, such as teacher and student to indicate the characters in the story, but also phrases such as "Oh, no, they missed the bus" to specify the occurrence.	I understood the reason for the student's current level of English proficiency is because he or she can properly use these verbs depending on the subject that he or she is writing about in the situation.	Traditional – no transition
Mandy	[The] student used a range of words including synonyms (big, love, sad) […] He uses descriptive words, subject specific, and academic related to curricular concepts.	For the Principles Structure, he uses some cause and effect thinking. […] He uses the conjunctions because, then and so. For the Sequence Structure, […] The student uses transitional words like next, then, now to show a step by step action.	Traditional towards Functional

Marilyn	The sentences were of a low level, simple structure with very little descriptive language and many of the verb tenses were incorrect…	This student's verb tenses were not accurate in most instances and she lacked many pronouns or helping words that would create fluidity in her writing.	Traditional – no transition
Raquel	The student needed to think about something she is good at (verb) and describe the talent using adjectives.	[The ELL] began talking about her talent by saying "First I will..." It's almost as if she is going to describe her talent step by step, however she doesn't use any other sequence words after that.	Traditional towards Functional
Olivia	My student should use nouns, verbs, adjectives, and prepositions. She should also use linking words to show the relationships between ideas.	She uses the thinking skill of classification to categorize which foods are eaten at different meals in different countries. […] My learner uses principles to hypothesize about a cause. […] She uses the thinking skill of sequence to structure the essay.	Traditional towards Functional
Sylvia	I would expect the students to be able to state their opinion in the first sentence of their work, utilizing the provided sentence structure "I like __________ because _________."	"I like" and "I can." These are exactly the types of verbs and phrases that I would expect my learner to utilize when writing an opinion piece. She also utilized the words "because" as well as "and," these are also words I would expect for her to rationalize and justify her response.	Traditional/ Functional towards Functional

[a] Aaron did not complete the online module, and Eloise completed the module in an unintended order.

> She utilizes the thinking skill of description to compare and contrast foods eaten in Colombia and the United States. To show comparison, she writes, "Colombian people love those dishes too." To contrast, she writes, "It's a big meal, contrary to Colombians, we prefer small dinners, maybe a hot coffee and a slice of bread, arepa and cheese." She could benefit from learning phrases such as "on the contrary" and other expressions that mark contrast.

In the excerpt, Olivia appropriately identifies the form-function relationship of language (i.e., *kinds of, too, contrary to*) associated with CLASSIFICATION and DESCRIPTION from the KF. She also seems to use her understanding to identify distinct weaknesses that the student could develop, such as the need for more linguistic resources to express formality and contrast.

Another student, Ashley, showed some indications of developing a functional shift in her perceptions of form as well, but glimpses of her traditional perspective towards grammar seemed to remain. As shown in the example excerpt, she says, "Because his sentence structure was so messy, I would also take the opportunity to reteach proper sentence structure." Without a clear explanation for why the ELL's sentence structure was "messy," Ashley's reflection seems to lack the contextualized, functional view towards language use.

Despite indications of a functional shift in the participants' analyses, two students, Cynthia and Marilyn, tended to remain within a traditional paradigm when describing their ELLs' language, both focusing on rule-based, accuracy judgments. Nevertheless, both were able to reflect on how the KF could be used in their instructional plans and identify specific knowledge structures they could address. We will revisit to what extent these two students, along with Ashley, adopted a functional approach when we introduce results for the second research question.

The TLC. Table 10.3 highlights representative excerpts from students' pre-module activation and post-module reflection activities where students were asked to first discuss perspectives towards explicit language teaching and later reflect on the importance of explicit teaching for literacy development. The final column represents students' transition between teaching-to-learn activities based on content analysis of responses to the activation and reflection activities.

For the activation activity, students tended to reflect on explicit teaching based on their own language learning and teaching experiences. Thus, it is without surprise that all students, with the exception of Eloise, associated explicit language teaching with judgments about accuracy or correctness and rules, for example:

Table 10.3 Summary of representative excerpts of individual's conceptions of literacy development in teaching–learning cycle online module

Name[a]	Pre-module Activation Activity	Post-module Reflection Activity	Transition
Allison	Teaching language "explicitly" involves a highly structured environment where teachers are focused on directing students' attention to a specific learning objective. For example, learning grammar, verb conjugations, [...], etc.	I now understand that explicit instruction is not solely the teacher's responsibility, but it is the inclusion of students too, allowing them to take the initiative to actively reflect on language they use in and across various contexts, ...	Traditional to Functional
Ashley	Explicit language teaching is when we deliberately teach specific language structures and grammar with close attention to accuracy and detail.	Explicit instruction, in the sense that ELs are taught explicitly how to navigate specific contexts effectively, is critical to their language growth.	Traditional to Functional
Cynthia	Explicit language teaching involves an educator to teach in a formal setting in which lessons are on grammar and other language aspects.	I now understand that explicit language teaching provides students with the independence to reflect on how language is used daily [...]	Traditional to Functional
Eloise	[Explicit teaching] outlines what the learning goals are for the student, and offers clear, unambiguous explanations of the skills and information structures they are presenting.	Explicit teaching is related to real-life use, so that understanding about language is developed in the context of actual language use.	General education perspective towards Functional

(Continued)

Table 10.3 *(Continued)*

Name[a]	**Pre-module Activation Activity**	**Post-module Reflection Activity**	**Transition**
Mandy	Growing up learning English language I think I was explicitly taught the rules about grammar, semantics, pronunciation, parts of speech and sentence structure.	Explicit teaching is guided by the teacher and fosters students' active involvement in learning and being able to critique an authentic text.	Traditional to Functional
Marilyn	Explicit teaching to me means strict vocabulary teaching and grammar components that students will need to know in order to help them acquire a new language with a new set of rules.	Having students focus on their form will allow them to have better understanding and efficacy for their learning and [. . .] more easily transition from one academic language to another.	Traditional to Functional
Raquel	It's more than just rote memorization or learning through translation; it's making language learning comprehensible.	I've learned that the more traditional approach to language teaching can be made more valuable to students by having students think about and reflect on the language that they are using.	Traditional to Functional
Olivia	While it is important for students to be able to guess at the meaning of words based on context clues, explicitly teaching the meanings of affixes may help students when they cannot guess the meaning solely based on the context.	I like the idea that explicit teaching means that "students can reflect on how language is used for a range of audience and for a range of purposes" and "teachers focus explicitly on those aspects of the language that allow students to do this."	Traditional to Functional
Sylvia	I would say explicit instruction is when a teacher accurately and precisely demonstrates a skill and is very direct in their presentation of knowledge and skills . . .	It is important to know that this systematic and functional model to instruction can indeed be carried out in an explicit manner.	Traditional to Functional

[a] Aaron did not complete the online module.

- Explicit language teaching is when we deliberately teach specific language structures and grammar with close attention to accuracy and detail. (Amy)
- [Explicit teaching] is successful for students' language learning when they comprehend when to use correct grammar. (Cynthia)
- Explicit teaching to me means strict vocabulary teaching and grammar components that students will need to know in order to help them acquire a new language with a new set of rules. (Marilyn)

Eloise's reflection about explicit teaching did not address language specifically; rather she referenced general teaching methods. Given that Eloise did not complete the previous module about the KF in the way it was intended, it is assumed that she was not able to internalize the key objectives of the online training. This lack of direction seems to have impacted her conceptualization of literacy development at the start of the TLC online module as well. In the post-module reflection activity, Eloise seems to begin her functional transition, as shown in Table 10.3; however, she continues to hold on to her general education mindset as well, which is indicative of her reference to explicit teaching as the need for presenting clear learning objectives.

For others, the post-module reflection illustrated a rather clear transition from traditional to functional conceptions of explicit, form-function instruction. Each of the students acknowledged their misconceptions about explicit teaching for the pre-module activation activity. For example, Marilyn stated, "I definitely had a misconception of what explicit language teaching could be at the start of this lesson and agree that I'm glad I now know what it can truly mean!" Similarly, Allison stated, "Along with others, I too had a complete misconception about what it meant to teach 'explicitly'." The responses after this second week of training seemed to indicate a clear shift from traditional to functional perspectives. As is evident from Marilyn's response above, students were excited to realize this shift, and Allison was glad to learn of a more contemporary perspective:

> In terms of grammar and vocabulary, sure, traditional approaches to this subject matter may have worked for the time being (or otherwise may have just gotten the job done!), but I too am glad that there are more developed, effective ways to allow students to build more of an explicit understanding of various subject matter and most of all, make meaning of it as well.

Others found the knowledge they gained was valuable and beneficial. However, it is unknown at this point whether students continue to demonstrate this functional shift for the social practice of teaching in the classroom. For this, we turn to our second research question.

Impact of Online Professional Development on Literacy Planning/ Instruction

The results of this study with regard to research question 2 (How do teachers integrate the KF and TLC for explicit teaching of form-function relationships into their literacy planning/instruction?) include several themes, as shown in Figure 10.3.

These themes reflect the frequency with which participants' final instructional plans included these different aspects. Key visuals (graphic organizers) were the most frequently used instructional strategy, mentioned in 25% of the final projects followed by multiple classroom applications of the course content mentioned in 20% of the projects. Genre stages/knowledge structures was the next most common theme, also mentioned in 20% of the projects followed by student engagement, mentioned in 15% of the projects, genre purpose in 10%, and form-function relationships in 10%. We will now elaborate on each of these themes individually.

Key Visuals (Graphic Organizers). Five of the 10 participants spoke directly to the importance of key visuals in their literacy plans. While key visuals are commonly used tools to help teachers scaffold learner understanding,

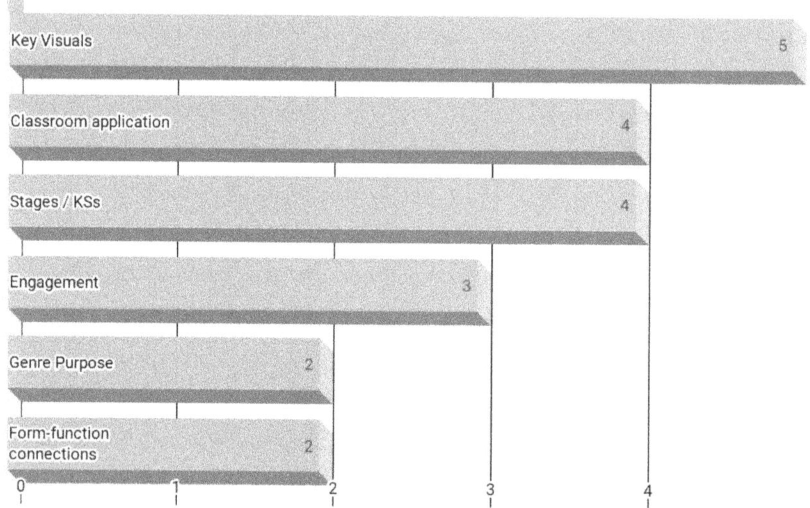

Figure 10.3 Frequency of teachers' integration of the KF and TLC into literacy planning

participants alluded to the unique function of key visuals as connected to the KF for mindfully assisting English learners' literacy development to convey specific thinking skills/knowledge structures and genre stages. Sylvia, for example, writes about the importance of webs for helping her bilingual kindergarten student brainstorm content before writing an informational report about cats, which involved the knowledge structures of CLASSIFICATION and DESCRIPTION. She states,

> The most concerning portion of [the student's] writing was that her writing was not logical...this can be done with the Knowledge Framework. I might ask [student] to draw a web telling me everything that she knows about cats. From the example, we can see that this activity can utilize a key visual with pictures and labels to help demonstrate her thoughts and organize them before writing.

Similarly, Allison writes about the utility of key visuals for helping her English learner to write in the personal recount genre,

> [Key visuals] can be useful in helping ELL students to retell a story as well. Those that illustrate a sequence with boxes each labeled with key words indicating sequence such as first, then, next, and last or beginning, middle, and end, make it easier for EL students to organize and order key story elements properly.

Another example of the importance of key visuals as connected to knowledge structures is illustrated in Marilyn's instructional plan. Marilyn, who teaches high school English writes about the importance of the key visuals involving the knowledge structures of PRINCIPLES and SEQUENCE for literacy development in the secondary language arts curriculum:

> The first [key visual] would include a procedure like listing of the step of the story following Freytag's Pyramid to mirror the construction of storytelling. [The student] would need to fill in a summary of the events that match each element of the story, such as exposition, rising action, climax, resolution, etc. I would also give her a graphic organizer that would focus on cause and effect in order to make sure that she doesn't just know how events took place, but further understand why they took place. This would enable her to better answer questions regarding meaning and author's purpose and help to organize her thoughts and understanding of the process.

Through these three excerpts, we can see that one of the main themes in participants' instructional plans included the importance of key visuals (graphic organizers) for developing students' literacy. While graphic organizers are commonly used across grade levels and subject areas, the participants in this study were able to speak to the careful selection of key visuals that connect to the specific ideas (thinking skills), written genres, and language forms in their curriculum.

Classroom Applications. The theme of classroom application was the next most frequently mentioned by the participants. Classroom applications of the ideas contained within the online modules included several innovative ideas, such as using the KF for text comprehension, using the knowledge structure of SEQUENCE within the personal recount genre, using less advanced personal recount genres to move students toward more advanced fictional narrative genres, and using assessment rubrics to help develop students' explicit knowledge of expository genre stages.

As Marilyn states, "While [my student] was reading a passage, I would also make use of different elements presented in the Knowledge Framework to make certain she is comprehending what she is reading when faced with a longer passage on her own." This comment alludes to the idea that knowledge structures can be used to help students comprehend the texts they read, an essential component of literacy development.

Another classroom application pertains to the use of oral language involving the knowledge structure of SEQUENCE for helping younger students in particular to move into procedural writing. As Sylvia writes,

> [Procedural] writing allows students to explain a sequence of events and explore precision in speaking and writing. As an educator at the kindergarten level it is best not to assume that all students have had experiences that would qualify them to speak fully on a topic. For this reason, it would be wise to model and practice with students before expecting them to write on a topic. For example, if I wanted to ask students to write about, "How do I brush my teeth?" I might model this for students and ask them to direct me with instructions on how to brush teeth. […] This activity can help them think of how they are communicating and writing messages for a reader.

A classroom application for learners at the elementary level is explored by Cynthia, who speaks about the importance of moving students from the simpler genre of personal recount to the more advanced and challenging genre of fictional narrative. "With the recount genre, [student] would need to improve on writing about the events that occurred in order to become prepared for many intensive genres such as narratives which require the much more advanced type of storytelling."

In high school, an important application that teachers can use is the use of functional assessment rubrics, that is rubrics that specifically delineate the appropriate genre stages and language. This is particularly applicable, as Marilyn relates in the following quote, to expository writing, which tends to be a major challenge for high school students across content areas. "The rubric would also be supplied with the prompt and graphic organizer to make sure that expectations are explicit and clear for the writer." As the participants in this study have indicated, there are numerous classroom applications for the form-function literacy development that are available to teachers.

Genre Stages/Knowledge Structures. A third theme that emerged from the literacy plans of participants included the importance of knowing the different genre stages, as well as understanding which knowledge structures are particularly prevalent within each stage. As both Olivia and Ashley note, elementary-level students will benefit greatly from knowledge of genre stages within informational reports, "[The student] could benefit from exposure to a variety of genres. In her future work, she will likely need to know how to read and produce information reports that include technical language" (Olivia). Similarly, Ashley, who also worked with an elementary-level learner writes,

> Being that [student] seemed to struggle most with informational texts during his reading assessments, I would implement a literacy plan based specifically on the genre of informational reports... He will be given ample opportunities to not only read various types of informational reports, but also to write them using appropriate text organization such as writing a clear and concise opening general statement/general classification and following it up with facts about various aspects of the subject.

In addition to informational reports, participants mentioned the importance of covering other genres, such as recounts, procedures, and explanations. As Olivia states, "Instructions shows how to do something, step by step, while explanations describe how something works. Studying recounts, which discuss past experiences, will also be useful for [my student]. As she is currently looking for work, she will need to produce cover letters, which include elements of recounts."

Within these varying genres, participants highlighted the complementary nature of knowledge structures and sentence-level form-function relationships. Olivia writes,

> [Student], in her interview, said she would like to be able to write without having as many doubts about the proper grammar and expressions to utilize. In her sample piece of writing, [the student] uses all the principles of the Knowledge Framework: classification, description, principles, sequence, evaluation and choice (Mohan, Early & Hooper, 1998 [incorrect citation]). She compares, informs, hypothesizes, evaluates and offers evidence. The sample shows a great deal of higher order thinking, but she uses little academic language.

These excerpts suggest participants' understanding of the importance of knowledge about genre stages and knowledge structures/thinking skills, as well as of the language features that are important therein. Taken as a whole, they indicate that participants took away important applications for their students' literacy development within a genre-based, functional model of language.

Student Engagement. Given that good teachers are constantly seeking ways to motivate their students, it is not surprising that many of the participants spoke to the importance of a form-functional model of literacy development for helping to engage their learners. Three participants alluded to the importance of a form-functional model for helping with this goal. As Ashley stated, choice of text is important for keeping student involvement. "To keep it fun and engaging, he will be allowed choice of text for both reading and writing lessons from an approved list of appropriately leveled texts containing subject matter that interests him."

Similarly, Cynthia writes about the importance of connecting genres to students' past experiences, "When I presented [the student] with the writing assessment to describe the event that she participated in over the weekend, it allowed her to remain focused on the task and become creative with not only her description but also her drawing of the event that happened during the period."

Finally, Mandy connects the instructional strategies recommended by the teaching–learning cycle for increasing student investment and learning: "Writing a joint construction of a personal recount with students can be very beneficial because students will give their input to write a story of their interest."

Genre Purpose. Another theme that emerged from students' instructional plans encompassed the importance of students writing with a purpose. Mandy writes, "I would go over personal recount genre and emphasis that the purpose of this genre is to entertain the audience and express personal feelings in the conclusion." Raquel also notes the importance of connecting this genre purpose to the actual assessment of student writing,

> After reading the short passage about a child entering a talent show, I created a writing assessment that was related to the topic that [the student] read about...This assessment falls under the genre of expository writing, more specifically "rhetorically expository." ...I used a rubric to assess [the student's] writing. According to the rubric criteria, she scored a 12/16 (75%)—mostly 3's out of 4. Her response was mostly question based, in that she answered each question that I asked, however she didn't go into much detail about each prompt.

By making concrete connections between purposeful writing and the assessment rubrics that teachers use, participants in this study knowingly made strides toward increasing the validity and reliability, not to mention the practicality and authenticity, of the assessments that they use to develop their students' literacy.

Form-Function Relationships. The next theme that emerged in participants' literacy plans related specifically to sentence-level form-function relationships. Mandy, for example, is able to make a specific connection between the genre stages of a recount and the language structures contained therein. She is also able to generate activities to target her student's struggles with function and form:

> According to Brisk (2015) there are different stages to recounts which are orientation, sequence of events and conclusion. I have also noticed that [the student] struggles with irregular verbs; therefore, creating different activities that would facilitate the skill would be beneficial. According to Brisk, making two columns labeled "-ed past" and "irregular past", to write the verbs under the corresponding column. Add irregular verbs like bought, taught, took, thought, sang, drove etc. (page 114). So, using all these activities would help to enhance [the student's] writing skills when he writes a personal/imaginative recount piece.

Similarly, Marilyn discusses the importance of evaluative vocabulary for helping to connect language function and form within expository writing. She states:

> One of the most beneficial ways to improve one's own vocabulary is by reading from others and evaluating the choices writers make to express themselves. By evaluating the word choice of different authors students are able to learn new vocabulary and understand the importance of choosing the best word to express meaning... I would select a passage

> for [the student] to read and then ask her to go back into the passage once she has competed it and fill out a chart based on the targeted understanding of the evaluative vocabulary. This activity would allow her to better understand the different ways we use language in writing and learn how to employ it in her own pieces.

By making connections between the word choices, grammar choices, language functions, and purposes of different text types, participants were able to generate form-function activities for their students' literacy development.

Depth of Application

The report of our findings would not be complete without mentioning the variability regarding the depth to which our participants integrated the KF and TLC for explicit teaching of form-function relationships into their literacy planning. Different participants were able to apply their newfound knowledge to varying degrees. The extent to which our participants were able to integrate ideas about form-function literacy development may have been impacted by their broad range of experience as teachers. As mentioned, our participants came from a number of different walks of life. Some of them came to the class with years of teaching experience, whereas others had zero years to only a matter of months inside the classroom.

The amount of classroom experience that our participants possessed inevitably influenced the extent to which they were able to integrate their knowledge. We might envision this as a continuum including on the one end participants who were able to understand and apply these ideas directly to their literacy plan and justify their curricular decision using evidence and examples, and on the other end, participants who struggled to incorporate their newfound knowledge of form-function literacy development.

Marilyn and Olivia were two such examples of participants who were able to make deep connections of their newfound knowledge to the classroom. In their literacy plan, both chose ideas contained in the online modules and elaborated on them to apply these ideas to their classroom. First of note is Marilyn's application of the knowledge structures of PRINCIPLES and SEQUENCE within fictional narratives. She writes,

> In order to aid [student] in more genre-specific functional writing, I would give her different graphic organizers that would explicitly aid her in setting up her paragraphs for an argument. For expository writing I would use a TEXT paragraph graphic organizer which matches

> the rubric that is used to grade such assessments. This organizer would explicitly state in the margins the steps to completing a full argumentative paragraph along with definitions of terms, suggestions for number of sentences, and questions to guide thinking and writing.... This organizer would help [student] to develop a thorough argument and make certain that she has a clear understanding of expectations. Within the organizer there is even a spot to remind students to cite their references and makes it clear how to properly do so in MLA format. I may also include an aid at the top of the page to aid the students in writing a claim for their paragraph, either giving a sentence starter or a fill in the blank sentence where they have to supply their argument and examples.

Within this example, we see a number of ways that Marilyn was able to connect her learnings to her instructional plan. First, she discusses the utility of specific graphic organizers for organizing logical/expository text. Next, she mentions the importance of formally assessing student writing using the notion of genre purpose and stages. Finally, she alludes to the importance of guiding students to choose and use appropriate language forms to accompany the varying stages of their expository essays.

The second noteworthy application was Olivia's deep ability to apply knowledge of the TLC to her own instructional context. This included both an awareness of genre purpose and stages, an ability to use graphic organizers purposefully, and an ability to distinguish knowledge structures within her English learner's assessment discourse. She writes,

> First, we will brainstorm items [student] can include in her cover letter... we will also review a list of action verbs commonly used in resumes and cover letters... next, I will ask [student] about what she knows about cover letters, and their purpose. I will give [student] an example of a cover letter for a position in her field... I will ask her what she notices about purpose of the different parts of the text. Building on her ideas, I will then show her the various elements of a cover letter... using the same cover letter, she could also mark key language features, including adjectives, action verbs, past tense and present perfect... in the joint construction phase, I will give [student] fictitious information about an individual seeking a particular job... Lastly, [student] will craft her own cover letter... We will talk about how cover letters should be modified based on the job.

Olivia's expert application of the TLC within her instructional literacy plan shows the extent to which she was capable of applying the ideas of the KF and the TLC to her own teaching practice.

On the other end of the continuum, participants with relatively little classroom experience may have struggled to incorporate their newfound knowledge of form-function literacy development. This is understandable given the fact that without practical real-world experiences, it is challenging if not impossible to apply theoretical ideas in a useful way. In Aaron's case, his lack of formal classroom teaching experience may have made it difficult to apply these concepts. In his reflection, he tended to associate student literacy development only with correct forms (e.g., spelling and capitalization). In Eloise's case, she seemed to struggle to justify her assertions. Although she states that she would use the KF in her grade 7 classroom, she lacks clear examples of how to do so, choosing instead to cite direct examples provided from another source, that of Slater and Gleason (2011). Aaron and Eloise's cases clearly suggest that the online training modules themselves may have created problems for them: Aaron failed to complete the modules and Eloise did not internalize the online contents.

Conclusion and Implications

Academic language development is a lasting concern across educational contexts. Central to the issue is the need to address teachers' professional development in order to improve classroom practices and thus student learning. This study evaluated the impact of online teacher development on pre-service teachers' conceptions towards literacy development and curricular planning. Using the Knowledge Framework and the teaching–learning cycle from a systemic functional approach to teaching and learning, teachers were exposed to two, week-long modules. Participants who were invested in appropriately completing learning-to-teach activities showed clear indications of understanding form-function relationships and explicit instruction of language use in social contexts. This investment, as well as the amount of prior teaching experiences, also impacted the depth of which participants were willing or able to utilize content from training in their instructional design. The findings seem to indicate that presenting pre-service teachers with even a limited amount of exposure to function-based, learning-to-teach activities can begin to transition their conceptions of language and language/content-based instruction. This transition was more evident among experienced teachers. Similar professional development opportunities are thus needed across institutional contexts, primarily with in-service teachers, while novice teachers should be exposed to more expanded learning opportunities to maximize impact and avoid superficial understanding of functional approaches to literacy development.

Despite participants' initial conception of form-focused instruction from a traditional perspective, participants' final instructional planning demonstrated successful application of the functional tools. The online training seemed to provide the majority of the pre-service teachers with opportunities to internalize the learning-to-teach activities for a transition into or at least towards a functional planning perspective. In other words, the online modules seemed to scaffold novice teachers' understanding of systemic functional literacy development. Further research is necessary to determine whether and how teachers utilize their training for teaching in the classroom.

The online format, however, was not without challenges. One participant in the study did not complete the online modules due to a lack of digital skills. By not gaining access to the content and also potentially due to his limited classroom experiences, he was not able to demonstrate an understanding of the KF and TLC and utilize that knowledge in instructional planning. To fill the gaps in teacher knowledge, this particular student would have benefited from immediate rather than delayed negotiation of meaning with an expert. With this said, the online platform provided students with constant access to content and interaction with classmates that has implications for more widespread distribution of learning-to-teach activities to a wider population of teachers. For the instructor of the online modules, the online platform enabled easier incorporation of materials and provided convenience due to the capability of replacing face-to-face time with autonomous work. The Canvas platform is also free, which can pave the way for future professional learning programs and potentially address the current lack of SFL-based resources for addressing literacy development.

References

Brisk, M.E. (2015). *Engaging students in academic literacies: Genre-based pedagogy for K-5 classrooms*. Routledge.

Butt, D., Fahey, R., Feez, S., Spinks, S., & Yallop, C. (2000). *Using functional grammar: An explorer's guide*. Macquarie University.

Charmaz, K. (2006). *Constructing grounded theory: A practical guide through qualitative analysis*. Sage Publications.

Christie, F., & Martin, J.R. (1997). *Genre and institutions: Social processes in the workplace and school.* Cassell.

Correa, D., & Echeverri, S. (2017). Using a systemic functional genre-based approach to promote a situated view of academic writing among EFL pre-service teachers. *HOW, 24*(1), 44–62. http://dx.doi.org/10.19183/ how.24.1.303.

Derewianka, B., & Jones, P. (2016). *Teaching Language in Context.* Oxford University Press.

Early, M. (1990). Enabling first and second language learners in the classroom. *Language Arts, 67*, 567–574.

Early, M., Mohan, B., & Hooper, H.R. (1988). The Vancouver School Board Language and Content Project. In J.H. Esling (Ed.), *Multicultural education and policy: ESL in the 1990s*, (pp. 107–122). Ontario Institute for Studies in Education.

Esterberg, K.G. (2002). *Qualitative methods in social research.* McGraw-Hill.

Freeman, D. (2004). A Framework for Teacher Learning and Development. *TESOL Symposium on English Teacher Development in EFL Contexts.* Retrieved from: http:// www.tesol.org/docs/default-source/new-resource-library/symposium-on-english-teacher-development-in-efl-5.pdf?sfvrsn=0

Freeman, D., & Johnson, K.E. (1998). Reconceptualizing the knowledge-base of language teacher education. *TESOL Quarterly, 32*, 397–417.

Gebhard, M. (2010). Teacher education in changing times: A systemic functional linguistics perspective. *TESOL Quarterly, 44*(4), 797–803.

Gebhard, M., Chen, I.-A., Graham, H., & Gunawan, W. (2013). Teaching to mean, writing to mean: SFL, L2 literacy and teacher education. *Journal of Second Language Writing, 22*, 107–124.

Gebhard, M. & Harman, R. (2011). Reconsidering genre theory in K–12 schools: A response to school reforms in the United States. *Journal of Second Language Writing, 20*(1), 45–55.

Gibbons, P. (2014). *Scaffolding language, scaffolding learning: Teaching second language learners in the mainstream classroom.* Heinemann

Halliday, M.A.K. (1978). *Language as social semiotic: The social interpretation of language and meaning.* Edward Arnold.

Halliday, M.A.K. (1985). *Introduction to functional grammar.* Routledge.

Humphrey, S., & Feez, S. (2016). Direct instruction fit for purpose: Applying a metalinguistic toolkit to enhance creative writing in the early secondary years. *Australian Journal of Language and Literacy, 39* (3), 207–219.

Hyland, K. (2003). Genre-based pedagogies: A social response to process. *Journal of Second Language Writing, 12*, 17–29.

Johns, A.M. (2011). The future of genre in L2 writing: fundamental, but contested, decisions. *Journal of Second Language Writing, 20*, 56–68.

Macken-Horarik, M. (2002). "Something to shoot for": A systemic functional approach to teaching genre in secondary school science. In A.M. Johns (Ed.), *Genre in the classroom* (pp. 21–46). Erlbaum.

Martin, J.R. (2009). Genre and language learning: A social semiotic perspective. *Linguistics and Education, 20,* 10–21.

Mohan, B.A. (1986). *Language and Content.* Addison-Wesley Publishing Company.

Paltridge, B. (2007). Approaches to genre in ELT. In J. Cummins & C. Davison (eds.), *The handbook of English language teaching. Volume 2* (pp. 931–943). Springer.

Rose, D. (2012). Genre in the Sydney school. In J.P. Gee & M. Handford (Eds.), *The Routledge handbook of discourse analysis* (pp. 209–225). Routledge.

Rothery, J. (1996). Making changes: Developing an educational linguistics. In R. Hasan & G. Williams (Eds.), *Literacy in society* (pp. 86–123). Longman.

Saldaña, J. (2016). *The coding manual for qualitative researchers.* Sage Publications.

Schleppegrell, M.J. (2013). The role of metalanguage in supporting academic language development. *Language Learning,* 63 (Supplement 1), 153–170.

Slater, T. & Gleason, J. (2011). Integrating language and content: The knowledge framework. In (J. Morrison Ed.), *Conference proceedings of MidTESOL: Gateway to global citizenship* (pp. 5–20). University of Saint Louis.

Slater, T., & McCrocklin, S. (2016). Learning to use systemic functional linguistics to teach literary analysis: Views on the effectiveness of a short professional development workshop. In L. de Oliveira, M. Shoffner (Eds.), *Teaching English language arts to English language learners* (pp. 193–214). Palgrave Macmillan.

Slater, T., Gleason, J. & Link, A. (2012, October). Creating integrated language-and-content units across the curriculum. Paper presented at the MIDTESOL Conference, Ames, Iowa.

Tang, G.M. (1997). From graphic literacy across languages to integrating English and content teaching in vocational settings. *Hong Kong Journal of Applied Linguists, 2*(1), pp. 97–114.

About the Authors

Stephanie Link is an associate professor of TESOL/applied linguistics at Oklahoma State University. Her research involves technology-mediated language learning with a focus on development and use of automated writing evaluation tools and learning systems for second language writing and writing for publication.

Jesse Gleason, PhD, is an associate professor of applied linguistics and Spanish at Southern Connecticut State University. Her teaching and research interests include bilingualism/biliteracy development and technology-mediated instruction. She has presented her research internationally in Australia, Belgium, Brazil, Canada, Chile, Germany, and the US as well as published research in a number of refereed journals, such as *CALICO, System,* and *Language, Culture and Curriculum.*

Appendix A: Rubric for Case Study/Instructional Literacy Plan

	A Done very well	A-/B+ Done well	B Satisfactory	C Minimally acceptable	F Not acceptable
Assessment Portion					
1. You have wisely selected your home language survey, reading assessment, and writing sample, and have explained your choices in the paper. 2. If appropriate, you have selected additional assessments, and have explained my reasoning for these supplemental assessments in the paper. 3. You have handed in actual "filled out" copies of each assessment. Also, the writing sample contains your responses to the writing, as if you were handing it back to the student.					
Analysis					
1. You have analyzed each of the assessments thoroughly, speaking to the various questions listed in the syllabus, as appropriate. 2. You have identified students' strengths exhibited in the assessments as well as their weaknesses. 3. Your references to the literature indicate that you have made good use of your newfound knowledge in your analysis. 4. You have considered traditional linguistic issues, genre-based functional linguistic issues as well has socio-cultural issues in your analysis.					

Development Plan
1. Your instructional plan clearly articulates the specific instructional strategies you will implement in the near future for both reading and writing. 2. You have convincingly explained WHY you have selected your particular instruction plan. 3. Your instructional recommendations are based specifically on your assessment analysis findings. 4. You have included a well-developed plan for reading/writing of a particular content area or genre.
Presentation
1. Your presentation meets the description requirements set out in the syllabus (page number, organization, etc.). 2. Your presentation is clear and written in good, academic English. 3. Your paper is organized and presented per graduate study standards.

11 Opportunities and Challenges of the Knowledge Framework for In-service Teacher Development: A Case Study

Jingzi Huang and Margaret Berg

Abstract

The growth of interest among teachers and schools seeking professional development that focuses on English Language Learners is a pressing challenge for the field of teacher education. Existing studies suggest that (1) there is a need to develop culturally responsive and linguistically sensitive teachers in order to facilitate emerging bilingual students' academic success; (2) existing research is limited on how teachers developed knowledge and skills in order to integrate language and content instruction for ESL students; (3) studies that recognize the importance of linguistic sensitivity in teacher professional development are extremely limited in their scope and do not cover school subject content areas; and (4) few studies connect teacher professional development effort to its impact on student performance. This chapter addresses the gap in both research and practice in teacher education by examining an in-service teacher development project in a variety of school contexts, including math, science, and social studies instruction where teachers typically do not see students' language development as their responsibility. The study, employing a mixed-methods approach to analyze the process of teacher development and document changes over time, examines the impact of the KF as a linguistically sensitive approach to teacher development on teachers' instructional practice and student performance in schools. The qualitative and quantitative evidence provided by the project strengthens the argument for the importance of incorporating culturally responsive and linguistically sensitive pedagogy into all teacher development programs. The findings shed light on opportunities and challenges with the use of the KF for in-service regular classroom teacher development.

Keywords: teacher development; CLD/ESL education; classroom research; academic language; disciplinary literacy

Mohan's Knowledge Framework (KF) is perhaps better known to teachers of English as a Second Language; however, as a guide for curriculum planning it can be powerful for regular classroom teachers. Since many of these teachers, particularly in the United States, are unprepared for the increasing linguistic diversity in their classrooms, they must learn more about the social practices of teaching that support academic language development in students. We have found the KF useful in the improvement of instruction and learning within the social context of schooling. This chapter is adapted from two previous publications by Berg and Huang (2015) and Huang, Berg, Romero, and Walker (2016) about an in-service K-12 teacher development program based on Mohan's KF for culturally and linguistically responsive pedagogy. To fit the purpose and scope of the book, the adaptation focuses on the impact of the KF on classroom teachers' social practices in the classroom for instructional design and classroom practice incorporating an academic language/literacy component to improve teaching effectiveness, particularly student writing in linguistically diverse classrooms.

Facing a dramatic increase of linguistically diverse student population, classroom teachers often feel professionally inadequate to do a good job with the knowledge and skills they received from a typical teacher preparation program that lacks attention to linguistically diverse learners (Balderrama, 2001; Darling-Hammond, Chung, & Frelow, 2002; Gandara, Maxwell-Jolly, & Driscoll, 2005). While available literature points to a need to prepare all teachers for culturally and linguistically diverse students (Garcia, Arias, Murri, & Serna, 2009), a large gap exists between the demand for classroom teachers who can work with English Language Learners (ELLs) and the supply of teachers educated to work with this population. This difference has led to an expansion of interest in teachers' professional development programs related to ELLs. Existing research efforts have been made to examine the factors contributing to professional development (PD) of classroom teachers in culturally and linguistically diverse settings, but most studies (see Garcia, Arias, Murri, & Serna, 2009) focus more on cultural responsiveness with little attention to the linguistic aspect for teacher development (see Aguirre-Munoz, Park, Amabisca, & Boscardin, 2008). This chapter examines a teacher development program that utilizes a functional linguistic approach (Halliday, 1976; Mohan, 1986; Schleppegrell, 2004, 2010) to equip teachers with knowledge and skills for students' academic language and literacy development. It examines the impact of such a program as evidenced by the change in participating teachers' instructional practice in the reality of their everyday teaching and their students' improved literacy performance. It also reveals challenges we are still facing at the implementation level.

Literature Review

In this chapter, we view literacy as a part of, and inseparable from, language development. Academic literacy, which is discipline-specific, is not a new concept in the field of literacy education. From a sociocultural perspective, the development of academic literacy takes place in specific academic content areas (Fang, 2014; Gee, 2007; Gibbons, 2009; Schleppegrell, 2004; Zwiers, 2008). Thus, instructional practice that separates literacy development from academic content learning becomes problematic. Existing research has shown that adequate development of academic language and literacy skills is crucial for students' school success (Fang, 2012; Schleppegrell, 2004; Schleppegrell & O'Hallaron, 2011; Zwiers, 2008). Many scholars, noticing that achievement disparities between ELLs and non-ELLs stem from the lack of instructional focus on academic language, argue for the need to make the linguistic structures of academic language explicit to ELLs (e.g., August & Shanahan, 2006; Fang, 2012, 2014; Gibbons, 2002, 2003; Wong & Snow, 2000). From the perspective of teacher development, a practical question is how to guide teachers to systematically incorporate students' academic language growth while teaching specific academic content such as math, science, and social studies.

Related to ELL education is the issue of systematic integration of language and content (Mohan, 1986). Linguistic and cultural aspects make an obvious impact on a student's language development and conceptual learning (de Jong & Harper, 2005; Harper & de Jong, 2004, 2009). Available studies have provided a strong argument for culturally responsive approaches to instruction (Cartledge & Kourea, 2008; Garcia & Ortiz, 2006), but a culturally responsive agenda with no emphasis on linguistically sensitive pedagogy will be insufficient to address the issue of culturally diverse students struggling in the use of mainstream linguistic resources for academic success (Schleppegrell, 2004). Thus, a linguistic focus is necessary in a culturally responsive pedagogy for all children to succeed in schools. Such an approach requires theory-informed and research-based instruction, and assessment strategies that make the connections between academic content and content-specific English explicit for the students. While studies from the socio-cultural perspectives (de Jong & Harper 2005; Gee, 2007; Halliday, 1976; Huang, 2004;

Mohan, 1986; Schleppegrell & de Oliveira, 2006) convincingly argue for the effectiveness of systematic integration of language and content in instruction for diverse students, the literature is limited on successful methods for developing teachers to implement this instructional integration.

Among those studies addressing in-service teacher development for content-specific literacy education, most are limited to teachers' beliefs, perceptions, and knowledge development (Glaeser, Leuer, & Grant, 2012; Pawan, 2008; Pytash, 2013). Some studies connect teacher perceptions to their development and professional practices (Aguirre-Munoz, et al., 2008; Huang, 2004; Hart & Okhee, 2003), such as Aguirre et al.'s study that provided evidence demonstrating the effectiveness of a systemic functional linguistic approach to teacher development for attention to academic language/literacy in teachers' instructional practice. However, the findings are limited to teacher development in the area of middle school language arts and provide no data on change in student performance as a result of teacher development.

In the past decade, Systemic Functional Linguistics (SFL), which has been widely used as a theoretical foundation for language and literacy education in international settings, has gradually made its way into the American educational field, partially due to the great effort made by American scholars in the field of ELL education. Zwiers's (2008) and Schleppegrell's (2004) work on academic language development in school settings have drawn attention to linguistic resources that we use to construct meaning in contextualized ways. The essence of the recent studies in literacy education from the SFL perspective is an emphasis on integration of language/literacy and content (e.g., Fang, 2012; Huang & Normandia, 2009; Schleppegrell, 1998, 2001, 2003, 2004).

Our approach to teacher development with a focus on students' academic language/literacy skills in the content-specific context is influenced by SFL, which views learning as a linguistic process. This linguistic view of learning results in a unified view of learning language, learning through language, and learning about language (Halliday, 2007). In this view, the child learning language for the first time is engaged in a process of language socialization (Ochs, 1988, Schieffelin & Ochs, 1986); the child is seen to be learning language and simultaneously learning through language, that is, learning about the world. Extending this view to ELL students learning science in a school setting, we see the learning of the language for science as related to the learning of science content, in a process of second language socialization.

Among the efforts to make connections between language and content from Halliday's functional view are register theory (Halliday, McIntosh, & Strevens, 1964), genre analysis (Martin, 1992), and the Knowledge Framework (Mohan, 1986, 2001). For our PD project, we chose Mohan's framework to guide teachers' instructional planning since it has been successfully used to help classroom teachers organize instruction that leads to a wide range of form-meaning connections (Early, 1991; Huang, 2000, Huang & Normandia, 2009; Tang, 2001). Also, while emphasizing the systematic integration of language and content, it addresses the psychological paradigm of Bloom's taxonomy (Anderson et al., 2000) which all of the teachers in our study were familiar with from their previous teacher education programs. An example of instructional design based on the KF developed by a participating teacher is presented in Figure 11.1 for a unit on Genetic Diseases. We will elaborate on this example in the methodology section.

Present Study

The literature review shows research gaps that include (1) the need to develop teachers' linguistic sensitivity (Commins & Miramontes, 2005; Jiménez & Rose, 2010; Sleeter, 2008) to provide culturally responsive and linguistically sensitive instruction to facilitate students' academic success; and (2) the need to expand studies to various school content areas and connect PD activities to the improvement of the teachers' practice and students' literacy performance. To address some of these research gaps, this study examines how a functional approach helps K-12 teachers in various content areas develop linguistic sensitivity to provide linguistically responsive instruction in the reality of their teaching. For the in-service teacher development project examined in the chapter, Mohan's KF, which systematically brings about wider form-function connections, was employed as the tool to help teachers gain understanding of the relation between language and content while developing teachers' linguistic sensitivity needed to integrate language and content in their classroom instruction. This study employs a mixed-methods approach to analyze the process of teacher development and document changes over time. It examines the impact of the KF as a linguistically sensitive approach to teacher development on teachers' instructional practice and student performance in schools. The specific question that guided this research effort is:

> How does PD with a functional linguistic focus effect teachers' instructional practice and their students' content-specific literacy development?

By addressing the question, we intend to present the power of the KF in helping classroom teachers while at the same time revealing challenges we are still facing when implementing the KF for teacher development.

Methodology

This study employs a mixed-methods design (Creswell, 2014: Johnson, Onwuegbuzie, & Turner, 2007), because qualitative and quantitative data together minimize "the limitations of both approaches" (Creswell, 2014, p. 218) and provides a deeper understanding of the change in the instructional practice. Data were collected through quantitative measures such as closed-question surveys and numeric rubrics related to PD assignments followed by an interview with open-ended questions. Data were interpreted by examining evidence from all the sources to build a "coherent justification" for themes (Creswell, 2014). The triangulation of data and the length of time spent with the teachers (six months) strengthen the validity of the findings.

Setting

The PD project, with the support from a Title II grant, was initiated by a conversation between the university's teacher preparation faculty and the school districts whose teachers are experiencing challenges working with culturally and linguistically diverse learners in the general education settings. The participating districts have at least 28% of the students designated as English Language Learners (ELL) and 60% as designated from a Spanish-speaking background but not necessarily designated as ELLs. These Hispanic students may speak fluent everyday English but struggle with academic language. Most of the teachers, facing a class with diverse learners as described, had never been formally trained to teach ELLs. At the same time, the state was adopting a new set of English language standards based on the WIDA Language Proficiency Standards (WIDA Consortium, 2012), which are heavily influenced by SFL (Halliday, 1976, 1994) and are content and grade specific.

The PD program, designed in partnership with the school districts, consisted of four 3-credit-hour courses, for a total of 12 credit hours of instruction, with a mandatory on-site coaching and mentoring component. The first two courses focused on instructional and assessment methods that emphasized a sociocultural perspective for second language development and have their theoretical foundation supported by SFL. The third course, coupled with a fourth course on the special needs of linguistically diverse learners, offered in the second semester, formally introduced the teachers to SFL for language education focusing on the functions of language in linguistic resources for meaning through application. Specifically, teachers were introduced to the concept of the KF and the six basic Knowledge Structures (KSs)—CLASSIFICATION, DESCRIPTION, PRINCIPLES, SEQUENCE, EVALUATION, and CHOICE. Then, using the KF, teachers designed instructional units that analyzed academic tasks for their functions and the associated linguistic features at the levels of lexicon (vocabulary), syntax (sentence), and discourse to provide linguistically responsive instruction. An example of the instructional design based on the KF developed by a participating teacher is presented in Figure 11.1 for a unit on Genetic Diseases. Teachers in this study were apprenticed into the use of the KF, which demands an analysis of academic tasks for their functions—what is being discussed (field), who/how it is being discussed (tenor), and the medium through which it is discussed (mode)—and the associated linguistic features at the levels of lexicon, syntax, and discourse. For example, in the Genetic Diseases example (Figure 11.1),

GENETIC DISEASES

CLASSIFICATION	PRINCIPLES	EVALUATION
Outcome: Classify genetic disorders into four categories **Thinking Process:** classifying **Activity:** Read materials about the categories of genetic disorders and briefly define characteristics of each one with appropriate sentence pattern. ***Essential Language:** chromosomal abnormalities, single genetic defects, multifactorial problems, teratogenic This disorder is a _______.	**Outcome:** State specific causes for specific genetic diseases, i.e., Radiation, genetics, etc. **Thinking Process:** explaining, inferring, interpreting **Activity:** Use defined characteristics notes and graphic organizer to discuss in small groups. ***Essential Language:** ...are known to cause... ...resulting in...	**Outcome:** Rate the pros and cons of a specific genetic disease? **Thinking Process:** analyzing, judging, evaluating **Activity:** Computer research with questions chart on a specific genetic disease and state the good and bad of it (if possible). Individual and whole class rating. ***Essential Language:** One advantage is... Although, this may also... The (dis)advantages include...
Outcome: Describe one genetic disorder from each of the four categories **Thinking Process:** compare/contrast **Activity:** Study and take notes one genetic disease from each category and be able to share notes and expand on them orally with small group. ***Essential Language:** ...may be inherited... ...chromosomes... inversion, translocation, deletion	**Outcome:** Tell how are these genetic disorders transmitted from one generation to the next? **Thinking Process:** ordering **Activity:** Find examples of genetic disorders and research how they are inherited. Complete sequence of events chain. ***Essential Language:** This leads to...	**Outcome:** Tell what are the benefits or detriment of knowing the human genome? **Thinking Process:** making a decision, analyzing, evaluating **Activity:** Computer group research on human genome, short PowerPoint presentation must include pros and cons
DESCRIPTION	**SEQUENCE**	**CHOICE**

*Essential language taken from a corresponding chart from teachers' unit design.

Figure 11.1 Sample of an instructional unit based on Mohan's KF—Biology

the field is biological science; the tenor will be informal when small groups of peers discuss the PRINCIPLES of genetic science, and more formal when the CHOICE around genetics is presented. The mode for conveying understanding of the PRINCIPLES is oral while there are at least two modes for the presentation: written messages on slides, and oral messages of support for those slides. To apprentice teachers into the social practice embracing students' academic language development, we pushed the teachers to never settle for non-native English speakers simply drawing a picture for the determination of understanding since success in schooling depends greatly upon linguistic means.

At the successful conclusion of the program, the participating teachers were awarded a CLD specialist certificate, with the courses potentially leading to a Master's degree in Culturally and Linguistically Diverse Education.

Participants

In this chapter, all participating teachers are referred to as teachers; all K-12 learners of those teachers are referred as students. Professors are those delivering the courses and mentoring the teachers in the classrooms. Twenty-three K-12 teachers, with teaching experience ranging 1–12 years, from one urban and three rural school districts, took part in this study. Of these, 13 were elementary level (K-6) teachers and 10 were secondary level (7–12) teachers. The content areas taught by these teachers included math, science, social studies, language arts, visual arts, computing/technology, family and consumer sciences, theatre/drama, health, music, special education (elementary, math, and literacy), world languages, pull-out English as a second language (ESL), and other subjects.

The research team included three university professors from a college of education and a doctoral candidate from the statistics department. The research professors' areas of focus were language, content literacy, and linguistically diverse education. We had taught in public schools within Canada or the United States prior to entering professorships.

Data Collection and Analysis

A comparative analysis of data collected at different stages of the program looks into the development of teachers' linguistic awareness and sensitivity and their ability to integrate subject matter instruction with language development activities at the levels of both instructional planning and instructional practice as a result of such a development. Examining data from teachers instructing different content areas at various grade levels could be challenging; however, the purpose of the study was to examine the change in the teachers' social practice in teaching their particular content areas. Although the curriculum content to be taught is different, the need for teachers to make the connections explicit for students, between meaning construction and language use, is the same. Thus, all the analytical tools for data analysis were designed to be inclusive of content and grade diversity. The researchers, with diverse experience and expertise in content-specific literacy, evaluated the teachers' sensitivity for and ability to incorporate appropriate language requirements in the data analysis focusing on teachers' attention to content-specific language/literacy skills.

Four different sources of data provided information for the study. A visual model of the embedded mixed-method design (Creswell, 2014) is provided in Figure 11.2 to show when data were collected in relation to the PD courses. For this chapter, we limit our focus to data on in-service teachers' instructional practice and their students' literacy performance.

Instructional Plans. Data in the form of lesson plans provide evidence of change in teachers' instructional planning. When teachers entered the program, they were asked to submit as baseline data a lesson plan they typically used. Then in the first course, the teachers were required, based on their current school curricula, to design two lesson plans for a content area (other than Language Arts if an elementary teacher) that included learner outcomes for oral language production and written language production among other elements. The basic requirements of the two initial lesson plans can be found in Figure 11.3. This assignment was given with a rubric that provided questions to have teachers consider the course work they had been doing. In the second semester, teachers were required to design an entire unit using Mohan's KF to identify aspects of a content topic (such as types and causes of genetic disorders, Figure 11.1) to be learned and the associated language functions to be realized using specific linguistic resources. Such instructional design pushes teachers to consider how the preferred thinking related to specific content learning could be realized linguistically. The baseline lesson plan, lesson plans after instruction in the first semester, and the unit design collected in the second semester were all analyzed using a pre-designed 1–4 rating scale, with 4 indicating the highest level of performance, followed by paired t-tests.

Classroom Observations. All teachers were observed at least twice during the period of the initial two courses: The baseline was taken within the first three weeks of entering the program, and the second observation took place toward the end or after the first semester. The far-left column of Table 11.1

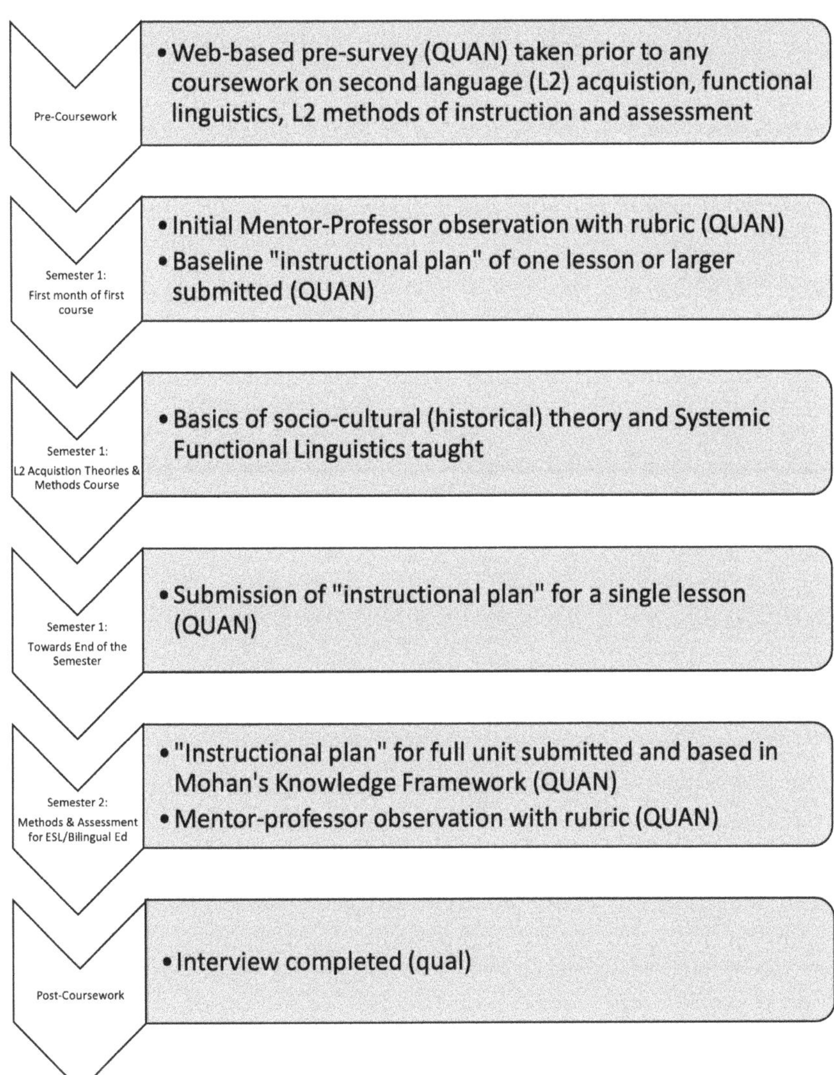

Figure 11.2 QUAN(qual) research design

shows the elements of the form used in observations. Modified to align with course content and the 2012 WIDA Standards, the form is loosely based on the Sheltered Instruction Observation Protocol, SIOP (Echevarria, Vogt, & Short, 2008). The pre-designed observation rating scale ranged from highly evident (4) to not evident (0). The completed observation rubric was analyzed using a paired t-test.

Requirements	Components	Materials
Planning for integration: Based on the curriculum you are currently using in the school, design two lessons that integrate content and language instruction at the level of objectives/outcomes, instructional activities, and assessment	• Identifying information: grade level, content area, learner description for accommodation/modification • Two lessons for the same content topic you want your students to learn about: one focusing on the development of spoken language; one on the development of written language; • For each lesson, objectives need to be explicit for both content outcomes and language outcomes (use Model Performance Indicator, WIDA); • For each lesson, student activities/formative assessments will require students to demonstrate the achievement of the content and language outcomes; • For each lesson, visuals/graphic organizers are used to facilitate students' thinking, comprehension, and communication; • A comment section on 1) principles of language development addressed by the lesson plans; 2) activities that engage students in various thinking processes; 3) activities that facilitate the development of CALP; 4) activities aligned with the established objectives/outcomes; 5) activities that facilitate both content learning and development of language associated with the target content.	Instructional materials you are currently using in the school; Course reading materials.

Figure 11.3 Basic requirements for the lesson plans

Finally, analysis of all data followed a recursive process as the researcher team read and reread the results of different data at different times to clarify their understandings of student work and the statistical results, and how these connected to the themes that emerged from interview data.

Student Writing Samples

Data in the form of writing samples from students were limited to the classes of teachers who taught the same subject and grade for two consecutive semesters. Six teachers instructing in subjects other than language arts submitted both a baseline student sample set and a second sample set. As a result, a total of 205 writing samples were collected from the students of six teachers teaching math or science in kindergarten to high school settings.

Table 11.1 Classroom observation

	Baseline		Second Assessment		Paired t-test results	
	Mean	**Std Dev**	**Mean**	**Std Dev**	**t-test**	**p-value**
Students' prior knowledge related to the new content activated and/or assessed	2.87	1.42	3.83	1.114	3.075	.006
Students' prior knowledge related to the new language features activated and/or assessed	2.09	1.54	2.91	1.443	2.413	.025
Background knowledge built to facilitate new learning when needed	2.65	1.61	3.91	1.164	3.051	.006
Key vocabulary, focus sentence structures, and salient discourse features highlighted, taught, and required to be used by students	2.96	1.49	3.74	1.010	2.657	.014
Prior Knowledge & Background	2.64	1.24	3.60	.913	3.626	<.001
Speech and written material appropriate for students' proficiency level	2.70	1.26	3.87	1.10	2.929	.008
A variety of techniques used to make content and requirements clear	3.09	1.04	4.13	1.18	3.006	.006
Student activities require student use of required language features in demonstration of content understanding	2.61	1.27	2.87	1.69	2.170	.041
Language output required to be in the form of both speaking and writing related to the content focus	2.22	1.51	3.30	1.46	2.737	.012

(Continued)

Table 11.1 (*Continued*)

	Baseline		Second Assessment		Paired t-test results	
	Mean	**Std Dev**	**Mean**	**Std Dev**	**t-test**	**p-value**
Comprehensible Input & Pushed Output	2.65	1.01	3.68	.751	4.041	<.001
Tasks conducted to promote higher-order thinking skills with a reduced linguistic demands for ELLs	1.91	1.31	3.43	1.16	6.076	<.0001
Graphic organizers, demonstrations, prompting techniques, etc. used to connect language functions to various thinking skills	1.91	1.28	3.00	1.57	3.014	.006
Appropriate graphic organizers used for organizing and communicating knowledge by both the teacher and the students, and to encourage students producing longer discourse related to the content focus	1.96	1.40	2.78	1.38	2.141	.004
Activities provided for students to demonstrate defined academic content learning and to use the required language features to achieve the lesson objectives in the classroom	1.91	1.13	3.35	1.43	3.813	<.001
Activities integrate the use of all language skills for communicating about the content focus	2.17	1.30	3.70	1.52	4.288	<.0001
Activities provide opportunities for interaction and discussion between teacher/student and among students, which encourage elaborated responses related to the lesson content objectives	2.13	1.29	3.48	1.28	3.496	.002
Grouping configuration support language and content objectives of the lesson	1.96	1.30	3.43	1.53	3.398	.003

	Baseline		**Second Assessment**		**Paired t-test results**	
	Mean	**Std Dev**	**Mean**	**Std Dev**	**t-test**	**p-value**
Strategies & Activities	1.99	1.14	3.31	1.09	4.710	<.0001
Student activities conducted as formative assessments for content learning relation to the lesson content objectives	2.39	1.53	3.96	1.11	4.281	<.0001
Student activities conducted as formative assessment for language development related to the lesson language objectives	1.96	1.43	2.87	1.58	2.192	.039
Regular feedback provided to students on their output	2.61	1.53	3.96	1.15	4.080	<.0001
On-going assessment of student comprehension and learning of all lesson objectives	2.87	1.69	4.04	1.15	3.127	.005
Review/Assessment	2.46	1.35	3.70	.990	4.257	<.0001
Overall Measurement Tool Results	2.37	1.07	3.53	.871	4.717	<.0001

Note: All p-values demonstrate a statistically significant increase in the mean at the second observation.

To measure the level of improvement in student writing, a rubric that highlights elements such as ideational content expressed and use of content-specific language (as shown in Table 11.2) was developed based on the Features of Academic Language in the 2012 version of the WIDA Standards. This rubric, having good reliability with regard to this project's sample population with a Cronbach alpha of .927, uses a Likert-like scale of 5 (clear and/ or detailed requirements/feedback was given to the student) to 1 (no requirements or feedback was given to the student). For students' writing samples, text analysis was conducted using an SFL lens, paying special attention to ideational meaning, or in other words, "meaning in the sense of content" (Halliday, 1985, p. 101), as conveyed by semantic relations expressed in writing and linguistic resources used in the form of lexicon, syntactical structures, and

Table 11.2 Summary of writing sample analysis: aggregated

		6 teachers	
Components	**Details**	**Base**	**Exit**
Ideational content expressed	Content related to the content area	24.37	25.25
	Content related to the topic	18.52	21.51
	Semantic relations expressed as required by the topic	12.69	18.36
Use of content-specific language	Vocabulary Usage (Specificity of word or phrase choice): • General, specific, and technical language • Multiple meanings of words and phrases • Formulaic and idiomatic expressions • Nuances and shades of meaning • Collocations	13.14	17.03
	Language Forms and Conventions (Types, array, and use of language structures): • Types and variety of grammatical structures • Conventions, mechanics, and fluency • Match of language forms to purpose/ perspective	12.78	16.16
	Linguistic Complexity: • Amount of speech/written text • Structure of speech/written text • Density of speech/written text • Organization and cohesion of ideas • Variety of sentence types	11.86	16.13

discourse features for meaning construction. The WIDA (2012) definition of Features of Academic Language serves as our guide for linguistic analysis of the collected writing samples. Specifically, an approach similar to knowledge structure analysis (Huang & Morgan, 2003; Mohan & Huang, 2002) was adopted as shown in the following steps for each writing sample analysis:

- Identify the topic of the writing (to see if it is as required);
- Identify the language function realized in the writing (i.e., compare/contrast, describe, explain, etc.);
- Identify semantic relations realized in writing and rate the richness of the expressed content;
- Rate the use of vocabulary, sentence, and discourse (as defined by WIDA) for appropriateness of grade level and the topic in the designated content area.

Findings

The results demonstrate the teachers' increased abilities to appropriately instruct linguistically diverse students. The interview data complement these findings and show teachers' greater knowledge of the linguistic complexity of schooling, the diversity of the immigrant experience, and their instructional responsibility. While survey and interview data revealed teachers' acquisition of knowledge and change of perceptions, the findings from instructional planning and classroom observations provide statistical evidence of the impact of the project on teachers' social practices in the classroom.

Instructional Planning that Integrates Language and Content

WIDA, adopting a functional linguistic view as its theoretical foundation for an understanding of language, emphasizes that language serves to perform different functions, such as classifying, comparing, explaining, justifying, and so on. Mohan's KF provides a principled account of how different language functions associated with a single content topic (e.g., Genetic Diseases) are realized by explicit linguistic features at the lexical, syntactical, and discourse levels. Thus, the introduction of the KF as a guide for instructional planning intended to draw teachers' attention to a variety of language functions that may be needed for students' demonstration of a more comprehensive understanding of a given topic. To examine teachers' change in instructional planning, the pre-designed rubric rated the teachers' use/appropriateness of content outcomes, language outcomes (including vocabulary, and sentence or discourse levels), accommodations for various language proficiency levels, activities/assessments to achieve both the outcome set and Bloom's higher thinking skills, and visual/graphic support for both input and output. The baseline lesson plan was compared to the lesson plans completed towards the end of the semester that integrated language and content. Both of these results were compared to the unit design that teachers were asked to create using the KF during second semester. Within the unit, all lesson plans should have included the components listed in the rubric. Table 11.3 displays the results of these paired t-tests.

The change between the initial baseline lesson and integrated lesson plans were statistically significant $t(22)=10.698$, $p<.0001$. While there was not a significant change from the integrated lesson plans to the unit design on the KF, the difference between the unit design and the baseline was statistically

Table 11.3 Instructional planning: baseline, content/language integrated lesson plans, unit design

Overall Results by Evaluation Guide			
	Baseline Lesson Plan	**Planning for Integration**	**Unit Design**
Sample Size	23	23	23
Cronbach Alpha	.783	.676	.741
Grand Mean	1.76	3.28	3.04
Standard Deviation	.56216	.44587	.57583

Overall Mean Score Differences by Evaluation Guide						
Pairs for Analysis:	**Mean Difference**	**Standard Deviation**	**t-test Value**	**df**	**Significance (2-tailed)**	**Comment**
Baseline Lesson Plan—Integrated Lesson Plans	−1.52	.68221	10.698	22	p < .0001	Significant
Integrated Lesson Plans—Unit Design	.239	.61919	1.852	22	p = .077	Not significant
Baseline Lesson Plan—Unit Design	−1.28	.84797	7.254	22	p < .0001	Significant

significant, t(22)=7.254, p<.0001, as shown by Table 11.3. The Cronbach Alpha reliability score for the pre-designed rubric was .783 for the baseline, and .741 for the unit design. A Cronbach Alpha requires a score of .70 or higher to demonstrate the reliability of a measurement tool. The rubric, however, came up slightly short, .676, when applied to the integration lesson plans; therefore, the significant growth from baseline to unit design—completed toward the end of both semesters—was the better indication of the teachers' ability to plan for linguistic diversity. Figure 11.4 provides an

Baseline Lesson Plan	Planning for Integration (mid-point)	Lesson from the Unit Design
Topic: None. **Objective:** Students demonstrate growth in writing from instruction based on previous formative writing sample. Review sequencing and demonstrate sample writing. Brainstorm ideas for topic. Students write as I roam room giving help and individual instruction. Students gather for share time. Volunteers read product. Grading done using district writing rubric.	**Topic:** What a tree needs to survive. **Model Performance Indicator:** Level 2 Students will practice using sentences with partners that tell things that a tree needs to stay healthy by using the sentence stem "A tree needs______." and visuals. **Language Objective:** **Listening** SWBAT point to pictures of what a tree needs to survive when prompted. **Speaking** Explain orally to a partner what a tree needs to survive using the following language features: sentences. **Vocabulary:** Sun, soil, rain, wind **Sentence structure:** noun/verb agreement in: "A tree needs______."	**Topic:** Seasons **Language Function:** Categorization **Content understanding to be demonstrated:** the clothing people wear changes as the seasons change **Language Features that are important for students to use when demonstrating understanding:** **MPI:** TSWBAT: sort clothing by the season in which they are typically worn by looking at a classroom graph of clothing **Language Objective:** **Vocabulary:** use "spring, summer, fall, winter, change" in speaking to categorize clothing by the season in which they are worn **Sentence:** use "Now the girl/boy is wearing (type of clothing) because it is (name of season)"in speaking to categorize clothing by the season in which they are worn **Discourse:** use "Now the girl/boy is wearing (describe clothing) because it is (name of season). Next it will be (name of season). In the (name of season), you can wear (type of clothing)."in speaking to categorize clothing by the season in which they are worn **Activities**:

Figure 11.4 An example of teacher's change in instructional planning

example of teachers' change in instructional planning that is typical of the participating teachers. The baseline lesson plan showed a focus on writing in isolation from ideational content. Neither the objectives nor the activities provided concrete guidance for desired student output. However, the lesson plans produced later revealed a much clearer focus on content related language development that not only tentatively addressed student's proficiency level, but also embraced explicit linguistic features desired for student use. Though still confused in the use of jargon (such as language functions), the increased attention to content-specific language development was evident.

When looking into the details of teachers' unit designs based on Mohan's KF, teachers' skill development in instructional planning was evident. While the lesson planning provided the opportunity to integrate language and content instruction for limited aspects of topic and language functions, an examination of the KF-based unit design showed teachers' competence in making systematic connections between a wide range of topic-related language functions and various content-specific linguistic resources. For instance, in the unit on Genetic Diseases as shown in Figure 11.1, we noticed a deliberate link between aspects of a chosen topic (such as types of genetic disorders) of which the students would demonstrate an understanding, and the various language functions (such as classifying, describing, explaining) that the students would need to use specific linguistic resources (i.e., vocabulary, sentence patterns, and discourse devices) to realize. It seems that the KF offered structured guidance for teachers to incorporate a language focus in the teaching of all aspects of a chosen content topic.

Classroom Observations. The results of the two observations, conducted at the beginning of the PD project and at the end of the first two courses, are shown in Table 11.1. The Cronbach Alpha for the assessment instrument shows reliability with a .931 score. The finding shows a significant effect of the teachers' PD on paired t-tests, $t(22) = 4.72$, $p<.0001$, based on the observational data. The teachers' increase in means at the second observation is statistically significant at the specified .05 level in relation to building prior knowledge at 3.60(.913), comprehensible input and pushed output at 3.68(.75), strategies and activities at 3.31(1.09), and review/assessment at 3.70(.99). The increase in strategies and activities, in particular, demonstrates that after the initial course the teachers provided greater support for language and thinking in connection to the content and language objectives.

This strengthened alignment between lesson planning and instructional practice is illustrated well with the comments of a mathematics teacher, Sofie. In the urban school district, the teachers had been using SIOP-inspired content and language objectives, but Sofie said, "I'd just write 'em up on the board and don't really know what to do with them. But now I know how to really use them." She then connected her expectation for students to sequence their steps for solving an algorithm with a model that was provided in the teacher development class: Sofie, and the other participants, had been shown how to use Mohan's work through lesson samples on acid rain, trees, and types of government structures. Sofie said it was the discussion of the formation of acid rain that she thought of when she chose to have students write about the formation of their thinking to solve an algorithm. In the PD course, signal words—*first, second, third, finally*—were taught for the Knowledge Structure of SEQUENCE. Sofie modeled the use of similar words in a whole class procedural recount before having students work on their own on a recount. On two occasions, she directed students' attention back to these signal words under the "objectives" on the board to assist them in writing their math recounts. In conferencing with teachers after observations, many of them expressed a greater sense of empowerment with the ability to make connections back to the lesson objectives.

Impact on Student Performance—Content-specific Writing

When introducing the KF in the PD project, all the teachers were encouraged to think about what they would actually teach in their own settings. Then they were guided to analyze a chosen content topic from the school curriculum into the six core KSs. It required the instructor to model first followed by the teachers' own analysis of a chosen topic. Figure 11.1 shows an example of a teacher's effort later in the course work. To help the teachers develop linguistic sensitivity so that they can implement instruction with attention to linguistic demand in writing tasks, the teachers were not only introduced to Mohan's KF for wider form-function connections, but also engaged in text analysis. At the level of text analysis, the KF draws upon register (Halliday, 1985, 1994) and genre (Martin, 1992) theories to identify linguistic features at the word, sentence, and discourse levels. To scaffold for the teachers how to engage in the text analysis for connection between content and language, a cause-effect text was used to model. The text and the guiding questions as part of the scaffold process can be seen in the Appendix. The participating teachers were required to work in groups to respond to the guiding questions with help from the instructor. Following this instructor-guided text analysis, the teachers were required to independently engage in the same process for a self-chosen text on a topic that they were likely to teach in their practice. The purpose is to acculturate/apprentice the teachers into the social practice in their own classrooms. This exercise seems to have helped the teachers carefully look at, instead of looking through, the specific linguistic resources that they would need to focus on when having their students engage in content-specific writing. While the observation data demonstrate an increase in teachers' attention to linguistic demand/need in their classroom instruction, the student writing shows that the change of teachers' instructional behavior made a positive impact on students' writing.

A comparison of baseline writing samples and exit writing samples reveals vast improvement in the students' content-specific writing. To measure the change in students' content-specific writing accompanying teachers' altered instructional practice, we focused on both ideational meaning expression in terms of richness and the use of language in terms of sophistication. The writing from a fourth-grade math class serves as an example.

Among all collected texts from the math class, 70.59% of the students used three to six required vocabulary words in the exit writing while only 31.82% of students did the same in the baseline data. Change in linguistic sophistication in the form of amount and density of the text is demonstrated by an increased number of clauses used in each text. In the baseline writing, 22.73% of the students produced texts that contained more than five clauses, including only one text (4.55%) with 10 clauses. In the exit writing, 88.24% of the students produced texts that contain more than five clauses including 47.06% of texts that contain 10 to 21 clauses.

Enriched content is also demonstrated by students' use of discourse features that convey more semantic relations in the exit writing. While the baseline writing mainly shows the use of "because" to indicate reasoning, the exit writing utilizes more linguistic choices in the form of both conjunctions and phrases to indicate a sequence such as "first," "second," "then," "to start with," and so on. In addition, conjunctions and lexicon are also used to reason or to justify:

1. *... so my answer should be near that* (Kness)
2. *I added...because...* (Fliana)
3. *If I moved...so my answer is..., that is not reasonable to my estimate... So...* (Cadenee)
4. *Therefore, the answer is...* (Emma)
5. *So I knew...* (Abby)

The use of an increased number of clauses may not necessarily come from an increased number of sentences in the exit writing. Very often, it is the use of complex sentences that increases the number of clauses:

6. *The number closest to 15 was 10.45 which is the answer.* (Kalab)
7. *I looked at my estimate which was 15 and placed the decimal between the 4 and 5* (Zack)
8. *Then I put the decimal back in according to what was closest to my estimate which was 14.5.* (Will)
9. *I made 15 into a decimal and put the decimal after the 5 in 15 which made 15.00* (Mckinnely)

A broader view can be taken to the students of all six teachers who were selected for this part of the study. From the six cases, a total of 114 baseline and 91 exit writing samples from six teachers were analyzed. Table 11.2 summarizes the result of the written discourse analysis of all the writing samples collected by the six teachers. Due to the limited data samples, statistical analysis for significance was not conducted; however, the aggregated data of students' writing as shown in Table 11.2 displays improvement in their ideational and content-specific writing. A re-examination of Figure 11.4 shows that a teacher, who had already been aware of the need for language objectives, increased her expectations for learners to a discourse level that included multiple sentences sequenced in relation to seasonal time after she had learned how to plan a unit of instruction with the KF. Deeper analysis of each teacher's practice and their student outcomes in writing is presented in Huang, Berg, Siegrist, and Chanaichon (2016).

Discussion

Mohan's KF provides a useful structure to aid teachers in designing units of instruction that meet the needs of their students to improve learning outcomes. Research shows that the simultaneous learning of language and content requires teacher development and knowledge across three areas: (a) understanding of how language works in content, (b) planning for it across a unit, and (c) supporting students' linguistic engagement in classroom activities (Schleppegrell & O'Hallaron, 2011). Our study drew upon a comprehensive set of data gathered through: (a) teacher pre/post surveys and interviews; (b) instructional plans at the beginning and end of the PD program; (c) classroom observations of the teachers; and (d) student writing samples from teachers in the program. Although we focused on the latter two points, analysis of these data—using paired t-tests, the SIOP observation protocol, and discourse analysis applying a systemic functional lens—has demonstrated how Mohan's KF approach can engage teachers in growth across all three areas. Specifically, this study documents that the use of the KF for in-service teacher development increases linguistic sensitivity leading to an expansion of teachers' knowledge about the different WIDA levels associated with content areas and the essential need for culturally responsive instruction (Cartledge & Kourea, 2008; Garcia & Ortiz, 2006). Moreover, the teachers' increased linguistic sensitivity was reflected in their design of instruction that in turn supported students' linguistic engagement in the process of content learning. Ultimately, instructional planning focusing on integrated content and language instruction made an impact on teachers' classroom practice and their ability to purposefully instruct for content-specific language/literacy, which translated into stronger writing performances from their students.

While American schools do not have enough graduates from traditional teacher education programs prepared to work with linguistically diverse populations (GAO, 2009), our study indicates the potential of a PD program that integrates a brief introduction to SFL theory, an explicit series of lessons on the KF for instructional design and text analysis, and a variety of activities/assessments for language learners, accompanied by on-site observation and mentoring. The rise of the Common Core and its emphasis on literacy in the content areas may push for increased preparation of all teachers for instructing the language of their discipline and providing the supports to help all students demonstrate it.

This research revealed that more attention to explicit language instruction increases teachers' abilities to teach their content. Since research shows that teachers must know both content and the language used to realize content (Gibbons, 2009; Schleppegrell, 2004), we hope this study can provide some resources and ideas to assist teacher educators. Colleges of teacher education need to give higher priority to ensure that all pre- and in-service programs develop teachers capable of designing appropriate instruction for linguistically diverse students struggling under traditional pedagogical practices that leave teachers feeling unprepared (Balderrama, 2001; Darling-Hammond et al. 2002; Gandara et al. 2005). Mohan's KF provides a structure for teachers to overcome such feelings and to think more deeply about their social practices in the classroom to prioritize students' academic language development.

While an increase in teachers' linguistic sensitivity in both planning and instruction is evident, our study also reveals challenges for teachers. For example, even when teachers became capable of framing very explicit language objectives at the vocabulary, sentence, or discourse levels, the rubrics that they tended to use for the written samples were at times too broad for the use of linguistic resources. Students who had missed the instruction on the target language for the assignment would have had difficulty meeting the intended outcome whether on the vocabulary, sentence, or discourse levels. A challenge that remains for researchers is how to help teachers better connect the assessment tool, particularly rubrics, to established learner outcomes for student language use (Berg & Huang, 2017).

The use of the KF enabled teachers to establish more content-based language objectives associated with a wider range of language functions. However, as pointed out by Berg and Huang (2017) drawing data from the same project, teachers still struggle with the identification of language objectives at the discourse level. A study by Huang and Laskowski (2014) revealed the same challenge facing pre-service teachers. How teacher educators can help teachers become more competent in identifying discourse level linguistics features remains a challenge of the KF as a tool for teacher development.

Finally, in our experience working with in-service teachers across different disciplinary content areas, we have found the teachers' lack of basic linguistic knowledge to be a huge challenge for both the teachers and the professors. Our PD program was designed to include a course in applied linguistics that devotes some attention to SFL. The methods course was developed to integrate theories and practice. Very often, the participating teachers would need to analyze salient linguistic features in content-specific texts to design language-focused classroom activities. We have found that our one introductory level linguistics course cannot fully prepare in-service teachers to engage in text analysis with ease. For example, in one lesson, we were analyzing a text about the effect of a hydrogen bomb that exploded in Japan. When one teacher pointed out that the text would provide the best opportunity to teach about the use of passive voice, a science teacher asked, "What is passive voice?" Typically, teachers who are native speakers of English seem to have a more difficult time pinpointing salient linguistic features since it is a language they never think about when using it and thus take for granted its meaning-making qualities. A challenge we face is the time needed to promote teacher development programs that raise linguistic awareness to a level of importance in education to better prepare the teachers to identify and instruct the grammatical resources for meaning making.

There are limitations to this study. Since data were collected within eight months after the launch of the program, the findings are limited in scope and depth. Also, the teachers who took part in this PD opportunity were either enticed by free college coursework and/or realized that they were not prepared for the growing linguistically diverse population in their classes; therefore, this sample may not be reflective of the many teachers in classrooms who similarly face such diversity but do not, for a myriad of reasons, seek development to serve these students.

Research Implications

For future research, longitudinal studies on the impacts of teacher development programs on student change in academic performance would be useful to address several questions: First, how can teachers augment and improve school-issued writing rubrics that do not take into consideration the needed linguistic resources? It was the linguistic analysis of the research team that showed an increased ability in writing by students as a result of improved teacher practice. We wonder how teachers would provide follow-up instruction without an assessment tool explicitly related to the specific three levels of language objectives. Second, what is the impact of such teacher development on students' academic performance over time in a school or district? Full cycles of instructional objectives, student performance, feedback from teachers, and follow-up student performance on similar tasks with the same group of educators and students across several years would provide data to reveal teacher effectiveness on student learning as a result of teacher development. Third, what is the lasting effect of such kinds of PD on the social practice of teaching? Three years from now, after having completed this study, it would benefit us to follow up with the teachers to determine whether or not they are still attentive to the language demands of the curriculum content they teach. Finally, how are state teacher evaluation systems compatible or not compatible with linguistically informed education across the curriculum? After all, teachers' performance is heavily influenced not only by their beliefs, but also by external forces coming from local, state, and federal authorities. An answer to this question would have implications for all stakeholders.

Authors' Note

Our gratitude goes to the journal of *Functional Linguistics* and the *Journal of the World Federation of Associations of Teacher Education* that have given the permission to adapt, remix, transform, and build upon the material for any purpose.

References

Aguirre-Munoz, Z., Park, J., Amabisca, A., & Boscardin, C.K. (2008). Developing teacher capacity for serving ELLs' writing instructional needs: A case for systemic functional linguistics. *Bilingual Research Journal, 31*(2), 295–322.

Anderson, L.W., Krathwohl, D.R., Airasian, P.W., Cruikshank, K.A., Mayer, R.E., Pintrich, P.R., Raths, J., & Wittrock, M.C. (2000). *A taxonomy for learning, teaching, and assessing: A revision of Bloom's taxonomy of educational objectives.* Pearson, Allyn & Bacon.

August, D., & Shanahan, T. (2006). *Developing literacy in second-language learners: Report of the National Literacy Panel on language-minority children and youth.* Lawrence Erlbaum Associates, Inc.

Balderrama, M. V. (2001). The (mis)preparation of teachers in the Proposition 227 era: Humanizing teacher roles and their practice. *The Urban Review, 33,* 255–267.

Berg, M.A. & Huang, J. (2015). Improving in-service teachers' effectiveness: K-12 academic literacy for the linguistically diverse. *Functional Linguistics, 2(5).* DOI 10.1186/s40554-015-0017-6

Berg, M.A. & Huang, J. (2017). Language objectives beyond vocabulary: Working with content area teachers for linguistically responsive instruction. In S. Neumann, R. Wegener, J. Fest, P. Niemietz, and N. Huzen (Eds.), *Challenging boundaries in linguistics: Systemic functional perspectives* (pp. 381–404). Peter Lang.

Cartledge, G., & Kourea, L. (2008). Culturally responsive classrooms for culturally diverse students with and at risk for disabilities. *Exceptional Children, 74*(3), 351–371.

Commins, N.L., & Miramontes, O.B. (2005). *Linguistic diversity and teaching.* Lawrence Erlbaum Associates, Inc.

Creswell, J.W. (2014). *Research design: Qualitative, quantitative, and mixed methods approaches.* Sage.

Darling-Hammond, L., Chung, R., & Frelow, F. (2002). Variation in teacher preparation: How well do different pathways prepare teachers to teach? *Journal of Teacher Education, 53,* 286–302.

de Jong, E.J. & Harper, C.A. (2005). Preparing mainstream teachers for English language learners: Is being a good teacher good enough? *Teacher Education Quarterly, 32*(2), 101–24.

Early, M. (1991). Language and content learning, K-12: The Vancouver School Board Project. *Cross Currents, 18,* 179–82.

Echevarria, J., Vogt, M., & Short, D.J. (2008). *Making content comprehensible for English learners: The SIOP model (3rd ed.).* Allyn & Bacon/ Merrill.

Fang, Z. (2012). The challenges of reading disciplinary texts. In T. Jetton & C. Shanahan (Eds.), *Adolescent literacy in the academic disciplines* (pp. 34–68). Guilford Press.

Fang, Z. (2014). Preparing content area teachers for disciplinary literacy instruction: The role of literacy teacher educators. *Journal of Adolescent & Adult Literacy, 57*(6), 444–448.

Gandara, P.C., Maxwell-Jolly, J., & Driscoll, A. (2005). *Listening to teachers of English language learners: A survey of California teachers' challenges, experiences, and professional development needs.* Center for the Future of Teaching and Learning.

GAO, Government Accountability Office. (2009). *Report to the Chairman, subcommittee on higher education, lifelong learning, and competitiveness committee on education and labor, house of representatives: Teacher preparation (Report Number GAO-09-573).* Retrieved from http://www.gao.gov/new.items/d09573.pdf

Garcia, E., Arias, M., Murri, N., & Serna, C. (2009). Developing responsive teachers: A challenge for a demographic reality. *Journal of Teacher Education, 61*(1–2), 132–142.

Garcia, S.B., & Ortiz, A.A. (2006). *Preventing disproportionate representation: Culturally and linguistically responsive prereferral interventions.* National Center for Culturally Responsive Educational Systems. Retrieved from http://www.nccrest.org/Briefs/Pre-referral_Brief.pdf, 1 20

Gee, J.P. (2007). *Social linguistics and literacies: Ideology in discourses.* Taylor & Francis.

Gibbons, P. (2002). *Scaffolding language, scaffolding learning: Teaching second language learners in the mainstream classroom.* Heinemann.

Gibbons, P. (2003). Mediating language learning: Teacher interaction with ESL students in a content-based classroom. *TESOL Quarterly, 37*(2), 247–273.

Gibbons, P. (2009). *English language learners' academic literacy and thinking: Learning in the challenge zone.* Heinemann.

Glaeser, B., Leuer, M., & Grant, M. (2012). Changing teacher beliefs about promoting literacy in content area classes. *Research in Higher Education Journal, 16*(1), 1–8.

Halliday, M.A.K. (1976). *System and function in language.* Oxford University Press.

Halliday, M.A.K. (1985). *An introduction to functional grammar.* Edward Arnold.

Halliday, M.A.K. (1994). *An introduction to functional grammar (2nd ed.).* Edward Arnold.

Halliday, M.A.K. (2007). *Language and education: Vol. 9.* A & C Black.

Halliday, M.A.K., McIntosh, A. & Strevens, P. (1964). *The linguistic sciences and language teaching.* Indiana University Press.

Harper, C., & de Jong, E.J. (2004). Misconceptions about teaching English language learners. *Journal of Adolescent and Adult Literacy, 48*(2), 152–162.

Harper C, & de Jong, E. J. (2009). English language teacher expertise: the elephant in the room. *Language and Education, 23*(2), 137–151.

Hart, J., & Okhee, L. (2003). Teacher professional development to improve the science and literacy achievement of English language learners. *Bilingual Research Journal, 27*(3), 475–501.

Huang, J. (2000). Integration of academic content learning and academic literacy skills development of L2 students: A case study of an ESL science class. *National Reading Conference Yearbook, 49,* 392–500.

Huang, J. (2004). Socializing ESL Students into the Discourse of School Science through Academic Writing. *Language and Education, 18*(2), 97–123.

Huang, J., & Laskowski, T. (2014). Developing linguistic sensitivity of ESL teacher candidates for linguistically responsive instruction. *The International Journal of Literacies, 20*(2), 29–50.

Huang, J., & Morgan, G. (2003). A functional approach to evaluating content knowledge and language development in ESL students' science classification texts. *International Journal of Applied Linguistics, 13*(2), 234–262.

Huang, J., & Normandia, B. (2009). Students' perceptions on communicating mathematically: A case study of a secondary mathematics classroom. *The International Journal of Learning, 16*(5), 1–21.

Huang, J., Berg, M., Romero, D., & Walker, D. (2016). In-service teacher development for culturally and linguistically diverse responsive pedagogy. *Journal of the World Federation of Associations of Teacher Education, 1*(1), 80–101.

Huang, J., Berg, M., Siegrist, M., & Chanaichon, D. (2016). Impact of a functional linguistic approach to teacher development on content area student writer. *International Journal of Applied Linguistics.* DOI 10.1111/ijal.12133

Jiménez, R.T., & Rose B.C. (2010). Knowing how to know: Building meaningful relationships through instruction that meets the needs of students learning English. *Journal of Teacher Education 61*(5), 403–412.

Johnson, R.B., Onwuegbuzie, A.J., & Turner, L.A. (2007). Toward a definition of mixed methods research. *Journal of Mixed Methods Research, 1*(2), 112–133.

Martin, J.R. (1992). *English text: System and structure.* John Benjamin.

Mohan, B. (1986). *Language and content.* Addison-Wesley.

Mohan, B., & Huang, J. (2002). Assessing the integration of language and content in a Mandarin as a foreign language classroom. *Linguistics and Education, 13*(3), 407–435.

Mohan, B. (2001). The second language as a medium of learning. In B. Mohan, C. Leung, & C. Davison (Eds.), *English as a second language in the mainstream* (pp. 107–126). Pearson.

Ochs, E. (1988). *Culture and language development: language acquisition and language socialization.* Cambridge University Press.

Pawan, F. (2008). Content-area teachers and scaffolded instruction for English language learners. *Teaching and Teacher Education, 24*(6), 1450–1462.

Pytash, K.E. (2013). Secondary preservice teachers' development of teaching scientific writing. *Journal of Science Teacher Education, 24*(5), 793–810.

Schieffelin, B.B., & Ochs, E. (1986). Language socialization. In B. Siegel (Ed.), *Annual Review of Anthropology* (pp. 163–191). Annual Reviews.

Schleppegrell, M.J., & de Oliveira, L. (2006). An integrated language and content approach for history teachers. *Journal of English for Academic Purposes, 5*, 254–268.

Schleppegrell, M.J., & O'Hallaron, C.L. (2011). Teaching Academic Language in L2 Secondary Settings. *Annual Review of Applied Linguistics, 31,* 3–18.

Schleppegrell, M.J. (2004). *The language of schooling: A functional linguistics perspective.* Lawrence Erlbaum.

Schleppegrell, M.J. (2010). Supporting a "reading to write" pedagogy with functional grammar. *NALDIC Quarterly, 8*(1), 26–31.

Schleppegrell, M.J. (1998). Grammar as a resource: Writing a description. *Research in the Teaching of English, 32*(3), 182–211.

Schleppegrell, M.J. (2001). Linguistic features of the language of schooling. *Linguistics and Education, 12*(4), 431–459.

Schleppegrell, M.J. (2003). *Grammar for writing: Academic language and the ELD standards.* UCLMRI Final Report. Santa Barbara, UC Language Minority Research Institute.

Sleeter, C. (2008). An invitation to support diverse students through teacher education. *Journal of Teacher Education, 59*(3), 212–219.

Tang, G. (2001). Knowledge framework and classroom action. In Mohan, B., Leung, C., & Davison C. (Eds.), *English as a second language in the mainstream* (pp. 127–136). Pearson.

WIDA Consortium (2012). *The WIDA standards framework and its theoretical foundations.* Board of Regents of the University of Wisconsin System. Retrieved from https://www.wida.us/

Wong, F.L., & Snow, C.E. (2000). *What teachers need to know about language?* ERIC Clearinghouse on Languages and Linguistics Special Report. US Department of Education, Office of Educational Research and Improvement.

Zwiers, J. (2008). *Building academic language: Essential practices for content classrooms.* Josey-Bass.

About the Authors

Jingzi (Ginny) Huang earned her PhD focusing on language education from the University of British Columbia, Canada. Having taught in elementary, secondary, and university settings in China, Canada, and the US, deeply involved in teacher education in the United States since 1997, she is currently leading the biggest teacher preparation program in Colorado as the School Director of Teacher Education at the University of Northern Colorado. Her major teaching and research interests include classroom discourse, second and foreign language education, language/literacy across the curriculum, high quality teacher development in general and second language education teacher development in particular.

Margaret Berg is a professor of Teacher Education at the University of Northern Colorado. She has taught at the secondary and tertiary levels in China, Russia, Ukraine, and in the inner city and on the Mexican border of the United States. She also taught general education classwork in a state-level, men's maximum security "correctional facility." Her area of research is educational linguistics.

Appendix A: Text Analysis as a Part of Scaffolding

> In 1954 a hydrogen bomb was tested at bikini. The explosion produced the expected radio-active fall-out on a number of Pacific Islands, and also scattered debris over thousands of square miles. As a result, dangerous radio-active materials appeared in the small plants which live in the surface of the sea; these were eaten by small animals which in turn were eaten by larger animals, notably the tuna fish which are an important article of diet in Japan. Hence a number of Japanese ingested quantities of radio-active food.
>
> S.A. Barnett, *The Human Species: A Biology of Man* (Harper & Row, 1971), p. 208

Read the passage and we will discuss in small groups the following:

1. What language function do you think the passage entails?
2. What is the ideational meaning that the passage constructs? Basically, if the passage needs to be retold, what is the content to be told about?
3. `Can you use a visual to represent the text? Think about knowledge structures and how visually they can be represented.
4. Can you frame a student outcome/objective for this retelling activity?
5. In order for your students to retell the passage, what would be the needed linguistic features that have to be used to express both the language functions and the ideational meaning?
   - Vocabulary?
   - Sentence structures?
   - Discourse features?

12 The Knowledge Framework for Building Teacher Awareness of Language in Content Instruction

Jesse Gleason and Elena Schmitt

Abstract

Learners' understanding of content develops alongside their ability to use language. Graduate programs in TESOL prepare teachers to work with language and content so that they may effectively help their students. This study examines the role of a participant observation and functional discourse analysis project for teacher education in ESOL. In-service teachers (N=19) received training with Mohan's Knowledge Framework, a linguistics-based tool for language-content integration, and completed four ethnographic observations in K-12 and adult classrooms, transcribing, analyzing, and reflecting on the discourse they had collected. Results revealed patterns of classroom discourse across content areas and grades, including patterns of knowledge structures for building knowledge of the classroom activity, of the content matter, as well as for developing interpersonal language. Major themes are discussed and implications are drawn for using the KF in conjunction with classroom observation for ESOL teacher training.

Keywords: ESOL teacher training; the Knowledge Framework; Systemic Functional Linguistics; discourse analysis; classroom observation

As the need for PreK-12 teachers of English language learners (ELLs) rises, graduate TESOL programs continue to prepare teachers to help all students succeed (de Oliveira, 2016; Hammond, 2006; Zwiers, 2014). As Mohan (1986) argues, "the integration of language and subject areas is relevant to all teachers, whether they teach language or subject matter, and whether they teach second language learners or native speakers" (p. iv). What and how much knowledge about language (KAL) do PreK-12 teachers need in order to help all students, but especially their ELLs, engage with content? A functional view of language, and in particular a tool called the Knowledge Framework (KF), has been shown to help teachers make connections between the content of their lessons and the language demands inherent therein (Huang & Laskowski, 2014; Schleppegrell, 2013). The types of learning experiences that in-service teachers in TESOL have during their graduate course work will undoubtedly influence their ability to help their students simultaneously learn language, learn content through language, and learn about language (Halliday, 1993). This project investigates the role of participant observation and knowledge structure discourse analysis for TESOL teacher preparation and demonstrates that as a result of KF training and field observations/analysis, our participants were able to: (a) achieve an awareness of the importance of linguistic aspects of classroom discourse on students' learning as well as to (b) apply the theoretical constructs of KSs to the analysis of actual discourse recorded in a variety of content classrooms. We argue that the development of teacher KAL is a necessary step to making content accessible for ELLs.

Classroom Discourse and Academic Language Development

PreK-12 classrooms are specialized learning sites involving numerous social practices and uses of language (Gibbons, 2015). Research on classroom language that views language development as the expansion of learners' meaning-making resources presents a unique perspective to the pervasive second language acquisition research, which tends to emphasize language development as the procurement and uptake of correct language forms (Derewianka, 2011). From the perspective of educational linguists working within a Systemic Functional Linguistics (SFL) approach, successful classroom integration of language and content involves explicit teaching of certain linguistic features—features that are key to students' academic literacies (Brisk, 2015).

Researchers generally agree that a decisive factor for school success is students' English language proficiency (Cazden, 1988; Cummins, 1984; Thomas and Collier, 2002), which ELLs often almost solely develop through their PreK-12 classroom interaction. As much research has shown, the language of the classroom tends to differ from the English that ELLs might encounter outside school in several important ways, including the reconfiguration of everyday experiences according to disciplinary expectations, specialized analytical subject matter, and high-density "written-like" discourse (Gibbons, 2015; Schleppegrell, 2004). Understanding how language use in the classroom is different from non-academic domains and how teachers can develop in-class discourse that would be conducive to developing both the language and the content/ways of thinking in their courses are key goals of TESOL teacher preparation.

Teachers' explicit knowledge about language has been shown to help combat the linguistic and scholarly disadvantages faced by ELLs (Jones & Chen, 2012; Macken-Horarik, Love & Unsworth, 2011). According to Johnson (1995), in order to understand the discursive patterns of language lessons, we must understand the discursive practices of L2 teachers because "patterns of classroom communication depend largely on how teachers use language to control the structure and content of classroom events" (p. 145). Walsh (2006) contends that even though classroom discourse is a collaborative effort constructed by both students and teachers, teachers are ultimately responsible for lesson orchestration. Thus, it is essential for teachers of ELLs to become cognizant of the use of language in classroom discourse, and its development should constitute an essential part of lesson planning.

Exemplary teachers have often been found to design and foster language learning opportunities in constructive and innovative ways in order to engage ELLs in classroom interaction (Hammond, 2006). Nonetheless, teachers from academic content areas such as math, science, or social studies who have not been trained in English for Speakers of Other Languages (ESOL) may encounter difficulty determining the language demands of their lessons (Humphrey & MacNaught, 2016) and the language needs of their ELLs. According to Huang and Laskowski (2014), developing teachers' "linguistic sensitivity" is essential for helping them to build language-content connections, that is, to see how the ideas of their disciplines are expressed linguistically. This in turn will help teachers determine what types of difficulties in writing and speaking specialized academic discourse their ELLs may encounter (Fang & Schleppegrell, 2008; Huang, Normandia, & Greer, 2005; Mohan & Slater, 2006).

Teacher *knowledge about language* (KAL) not only helps support ELLs but also mainstream students, promoting the kinds of consciousness-raising talk that has been shown to develop academic language (Schleppegrell, 2013). Moreover, training teachers to integrate the teaching of language with the teaching of content *through* language entails first developing teachers' own linguistic sensitivity (Huang & Laskowski, 2014). To help students develop their academic literacies, teachers need a working KAL, "a metalanguage based on the careful study of grammar—a way of thinking with grammar in mind" (Macken-Horarik et al., 2011, p. 9). With the increased linguistic demands of the Common Core State Standards (CCSS), it has been argued that all teachers would benefit from focused, linguistically sensitive training to develop their KAL (Brisk, 2015; Samson & Collins, 2012). Such an awareness of language-content connections is essential for developing language-and-content–integrated lessons that target a variety of essential skills and provide students with ample opportunities to engage in discussions with peers.

Constructive and supportive student–teacher interactions make up the core of every successful classroom environment (Muntner, 2008). However, many studies of ELL classroom discourse have shown that teachers produce significantly more language than do their students (Harklau, 2005). In addition to quantity of talk, it becomes necessary to explore the qualitative features of in-class student and teacher interaction that promote language and content learning. The present study aims to address this need by posing the following overarching question: How does participant observation combined with social practice analysis help graduate-student participants, many of them in-service PreK-12 teachers, to understand the role of oral discourse in classroom settings, thus potentially helping them design classroom activities that will engage students and get them talking, thereby developing their English abilities and their academic knowledge?

Methods

This study showcases a classroom project that involved the training of in-service teacher candidates enrolled in a MS TESOL program to use the KF for their analysis of language-content integration in K-12 and adult ESL classroom observations. The following question guided our study: How can training with the KF help teachers become more cognizant of the use of specific knowledge structures (KSs), including the relevant linguistic tools involved in their use, in classroom discourse? This question reflects the current gap between the value of KSs (Mohan, 1986) and the lack of explicit focus on them for instructional purposes (Huang & Laskowski, 2014; Huang, Normandia & Greer, 2005).

Participants

The participants in this study were 20 in-service teacher candidates who were graduate students enrolled in a third-semester course sequence of an MS TESOL program. Table 12.1 illustrates key information about these individuals.

The participants engaged in a hands-on workshop on the KF and its application to discourse analysis during two 2.5-hour class periods. During these sessions, they focused mainly on the use of the KF as a discourse analysis tool

Table 12.1 Key participant information

Participant (Pseudonym)	Current Teaching Position/Certification
Riley	Elementary certified
Mary	Secondary special ed
Jamie	2nd grade mainstream
Megan	3rd grade mainstream
Lori	Not currently teaching
Kenny	University level
Jane	10th grade social studies
Duah	Elementary certified
Paula	Adult education
John	8th grade mathematics
Katie	3rd grade mainstream
Lea	2nd grade mainstream
Kristy	4th grade mainstream
Amalia	3rd grade mainstream
Kim	3rd grade mainstream
Niki	Secondary special ed
Raquel	3rd grade bilingual
Alissa	Adult education
Julie	Adult education
Natasha	8th grade mathematics

and were provided content and lexicogrammatical features of KSs and examples of KS analysis applied in various studies (e.g., Mohan & Slater, 2006). Upon completion of the KF training, participants were tasked with observing four different ESOL classrooms, and recording, transcribing, and analyzing the oral discourse therein, reflecting on the role of KSs in the classroom discourse they captured.

Using these same transcriptions, researchers applied both top-down and bottom-up discourse analysis strategies for KS identification. Bottom-up strategies relied mainly on lexical and structural clues for specific KSs; for example participants were given a sentence and asked to parse it out and identify the different types of verbs (e.g., being/having, doing, or feeling/sensing). Top-down discourse analytic strategies involved both linguistic and a discourse context for the analysis of KSs; for example participants were provided with a short text and asked to guess the context in which it was created as well as the purpose of the text and potential audiences.

Data Collection

Data collection for this study was two-pronged. First, observational data, analyzed within the KF, were collected by the participants in a range of classroom settings, as shown in Table 12.2, as a part of the classroom observation project in a graduate-level course on TESOL methodology. As Table 12.2 shows, participants observed a broad range of classroom types, some with smaller percentages of ELLs (Primary=27%) and others consisting of only ELLs (Adult education=100%).

Second, post-observation semi-structured focus group interviews were conducted by the researchers as a way to understand graduate-student participants' perceptions of the KF and its role in the classroom discourse and to compare these perceptions to the results of the observation analysis produced by the participants. Data collection procedures consisted of classroom observations, transcriptions, and reports conducted by participants, post-semester in-depth focus group interviews with the participants, and a variety of textual documents, including training materials used during the two KF training sessions. Table 12.3 outlines these procedures, including the numbers of classes observed and interviews.

Observations. Teacher participant observation has been shown to be particularly advantageous for shedding light on classroom language use (Stillwell et al., 2011). Studies using participant observation have grown in popularity over the past three decades and are often performed in conjunction with

Table 12.2 Number of students and ELLs across classroom settings

Type of Classroom Setting	Total # of Students	# of ELLs	% of ELLs
Primary (K-5)	190	52	27
Secondary (6–12)	115	41	36
Adult	131	131	100
Total	436	224	51

Table 12.3 The database

	Observations	Focus Group Interviews	Textual Documents
Methods course 1	13	3	Training materials, field notes, student reflections
Methods course 2	16	5	
Total	29	8	

Table 12.4 Distribution of observations across primary, secondary, and adult classrooms

Type of Classroom Setting	# Classroom Observations	%
Primary (K-5)	10	34.5%
Secondary (6–12)	7	24.1%
Adult	12	41.4%
Total	29	100%

Table 12.5 Number and types of lessons observed across research sites

Lesson Type	# of Lessons	%
ESL	15	52
Language Arts	7	24
Math	4	14
Science	2	7
Social Studies	1	6
Total	29	100

discourse analysis (Tsui, 2012). Over the course of the semester, our graduate-student participants conducted 29 classroom observations in a variety of classrooms as shown in Table 12.4. Given the broad range of classrooms observed, there were five main lesson types as portrayed in Table 12.5.

Over the semester, participants digitally recorded, formatted, and transcribed over 20 total hours of classroom discourse. To supplement the recordings, they took detailed field notes and sketched out the layout of the classrooms, as seen in Figure 12.1 below, in order to capture information about how students and teachers interacted in small and large groups. As such, participants were deeply involved in understanding and practicing the role of participant observer.

As Charmaz (2006) and other qualitative researchers recommend, field notes should attempt to represent the classroom surroundings and space in order for participant observers to be able to later effectively reconstruct the happenings and interactions of students and teachers. This multimodal representation aligns with the notion that all language occurs for a purpose and within an ecological setting. By enacting the various steps of participant observation, including sketching out the classroom environment and taking detailed field notes alongside transcription, the graduate-student participants in this study were able to hone their ethnographic research skills and thus

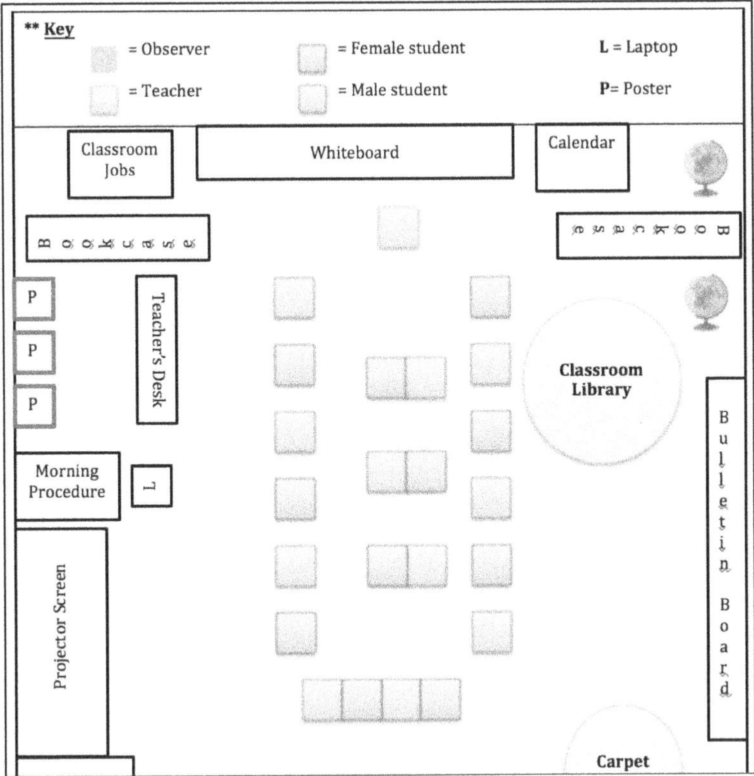

Figure 12.1 One participant's example depiction of a classroom layout

engage in the assignment involving participant observation combined with social practice analysis more holistically.

Transcribed recordings were analyzed within the KF by the participants, who focused on the content of the observed lessons, the language used in the classroom to explore that content, and the types of key visuals (KVs) present in the lesson. Specifically, the analysis involved (a) identification of the KSs that the teacher used during the lesson as present in the transcription of classroom discourse, (b) identification of the lexicogrammar used to enact these KSs (e.g., "being/having" verbs), and (c) association of any KVs that the teacher used in the lesson with the KSs and language identified therein.

Interviews. Upon completing the course, the researchers conducted eight 30- to 45-minute semi-structured focus group interviews with participants. These interviews focused on several general ideas, as seen in the Interview Protocol in the Appendix. In addition to the discussions that took place during the focus groups, participants were asked to analyze a sample of their own classroom texts using the KF. These sample texts provided grist for further analysis and interpretation of what was occurring in the discourse of the observed classrooms.

Textual Documents. The textual documents used in this study consisted of teacher-training materials (lesson plans, PowerPoint Presentations, example texts), observer field notes, and participants' written reflections. These documents were used to understand and compare the ways in which the participants analyzed classroom observation transcripts with the training they received prior to conducting the observations.

Data Analysis

Data analysis for this project included systematic coding and cross-referencing of KSs within the transcripts of classroom discourse appearing in the observed lessons. After analyzing transcripts using the techniques for knowledge structure analysis learned during their training workshop, participants wrote reflections grounded in the KF. Later, researchers revisited their transcripts evaluating their analyses and comparing them against their own interpretations of the data.

Results

This study examined the role of participant observation and social practice analysis in ESOL teacher preparation, thus these results focus on what participants learned from the assignments involving classroom observation analysis within the KF framework as well as on their understanding of the role of discourse in a content classroom. Primary data include participants' observation transcripts, their analyses of these transcripts, and their oral discourse as captured during in-depth focus group interviews. Three main themes (the KF for teaching, the KF for analysis, and challenges) and 11 sub-themes emerged from the focus group interviews as shown in Table 12.6.

The KF for Teaching

Managing Classroom Behavior. The first sub-theme within the major theme of using the KF for teaching was about managing classroom behavior. Participants' interviews indicated their beliefs that SEQUENCE, PRINCIPLES, and EVALUATION were often used to perform a directive function,

Table 12.6 Themes of focus group interviews surrounding the use of the KF for teacher training

Theme	**KF for Teaching**	**KF for Analysis**	**Challenges**
Sub-Theme	Managing classroom behavior	Ease and difficulty enacting KSs for ELLs	Time
	Focus and organization	Ease and difficulty identifying KSs	Individual analysis (versus working with a buddy)
	Lesson planning	KSs across content areas and grade levels	Linguistic notions
	Key visuals	Bottom-up / Top-down processing	

that is to manage students' classroom behavior. Lori, for example, asserted: "In the beginning of the lesson she used the knowledge structures of PRINCIPLES and SEQUENCE to explain what the students were going to do in the lesson" (Obs#4, Middle school).

Lori's claim can be corroborated with actual classroom discourse from participants' transcripts. As shown in Text 1, below, a teacher from Grade 4–5 ESL pull-out uses Sequence (note the use of "doing" processes: *we're going to watch, it's going to tell you, we're going to practice…*), to manage the classroom activity of the lesson. Discourse marked in **bold** indicates CLASSIFICATION and DESCRIPTION, *italics* indicate PRINCIPLES and SEQUENCE, and <u>underlined text</u> indicates EVALUATION and CHOICE.
Text 1: Grade 4–5 ESL pull-out

> Teacher: Ok, remember that we're talking about peer pressure. And just so that we remember…*we're going to watch this anger video…* [plays video] Alright, so, that was just to give you a little preview like we're at the movies of what this article is going to be about. And this sheet I'm going to give you…*it's going to tell you what our plan is for today and give you somewhere to write something down…* So, our objective for today is *we're going to practice identifying problem and solution* and *we're going to read a magazine article.*

While participants such as Lori claimed that they believed that SEQUENCE and PRINCIPLES were used to give instructions and directions for a task toward the beginning of the lesson, others suggested that PRINCIPLES was also used to increase student investment in classroom tasks. Jane for example stated, "The language that went along with the "PRINCIPLES"... helped students better understand why they are asked to do certain activities, such as writing the example of the math problem on their worksheet" (Obs#7, 6th grade mainstream, math).

Participants also asserted that the KS of EVALUATION, in particular was used by teachers in the beginning part of a lesson. As Jane states: "I found that Mrs. McKain used significantly more evaluation discourse in the earlier part of the lesson...While evaluative feedback to students' responses was frequent early in the lesson, as the lesson continued, she provided significantly less...(Obs#6, Adult ESL).

Jane and others stated in their interviews that this ample use of EVALUATION could serve to encourage student behavior: "It appears that as the students become oriented in the lesson, she [the teacher] does not feel the need to provide them with as much positive feedback to encourage them" (Jane, Obs#6, Adult ESL). These quotes suggest their understanding of EVALUATION as a directive tool for classroom management, and one that perhaps needed to appear more frequently in the beginning of the lesson. This can be corroborated by the teacher's use of EVALUATION in Text 2 below.
Text 2: Grade 3 language arts

S2: The last time my cousin *came over* my house and she *made* a mess, but my mom said that**'s** still **rude**, even if she's a guest.
T: That's a nice connection you've made. What **kind** of person would say that? How *was* your cousin *acting*?
S2: **Mean** and **rude**
T: Yeah. Would we want to act like Ce-Ce?
Ss: No.
T: Would you get upset? ... So, what **type** of guest would you want to be? Would you be a **grateful**, **patient** guest or **rude** and **selfish** guest?
S1: Patient
T: And how about you?
S2: **Patient** too

Participants' understanding of how the KSs of SEQUENCE, PRINCIPLES, and EVALUATION to manage learning tasks and student behavior alongside these examples of classroom discourse verify their claims. Furthermore, they shed light on the importance of KSs for setting up social practices within PreK-12 classrooms.

The KF for Focus and Organization of Lessons. The second sub-theme involved focus and organization of social practices within the classroom. During interviews, most participants expressed an interest in using the KF in their own teaching. Their comments focused on the application of the KF for lesson organization, lesson planning, and the appropriate incorporation of key visuals. Participants spoke at length about the valuable scaffolding that the KF provided them in focusing and organizing the lessons they observed. They felt that the KF allowed them to identify KSs that may have been missing from the lessons. Several participant quotes to support this sub-theme can be seen in Table 12.7.

Participants voiced their perceptions that (a) having the KF was helpful for focusing on specific elements of classroom discourse (e.g., KSs) and ensuring that they are consistently present; (b) the KF was an important heuristic for bringing language and content together instead of only working through the content that precluded an awareness of language; and (c) relying on the KF brought about more structured meaning to the classroom interaction. These ideas point to the centrality of the KF for helping in-service teachers to focus on content and language of the lesson.

Table 12.7 Quotes on the KF for helping increase teaching organization and focus

Teacher	Comments
Kim	"the Knowledge Framework… kind of just helps you focus more, like you knew what you were looking for..."
John	"Knowing the framework made analyzing the class easier. These words are measurable, so then… Just the language, for example, if we're talking about EVALUATION in CHOICE or PRINCIPLES in SEQUENCE, if you know the terminology, the language, you can understand how the teacher is trying to present. Prior to know this, trying to analyze, I found myself just all over the place. I just did not really have a Sequence of how I was going to analyze the class from the objective. With the framework, it just gave me… It was another tool that I can organize my understanding better. It was very helpful."
Megan	"It's nice to have the CLASSIFICATION PRINCIPLES. The title of what's happening and what you notice in discourse. You can give meaning to it."
Duah	"It really allowed me to zone in more so on language. We tend to as teachers focus more so on content. It was nice to take a closer look at not just what they're learning overall, but rather the language used to relay the messages, but also what we're receiving from the students. It was nice to see language and content intertwined."

Table 12.8 Quotes on the KF for lesson planning

Teacher	Comments
Megan	"Because no teacher wants to spend too much time on DESCRIPTION or too much time on EVALUATION. It can show you how to evenly distribute it among your lesson. Each one of those aspects needs to be present, but I think that each is just as important as the one before it. You shouldn't spend too much time on one or too little time on another. You can go back, analyze the discourse with that, and see what areas you need to strengthen and which areas you need to cut back on."
Kristy	"I think too, when planning, you're more mindful now when planning because you think about, "How much do I really want to be talking?" And "How much do I want the kids to be talking?" I think planning is also a part where I've opened my eyes to where kids should be talking more... if I wanted to implement more CHOICE in a lesson, I would then know what to gear it towards. What kind of language I would want to use, what I'm looking for from the student, things like that. I think it would be helpful in planning."
Jane	"the way I interpreted the Knowledge Framework it's really working you know from this basic concrete. You're classifying, you're describing, and then you're going all the way up to that EVALUATION and CHOICE. So this I could see helping me with lesson planning, thinking about what kind of questioning I'm using."

Lesson Planning. A third sub-theme within the major theme of using the KF in the classroom, was the importance of the KF for helping to plan lessons and curricular units. Lesson planning was an area that excited our participants as evident from a sample of their responses presented in Table 12.8 below. Here they focused mainly on the role of the KF in teaching and making language comprehensible during content-based lessons.

Jane's quote in particular showed her understanding of the dynamic and progressive nature of KSs, emphasizing the directional movement from one structure to the next. Megan stressed the need to balance KSs throughout the lesson. Finally, Kristy used the KF to help her gauge the amount and quality of language used by the teacher and by the students.

Key Visuals. The fourth sub-theme within this category was the value of the KF for discerning types of key visuals (KVs) used in the classroom. Key visuals are graphic organizers that are used to model target language and provide a structure to support understanding. Unlike language input flooding (Mizapour, 2016), KVs present an important link between language and content, when used systematically. Participants reported that KVs were not often used during the lessons they observed. As Paula, stated "For me, what was very interesting is there were absolutely no visuals and when we were analyzing I realized how much it would have helped and how it would have increased the language production" (Paula, Interview 1).

Similarly, Julie stated that KVs while useful took up a great deal of time to develop and may not be used by more experienced teachers: "Again, if you are doing real world teaching, blending of so many visuals for every step takes time. The more experience you have, the less visuals you actually need" (Julie, Interview 2). Lastly, Niki emphasized the importance of KVs and their role in better comprehension of content by ELLs. "I especially like looking at the graphic organizers that were different for each component. That visual stuff is really, really important. No matter what you're doing there's some visual that you can be using" (Niki, Interview 2). It is clear through these quotes that the KF, and its particular integration of language functions, structures, and visuals helped our participants to see these elements and their interplay in the classroom in a wholistic way.

The KF for Analysis

While the utility of the KF for exploring issues of classroom management, lesson planning, and more was shown in the previous sections, several sub-themes related to the benefit of the KF for discourse analysis assignments also emerged, such as the ones they conducted for part of their methods course. Firstly, participants observed a variety of KSs in the transcripts of their lessons. In fact, a careful examination of the participants' analysis of their observation transcript indicates that the participants witnessed the use all six KSs across the observations: CLASSIFICATION, DESCRIPTION, PRINCIPLES, SEQUENCE, EVALUATION, and CHOICE, which is perhaps unsurprising given the fact that Mohan (2007) asserts that every complete social practice should involve all six KSs. We will now expand upon participants' use of the KF for self-reflection and analysis as well as for engagement with the language of the observed content classes. Four major sub-themes developed in this area.

Ease and Difficulty of KSs for ELLs. Participants thought that certain KSs tended to be challenging for English learners. In their written reflections, for example, participants emphasized their belief that within the content of the lesson ELLs tended to struggle most with three key KSs: CHOICE, PRINCIPLES, and EVALUATION. As Niki states, "Students probably had the most difficulty with CHOICE. They struggled to come up with their own examples of being a good friend and most of them borrowed the teacher's example of a student falling on the playground and another student helping that person up" (Obs#14, Kindergarten, Language Arts).

As shown in Text 3, below, Riley also noticed that the ELLs in her classroom had difficulty with CHOICE together with PRINCIPLES, "I think they were facing difficulties to understand and answer the last question 'I wanna know what is your favorite math strategy for addition and subtraction and why?' (lines#82+83). They couldn't tell the reasons behind their preference" (Obs#1, 3rd grade mainstream, math lesson).

Text 3: Grade 3 Math lesson

Teacher: I <u>wanna know</u> what **is** your <u>favorite</u> math strategy for addition and *why*
Student: My <u>favorite</u> strategy is number line *because*...like *something plus equals*
Teacher: *Why* <u>do</u> you <u>like</u> stacking and adding?
Student: *Because* it'**s** <u>easy</u> to figure it out.

Natasha also noted the difficulty the students she observed had with PRINCIPLES and CHOICE, stating "Principles requires a good understanding of the lesson in order to make predictions and draw conclusions, and CHOICE requires the ELLs to [later] articulate their decisions and to explain the reason why they made that decision" (Obs#17, Adult ESL).

Similarly, Lori stated "They [the English learner students] also had difficulty with and expressing their viewpoint on what they believed to be true or not as well as explaining their choices" (Obs#4, Middle school, ESL pull-out). As Lori pointed out, that the reason the English learners she observed had particular difficulty expressing CHOICE may not have been due not to the actual choice itself, but rather the difficulty in providing a rationale for that choice later on.

From the above quotes, we see a pattern in our participants' understanding of classroom use of KSs. When called on in class to demonstrate their knowledge orally, our participants noted that ELLs were reported to have frequently had difficulty supporting their answers with evidence. In other words, when prompted with CHOICE, students had difficulty using the KSs of PRINCIPLES and EVALUATION to justify their answers.

Ease and Difficulty Identifying KSs. In addition to the realization that ELLs may have certain difficulties enacting certain KSs, participants themselves had difficulties identifying them in their transcribed discourse. Many participants indicated that some KSs stood out to them more than others.

For example, during Duah's observation of a math lesson, she found that SEQUENCE was easy to identify. This may be due to lexical markers like *first*, *second*, and *next*, which tended to not be embedded in verb phrases, thus requiring a less sophisticated analysis of discourse.

Several participants reported that some math classes tended to use SEQUENCE and CHOICE while others focused on DESCRIPTION and CLASSIFICATION. Kim found CHOICE to be a particularly salient KS. CHOICE has a straightforward lexical marker *or*, which helped participants to immediately identify it among other KSs. Participants found EVALUATION, often expressed lexically using evaluative expressions such as *good* and *nice job*, to be present across subject areas and grade levels.

KSs Across Content areas and Grade Levels. The third sub-theme involved pertained to the use of certain KSs across content areas and grade levels. For example, Riley asserted that in mathematics, there tended to be ample use of SEQUENCE, "with math there's a lot of SEQUENCE *first, next, then*" (Riley, Interview 1) This is supported by other participants such as Kim who reasoned that in math, "the children are asked to sequence every day with the numbers" (Kim, Interview 2). CHOICE and EVALUATION were two other KSs that seemed to participants to be important for the math content area. As Kim states, "Also in math, the children are allowed to choose because we have centers. Which skills to use? The students are involved. They're given a choice of maybe six or seven centers and they're able to choose which ones" (Interview 2).

A belief among participants held that certain KSs tended to be used more frequently depending on the age group or grade level of students. For example, CHOICE was thought to be more common in the lower grades whereas in the upper grades or in classrooms that were more teacher-fronted, fewer CHOICE features were used. "There was CHOICE for the younger kids. They were given more options in front of them, whereas in the classrooms that I realize were much more teacher-fronted or teacher-centered. They didn't have much room for choosing. It's more of, "Okay, I'm here to evaluate you" (Duah, Interview 1). Interestingly, Duah also associates CHOICE and EVALUATION as aligned with freedom of choice and EVALUATION with teacher-directedness: In "adult ed, they had a sense of independence. There was a lot more room for CHOICE, but with the younger grades I noticed a lot CLASSIFICATION, and DESCRIPTION and the content that they were working with. It required for them to be able to classify and describe" (Duah, Int. 1). This comment may suggest that participants tend to evaluate certain KSs as positive and others to be avoided, rather than seeing them within a synergistic framework where each has importance.

Bottom-Up Versus Top-Down Processing. Our analysis of participants' reports on the classroom observations and their interviews indicates that they struggled to combine bottom-up (focus on lexicogrammatical features of discourse) and top-down strategies (focusing on discourse/knowledge structures) to identify KSs within student and teacher discourse. This was especially prevalent during their first observation, where they had to do the analysis on their own, without a buddy, as explored below. On the one hand, their training in the KF provided them with lexicogrammatical indicators of various KSs; but on the other hand, they had to read into the content and context of the lessons to understand which KSs were reflected by particular linguistic processes. As shown in Table 12.9, in the first classroom observation most participants looked at lexicogrammatical resources as a signal of KSs without paying much attention to context. It appeared from the reflections, however, that participants tended to consider parts of speech (e.g., verbs, connectors) used in the discourse to assign a specific KS to that linguistic feature, without first consulting the context.

In terms of ease and difficulty, participants found that the KF was relatively easy to use for the analysis of classroom discourse. Jane, for example, described the application of KSs as intuitive and "mirroring how sort of discourse pragmatics normally works" (Interview 1). In relation to the use of KSs by school children, participants relied on their intuition and experience to

Table 12.9 Quotes about bottom-up/top-down processing

Participant	Statements about Analysis
Paula	"The first one, what I did, I tried to look for all of the knowledge structures in the discourse and then I was actually looking at language and trying to... I think the constructions from coming from the other direction and the force of the ritual we did, we actually looked for the language and then attached it to the knowledge structures."
John	"What I noticed with the third is what the adult ed, and he teaching the 'if' clause. If this happens, then you do that. That was PRINCIPLES and SEQUENCE, and I didn't realize that until after I did [observation]. I was doing my analysis. We had class. I think I even wrote, "I didn't know this was going on until that particular class... It was just another tool that helped me to understand what the teachers trying to get across just from the verbiage, just from the language."
Megan	"I had that in front of me when I was watching the class, but I had to stop because I wasn't paying enough attention to what was going on in the classroom with the kids. I was paying more attention to just words."

rank them as more or less difficult. For example, they stated that DESCRIPTION was probably the easiest, whereas EVALUATION and PRINCIPLES were the most challenging. Participants reasoned that when using DESCRIPTION, students relied on vocabulary provided by the teacher and often simply repeated what the teacher said. In EVALUATION and other KSs, students had to provide explanations using novel cognitive and linguistic structures, with which they may have been unfamiliar.

Challenges of Learning Using the KF

Our analysis would not be complete without bringing up the third major theme discussed by the participants—the challenges of using the KF as they relate to the present study. The major challenges identified pertain to (a) lack of time spent on training using the KF (b) analysis with the KF, and (c) teachers' preconceived linguistic notions.

Time. During the semester and in a methods course that aims to pack as much in as possible in order to reap the benefits of increased methodological understanding and application, the challenge of time was certainly understandable. As Megan stated, "I feel like something as in depth as this could be its own course" (Interview 3). Indeed, the KF is a powerful organizational tool that involves a range of KSs, thinking skills, and linguistic means of expression. As such it may be most effectively studied in its own right or laced through a number of courses that prepare teachers in TESOL.

Individual Analysis. A second challenge which came up was the difficulty of teasing out KSs within the transcripts of classroom discourse. In this regard, participants mentioned the difficulty of working individually on the first observation and analysis. This difficulty became less of a challenge during the second observation in which they were permitted to work in pairs or small groups to complete the analysis. Jane's remark "It was really helpful because it just opened my eyes a little bit more...this kind of gave me a better understanding... It was really helpful working together" (Interview 2) makes it clear that some participants found it beneficial to work with peers.

Linguistic Notions. The analysis of classroom discourse grounded in the KF presented an additional challenge to several participants who struggled with the functional grammatical descriptors. For example, Lori mentioned, "For me the hardest part was I think CLASSIFICATION and DESCRIPTION. Especially when it came to the grammar part like where it fits in I wasn't, I'm still kind of confused as to how that fits in with CLASSIFICATION and DESCRIPTION. How those verbs fit" (Interview 1). Lori's comment is an indication that some participants may have struggled with the interconnection between lexicogrammar and thinking skills across subjects and grade levels.

Discussion

Based on the data presented, we can now answer the research question: How does participant observation combined with social practice analysis help graduate-student participants to understand the role of oral discourse in classroom settings? As a result of KF professional development and field observations/analysis assignments, our participants were able to demonstrate: (a) awareness of the importance of functional linguistic aspects of oral classroom discourse on students' learning; (b) an emergent ability to apply the theoretical constructs of KSs to the actual discourse recorded in a variety of content classrooms; and (c) a nascent knowledge about language, which we believe will lay the groundwork for strategies that have been shown to be particularly relevant for making content comprehensible for ELLs in mainstream classrooms.

The results indicate that even a brief training provided to our participants with the KF leads to the development of awareness of classroom discourse from a linguistically sensitive perspective that integrates language and content through the classroom interaction among teachers and students (Huang & Laskowski, 2014). In this section, we would like to discuss this finding in a more nuanced way by addressing the role of teacher education projects involving classroom observations, specifically those that use the KF as a guide.

Awareness of KSs in Classroom Discourse

Stillwell et al. (2011) herald the benefits of hands-on practice with participant observation and transcription. The participants in our study took this a step further. Not only did they engage in participant observation and transcription of classroom discourse, they applied the KF to examine this discourse functionally. As a result, our participants were able to make discoveries about how the KSs played a role in classroom learning. Their insights into the nature of the KSs, the linguistic expression of KSs, and their use in the classroom is a necessary step in helping them to understand the role of academic language in oral classroom discourse.

Previous research has identified cognitive and discourse structures for language and content integration (Beacco et al., 2010; Bloom et al., 1956;

Dalton-Puffer, 2016). This study builds on this work by showing which discourse structures are more easily identified by teachers. In fact, participants' comments clearly indicate that certain KSs tend to be more easily identifiable than others. This preliminary finding underscored the perception that certain KSs appeared more salient to teachers, including the "action" KSs, such as SEQUENCE and CHOICE. On the other hand, the "reflection" KSs, such as PRINCIPLES and EVALUATION, which can draw on cause-effect and means-end relationships, were less frequently identified by our participants. This difficulty supports ample research that points out a difference between everyday and academic linguistic modes (Cummins, 1984; Gibbons, 2015; Halliday, 1993), and leads to a two-pronged issue. On the one hand, the KF requires knowledge of functional discourse features that teachers need to learn in order to apply it to the analysis of discourse. On the other hand, to fully apply the KF to lesson planning and teaching, teachers may need overt and focused instruction on these same features. Given that the "reflection" KSs are troublesome for participants to spot, it may be beneficial to target instruction in the functional linguistic resources within CLASSIFICATION, PRINCIPLES, and EVALUATION specifically, perhaps linking each "reflection" KS to its "action" KS pair.

Hands-on Identification of KSs through Knowledge Structure Analysis

One of the benefits of the KF is the connections it makes between knowledge/discourse structures and lexicogrammar (Early, Mohan & Hooper, 1989; Mohan, 2007; Mohan et al., 2015). This integrated classification allows users to work both top-down, that is from the discourse/knowledge structure down, as well as bottom-up, starting with lexicogrammatical features. With regard to the analysis of classroom transcripts, it was clear that our participants were able to apply their knowledge of KSs to classroom discourse. Moreover, in the paired analysis of the second observation, they combined top-down strategies for KS identification with bottom-up processing of KSs using functional language features. This indicates that participants were able to examine both the content and the language of the classroom in an integrated way. Participants exhibited a heightened awareness of the relationship between content, thinking skills, lexicogrammar, and key visuals.

The procedural aspect of the classroom observation project gave us a glimpse at what participants experience when working individually versus in a small group. From the perspective of sociocultural theory (Vygotsky, 1962; Walqui & van Lier, 2010), participant comments about the positive experiences of partner-supported classroom discourse analysis have implications for implementation. According to Vygotskyan views of learning, interaction with peers helps expand the zone of proximal development while negotiating meaning and constructing knowledge. Therefore, peer work generally results in a more efficient processing of the information than individual work. This is especially significant in light of participants' difficulty identifying the "reflection" KSs which leads us to believe that working together on the analysis of classroom discourse is more beneficial than working alone.

From Linguistic Sensitivity to Making Content Accessible for ELLs

It is the aim of any teaching methods course to increase teacher candidates' awareness of the tools with which they can become more effective educators (Muntner, 2008; Samson & Collins, 2012). During initial teacher preparation programs, teachers generally are not trained to work with students on language resources outside the designated time for language arts. In addition to this lack of language focus, school tests and standardized assessments also focus on content assuming that language skills are already present (Gottlieb, 2016). This lack of explicit language focus adds to the well-documented problem of a hidden/invisible curriculum, where traditional pedagogical practices and decontextualized high-stakes assessment tasks have been found to limit the achievement of historically underserved learners (Humphrey, 2018). Hence, teachers' main concern in lesson planning and in initial classroom observations is on content. Through the study of the KF and careful analysis of the recordings of classroom discourse, participants were able to develop keen awareness of the salience of language for content comprehension and learning, particularly among ELLs.

The results of this study point to the likelihood that a major benefit of the KF is in helping teachers to see the connection between classroom oral language and the content covered in the classroom (Humphrey & McNaught, 2016; Mohan & Slater, 2006). This is achieved by helping to make teachers cognizant of how KSs play a role in the oral discourse of the classrooms that they observe. An additional benefit—and one that is particularly relevant to sheltered language classrooms—is the presence of key visuals that help structure students' thinking (Tang, 1997). These tools make the KF an invaluable and powerful resource for any classroom, but even more so for classrooms with integrated ELLs.

Finally, when the analysis of classroom discourse is supported by the KF, participants identify patterns of KSs in teacher discourse and student discourse thus becoming more cognizant of not only student/teacher talk ratios, but also of the linguistic quality of talk (Huang & Laskowski, 2014).

Therefore, training teachers in the KF is important in order to provide them with tools to integrate language and content in a meaningful and systematic way. This is particularly essential for teacher education programs that prepare ESOL teachers as well as mainstream teachers for bilingual and bicultural tracks.

Conclusion

It is through a close and detailed analysis of classroom discourse that teachers are able to grasp the intricacies of language and content ties (Stillwell et al, 2011; Tsui, 2012). Classroom observations, their transcription, and analysis for teacher training, provide the grist for such analysis. Combined with introduction to the KF as a tool for functional classroom discourse analysis, classroom observation and analysis assignments can help teachers draw theoretically informed conclusions about how to foster learners' language-and-content knowledge during in-class oral conversations.

For future research, two aspects pertain to the application of KSs. First, it is essential to investigate how awareness of KSs and their corresponding linguistic features allows teachers to effectively plan and implement lessons with ELLs in mind (Hammond, 2006). Second, the development of familiarity with and use of KSs in school children is increasingly important for their academic success. Teachers can help their students become aware of KSs in academic language (Early, Mohan & Hooper, 1989; Huang & Laskowski, 2014). Future studies can investigate how extensive teacher training fosters effective student use of KSs, both in written and spoken genres. More specifically, future research should study the relationship between such opportunities for professional development and participants' own growth as teachers.

It would also be helpful to better understand the patterns of use of KSs across content-based classrooms. This study has shown that several of the KSs (CLASSIFICATION, DESCRIPTION, and SEQUENCE) may be more prevalent in teacher discourse, but other KSs (PRINCIPLES, EVALUATION, and CHOICE) may be used less systematically and holistically in the classroom. It also appears that ELLs may have difficulty with EVALUATION that elaborates on CHOICE. Following these emergent findings, we suggest that future research should analyze and understand difficulties that students and teachers have with these particular KSs, which would have value for ELLs and other students across disciplines.

We cannot claim that knowledge is always created in the same way in every classroom. Nonetheless, our data may help teacher educators plan projects to help teachers become more cognizant of how students learn content and language in an integrated manner. While the KF is clearly no quick fix to teaching or learning academic language, it certainly is a clear-cut and usable tool that should be considered for ESOL teacher preparation. The specific patterns of discourse highlighted here provide a roadmap for understanding how knowledge is built linguistically in classrooms across content areas and grade levels. Once teachers are aware of the linguistic aspects of building academic knowledge, they can carry out lessons more effectively, better serving their growing population of ELLs.

References

Beacco, J.-C., Coste, D., van de Ven, P.-H. & Vollmer, H. (2010). *Language and school subjects. Linguistic dimensions of knowledge building in school curricula. Language Policy Division.* Directorate of Education and Languages, DGIV. Council of Europe, Strasbourg. Retrieved from https://www.coe.int/t/dg4/linguistic/Source/Source2010_ForumGeneva/KnowledgeBuilding2010_en.pdf

Bloom, B.S., Engelhart, M.D., Furst, E.J., Hill, W.H. & Krathwohl, D.R. (1956). *Taxonomy of educational objectives: The classification of educational goals. Handbook I: Cognitive domain.* David McKay Company.

Brisk, M. (2015). *Engaging students in academic literacies. Genre-based pedagogy for K-5 classrooms.* Routledge.

Cazden, C.B. (1988). *Classroom discourse. The language of teaching and learning.* Heinemann.

Charmaz, K. (2006). *Constructing grounded theory.* SAGE.

Cummins, J. (1984). *Bilingualism and special education: Issues in assessment and pedagogy.* Multilingual Matters.

Dalton-Puffer, C. (2016). Cognitive discourse functions: Specifying an integrative interdisciplinary construct. In T. Nikula, E. Dafouz, P. Moore & Smit, U. (Eds.), *Conceptualising integration CLIL and multilingual education* (pp. 29–54). Multilingual Matters.

de Oliviera, L. (2016). A language-based approach to content instruction (LACI) for English language learners: Examples from two elementary teachers. *International Multilingual Research Journal, 10*(3), 217–231.

Derewianka, B. (2011). *A new grammar companion for teachers.* PETA.

Early, M., Mohan, B., & Hooper, H.R. (1989). The Vancouver School Board Language and Content Project. In J.H. Esling (Ed.), *Multicultural education and policy: ESL in the 1990's,* (pp. 107–122). Ontario Institute for Studies in Education.

Fang, Z., & Schleppegrell, M.J. (2008). Disciplinary literacies across content areas: Supporting secondary reading through functional language analysis. *Journal of Adolescent & Adult Literacy, 53*(7), 587–597. DOI:10.1598/JAAL.53.7.6

Gibbons, P. (2015). *Scaffolding language, scaffolding learning* (2nd Ed.). Heinemann.

Gottlieb, M. (2016). *Assessing English language learners. Bridges from language proficiency to academic achievement.* Corwin Press.

Halliday, M.A.K. (1993). Towards a language-based theory of learning. *Linguistics and Education, 5*, 93–116.

Hammond, J. (2006). High challenge, high support: Integrating language and content instruction for diverse learners in an English literature classroom. *Journal of English for Specific Purposes, 5*, 269–283.

Harklau, L. (2005). Ethnography and ethnographic research on second language teaching and learning. In E. Hinkel (Ed.), *Handbook of research in second language teaching and learning* (pp. 179–194). Lawrence Erlbaum.

Huang, J. & Laskowski, T. (2014). Developing linguistic sensitivity of ESL teacher candidates for linguistically responsive instruction. *The International Journal of Literacies, 20*(2), 29–50.

Huang, J., Normandia, B., & Greer, S. (2005). Communicating mathematically: comparison of knowledge structures in teacher and student discourse in a secondary math classroom. *Communication Education, 54*(1), 34–51.

Humphrey, S. (2018). "We can speak to the world": Applying meta-linguistic knowledge for specialized and reflexive literacies. In R. Harman (Ed.), *Bilingual learners and social equity: Critical approaches to Systemic Functional Linguistics*, (pp. 45–70). Springer. https://doi.org/10.1007/978-3-319-60953-9_3

Humphrey, S. & Macnaught, L. (2016). Developing teachers' professional knowledge of language for discipline literacy instruction. In H. de Silva Joyce (Ed.) *Language at work in social contexts: Analysing language use in work, educational, medical and museum contexts* (pp. 68–87). Cambridge Scholars Publishing.

Johnson, K.E. (1995). *Understanding communication in second language classrooms.* Cambridge University Press.

Jones, P. & Chen, H. (2012). Teachers' knowledge about language: Issues of pedagogy and expertise. *Australian Journal of Language & Literacy, 35*(2), 147–172.

Macken-Horarik, M., Love, K. & Unsworth, L. (2011). A grammatics "good enough" for school English in the 21st century: Four challenges in realising the potential. *Australian Journal of Language and Literacy, 34*(1), 9–23.

Mizapour, M. (2016). A critical perspective at the role of input flooding in the acquisition of linguistic forms by EFL learners. *International Journal of Modern Language Teaching and Learning, 1*(5), 197–201.

Mohan, B.A. (1986). *Language and content.* Addison Wesley.

Mohan, B.A. (2007). Knowledge structures in social practices. In J. Cummins & C. Davison (Eds.), *International handbook of English language teaching, Volume 15* (pp. 303–315). Springer.

Mohan, B.A., Beckett, G., Slater, T. & Tong, E.K.M. (2015). Tasks, experiential learning, and meaning making activities. In M. Bygate, J.M. Norris & K. Van den Branden (Eds.) *Domains and directions in the development of TBLT* (pp. 157–192). John Benjamins.

Mohan, B. & Slater, T. (2006). Examining the theory/practice relation in a high school science register: A functional linguistic perspective. *Journal of English for Academic Purposes, 5*, 302–316.

Muntner, M. (2008). *Teacher-student interactions: The key to quality classrooms.* The University of Virginia Center for Advanced Study of Teaching and Learning (CASTL). Retrieved from http://www.readingrockets.org/article/teacher-student-interactions-key-quality-classrooms

Samson, J.F., & Collins, B.A. (2012). Preparing all teachers to meet the needs of English language learners: Applying research to policy and practice for teacher effectiveness. *Center for American Progress.* Retrieved from http://files.eric.ed.gov/fulltext/ED535608.pdf

Schleppegrell, M. (2004). *The language of schooling.* Routledge.

Schleppegrell, M. (2013). The role of meta-language in supporting academic language development. *Language Learning, 63*(1), 153–170. doi:10.1111/j.1467-9922.2012.00742.x

Stillwell, C., Curabba, B., Alexander, K., Kidd, A., Kim, E., Stone, P., & Wyle, C. (2011). Students transcribing tasks: Noticing fluency, accuracy, and complexity. *ELT Journal, 64*(4), 445–455.

Tang, G.M. (1997). From graphic literacy across languages to integrating language and content teaching in vocational settings. *Hong Kong Journal of Applied Linguistics, 2*(1), 97–114.

Thomas, W.P., & Collier, V.P. (2002). *A national study of school effectiveness for language minority students' long-term academic achievement.* Center for Research on Education, Diversity and Excellence, University of California Santa Cruz.

Tsui, A.B.M. (2012). Ethnography and classroom discourse. In J. P. Gee, & M. Handford (Eds.), *The Routledge handbook of discourse analysis* (pp. 383–395). Routledge.

Vygotsky, L.S. (1962). *Thought and language.* MIT Press.

Walsh, S. (2006). *Investigating classroom discourse.* Routledge.

Walqui, A., and van Lier, L. (2010). *Scaffolding the academic success of adolescent English language learners: A pedagogy of promise.* WestEd.

Zwiers, J. (2014). *Building academic language: Meeting Common Core Standards across disciplines.* Jossey-Bass.

About the Authors

Jesse Gleason, PhD, is an associate professor of applied linguistics and Spanish at Southern Connecticut State University. Her teaching and research interests include bilingualism/biliteracy development and technology-mediated instruction. She has presented her research internationally in Australia, Belgium, Brazil, Canada, Chile, Germany, and the U.S. as well as published research in a number of refereed journals, such as *CALICO*, *System*, and *Language, Culture and Curriculum*.

Dr. Elena Schmitt is a professor of applied linguistics and coordinator of the Master's Program in TESOL, Bilingual, and Multicultural Education at Southern Connecticut State University. Her teaching focuses on linguistic theory and its application to classroom learning. She publishes on the issues of bilingualism, including first language attrition, classroom interaction, technology-mediated instruction, and teacher development.

Appendix: Interview Protocol

1. How did you feel using the KF to analyze discourse?
2. Was there a change in your ability to use it from the 3rd to the 4th ethnographic observation?
3. In your experience, what were the most challenging aspects to grasp about the KF? What were the easiest or most useful aspects?
4. Do you think you will use the KF in the future, either for lesson planning or as a discourse analyst?
5. Would you be willing to study the KF further? And if so, how would it contribute to your lesson planning and/or discourse analysis?
6. Was there anything that we could do to make the KF easier to understand? In other words, as learners about of the KF, what (if anything) would you have made it easier to understand and use?
7. In your opinion, how could future MS TESOL students benefit (if at all) from learning how to use the KF? What advice would you have for them about this assignment?
8. Specific questions.

13 Learning and Using the Knowledge Framework as a Language and Content Teaching Unit Project: A Case Study

Amy Walton and Gulbahar H. Beckett

Abstract

Limited research has been carried out on the integration of the Knowledge Framework (KF) and project work for language, content, and skills teaching and learning. A study that explores how pre-service teachers appropriate the KF in their unit plan projects during short-term training contexts thus offers a welcome addition to the field. This chapter discusses a qualitative case study of a class of 17 pre-service teachers participating in a four-week training session designed to teach them enough about the KF to create KF unit-based projects. The study examined their understanding of these projects, their reflections on the challenges involved in creating KF unit-based projects as an undergraduate course requirement, and their future plans for language and content teaching with these types of projects. Findings of the study suggested that although the teachers demonstrated that they learned much about the KF and were enthusiastic about experimenting more with it, having them learn about the KF by carrying out and reflecting on a unit planning project of their own, one that implements their knowledge of the KF, helped highlight issues and challenges that arose in their understanding of the theory. The implications of the study suggest that explicitly connecting theory and practice through this type of learning activity may help raise pre-service teachers' confidence about using blended KF unit-based projects in their future careers as well as offer valuable feedback to instructors regarding the areas that appear the most challenging.

Keywords: Knowledge Framework; project work; language and content; pre-service teachers; short-term training; educational activity; sociocultural activity

Background

Teacher education programs prepare pre-service teachers, including English as a Second Language (ESL) teachers, to develop, implement, and evaluate instruction in general as well as present them with tools to teach their students content knowledge and language skills (Snow & Brinton, 1997). Mohan's (1986) Knowledge Framework (KF) is heralded as a way address the latter objectives, providing a useful heuristic for creating lessons, units, and instructional *activities* that teach language, content, and thinking skills in an integrated way (Slater & Mohan, 2019). Furthermore, research has shown that project work is a natural educational *activity* for language, content, and skills development (Beckett, 1999; Beckett, 2006; Beckett, Slater, & Mohan, 2020; Slater & Mohan, 2019); thus project work presents a natural context for implementing the KF (Beckett et al., 2015; Slater, 2020). However, little work has been carried out to investigate how the KF can be taught through projects, instead focusing on the benefits of the KF for teachers and students (e.g., Early, Potts, and Mohan, 2005; Huang, 2000; Tang, 1994). Given that project-based language teaching and the KF appear to connect closely through the concept of *activity*, the two approaches can benefit from research that addresses how pre-service teachers appropriate the KF heuristic through project work. Such an investigation into project implementation can highlight pre-service teachers' understanding of the KF and how they may implement it into their own teaching practice and materials creation.

Existing work offers examples that show how KF teacher training has been implemented during substantial professional development sessions (e.g., Berg & Huang, 2015; Huang & Berg, in this volume). While professional development with any model deserves substantial amounts of time, teacher education programs are typically packed with required courses that introduce the most prominent models and frameworks so that the program meets required objectives and standards. As such, each model or framework may be granted only a few weeks of teaching and learning, with each topic often culminating with assignments such as a unit plan project. Not all programs have time to implement models that promote the integration of language and content, such as the KF; moreover, research indicates a need for teacher training in the effective implementation of project-based instruction throughout all content areas (see Beckett et al., 2015; Beckett, Slater, & Mohan, 2020; Slater & Beckett, 2019). These reasons reinforce the need for research to explore the potential value of using a project-based approach to teaching with the KF.

This chapter discusses a qualitative case study of a four-week training session that took place in a single class of 17 undergraduate students in an English as a second language (ESL) Literacy Methods course that involved pre-service teachers learning how to create KF unit projects. The study examined their understanding of the KF as it applied to their unit plans, their reflections on the challenges they faced during the creation and application of these KF unit projects, and their future plans for teaching language and content using KF-based projects. The chapter will begin with a discussion of language, content, and skills development using KF-based projects, followed by a description of the research methods involved in the study. It will then present and discuss the research findings. It will conclude with implications for further research and practice.

Teaching Language, Content, and Skills with Knowledge Framework Projects

Literacy instruction needs to help students deconstruct often complex academic content and teach them how to reconstruct their understanding using academic language through which content knowledge is taught and assessed (Fang, Schleppegrell, & Moore, 2014; Halliday, 2007). To do this, teachers need training and tools that can help their students analyze the academic language they encounter as they address curriculum standards (Fang, 2014; Love, 2009). Two such tools are considered in this chapter: Mohan's KF (Mohan, 1986) and project work (Beckett, 1999). Each will be addressed below.

Knowledge Framework

As discussed in the first chapter of this book, the Knowledge Framework (KF) (Mohan, 1986) takes a functional view of language as it relates to content and has six knowledge structures (KSs). According to Slater and Mohan (2019), these "KSs and the associated thinking skills are common to most subject areas and student levels, and follow Dewey's (1911, 1913) concept of an activity and its theory and practice (action situations)" (p. 1). Research has demonstrated that the six KSs are prevalent in classroom activities and educational materials (e.g., Early, Thew, & Wakefield, 1986; Early, Mohan, & Hooper, 1988; Mohan & Slater, 2005, 2006).

Scholars have provided ample examples of the visuals and linguistic features associated with these KSs and their associated thinking skills (e.g., Cummins & Early, 2015; Mohan, 1986; Slater & Beckett, 2019; Slater & Gleason, 2011). The use of visuals has shown promise in activating students' background knowledge and demonstrating underlying relationships within knowledge structures, with the capability to support learning across cultures (Early & Tang, 1991; Tang, 1994) and to increase engagement with content (Early, 1989) for all students, including lower-proficiency students. The use of visuals has also been positively associated with language development (Tang, 1994).

Decades of research have in fact shown that many teachers find the KF to be an effective organizational tool for planning units, lessons, and tasks to help their students construct their thinking skills linguistically and visually as well as gain the knowledge to deconstruct and reconstruct academic discourse multimodally (Berg & Huang, 2015; Slater & Mohan, 2019). A Huang and Laskowski (2014) study of pre-service teachers noted that an introduction to and training with the KF aided teacher education candidates' linguistic awareness in different texts. Berg and Huang's (2015) study of 23 experienced in-service K-12 teachers in four graduate content courses revealed that KF training improved classroom instruction and lesson planning and brought more attention to students' language development, thus increasing their preparedness for differentiated instruction. (See also the chapter by Huang & Berg in this volume.) To date, however, the lack of studies that explore the teaching of the KF to pre-service teachers points to a need for more studies that focus on short-term training.

Project-based Learning

Project-based learning (PBL) is a Deweyan sociocultural activity that "teachers and students carry out to achieve various goals" (Beckett, 1999, p. 19) by purposefully working on real-world problems and creating knowledge through activities such as designing a curriculum (Dionne & Horth, 1994). PBL can be "a series of individual or group activities that involve language/content learning through planning, researching (empirical and/or document), analyzing and synthesizing data, and reflecting on the process and product orally and/or in writing by comparing, contrasting, and justifying alternatives" (Beckett, 1999, p. 4). This definition of PBL resonates with Deweyan and Hallidayan functional views of language and draws on language socialization theory (Ochs, 1988, Schieffelin & Ochs, 1986) which holds that we learn about language (linguistic knowledge) by engaging in sociocultural activities (e.g., working on KF unit projects) by socializing with others (teachers and peers) and by using language (Beckett, 1999).

Activity is "a unit of inquiry in social science research" (Beckett, 1999, p. 71). Ochs (1988) sees activity as "a behavioral unit, in the sense of a sequence of actions associated with particular motivations and goals... and a process in the sense of praxis" (p. 14). According to Beckett (1999), activity is seen to have both "theoretical and practical aspects" (Mohan, 1986, p. 43) because it is a "mode of thought and conduct" that "has a pattern of action" (p. vi), both of which is necessary for education because "without the practical, students cannot apply what they know; without the theoretical, students cannot understand what they are doing, nor transfer what they know" (Mohan, 1986, p. 43).

The Need for Knowledge Framework Project Work

Research in both general education and second language education has shown how PBL affords language socialization opportunities (e.g., Beckett, 1999; Beckett & Miller, 2006; Beckett, Slater, & Mohan, 2020). However, in response to teacher training needs in implementing the KF and PBL, scholars (e.g., Beckett & Slater, 2017; Gleason & Link, 2020; Slater, 2020; Slater & Beckett, 2019) have proposed KF projects. Acknowledging the power of PBL in language socialization as well as skills and content knowledge development within authentic sociocultural contexts and in response to research findings that students can find it difficult to see language development through PBL (Beckett, 1999, 2005, 2006), Beckett and Slater (2017) and Slater and Beckett (2019) proposed a blended framework. They discussed how Mohan's (1986) KF and Beckett and Slater's (2005) Project Framework can be "combined to create unit plans that explicitly integrate language, content, skills, and technology" (p. 1) to help students see how each component, including language, is being taught. The authors illustrated how the blending of the two frameworks can work through the model of an 11-lesson unit plan about applying for American graduate schools as the content. These lessons focus on "sequences, tasks, and learning objectives for the content, language, academic skills, and technological understandings that the unit comprises" (p. 1).

Gleason and Link (2020) developed a technology-enhanced form-function project-based language learning (TEFF PBLL) heuristic to help K–12 teachers attend to language, content, technology, and state standards through projects that also enhance multiliteracies and career readiness. Gleason and

Link illustrated their heuristic with a third-grade classroom learning segment guided by the KF and the teaching-learning cycle (TLC) for genre pedagogy, with ideas for modification to other contexts.

Slater (2020) showed how project-based language learning (PBLL) with Mohan's (1986) KF can be made explicit. She also demonstrated how content-relevant technology can be incorporated into PBLL. Slater's arguments and illustration are based on a KF analysis of two semesters of data collected in a university-level intensive English bridge class designed to prepare students for regular university credit courses. She argued that a KF analysis shows how "the program's learning objectives, discussions, lectures, and assignments can be described in terms of knowledge structures, thus offering opportunities for instructors to develop and reinforce new, more academic ways for students to construct content through language" (Beckett, Slater, & Mohan, 2020, p. 13).

Little work has been carried out to investigate how students in a university-level pre-service teacher education program understand and make use of the tools that KF-based project work offers. PBLL, which promotes student-centered activity, focuses on students' needs and interests. Helping pre-service teachers utilize the KF as a tool for planning PBLL-based units and lessons that help develop their students' linguistic and visual resources that meet their needs and interests is a worthy endeavor (for elaboration, see Slater, 2020; Slater & Beckett, 2019). The blending of the KF into PBLL shows promise, but more work needs to be done. This chapter addresses that need.

Research Methods

Participants and Research Context

The participants of the study were 17 pre-service teachers enrolled in an undergraduate ESL Literacy Methods course at a large Midwestern University. The participants volunteered for the study and understood that the data being collected would be analyzed after final grades were calculated. The participants came from a variety of programs of study, including Linguistics (7), English Education (3), English (2), World Languages (2), Journalism (2), and Global Resource Systems (1). Of the 17 participants, six had some prior teaching experience, three had at least six hours of one-on-one tutoring through another methods course, and three had participated in a teaching practicum in a K-12 school. The other 11 participants self-identified as having no prior teaching experience.

The course introduced key ESL Literacy research issues and approaches, including the Knowledge Framework (KF), pertaining to literacy instruction and assessment. The ESL Literacy Methods course met twice a week for 80 minutes over a 15-week semester. The participants learned and practiced ways to adapt teaching materials and methods to different age and proficiency levels and to identify the linguistic characteristics of various text types and offer ideas for teaching them. This was done through lectures, small-group discussions and projects, and individual and team teaching. Major projects within the course included a comparison of oral and written text; a written midterm and final exam; journals used to respond to required readings and try out different literacy building techniques; a tutoring project and reflection; and a six-lesson KF unit project that included all six knowledge structures. This latter project is the focus of this chapter. Four weeks were devoted the KF: One week (week 11) was devoted to explicit instruction in the KF, followed by three weeks during which students worked on and presented their KF unit planning projects.

The two lessons in week 11, in which participants learned about the KF and creating KF projects, started with an overview of the framework and a discussion of ideas and activities for an example KF unit project on *Romeo and Juliet*. Students read Slater and Gleason (2011) and Early (1990) and reflected on them in journal entries. They also examined different genres for different purposes and the six knowledge structures (KSs) associated with the KF: CLASSIFICATION, DESCRIPTION, PRINCIPLES, SEQUENCES, EVALUATION, and CHOICE. In groups, the class explored other texts, activities, and visuals for a KF unit on whales. Students then had a week to work, either individually or in pairs, on planning their KF unit projects after which they brought in their initial drafts for peer response. In week 14, three weeks after the start of the project, students submitted their units in writing. In week 15, students presented their work in informal poster sessions for their classmates.

Amy, the first author of this chapter, was the instructor of the ESL Literacy Method course. Her goal for the course was to further students' progress through the stated objectives; her related research goal was to collect data on how the topic of the KF was received and integrated into the students' project work. Amy had taught the ESL Literacy Methods course three times consecutively and the KF unit project was a course assignment each time she taught it. Nothing was altered for the purpose of this study except for the data collection, as described below.

Data Sources, Collection, and Analysis

Data sources for this qualitative case study included ethnographic observations (field notes of class meetings, office hours, and poster sessions), document collection (students' summary response journals on Knowledge Framework readings and their rationales for their lesson plans and posters that comprised their KF unit projects), and interviews (Guba & Lincoln, 1989; Spradley, 1980). Observational and document data were collected to understand what the participants did (practice). Interview data were collected to understand what the participants knew or did not know, and why (theory) (Spradley, 1979).

Observations, consisting of in-class observations, office hour feedback, poster presentations, were conducted and field-noted (25 pages of notes) by Amy and an additional researcher. The additional researcher visited the course, took field notes, and recorded four class sessions in order to document the teaching of the KF and the students' introductory thoughts on the framework as well as questions students had over the course of the teaching and project creation. Documents, 19 pages of participants' journal responses and 18 rough drafts of their projects (two of which were submitted as pair projects) were also collected by Amy. Interviews with 15 participants (not all students were interviewed due to the time constraints of the poster session) were conducted by Amy and the additional researcher to find out students' thoughts about the KF, including its benefits and drawbacks; challenges they experienced in creating a KF-based project unit integrating visuals; if and how they would use KF projects in their future teaching, and why they would or would not; and what more they needed to learn to use the blended approach in their future careers. These semi-structured interviews were conducted by Amy and the additional researcher during the participants' poster sessions for their projects.

These in-class observations were audiotaped with digital voice recorders worn by Amy and the additional researcher as well as other larger recording devices set at the front of the classroom. The data were transcribed verbatim by the two researchers and analyzed for key issues (Patton, 1990) by Amy. The findings of these observations and fieldnotes informed the development of questions for the interviews. The recordings of the interviews were also transcribed and examined for recurring themes (Strauss & Corbin, 1990; Spradley, 1980) by Amy. After this, the contents of the participants' KF unit plan project rationales were examined for key issues (Patton, 1990) and themes (Spradley, 1980), also by Amy, to offer insights into students' understandings of the KF as well as how and why they might use it in their future teaching.

Findings

The themes that arose from a close analysis of the data could be classified into three general areas: participants' understanding of the KF for unit planning, their views of the KF for their own future teaching, and the challenges they faced in the creation of their projects. Each of these will be considered in turn.

Participants' Understanding of the KF for Unit Planning

As articulated in their KF unit plan project rationale, all 17 participants considered the KF to be a powerful organizational tool for systematic lesson and unit planning that offered simultaneous teaching and learning of language and content across the curriculum. In their rationale, nine participants indicated that the knowledge structures (KSs) offered dynamic and flexible tools for teaching generalizable and transferable thinking skills for developing language that can be modified for different teaching contexts. For example, when learning about the KF, Margot stated that "this works so much better because you know that you're hitting everything," highlighting her conception of the usefulness of the heuristic for planning unit projects that address the development of language, content, and thinking skills together. Margot's classmate, Bella, focused on how the KF is a tool that can be used for students' language development, writing that "things are already clearly defined and categorized in the Knowledge Framework… It also gives great tools to expand literacy such as adjectives and other grammatical structures and how to use them, different thinking skills, and what kids of connections can or should be made by students in the activities." Eva observed that "zoning into each part of the framework allows for instructors to think about a subject and divide it according to the main components. This focuses each lesson plan and actually helps develop its structure and what to include." Barbara considered the six knowledge structures as forms that "seemed to fit well" with her learning objectives and the activities she planned to do within her class time.

While the comments of many of the participants reiterated closely what had been presented in class and in their readings, a few made observations that were novel and insightful. For example, Carmen and Todd speculated that "when a topic is addressed in multiple ways, it is more likely that the information will be retained." In other words, planning unit projects for their own future students to complete, and using the KF to organize these projects, can offer teachers ways to systematically design tasks and visuals that will help their students learn and remember both the topic and the language associated with that topic.

Chad reflected on the benefits of the KF for both novice and experienced teachers, a topic which had not been addressed in class:

> As a tool, the Knowledge Framework is not only helpful to new teachers who may be looking for guidance in lesson, activity, and unit planning, but also to experienced teachers who may be looking for a consistent framework that can be applied to speed up unit planning.

Chad also commented on the potential of the KF for the modification of lessons "to fit the many variables that teachers encounter in different teaching contexts (classroom size, student's age, L2, proficiency, etc.)," which he believed to be a design perk of the KF that is "an attractive feature to teachers."

The above excerpts show that the participants regarded the KF as an appealing tool with which to plan engaging teaching units that incorporate specific thinking skills, associated linguistics features, and representative visuals that can be modified to a variety of levels and contexts. For example, Bella wrote in her unit plan rationale that "the approach that the Knowledge Framework gives makes it possible to better define, acknowledge, and understand all of the holidays, their histories, and their unique celebrations." Margot thought "it's definitely an improvement over what I grew up with, because I definitely didn't get sequence a whole lot, or like, classification, because I didn't have anything to draw from." Other participants (e.g., Stan) realized that the KF can be a useful guide for the "completeness" of a language and content teaching unit, with each KS focusing on different aspect of the curriculum.

As their comments suggested, the pre-service teachers seemed to exude enthusiasm about the benefits of the KF for unit planning. They appreciated being introduced to a tool that they could use to help ensure that the language of the six knowledge structures would be included in their projects. They also offered their understandings of how their future students could benefit from the KF approach as well.

Participants' Views on the KF for Their Future Teaching

Highlighted in the participants' comments was the benefit of the heuristic for supporting their future students' development of language and content. Charlie pointed out the value of the KF for students due to its transferability to other courses and content across the curriculum, an observation that was made evident through the variety of unit projects that these pre-service teachers produced for the course, as highlighted in Table 13.1. Cody appreciated the heuristic because it "broke down different verb tenses and activities that students could work on to gain knowledge in those areas." Bella reflected this idea, saying "all in all, I find that the Knowledge Framework is very flexible to any kind of classroom, unit, or lesson." As suggested by these comments, the pre-service teachers generally appeared to see the KF as a valuable tool to help their future students learn content and language. Stan claimed that by using the KF, he could create units that build on earlier units, with activities that are "different and engaging" and focus on different language, and that consequently, "students will not only be interested throughout, but also learning throughout."

Three other participants noted in their unit plan rationales that the KF and the activities created for each knowledge structure lent themselves to a dynamic "blend" or "engaging" and "balanced" teaching. Two others discussed how the KF helped them realize that using key visuals can be a means of supporting student retention of the materials being taught, helping the to add context to content learning. Carmen and Todd commented that using the visuals advocated in the KF "provide room for a wider variety of learners... which made the KF an appealing option when we considered the wide range of learners." Lily considered the KF as a "great choice" for the unit she developed on dinosaurs because "not only are students engaging in vocabulary related to each [knowledge] structure, they are also seeing a visual that breaks down the information further." Lily argued that the KF helped her lessons

Table 13.1 Topics for the KF unit plan projects

Project Topic	Project Audience
Genealogy	High school ESL
King Arthur Myth	High school ESL
Film	High school ESL
Information Literacy	High school English
Daily Routine	Middle/high school ESL
Endangered Animals	Middle school EFL
Dinosaurs	Elementary ESL
Holidays	Elementary ESL
Food: Restaurants and Grocery Stores	Elementary ESL
Conversational English	Intensive English Program
"Choose Your Own Adventure" Stories	College academic writing ESL course
Helping Tourists in Ho Chi Minh City	Vietnamese adult EFL class
Yu-Gi-Oh!	Unspecified

become more directed to language development for her students, and its use of key visuals assisted with content development.

When asked whether they would apply KF-based projects in their future teaching of the language and content, all participants interviewed responded positively. One participant, Eva, explained that she could see the benefits of using the KF, but that she still had much to learn about lesson planning:

> Yeah, I think it's good. It has direction and it abides by the thinking skills that are fundamental for the classroom. So, I think that's a strength. It does follow a certain theory and there are other theories that go a different direction. I would have to develop my own opinion. I thought this was good, especially for my first experience with lesson plans.

Bella stated she would also employ the KF in her future teaching, saying "it's a nice way to pinpoint the language I want to use" and Margot felt it was a "very usable framework." Sammi, who had some experience in the classroom, asserted strongly, "I wish that I had learned about this before I did my teaching!"

Although the participants were generally enthusiastic about implementing the KF into their unit planning projects, a few participants also felt challenges. For example, Margot said that "a lot of the stuff fell into multiple categories, so it was hard to wrap your brain around at first." Such challenges caused some anxiety for the less experienced participants, as addressed in the next section.

Challenges in Creating KF Unit Plan Projects

When reflecting in interviews on the challenges of creating KF unit projects, seven participants reported struggles with lesson planning in general and working with KS in particular. Even students like Cody, who had some prior teaching and planning experience, noted apprehension about being able to "work the models into [his] lesson plan and have it make sense." Others such as Margot, for whom this was the first unit planning project, found the KF served as a useful direction, but she had trouble recognizing the KS on her own because other lesson planning models she knew "[weren't] set up like that" and she found it was difficult to choose KSs for her lessons because they "fell into multiple categories so it was hard to wrap your brain around at first." Bella worked through a similar issue. She had difficulty keeping KSs separate when working on her CHOICE and EVALUATION lessons and came in for additional help during office hours.

Field notes from an observation of the second KF lesson as well as interviews indicated that some participants struggled to differentiate between theory and practice pairs. Sammi, for example, specifically mentioned struggling with the KS PRINCIPLE over SEQUENCE, saying "I feel like it's easier for me to explain how you do something, instead of why you do something."

In class, Arthur asked for further clarification between the structures of SEQUENCE and PRINCIPLE. He mentioned this challenge in his interview, when asked about any difficulties he had, noting that "the lower of the six-box row—those seemed to be more concrete. For some reason the theoretical ones don't make as much sense to me as the concrete ones. I can sequence, I can classify, I can't 'principle.'" Arthur's difficulties with this theory/practice issue persisted into his final unit plan which, although earning him a grade of A (the top grade possible), elicited a comment from Amy that "for a few of the lessons, a bit more detail about what language you want the students to use would help me see whether the KF lesson matches the structure." Moreover, a follow-up sentence in the feedback suggested that Arthur's observation about the lower three knowledge structures being easier to understand could be contested by Amy's comment that she had questions about his presentation of DESCRIPTION language, one of the more concrete structures. In fact, one of the most frequent knowledge structures targeted by Amy's feedback for all submitted unit plans was CHOICE, also a "practice" knowledge structure.

Data collected in class, through peer responses, during the poster presentation interviews, and from Amy's formal feedback on the completed unit plans also indicated that some participants had trouble seeing or showing where the KF language actually was in their lesson plans. During the interviews, four participants relayed that they consulted supplemental materials that were part of the instructor's KF lesson plans that were included in her PowerPoint slides and the examples provided in-class activities. Some participants also said they consulted the Slater and Gleason (2011) chart of the verbs, thinking skills, and key visuals that align with each KS and found it helpful in addressing challenges they faced. For example, Sammi said, "I was able to just go back to her PowerPoint presentations to find everything I needed."

Nevertheless, two participants commented that they could have benefited from more instruction on the KF. Margot struggled to write both language and content objectives and did not include key visuals in her unit. She felt she could have been able to do better, "if we had a whole class on the Knowledge Framework, or if Amy had showed us all the different things we could

Table 13.2 Grade spread for the KF unit project

Letter Grade	Value (as per University Guidelines)	Number of Participants Receiving Grade
A	4	6
A-	3.67	2
B+	3.33	1
B	3	2
B-	2.67	3
C	2	1
F	0	2

do for a unit." Arthur also said he would use the KF "assuming I got more practice with it."

At the end of the four-week training session, fifteen of the pre-service teachers submitted what Amy judged as complete KF-based unit plans that presented their ideas for teaching topics of their choices. Table 13.2 summarizes the grades that participants received for their projects. Although most students received the top grade of an A, the mean letter grade is close to a B with a standard deviation of 1.25, a little more than the value of a letter grade. The two participants who received a failing grade (F) did not submit a plan or did not present a completed plan.

Discussion

The findings from this qualitative case study suggest that after four weeks of training on the application of the KF heuristic to a unit planning project of the pre-service teachers' choice, most participants were able to articulate an understanding of the KF that reflected both what they were taught and their favorable views of it as a powerful tool for unit planning and teaching. Their comments about its transferability across curricular areas align with Stewart (1997) who argued that the KF "gives instructor teams from different disciplines a way to discuss and plan common lessons in a comprehensive way [which] leads to highly structured lessons where content and language learning are naturally combined" (p. 18). The participants' understandings were generally confirmed by the grades they received for their unit plans. Yet even though the participants could describe the KF and discuss its potential for their practice, they addressed challenges, primarily the connection between linguistic resources and the most likely knowledge structures. Their reflections served the purpose of offering Amy insight into areas that may need more focus in future similar short-term training sessions. As described earlier in this chapter, these challenges were proposed by a few participants and the issues were made apparent in much of Amy's feedback on the unit plans.

Having students reflect on what they were learning was thus a valuable part of the project that Amy provided for her students and a powerful tool for her to use to evaluate the four-week training session. Mohan (2007) would consider Amy's teaching activity a social practice, which (like the KF) has a theory side—learning about the KF—and a practice side, creating a KF unit. Amy's evaluation of her own social practice of teaching the KF as a language and content teaching unit project involves probing what her participants said they learned about the KF (their theories) and exploring what these same participants did with the KF (their actual unit plan projects). Her students' theories were articulated through their interviews, the questions, asked during classes, their reflections, and the justifications written in their introductions to their unit plans, all of which were generally positive and suggested they were relatively confident about the potential of the KF, despite the challenges participants addressed. Their practice was manifested through the unit plans they created, which appeared to have a number of problems that both matched and did not match the observations that the pre-service teachers had made, including the presence of tasks that did not, to Amy's understanding, appear to elicit the language features of the targeted knowledge structures. Such observations highlight the importance of incorporating both interviews and projects into these types of theory-driven training programs.

The Role of Projects in Learning the KF

The projects in the KF unit plan projects served as a sociocultural and educational activity or social practice through which participants learned practical pedagogical skills to create unit plans for the first time, for most, while also learning about the KF, theoretical knowledge that was intended to inform their practical kills. Participants noted that the unit planning projects and the KF were a natural fit as they learned to be critical thinkers and attempted to utilize KF visuals to articulate their thoughts creatively. According to Hope, for example, the project worked "well with the Knowledge Framework, because it is a lot of critical thinking, and the visuals work because it sort of creates the project."

The language and content teaching KF unit projects activity afforded the participants opportunities to experiment with how various parts of the assignment, such as language objectives and content objectives, can come together as a whole unit. The projects allowed students to learn about the KF and apply the heuristic to their chosen interest contextually, a hallmark of project work. What Carmen and Eva said during interview represents such sentiments. Carmen thought "it was cool that we each got to explore it on our own," a sentiment reflected by Eva, who found the individual project motivating to work through: "Thinking of what would relate to the structures takes a little time, but I think that's more about really pausing and letting your creativity come through. You have your general outline and it allows for different directions."

The projects served as a unit of activity that helped the participants see how they could apply the six knowledge structures—the theory—to the development of their lessons and engage in self-assessment of their understanding of each structure, the related thinking skills, and the associated linguistic features. Projects also served as a way for Amy to see which areas specifically caused difficulties, as what students said did not always reflect what they did. By working on their KF projects as an activity, the participants came to understand more about how the six knowledge structures combine in a language and content teaching unit project, which added to their existing knowledge of unit planning for language and content integration. Margot noted this connection of the new theory with her background knowledge by observing that she started with activities she was familiar with as a student and worked with the KF from there.

Indications surfaced that the KF language and content teaching project helped participants learn knowledge about language; in other words, they became socialized to the linguistic discourse needed to articulate their understanding of the KF. Bella's note in her KF unit project rationale is an example of how participants' language reflected her evolving knowledge of the KF. She wrote:

> If I want to teach my students different thinking verbs (such as *believe, think, like,* and *want*) but I also want to teach them action verbs (like *singing, running, celebrating, dressing up, scaring, receiving,* and *giving*) I can do that through the Knowledge Framework. Things are already clearly defined and categorized in the Knowledge Framework, but not just for verb usage. It also gives great tools to expand literacy such as adjectives and other grammatical structures and how to use them, different thinking skills, and what kinds of connections can or should be made by the students in the activities.

Indeed, the participants' *reflections* on the meaning, value, and potential of a tool such as the KF, with the types of linguistic resources it comprises, was valuable, especially when the theory was new to them and a continuing topic year to year in Amy's methods course. Just as important, however, were pre-service teachers' *actions* that made use of the KF in a project-based approach that saw them appropriating the theory as they understood it to create potential projects for their future students. Such a connection between action and reflection offers both the instructor and her students' information about the success—or the shortcomings—of the short-term training.

Implications for Further Research and Practice

This qualitative case study examined how students in a university-level teacher education ESL Literacy Methods course understood and made use of the KF within a project that had them create a unit plan that exemplifies how they might later teach a topic of their choice. To the best of our knowledge, this is the first study to explore the teaching and learning of the KF through projects and also the first to involve pre-service teachers with little prior teaching or curriculum development experience in a short-term introduction to the theory of the KF. As it was conducted in a sociocultural and socioeconomically homogeneous state with relatively little diversity, we hope that more studies in different contexts will be carried out to offer opportunities for across-case comparison.

This study's findings also indicated that a four-week training session may not be idea for all students, as several expressed challenges in identifying the various knowledge structures and their linguistic features despite fulfilling the prerequisite of an introduction to linguistics course. Despite Stewart's (1997) assertion that "it is not overly time consuming to plan units with the KF" (p. 11), it can be difficult to understand fully the theory and process behind such planning; thus we concur with the participants in this study as well as with scholars such as Beckett et al. (2015) who argued that teachers can benefit from long-term and ongoing support, and with Fang et al. (2014), whose similar claim suggests that longer training sessions may help address the challenges that the participants in the current study faced.

Some students' perceived difficulties distinguishing theory discourse and action discourse is a finding that may provide insight into the teaching of research writing to graduate students. Understanding from a linguistic perspective how research findings connect to or become theory through language use can be confusing to emerging scholars who may find it easy to describe and sequence, but perhaps face dilemmas when attempting to classify (an inherent part of qualitative analysis, especially in ethnographic research; see Spradley, 1980) and to construct PRINCIPLES (i.e., to explain findings or causality and to produce theory). It is important for writers to realize that their language choices—in other words, the knowledge structures that they choose—construct the meanings of their utterances; showing a sequence of events can provide much less useful theory than showing causal connections among such events (see, for example, Mohan & Slater, 2004).

The framing of training sessions as social practices with both a theory side and a practice side has provided a useful way to examine other such teaching and learning contexts. Having instructors build in formal student reflections about the theory they are learning and creating a project assignment that can reveal successful learning as well as challenges, provides the framework and context for an action learning cycle (for action research design, see, for example, Berg, 2004, Chapter 7). In other words, in this study, Amy collected valuable feedback to inform her success as an instructor (i.e., she was able to form new theories about the teaching of the KF), feedback that can inform her teaching in its next iteration (i.e., her future practice).

This study revealed encouraging findings regarding pre-service teachers' enthusiasm towards using the KF to plan innovative units and projects that can help develop their future students' language and critical thinking skills across curricular areas. Despite the challenges that these teachers identified as they worked towards the completion of their projects, the participants remained confident that the KF projects offered a tool that they could implement in their future teaching to organize their units in a theoretically sound way.

References

Beckett, G.H. (1999). *Project-based instruction in a Canadian secondary school's ESL classes: Goals and evaluations.* (Unpublished doctoral dissertation). University of British Columbia, Canada.

Beckett, G.H. (2005). Academic language and literacy socialization of secondary school Chinese immigrant students: Practices and perspectives. *Journal of Asian Pacific Communication, 15*(1), 191–206.

Beckett, G.H. (2006). Beyond second language acquisition: Secondary school ESL teacher goals and actions for project-based instruction. In G.H. Beckett & P. Miller (Eds.), *Project-based second and foreign language education: Past, present, and future* (pp. 55–70). Information Age Publishing, Inc.

Beckett, G.H. & Miller, P. (2006). (Eds.), *Project-based second and foreign language education: Past, present, and future*. Information Age Publishing, Inc.

Beckett, G.H., Hemmings, A. Maltbie, C., Wright, K., Sherman, M., Sersion, B., & Jorgenson, S. (2015). An evaluation study of the CincySTEM iTEST projects: Experience, peer support, professional development, and sustainability. *Journal of STEM Teacher Education, 50*(1), 3–17.

Beckett, G.H., & Slater, T. (2005). The project framework: A tool for language, content, and skills integration, *ELT Journal, 59*(2), 108–116.

Beckett, G.H., & Slater, T. (2017). *A synthesis of project-based language learning: Research-based teaching ideas.* Paper presented at the meeting of the Teachers of English as a Second or Other Language (TESOL), Seattle, Washington.

Beckett, G.H., Slater, T., & Mohan, B. (2020). Philosophical foundation, theoretical approaches, and research gaps. In G.H. Beckett & T. Slater (Eds.), *Global perspectives on project-based language learning, teaching, and assessment: Key approaches, technology tools and frameworks* (pp. 3–22). Routledge.

Berg, B.L. (2004). *Qualitative research methods for the social sciences.* Pearson.

Berg, M. & Huang, J. (2015). Improving in-service teachers' effectiveness: K-12 academic literacy for the linguistically diverse. *Functional Linguistics, 2*(5), 1–21.

Cummins, J., & Early, M. (2015). *Big ideas for expanding minds: Teaching English language learners across the curriculum.* Pearson Canada.

Dewey, J. (1911). Activity, logical theory and educational implications of. In P. Monroe (Ed.), *A cyclopedia of education, Vol. I* (pp. 33–4). The Macmillan Company.

Dewey, J. (1913). Theory and practice. In P. Monroe (Ed.), *A cyclopedia of education* (pp. 606–607). The Macmillan Company.

Dionne, H., & Horth, R. (1994). Challenges of literacy and development in rural Quebec. In J.-P. Hautecoeur (Ed.), *Literacy and cultural development strategies in rural areas* (pp. 249–268). Culture Concepts.

Early, M. (1989). Using key visuals to aid ESL students' comprehension of content classroom texts. *Reading-Canada-Lecture, 7*(4), 202–212.

Early, M. (1990). Enabling first and second language learners in the classroom. *Language Arts, 67*, 567–574.

Early, M., Mohan, B.A. & Hooper, H.R. (1988). The Vancouver school board language and content project. In J.M. Esling (Ed.), *Multicultural education and policy: ESL in the 90s* (pp. 107–125). Ontario Institute for Studies in Education.

Early, M., Potts, D., & Mohan, B. (2005). Teachers' professional knowledge in scaffolding academic literacies for English language learners. *Prospect, 20*(3), 63–76.

Early, M. & Tang, G. (1991). Helping ESL students cope with content-based texts. *TESL Canada Journal, 8*(2), 34–44.

Early, M., Thew, C. & Wakefield, P. (1986). *Integrating language and content instruction K–12; An E.S.L. resource book, vol. 1.* Victoria, B. C. Ministry of Education, Modern Language Services Branch.

Fang, Z. (2014). Preparing content area teachers for disciplinary literacy instruction: The role of literacy teacher educators. *Journal of Adolescent & Adult Literacy, 57*(6), 444–448.

Fang, Z., Schleppegrell, M.J., & Moore, J. (2014). The linguistic challenges of learning across academic disciplines. In C.A. Stone, E.R. Silliman, B.J. Ehren, & G.P. Wallace (Eds.), *Handbook of language and literacy: Development and disorders* (2nd ed., pp. 302–322). Guilford.

Gleason, J. & Link, S. (2020). Using the Knowledge Framework and Genre Pedagogy for technology-enhanced form-function project-based language learning. In G.H. Beckett & T. Slater (Eds.), *Global perspectives on project-based learning, teaching, and assessment: Key approaches, technology tools, and frameworks* (pp. 185–203). Routledge.

Guba, E.G., & Lincoln, Y.S. (1989). *Fourth generation evaluation.* SAGE Publications.

Halliday, M.A.K. (2007). *Language and education: Volume 9 in the collected works of M.A.K. Halliday.* Continuum.

Huang, J. (2000). Integration of academic content learning and academic literacy skills development of L2 students: A case study of an ESL science class. *National Reading Conference Yearbook, 49*, 392–500.

Huang, J. & Laskowski, T. (2014). Developing Linguistic Sensitivity of ESL Teacher Candidates for Linguistically Responsive Instruction. *The International Journal of Literacies, 20*(2), 29–50.

Ochs, E. (1988). *Culture and language development: Language acquisition and language socialization in a Samoan village.* Cambridge University Press.

Patton, M.Q. (1990). *Qualitative evaluation and research methods* (2nd ed.). SAGE Publications Ltd.

Love, K. (2009). Literacy pedagogical content knowledge in secondary teacher education: Reflecting on oral language and learning across the disciplines. *Language and Education, 23*(6), 541–560.

Mohan, B.A. (1986). *Language and content.* Addison-Wesley.

Mohan, B.A. (2007). Knowledge structures in social practices. In J. Cummins & C. Davison (Eds.), *International handbook of English language teaching, Part 1* (pp. 303–315). Springer.

Mohan, B., & Slater, T. (2004). The evaluation of causal discourse and language as a resource for meaning. In J. Foley (Ed.) *Functional perspectives on education and discourse* (pp. 255–269). Continuum.

Mohan, B., & Slater, T. (2005). A functional perspective on the critical "theory/practice" relation in teaching language and science. *Linguistics and Education, 16*, 151–172.

Mohan, B., & Slater, T. (2006). Examining the theory/practice relation in a high school science register: A functional linguistic perspective. *Journal of English for Academic Purposes, 5*, 302–316.

Schieffelin, B.B., & Ochs, E. (1986). (Eds.). *Language socialization across cultures.* Cambridge University Press.

Slater, T. (2020). The Knowledge Framework: An organizational tool for highlighting the "LL" in technology-integrated PBLL. In G.H. Beckett & T. Slater (Eds.), *Global perspectives on project-based learning, teaching, and assessment: Key approaches, technology tools, and frameworks* (pp. 185–203). Routledge.

Slater, T., & Beckett, G. H. (2019). Integrating language, content, technology, and skills development through project-based language learning: Blending frameworks for successful unit planning. *MEXTESOL Journal, 43*(1), 1–14. Retrieved from http:// www.mextesol.net/journal/index.php?page=journal&id_article=5557

Slater, T., & Gleason, J. (2011). Integrating language and content: The knowledge framework. *The conference proceedings of MidTESOL*. Retrieved from http:// www. midtesol.org/docs/MIDTESOLProceedings_2011.pdf

Slater, T. & Mohan, B. (2019). The Knowledge Framework approach to developing language and content. *The TESOL encyclopedia of English language teaching*. Wiley Blackwell.

Snow, M. A., & Brinton, D. M. (Eds.) (1997). *The content-based classroom*. Addison Wesley Longman.

Spradley, J. (1979). *The ethnographic interview*. Holt, Rinehart and Winston.

Spradley, J. (1980). *Participant observation*. Holt, Rinehart, and Winston.

Stewart, T. (1997). *Integrating language and content instruction: A framework to guide cross-disciplinary team teaching*. Retrieved from ERIC Database. (ERIC document number ED 403 7851).

Strauss, A., & Corbin, J. (1990). *Basics of qualitative research: Grounded theory procedures and techniques*. SAGE Publications.

Tang, G.M. (1994). Textbook illustrations: A cross-cultural study and its implications for teachers of language minority students. *The Journal of Educational Issues of Language Minority Students, 13*, 175–194.

About the Authors

Amy Walton (MA TESL) is an associate teaching professor and Assistant Director of ISUComm Foundation Courses at Iowa State University. She has taught English, French, and Computer Science at the high school level. At Iowa State, she incorporates her classroom experience and interests in Computer-Assisted Language Learning, Literacy Education, and Cross-Cultural Communication in her teaching of English pedagogy, grammar, and composition courses.

Gulbahar H. Beckett (PhD), Professor of TESL/Applied Linguistics, focuses on project-based second/foreign language acquisition and socialization; Content-based second/foreign language (a.k.a. English as a medium of instruction/learning); Second and minority language policies; Technology integrated teaching and learning; and Academic literacy. She has numerous publications including books, chapters, and journal articles. Her latest book is Beckett, G. H. & Slater, T. (Eds.) (2020). *Global perspectives on project-based language learning, teaching, and assessment: Key approaches, technology tools, and frameworks.* NY: Routledge. She is an associate editor of Diaspora, Indigenous, and Minority Education Journal.

14 Enhancing Disciplinary Learning Experience through an Adjunct English-across-the-curriculum Model

Esther Ka-man Tong, Cecilia Fung-Kan Pun, and Phoebe Siu

Abstract

Tertiary education programs are often designed to prepare students for active engagement in the evolving practices of disciplinary communities. Academic success in these programs means not only the mastery of disciplinary knowledge and skills but also the appropriate selection of multimodal resources to represent disciplinary ways of thinking, doing, and knowledge sharing. Responding to the call for supporting students' development of English academic literacy in English-medium College programs in Hong Kong, this chapter discusses the effectiveness of an adjunct English-across-the-curriculum (EAC) instructional model which uses Mohan's Knowledge Framework as a needs/task analysis tool to identify the specific cognitive, linguistic, and multimodal representation needs of college students in Engineering and to plan explicit instruction on program-specific writing and speaking genres. The data reveal how a Knowledge Framework analysis provides a comprehensive account of the academic literacy demands of the Engineering program and facilitates the development of an integrated instructional model that offers language support needed for students' academic success.

Keywords: adjunct English-across-the-curriculum model; Knowledge Framework analysis; English as a second/additional language; multimodality; engineering discourse

English-medium instruction (EMI) in tertiary education as an expanding global educational phenomenon has captured the attention of researchers, especially applied linguists (Airey, 2020; Dafouz and Smit, 2016; Doiz, Lasagabaster & Sierra, 2013; Macaro et al., 2018). In Hong Kong, many students with modest English abilities are keen on pursuing tertiary education in community colleges and universities. As English is a predominant medium of instruction in these tertiary programs, it has become increasingly important to create instructional approaches that can socialize students into various disciplines through English at the same time as they scaffold discourse development. Mohan (2007) asserts that "learning is a linguistic process" (p. 305) and thus the task of learning the language of the discipline is indivisible from that of learning to practice the distinctive modes of analysis in the discipline. In affirming the indispensable link between language and disciplinary learning, Mohan (1989) called for research on academic tasks to provide "insights into the quantity and quality of student language use" (p. 116). The aim of this chapter is to use a qualitative case study of an engineering program at a college in Hong Kong to illustrate how the Knowledge Framework (KF) (Mohan, 1986) was used as a needs/task analysis tool in an adjunct English across-the curriculum model to help identify the specific cognitive, linguistic, and multimodal representation needs of college students at the program and subject level. At the program level, the KF, as a social practice analysis tool, is used to identify and organize the major common cognitive/linguistics/multimodal literacy skills demanded in an academic program. At the subject level, the KF is used to identify the content/language training needs in discipline-specific subjects. We shall first provide the contextual background of the curriculum for an adjunct English-across-the-curriculum (EAC) instructional model arranged around the KF to illustrate the indispensable link between language and disciplinary knowledge outcomes in an Engineering higher diploma program. Next, we shall present a KF analysis of the program-specific writing/speaking genres to showcase the interdependent relationship of multimodal meaning-making resources, disciplinary knowledge, and disciplinary reasoning. In an attempt to demonstrate how such information can be used to explicate the content–language link, we shall then exemplify how the KF analysis provides implications for a course design that can foster students' active engagement with academic discourse. A description of authentic materials designed for the Engineering higher diploma program will be used to illustrate the teaching of the knowledge structure and the lexicogrammatical features of the key disciplinary writing tasks. Finally, the paper will evaluate the effectiveness of an KF-informed adjunct model by drawing on multiple sources of data, including both quantitative and qualitative.

Content–Language Integration in Disciplinary Learning Practices

This section will provide a basis to rationalize the curriculum for an adjunct instructional model arranged around the KF to enhance students' disciplinary learning experience at the program level.

A Curriculum of Content and Language Integration

In response to the call for substantial scaffolded language support for English as a second language (ESL) students' learning in English-medium institutions, a variety of content-based instructional models have been adopted in Canada, The United Kingdom, and the United States (Lyster, 2017). Among these content-based models, the adjunct language-across-the-curriculum (LAC) approach has a balanced focus on the values of language-driven and content-driven learning. It maps adjunct (parallel) courses of language instruction with subject courses and enrolls students "concurrently in two linked courses—a language course and a content course—with the idea being that the two courses share the content and complement each other in terms of mutually coordinated assignments" (Brinton, Snow, & Wesche, 1989, p. 16). It is worth noting that bringing about the outcomes of such adjunct courses depends on the degree of language–content integration and the way it is practiced. In fact, one key challenge faced by the advocates of the adjunct model (e.g., Roquet et al., 2020; Snow & Brinton, 1988; Zappa-Hollman & Duff, 2017) rests on how to arrange a curriculum that promotes the integration of content and language learning through the explication of the features of knowledge structures embedded in the key disciplinary genres. To understand how the KF can be used to help arrange an integrated content and language curriculum, the next section will illustrate how the six main knowledge structures fit together dynamically to model an academic activity, or social practice, in higher education contexts.

The Dynamics of the Knowledge Structures

In higher education, students are expected to be able to put theories learned in their academic programs into simulated or real-life practice of the target disciplinary community. Mohan's (2007) view of literacy as a social activity considers a social practice as "a unit of culture that involves cultural knowledge and cultural action in a theory/practice, reflection/action relation" (p. 303) which provides learners a framework to understand, interpret, and generate behaviors/actions in a discipline-specific learning or workplace environment (Mohan, 2011; Spradley, 1980; see also Chapter 1, this volume). To understand the actual language demand of academic tasks in higher education contexts, Mohan (2011) calls for more linguistic research on social practices to provide a linguistic account of learners' experience in the theory–practice dialectic.

Highlighting the heteroglossic nature of language and semiosis in disciplinary meaning-making activities, Tong (2014) addresses the need for students to use appropriate lexicogrammatical resources to cope with the theory/practice dialectic of different subjects, to comprehend and apply the theory of an academic discipline, and to fully function in the disciplinary discourse community by enacting the principles governing the practices. As Mohan (1998) suggested, "the interplay between theory and practice is very noticeable in education" (p. 521). Observing that many academic tasks in higher education require students to demonstrate their understanding of the theory–practice dialectic through a case analysis, Tong (2014) further suggested analyzing the semantic and linguistic demands of academic tasks using an adapted Knowledge Framework analysis model as shown in Figure 14.1.

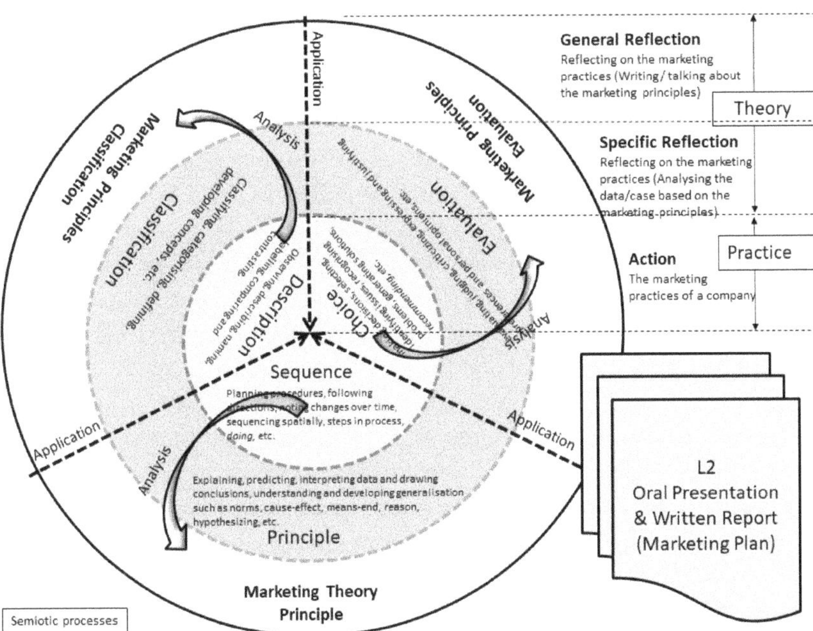

Figure 14.1 Semantic and linguistic competence demanded in a marketing project (Tong 2014)

One key objective of tertiary education programs is to equip students with field-related communication skills and disciplinary knowledge to help them function fully in the target professions. The demand on the application of academic theories is represented by the dotted line inward pointing arrows in Figure 14.1. Meanwhile, as apprentices to a disciplinary community, tertiary-level students are often asked to analyze a case in the real world or to engage in simulated practices to develop their understanding of the theory–practice dialectics. The three-ring adapted KF model (Tong, 2014) in Figure 14.1 describes the dynamic processes and relationships of Mohan's six knowledge structures embedded in each discipline-related academic task. The outer ring in the adapted KF model represents the theories of the field, or in other words the knowledge within the context of culture in Halliday's (1994, 2007) meaning-oriented systemic functional model of language within which disciplinary activities are grounded and understood (Mohan, 1986). The middle and inner rings depict the situational context where a real-life case is practiced, or in other words the immediate context from which disciplinary texts and the accompanying social processes are introduced and produced. Disciplinary texts, as evidence of students' learning of disciplinary theories and practices, demand learners' careful selection of language and other semiotic choices to realize the semantic relationships (disciplinary processes) specific to the immediate context. Learners are expected to use more cognitively demanding linguistic and non-linguistic features to illustrate and justify their analysis of the case they researched in tertiary education courses.

While students are exposed to recurring disciplinary texts illustrating the dialectics of theory and practice in the discipline through lectures, they are often required to demonstrate their comprehension of the theory–practice dialectic and mastery of the linguistics practices in case analysis tasks in tutorials and subject assessments. Such analytical processes are represented by the outward pointing arrows from the center in the model, starting from factual descriptions of the target company's practices to using theories to rationalize its practices and proposing innovative solutions to the problems identified. Through constant engagement of students in such case analysis tasks, students are expected to be able to transfer their learning to practice—to apply theories to practice, to make theory-informed disciplinary decisions in a specific case, and to implement disciplinary practices guided by theories in the field. While the inner ring represents the practice side of Mohan's (1986) Knowledge Framework, the middle ring involves students in more cognitively demanding analysis of the case founded on the theories of the discipline described in the outer ring. With the goal to initiate students into the target disciplinary community, careful alignment of the subjects with the program learning outcomes is required for a full coverage of knowledge structure training in an academic program. The next section will illustrate how the KF can be used to help arrange an integrated content and language curriculum at the program level, or how to articulate explicitly the expected learning outcomes of the target programs with dual focus on language development and disciplinary knowledge construction.

Language and Other Semiotic Demands of a Decision-Making Curriculum

Graduates of tertiary education programs are often expected to be able to perform disciplinary tasks that require them to exercise higher order thinking skills specific to their disciplinary knowledge. In particular, tertiary-level students are involved in reasoned decision making (Mohan, Slater, Beckett, and Tong, 2015). A close look at the intended learning outcomes of the Engineering program reveals that students are often expected to make informed and creative decisions on ways to tackle issues and problems in the discipline. For example, students in the Higher Diploma in Mechanical Engineering program (HDME) are expected to be able to "apply engineering and computing principles, tools and analytical skills and **suggest workable solutions to deal with problems in engineering and daily contexts** [emphasis added]" and to "**design engineering components, processes or systems** [emphasis added] to meet desired needs" (Hong Kong Community College, 2015a, p. 3).

The examination of the program outcome statements points to the importance of supporting not only students' development of generic English communication skills but also the use of multimodal resources to (re)construct and enact the logical thinking, knowledge, and practice in the discipline. In fact, to prepare students for success in the target professions, many academic programs, including those offered by Hong Kong tertiary institutions, consider the ability to communicate clearly and effectively in professional contexts as one of their graduates' attributes. The critical need to develop disciplinary communication skills calls for the explicit statement of specific Intended English Language Learning Outcomes (IELOs) for each academic program. How lexicogrammatical and other multimodal resources are orchestrated to represent the knowledge structures in key disciplinary texts and practices embedded in the curriculum of the target academic programs needs to be specifically defined. The IELOs explored in this chapter are presented below.

Higher Diploma in Mechanical Engineering. Listed here are five IELOs with their key goals summarized in brackets.

1. Compose basic types of writing genres commonly used in the field of Engineering, for example, lab reports, design reports/review, and proposals [Writing genres in Engineering].
2. Use appropriate lexicogrammatical and non-linguistic resources to represent their disciplinary knowledge, for example, to report on the experiment, to illustrate the engineering design process (sequence), to propose a new design to meet a stated objective, to interpret calculation results, and so on. [Representations of knowledge structures]
3. Research, read, and interpret findings/analysis (research specifications, product descriptions, methodologies) in texts and visual images [Critical reading skills]
4. Use conventions of the Engineering disciplines, for example, Institute of Electrical and Electronics Engineers (IEEE) documentation style (IEEE, 2018) [Engineering conventions]
5. Present disciplinary knowledge clearly in oral communication contexts [Oral communication]

Genre, as defined in this paper, is a means to an end instead of an end in itself. As defined by Martin (2009), genre "coordinates resources, to specify just how a given culture organizes this meaning potential into recurrent configuration of meaning, and phrases meaning through stages in each genre" (p. 12). From this functional view, the ultimate purpose of texts is achieved through learners' active engagement in disciplinary moves of doing, thinking, and meaning making or "assembling meaning as we go" (Martin, 2009, p.12). The processes of knowledge structure construction specific to each disciplinary move build the genre elements one by one, guide the learners to perform disciplinary thinking and practice step by step, and ultimately enable the selection of the best-informed disciplinary choices that achieve the communicative goals of the discipline. Detailed scrutiny of the knowledge structures embedded in key disciplinary genres will facilitate the full implementation of the integrated content and language curriculum.

The Knowledge Framework as a Collaborative Tool for Disciplinary Genre Analysis

One key factor that may influence the effectiveness of the Adjunct Language-across-the-curriculum Instructional Model is the collaborative communication between language specialists and disciplinary faculty, which may be affected by conflicts of assigned roles, duties, and the ownership of teaching and assessment materials along with time and labor cost (Lin & Lo, 2018). It is crucial to develop a communicative platform for mediating the knowledge structure awareness of both the language specialists and disciplinary faculty. Mohan's Knowledge Framework (Mohan, 1986) highlights the form–meaning relationships in academic texts. It can be used as a communicative and pedagogical tool to facilitate the unfolding of the cognitive and linguistic and multimodal demands of the "mutually coordinated assignments" (Brinton et al., 1989, p. 16) in the mapped content subjects in the adjunct model. The dynamic nature of the six knowledge structures, as presented in Tong's adapted KF model (Tong, 2014), enables a more specific description of how knowledge structures and their corresponding linguistic and non-linguistic resources interact to bring about the ultimate objective of making reasoned decisions.

Lin (2012) emphasized that discipline-specific genres are keys to building up L2 students' capability to pack, unpack, and repack English to consolidate the knowledge patterns of various genres of academic texts for "co-textualization" and "contextualization." For instance, in a content subject such as Introduction to Marketing, learners who have never studied marketing-oriented content may feel puzzled when engaged in the various knowledge structure processes in different disciplinary genres embedded in the program curriculum. Through the KF analysis co-performed by both language specialists and disciplinary faculty at the subject level, the hidden disciplinary learning demand on writing a marketing proposal, performing case-study research on a particular brand/ corporate/organization in English, and delivering an oral presentation for a marketing plan in English can be underscored and be stipulated explicitly as intended disciplinary/language learning outcomes of the adjunct language courses.

According to Mohan (2001), learning is a social practice into which students are socialized through their active engagement in a series of activities which construct and nurture disciplinary knowledge and behavior through discourse. This social practice view considers learning activities in an adjunct EAC course/content course as a social practice which consists of a combination of the six main knowledge structures, the semantic patterns of disciplinary discourse (the recurring and patterned ways of engaging with disciplinary knowledge, procedures, and thinking). To function effectively in a social practice, students need to be able to select appropriate semiotic resources that characterize the register of a disciplinary practice to perform different discipline-related functions in the theory–practice dialect of the discipline.

Figure 14.2 presents a KF-embedded framework. This framework, which highlights the relationship between the knowledge structure processes that

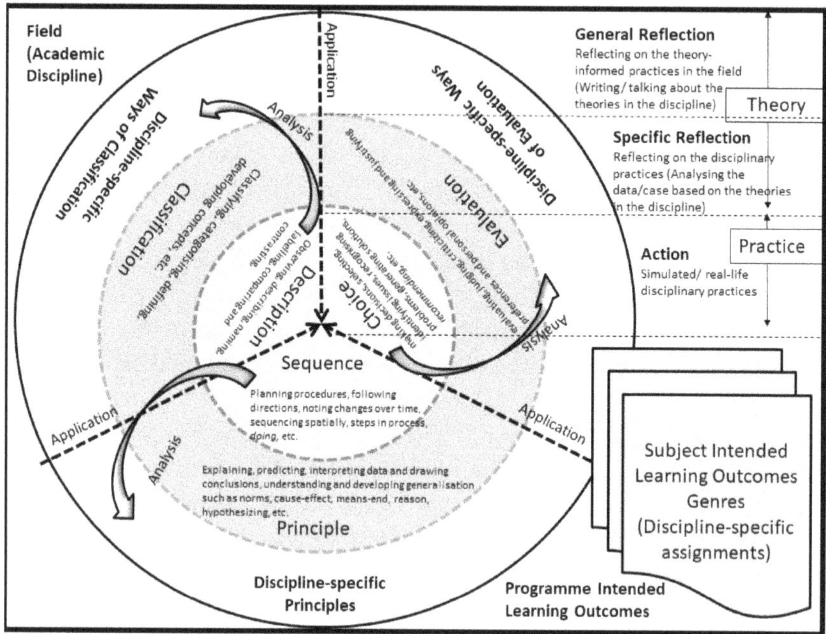

Figure 14.2 Linguistic/Semiotic analysis of the social practice in an academic discipline

underlie the disciplinary activities/genres and program/subject intended learning outcomes (communication and learning goals of the disciplinary activities/genres), can serve as a blueprint to a collaborative tool which engages both language specialists and disciplinary faculty in a meaningful dialogue for the strategic planning of scaffolded support to be provided in the adjunct courses to promote learners' academic discourse development (See Figure 14.3).

First, the field of the adjunct course (what is being talked about, the genre through which meaning is (co-)created, and the learning outcomes of the activities) is considered. With a shared understanding of the learning goals of disciplinary activities, the language specialists and disciplinary faculty can identify the types of multimodal resources learners are required to use for effective functioning in the disciplinary community. Second, the form–meaning analysis based on the KF can explicate the knowledge structures processes embedded in the disciplinary genres and identify the register-specific multimodal resources that learners need to use to engage in simulated disciplinary decision-making procedures in an assignment.

In the next section, we shall present an example of how the KF can be used to promote a more systematic and robust integration of language and content that covers all six knowledge structures in the design of an adjunct course.

Implementation of the Adjunct Model: Knowledge Framework Analysis for Strategic Planning of Scaffolded Language Support

The findings presented in this chapter were drawn from a project that aimed to identify the students' discipline-specific language needs and to gain insights into the provision of enhanced scaffolded integrated language and content learning support to students in Mechanical Engineering. Data were collected in three phases through questionnaires, documentary evidence, and individual interviews to capture the views of the program leaders, subject leaders, and students. This chapter presents the data collected from interviews and questionnaires in the first phase of the study in an attempt to identify the knowledge structure processes embedded across the curriculum of an Engineering program. The first subsection below summarizes the key views of the HKME program leader and subject leaders on language issues pertinent to students' learning in the subjects as well as the students' voices on their perceived challenges in meeting the language demands of the program. The subsection after that presents an analysis of the intended learning outcomes and discipline-specific genres of the subjects identified to be most challenging to students.

Program Leader's View

The program leader described the demand for "higher order semantic processes" in the KF as the need to digest what is taught in the readings (Engineering theories—CLASSIFICATIONS and PRINCIPLES), and to learn new methods (CHOICE) and new products (EVALUATION of an improved solution to a problem identified). The leader stated:

> Students will have to complete an engineering project in the final semester of the program... students will need to use what they have found [from readings and research] and digest [what they have learnt in the program]. In that regard, they would learn new things, such as new methods or an item or a product.

The knowledge structures of CHOICE and EVALUATION were identified through the interview as key skills expected among Mechanical Engineering students in language such as:

> [The design of the proposed product] involves different design methods. These design methods come with pros and cons.

In addition to the KF processes, the program leader also highlighted the need to provide language support on writing discipline-specific genres and pointed to the demand in comprehending graphs and figures beyond English texts:

> [Students] often have to write reports. Aside from this, sometimes they may write a brief proposal or analysis.
>
> They (students) have to understand that (graph). This is typical in Engineering.

Subject Leaders' Views

The respondents were supportive of the need to improve students' abilities in the various genres that are characteristic of Engineering subjects.

> How to write a persuasive proposal with strength and weakness analysis (Preston)

> Writing the answers for discussion, or long / essay-type questions in a precise and organized manner, with effective communication (Wilfred)

> Appropriate format and use of discipline-specific terminology/verb in technical report (Freeman)

> Organization and format on report writing (Stephen)

Students' Views

Students observed that writing-intensive assignments such as Engineering proposals, Engineering project reports, Engineering lab reports, and Engineering case analysis/questions were apparent in Engineering subjects, which involved them in drawing and elaborating on engineering concepts to justify their designs, ideas, and mechanical processes. First-year students in the Mechanical Engineering program rated three assignments in the Engineering subjects as the most challenging: the Engineering proposal in Applied Computing for Engineers course, the lab report in Engineering Materials, and the design report in the Engineering Design Fundamentals course.

Adjunct Course for a Core Engineering Subject Titled "Engineering Design Fundamentals"

To develop a fuller understanding of the objectives of the target assignment genre for which scaffolded support would be provided, a KF analysis of a core Engineering subject's ("Engineering Design Fundamentals") was carried out. Table 14.1 shows the results of this analysis.

Table 14.1 KF analysis of subject intended learning outcomes of a content subject (engineering design fundamentals)

Subject Intended Learning Outcomes (SILOs) Assessed	Knowledge Structure Processes Students Are Expected to Perform (Linguistic analysis of the SILOs)
a) Search for design related/ needed data, information and knowledge for decision-making	**SEQUENCE** (***Search*** for the related and needed data, information and knowledge) (Doing process) > **CHOICE** (…for ***decision making***) (choice lexis)
b) Comprehend and select appropriate design process for different design problems	**SEQUENCE/ PRINCIPLES** (***Comprehend…design process*** for different design problems) (sequence lexis) > **DESCRIPTION/ CLASSIFICATION** (***Comprehend… <u>different</u> design problems***) (Taxonomy lexis) > EVALUATION/ CHOICE (***Select <u>appropriate</u> design process***) (choice lexis; evaluation lexis)
c) Apply the design solution generation methods in different design processes and product development	**PRINCIPLES** (Apply ***design solution generation methods***) (Technicalities) > **CLASSIFICATION** (*Apply* the design solution generation methods *in* ***<u>different</u> design processes***) (Taxonomy lexis) > **SEQUENCE** (***Apply*** the design solution generation methods ***in*** different ***design processes***) (Sequence lexis) > **CHOICE** (***Apply*** the design solution generation methods ***in product development*** [designing a new product]) (Alternative lexis)

The analysis shows that students are expected to engage in all six core knowledge structures in the Engineering-specific assignment. Learners are trained in the academic programs to be able to apply what they have learned to make theory-grounded decisions, and in the case of this Engineering adjunct course, to perform simulated disciplinary decision-making procedures to develop an enhanced product design that helps to solve a specific problem relevant to the discipline.

Students are expected to show evidence of their learning in a group assignment which requires them to follow "a series of steps that engineers follow to come up with a solution to a specific problem" (Hong Kong Community College, 2015b). This assignment, in other words, requires learners to engage in the knowledge structures of SEQUENCE (***[follow] a series of steps;*** a series of steps ***that engineers follow***) and PRINCIPLES (adhere to ***the theory of inventive problem solving (the TRIZ approach)*** which would ultimately assist the learners to enact the knowledge structure of CHOICE (to ***come up with a solution*** to a specific problem). Tables 14.2 and 14.3 illustrate how a detailed KF analysis of the sample assignment was performed to identify the cognitive, linguistic, and multimodal demands of the knowledge structure processes embedded in different parts of an Engineering proposal assignment in the mapped discipline-specific subject titled Engineering Design Fundamentals.

The KF analysis of this Engineering proposal writing task as shown in Table 14.2 reveals that knowledge structures are embedded in the disciplinary genre. Different sections (i.e., different parts in the Engineering proposal) demand the use of different linguistic/ multimodal features to realize the disciplinary knowledge, practice, thinking, and logical reasoning represented in the genre. Table 14.3 shows that students need to use lexicogrammatical resources as well as other semiotic resources specific to the Engineering discipline, including decision matrices and sketches of the final and alternative design of the product. For example, verbs of being/ having processes (i.e., verb-to-be and "there is/are") and attribution lexis are used to describe the needs of the target group and the problems of the existing products, for example, that umbrellas are (verbs of being) clammy (attribution lexis). CHOICE lexis such as what "aims at" can be considered in context is used to introduce the project objectives. In the "Research on Previous Works" section, students need to report on their survey of existing products/ patents relevant to the proposed problem. They need to present their findings—the pros and cons of the existing products—in a table format. The table, as a semiotic resource in this section of the Engineering proposal, can guide the disciplinary way of organizing information and evaluating the existing products based on the selected features essential to the alleviation of the problem. To describe the

Table 14.2 KF analysis of the cognitive demands (semiotic processes) of an engineering proposal writing task

Genre: Engineering Proposal	Embedded Knowledge Structures
Cover page	N/A
Table of Contents page	N/A
I. Project Background	**(1)** Identify **an engineering problem** (or a need in daily life) **(CLASSIFICATION)**
	(2) **Observe and describe** an engineering problem (or a need in daily life) **(DESCRIPTION)**
II. Project aim and objectives	**(3)** **Formulate project objectives** to support the corresponding aim **(CHOICE)**
III. Research on Previous Works	**(4)** Survey of **existing products/ patents** relevant to the proposed problem **(DESCRIPTION)**
IV. Concept Evolution Map	**(5)** **Classify** the previous works based on their features **(CLASSIFICATION)**
	(6) **Create a concept evolution map (CHOICE)**
V. Design Constraints and Specifications	**(7)** Use **the TRIZ approach** to identify physical and technical contradictions **(PRINCIPLES)**
	(8) Use the TRIZ approach to **identify physical and technical contradictions (DESCRIPTION)**
VI. Alternative Design Ideas with sketches and descriptions	**(9)** Create alternative design ideas with the aids of the **40 inventive principles (SEQUENCE – the innovation; PRINCIPLES)**
	(10) **Create alternative design ideas** with the aids of the 40 inventive principles **(CHOICE)**
	(11) **Evaluate** the alternative design ideas with respect to the constraints and criteria by using the decision matrix **(EVALUATION)**
VIII. Decision Matrix	**(12)** **Follow a series of steps that Engineers follow (SEQUENCE)**
	(13) **Identify the most preferred product design (CHOICE)**
	(14) List out the **design constraints and specifications** for the coming design **(DESCRIPTION/ EVALUATION)**
IX. Layout drawing of most preferred design	**(15)** **Use hand drawing technique or CAD software** to present the layout drawing of the preferred [solution] **(DESCRIPTION)**
References	N/A

Table 14.3 KF analysis of the linguistic and multimodal demands of an engineering proposal writing task

Genre: Engineering Proposal	**Linguistic and Other Semiotic Resources Used**
Cover page	Standard format of a cover page for an assignment
Table of Contents page	**(1)** Standard format of a Table of Content page **(2)** Use of headings and sub-headings
I. Project Background	**(3)** **Being processes** *(e.g., Nowadays, because of unhealthy diet and lifestyle, some people* ***will have*** *different sickness like diabetes and heart disease when they are old.) (e.g.,* ***There are*** *so many rainy days in the summer in Hong Kong.)* **(4)** **Taxonomy lexis** (e.g., Our group will focus on **the need of elderly**, especially those having problems with taking medicine **(5)** **Attribution lexis** (e.g., **clammy** umbrella.)
II. Project aim and objectives	**Choice lexis (Language of goal statements)** (e.g. **The project aim is to** design an umbrella ***that will not moisten your bag***. (e.g.) **This project aims at** designing a new pill-box ***that can remind the elderly to take medicine punctually***. - **Attribution lexis** *(description of the enhanced feature of the new product in "that clauses")*
III. Research on Previous Works	**(6)** **Being process** (e.g., *verb to have (possessive), is used to (function)* **(7)** **Attribution lexis** (modifiers) (e.g., Existing pill boxes... **are** ***not convenient***.) (e.g., The sample pill-boxes **are** not good enough; they are ***small but heavy***.) - **[Multimodal resources]** Pros and Cons Table (Comparison of the features of existing products) - **[Multi-modal]** Still images (e.g., case imagery of objects – existing products)
IV. Concept Evolution Map	**(8)** **Taxonomy lexis** (e.g., Enhanced convenience, enhanced portability) **(9)** **[Multimodal resources]** Concept evolution map
V. Design Constraints and Specifications	**(10)** **Technicality** (e.g., To solve the problem, we focus on **technical contradiction [of the TRIZ approach]**.) - **Descriptive/ attributive lexis** (e.g., non-toxic, toughness, non-oxidation, water-resistant)

(Continued)

Table 14.3 *(Continued)*

Genre: Engineering Proposal		Linguistic and Other Semiotic Resources Used
VI. Alternative Design Ideas with sketches and descriptions	**(11)**	**Doing process** *(e.g., action verbs such as add, set up, install, divide, combine, control* - **Casual/ Consequential lexis** (e.g., **As a result of** shaft rotation, a torque will ....) (e.g., **Due to** the effect of inertia, the water drops will...) - **Being process** (e.g., **There is** a power plug for the heating wire on the top of the umbrella.) - **Evaluative lexis** (e.g., Advantages, disadvantages, strange appearance) - **Descriptive/ attributive lexis (to describe the design alternatives)** (e.g., a **fixable** handle) - **Language of comparison/contrast** *(e.g., similar to, compared with, comparatives such as easier, lighter, lower)*
	(12)	**Reference to the visuals**
	(13)	**[Multi-modal]** Sketches of the alternative design ideas
VIII. Decision Matrix		- **Descriptive/ attributive lexis (to describe the design alternatives)** (e.g., easy to open, light weight, small in size)
	(14)	**Choice Lexis (To introduce the preferred design** *(e.g., In conclusion, our decision is...)*
	(15)	**Reference to the visuals**
	(16)	**[Multi-modal]** Tables (decision matrix)
IX. Layout drawing of most preferred design	**(17)**	**[Multi-modal]** Still images (layout drawing of final decision)
References		In IEEE formatting style
Throughout the Engineering proposal	**(18)**	**Discipline-specific vocabulary (Engineering terms)** *(e.g., TRIZ approach, decision matrix, design constraints and specifications, 40 inventive principles, materials, insulator, motor, preliminary anti-action, mediator, mechanical vibration, user-interface, local quality)*

features of the existing products, being processes and attribution lexis (e.g., small but heavy) have to be used. Through reflecting on the features of the existing products, taxonomy lexis is used to classify the existing products and describe their evolution in a concept evolution map. Technicality (the use of technical terms in the field of Engineering) is apparent in the "Design

Constraints and Specifications" section to use the Engineering theory of the resolution of invention-related tasks (the TRIZ approach) to identify physical and technical contradictions in descriptive and attributive texts. Attributive lexis such as water-resistant, non-toxic, are used to describe the expected product qualities. These opening sections justify the need for an alternative and enhanced design, so lexical and grammatical items of EVALUATION (e.g., evaluative lexis such as advantages and disadvantages), PRINCIPLES (causal/consequential lexis such as due to and as a result of), DESCRIPTION (descriptive/attributive lexis such as fixable) and CHOICE (CHOICE lexis such as decision and preferred) are used when the alternative designs are proposed and chosen. The KF analysis can be used to "describe the features of academic genres so [teachers] can make these explicit to students" (Hyland, 2013, p.59). The semiotic roles the visuals (table, sketches of the alternative designs, decision matrix, layout drawing of the most preferred design) play and how they interact with the texts in the Engineering proposal need to be highlighted to prepare students for full participation in the disciplinary community (Paltridge, 2013).

Additionally, learners are required to engage in the six knowledge structure processes embedded in different parts of the disciplinary genre to create meaning on the go in the discipline, which includes higher order knowledge structures on the theory side. The six knowledge structures fit together dynamically to help achieve the ultimate communication goal of the activity, to identify the most preferred product design that can address the problem identified more adequately. Figure 14.3 summarizes the on-the-go meaning-making processes in the Engineering proposal writing activity using the KF and illustrates the dynamic yet intertwined relationship between the knowledge structures on the theory side and those on the practice side in the disciplinary genre, highlighting the demand for active engagement with the theory–practice dialectic in different genre stages as students reason their decision-making in the discipline.

Materials for Explicating the Content–Language Links

The examples given in the last section demonstrate how the KF can be used to identify linguistic and other multimodal resources that learners are expected to use to achieve the disciplinary outcomes of an activity. The findings exemplify how the six knowledge structures embedded in a genre interact dynamically within a discipline-specific activity. Especially for higher education programs, it is critical that the adjunct courses incorporate learning activities

Field/Disciplinary Genre:

Knowledge Structure	**Specific Reference** Case/ Contextual Information		**Generic Reference** (Theory; Ways of Knowing, Doing and Reasoning in the Discipline)	Knowledge Structure
	Action (What the participants are doing)	**Specific Reflection** (Commenting on the action)	**General Reflection** (Writing/Talking about knowledge/ theories)	
Description				Classification
Sequence				Principles
Choice				Evaluation

Figure 14.3 A collaborative tool for linguistic/semiotic analysis of a content and language integrated activity

that address all six areas of thinking skills, including the more cognitive demanding (i.e., theory) ones. Also, learners need to be taught explicitly how different semiotic representational systems are orchestrated to aid their disciplinary engagement and learning across the curriculum. The following section uses examples from the data to illustrate how the analysis informed the material design for the adjunct course.

Session One: Representing the Engineering Design Process in a Proposal

The adjunct course was designed to facilitate integrated content-and-language learning. Therefore, it was crucial to "set the stage" for students' active engagement in the target disciplinary discourse in the first session of the unit. Within this first session, the first task (Activity 1.1) was a diagnostic writing practice designed to help the lecturers assess students' prior learning. Students were asked to describe the Engineering design process based on what they had learned in the content subject. Such written texts could help the lecturer gain information about not only students' disciplinary writing abilities but their understanding of the concepts. Activity 1.2 was a video-watching activity the purpose of which was to introduce the Engineering design process (SEQUENCE) and the disciplinary reasoning/problem-solving skills (PRINCIPLE, CHOICE, and EVALUATION) to prepare students to understand why the Engineering proposal is structured the way it has been. To link the Engineering thinking and procedures with the features at the genre level, students were asked in Activity 1.3 to put the pictures of the Engineering design process in order. This activity provides students with an opportunity for practicing the knowledge structure of SEQUENCE in an oral communication task. Drawing on the results of Activity 1.3, students were then asked to analyze the assessment guidelines and to identify the different parts of the design process (CLASSIFICATION) that they were being assessed on in their written assignment (Activity 1.4). This activity linked the adjunct course to the content goals and motivated students to complete this non-credit bearing subject to address their language learning needs. To check students' comprehension, students were then asked to write a Table of Contents for their assignment (Activity 1.5). To make explicit the independent relationship between the text structure of an Engineering proposal and the design process as analyzed in Tables 14.2 and 14.3, a mini-lecture was then delivered.

In the last activity of this session, students were asked to view a video about an Engineering problem (a slow boat) and to describe in writing how they might use the design process to fix the identified problem. As can be seen through this section, the first session of this topic of the adjunct English course moved from the diagnostic stage to the deconstruction and joint construction of knowledge through group discussion/pair practices of the Engineering design process before students independently constructed their written texts realizing the knowledge structure of SEQUENCE in the core concept of the linked Engineering subject—the Engineering design process.

Sessions Two and Three: Writing an Engineering Proposal

After building a basic understanding of how the Engineering proposal is structured to represent the Engineering design process in Session One, the next two sessions introduced students to the language–content links in various sections of the proposal. Session Two started with revision practice on the structure of an Engineering proposal (Activity 2.1), followed by discussion practice (Activity 2.2) on samples of good and bad Tables of Contents provided by the disciplinary faculty to consolidate students' learning. Next, in Activity 2.3, an example of the case of the "slow boat" that students worked on in Session One was used to illustrate how a problem could be defined: "who" needs "what" because "why," which engaged students in an array of knowledge structures, including the description of the problem (DESCRIPTION), the definition of the problem (CLASSIFICATION), the analysis of the cause and effect of the problem (PRINCIPLES), the identification of existing solutions to the problems (DESCRIPTION), an analysis of the advantages and disadvantages of the existing problem (PRINCIPLES), and a statement of potential project aims and objectives (CHOICE). It was expected that this would pose a challenge to many students that had limited experience with Engineering; a sample problem statement was therefore given in Activity 2.3 to engage students in the deconstruction of the sample to develop a better understanding of the content-based language. A graphic organizer (Figure 14.4) was used to facilitate students' deconstruction of the knowledge structures in the sample text.

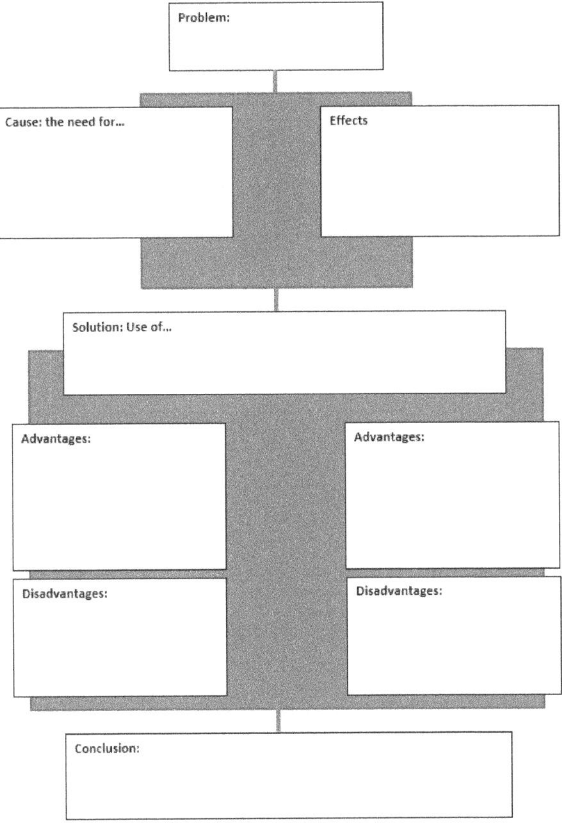

Figure 14.4 Graphic organizer used to help learners deconstruct the knowledge structures of the problem statement in engineering proposals

To highlight the content–language links and to offer explicit instruction on the language for "repacking" the academic text, the language specialist provided language scaffolds when building the graphic organizer with the students after the discussion practice. The students' language awareness was built by highlighting common lexical items and grammatical structures specific to the corresponding knowledge structures. Alternative lexicogrammatical features were introduced and taught when limited features were found in the student samples. Having developed awareness of the language features and structure of the problem statement, students were then asked to write the background (problem statement) of their projects. Acknowledging that the progress of students' projects may vary, students were given the option to develop the text based on the graphic organizer to practice realizing the relevant knowledge structures using the lexicogrammatical resources learned from the sample and lecture. Similarly, in Activity 2.4, students were asked to analyze sample goal statements to identify the aim and objectives. The language features were analyzed, and alterative lexicogrammatical features were introduced before students were asked to write the aim and objectives for their own projects.

Session Three was planned using the same approach. In Activity 3.1, Students were asked to read and analyze a sample Research of Previous Works given by the disciplinary faculty. Guided questions on the functions and structure of the section were given to guide students' analysis:

1. What is the function of the first paragraph [in this section]?
2. How does the writer structure the review of each previous design?

Table 14.4 Example of the explication of features of the knowledge structures embedded in the genre

Section (Sub-genre)	**Research of Previous Works**
Knowledge Structures (Semantic Relations)	(a) Introduce the section ***(CLASSIFICATION)*** (b) Describe the product - Its definition ***(DESCRIPTION)*** - Its uses (its practical functions) ***(SEQUENCE; how it works)*** - Its parts ***(DESCRIPTION)*** (c) Compare and contrast the different designs ***(DESCRIPTION)*** (d) Analyze the advantages and disadvantages of each design ***(PRINCIPLES)***

(Continued)

Table 14.4 *(Continued)*

Section (Sub-genre)	Research of Previous Works
Lexicogrammatical Features (Analysis of Excerpts from Sample Student Texts)	(a) Various **previous works** ***(discipline-specific vocabulary)*** are found for improving the hand motor function of stroke patients. They can mainly **be divided into** ***(verb of classification)*** four different **categories** **(nouns of classification)** which are **(i)** by stimulation, **(ii)** by wearing gloves, **(iii)** by wearing a robotic hand, and **(iv)** ***(numbering for improving readability)*** by other methods. (b) Electrical stimulation **uses** electrical currents to activate nerves of stroke patients ***(Verbs of defining)***. Electric pads ***(labels of parts)*** of the device are **placed** ***(verbs of material process)*** on the user's forearm. The device **generates** ***(verbs of material process)*** electrical impulse and **delivers** ***(verbs of material process)*** through the **electrodes** ***(labels of parts)*** to the muscles **to be stimulated** ***(verbs of material process)***. The impulse **acts as** ***(verbs of defining)*** action potential coming from the central nervous system, **causing** ***(causal verbs)*** the muscles to contract. (d) **Advantages** ***(Use of sub-headings)*** – **Relatively low[er]** ***(language of comparison)*** medical costs **Disadvantages** ***(Use of sub-headings)*** **(1)** The device **may cause** ***(hedging; causal verbs)*** muscle tears, blisters, burns and dizziness. **(2)** Users **may feel** ***(hedging)*** discomfort **due to** ***(causal verbs)*** the flow of electrical currents flowing through their body. **(3)** Time **is needed** ***(criteria statement)*** to place the electric pads in proper position. (Other features: use of **point form** is acceptable.)
Use of Other Multimodal Resources	Labelled diagram (Electrical Stimulation Device) 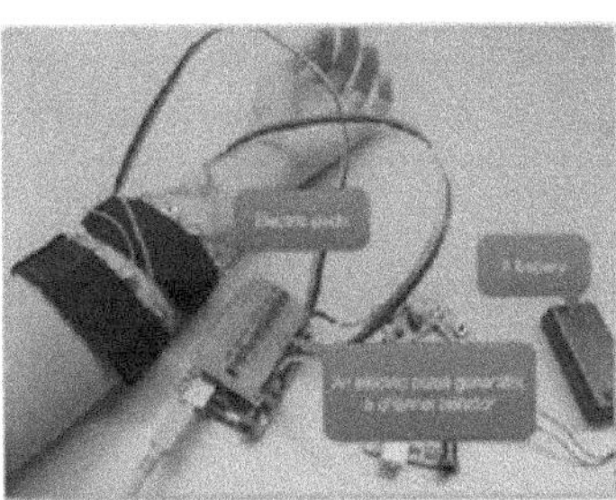

While going through the analysis with the students, the language specialist reminded students about the text structure, the function, the linguistic features of the texts, and the use of other semiotic resources such as tables (if any) in each section of the text. For instance, students' awareness of the sub-genre of the Research of Previous Works section and its lexicogrammatical features as well as the use of other multimodal representations was aroused through sample text analysis.

Next, the discussion was moved forward by drawing students' attention to areas for further improvement. Through dialogues about the student samples, awareness of the content and language requirements could be built. While the analysis of the good samples could make explicit the language resources used for realizing different knowledge structures of the sub-genres in the Engineering proposal, discussion of the weaker samples could create "teachable moments" in which students' attention could be drawn to the common mistakes made. Targeted language exercises which required students to match useful expressions for stating the definition, to describe the uses of the various parts of the text, and to refer to the parts of the texts with their functions (Activity 3.2) offered a way to help students enrich their resources for meaning representations in their discipline. After building students' awareness of the content–language links, instructors had students complete a joint writing task near the end of each class with the belief that this would help them prepare their readiness and confidence for independent writing in the future.

Effectiveness of the Adjunct Instructional Model

The effectiveness of the adjunct model was determined using different tools and approaches, including surveys, interview comments, and documentary evidence drawn from a variety of sources. An average Student Activity Questionnaire (SAQ) score of 4.07 (out of 5) on the question "Overall, this [adjunct] course is useful to my study and future career" was obtained for the Engineering adjunct course. Through interviews, 88% of the Mechanical Engineering students confirmed (i.e., those who indicated 4 or above) that after taking this adjunct course, they could compose an Engineering proposal, a number that the instructors found satisfyingly high. The interview data echoed the positive SAQ results reported above. The student participants of the study asserted that the adjunct course was effective in helping them fulfil the requirements of their discipline-specific subjects and the language demands of the Engineering discipline. They stated that they found the language teachers' feedback and the materials of the adjunct courses were useful to their learning of the discipline, as one student claimed:

> The writing samples were useful in helping me handle the demands of the assignments. The course could help me enhance the quality of my project/assignment by collecting feedback from my adjunct course teacher.

In particular, students found the adjunct courses effective in helping them develop their discipline-specific English language skills, including learning about "the structure of an Engineering proposal/report," acquiring "useful expressions that help me express my Engineering ideas," and understanding how to compose the "IEEE referencing style."

In addition to the positive student feedback, the program leaders in HDME, the leaders in the Engineering subjects, and the language teachers were all very supportive of the KF-based adjunct courses. They welcomed the collaboration opportunity and agreed that the courses served as a platform that could help them better understand the students' learning needs and better learn from other colleagues about the language/disciplinary requirements of the assignments through the sharing of teaching materials, assessment guidelines, and student samples. In addition, these stakeholders also learned about the good teaching practices adopted by other colleagues as well as integrated content-and-language teaching strategies such as interactive teaching methods and the use of videos as writing prompts. All of the subject leaders commented that they felt the adjunct course could enhance the language performance (e.g., choice of words, sentence structures, organization of the assignment) of those students who attended the non-credit-bearing adjunct courses regularly, as the following comment suggests:

> Students could use more accurate and specific expressions to explain their observations in the reports. In the past, some students simply plotted the graphs and put them in the reports while expecting the readers to interpret the graphs themselves. Some even wrote in points form. Now they could explain their observations using the technical terms and concepts learnt in class.

The analysis of the written texts also shows that the students became able to use a wider range of linguistic and multimodal resources such as tables and labeled diagrams to realize the knowledge structures specific to different parts of their final Engineering proposal. Students who took the adjunct classes were also able to use IEEE referencing style when making references to other sources.

Conclusion

The results of the research, both from the smaller discussion presented in this chapter and the larger study, strongly suggest that a KF-based adjunct instructional model can be regarded as successful in aiding students' development of the academic discourse of their targeted discipline. The results support the idea that college students can benefit from English language instruction which is KF-based and grounded in disciplinary practices. Doing a Knowledge Framework analysis can not only help content and language teachers identify the linguistic and cognitive demands of the extensive writing tasks in the disciplines, it can also help highlight the functions of other multimodal tools employed for additive and supplementary meaning representations in written disciplinary genres. To promote real content–language integrated learning, the language specialists and disciplinary faculty need to continue close collaborative partnerships. This chapter detailed the effective use of the Knowledge Framework as a platform for facilitating the meaning negotiation and knowledge sharing between language specialists and disciplinary faculty. Strategic planning regarding how the student samples (both the exemplars and the weaker samples) can be used in class should be promoted to facilitate students' integrated content-and-language learning in the adjunct English-across-the-curriculum model. This chapter has focused on illustrative examples from the Mechanical Engineering adjunct course, but further KF analyses of the practices in other disciplines—both related and unrelated—would shed light on the ontological preferences of a wider range of disciplines.

References

Airey, J. (2020). The content lecturer and English-medium instruction (EMI): Epilogue to the special issue on EMI in higher education. *International Journal of Bilingual Education and Bilingualism, 23*(3), 340–346. doi:10.1080/13670050.2020.1732290

Brinton, D.M., Snow, M.A., & Wesche, M.B. (1989). *Content-based second language instruction*. Newbury House.

Dafouz, E., & Smit, U. (2016). Towards a dynamic conceptual framework for English-medium education in multilingual university settings. *Applied Linguistics, 37*(3), 397–415. DOI:10.1093/applin/amu034

Doiz, A., Lasagabaster, D., & Sierra, J. (2013). Globalisation, internationalisation, multilingualism and linguistic strains in higher education. *Studies in Higher Education, 38*(9), 1407–1421. DOI:10.1080/03075079.2011.642349

Halliday, M.A.K. (1994). *An introduction to functional grammar* (2nd ed.). Edward Arnold.

Halliday, M.A.K. (2007). On grammar and grammatics. In R. Hasan, C. Cloran, & D.G. Butt (Eds.), *Functional descriptions: Theory in practice* (pp. 1–38). John Benjamins.

Hong Kong Community College. (2015a, September). *Definitive programme document for 8C118 Higher Diploma in Mechanical Engineering.* Hong Kong Community College.

Hong Kong Community College. (2015b, September). *Assessment Guidelines, Group Project for CCN2248 Engineering Design Fundamentals.* Hong Kong Community College.

Institute of Electrical and Electronics Engineers (IEEE). (2018). *IEEE Reference Guide.* Piscataway, NJ: Institute of Electrical and Electronics Engineers. https://ieeeauthorcenter.ieee.org/wp-content/uploads/IEEE-Reference-Guide.pdf

Hyland, K. (2013). Writing in the university: Education, knowledge and reputation. *Language Teaching, 46*, 53–70.

Lin, A.M.Y. (2012). Multilingual and multimodal resources in L2 English content classrooms. In C. Leung & B. Street (Eds.), *"English"—A changing medium for education* (pp. 79–103). Multilingual Matters.

Lin, A.M.Y., & Lo, Y.Y. (2018). The spread of English Medium Instruction programmes: educational and research implications. In Barnard, R. & Hasim, Z. (Eds.), *English medium instruction programmes: Perspectives from South East Asian Universities* (pp. 87–103). Routledge.

Lyster, R. (2017). Language-focused instruction in content-based classrooms. In M.A. Snow & D.M. Brinton (Eds.), *The content-based classroom: New perspectives on integrating language and content* (pp. 109–123). University of Michigan Press.

Macaro, E., Curle, S., Pun, J., An, J., & Dearden, J. (2018). A systematic review of English medium instruction in higher education. *Language Teaching, 51*(1), 36–76. doi:10.1017/S0261444817000350

Martin, J.R. (2009). Genre and language learning: A social semiotic perspective. *Linguistics and Education, 20*(1), pp. 10–21. Retrieved from https://doi-org.ezproxy.lb.polyu.edu.hk/10.1016/j.linged.2009.01.003

Mohan, B.A. (1986). *Language and content.* Addison-Wesley.

Mohan, B.A. (1989). Knowledge structures and academic discourse. *Word, 40*(1–2), 99–115,

Mohan, B.A. (1998). Knowledge structures in oral proficiency interviews for international teaching assistants. In R. Young, and A. He (Eds.), *Talking and testing* (pp. 173–204). John Benjamins.

Mohan, B.A. (2001). The second language as a medium of learning. In B. Mohan, C. Leung, & C. Davison (Eds.), *English as a second language in the mainstream: Teaching, learning and identity* (pp. 107–126). Pearson Education Limited.

Mohan, B.A. (2007). Knowledge structures in social practices. In J. Cummins & C. Davison (Eds.). *International handbook of English language teaching* (pp. 303–315). Springer.

Mohan, B.A. (2011). Social Practice and Register: Language as a Means of Learning. In E. Hinkel (Ed.), *Handbook of research in second language teaching and learning, Vol. 2* (pp. 57–74). Taylor & Francis.

Mohan, B., Slater, T., Beckett, G., & Tong, E. (2015). Tasks as meaning-making activities: A functional approach. In M. Bygate (Ed.), *Domains and directions in the development of task-based language teaching: A decade of plenaries from the international conference* (pp. 157–192). John Benjamins Publishing Company.

Paltridge, B. (2013). Genre and English for specific purposes. In B. Paltridge, and Starfield, S. (Ed.). *The handbook of English for specific purposes* (pp. 347–364). John Wiley & Sons.

Roquet, H., Vraciu, A., Nicolás-Conesa, F., & C. Pérez-Vidal. (2020). Adjunct instruction in higher education: examining the effects on English foreign language proficiency. *International Journal of Bilingual Education and Bilingualism*, 1–22. DO I:10.1080/13670050.2020.1765967

Snow, M.A., & Brinton, D.M. (1988). The adjunct model of language instruction: An ideal EAP framework. In S. Benesch (Ed.), *Ending remediation: Linking ESL and content in higher education* (pp. 33–52). TESOL. 93.

Spradley, J. (1980). *Participant observation.* Holt, Rinehart and Winston.

Tong, E.K.M. (2014). *Mediating academic discourse development in a marketing course in Hong Kong: The role of bilingual resources.* Unpublished doctoral dissertation, The University of Hong Kong, Hong Kong.

Zappa-Hollman, S., & Duff, P. (2017). Conducting research on content-based language instruction. In A.A. Snow & D.M. Brinton (Eds.), *The content-based classroom: perspectives on integrating language and content (2nd ed)* (pp. 309–321). University of Michigan Press.

About the Authors

Dr. Esther Ka-man Tong is Head of Division of Languages and Communication and Director of Centre for Pedagogic Research at College of Professional and Continuing Education, The Hong Kong Polytechnic University. She was the recipient of CPCE Dean's Award for Outstanding Teaching Performance/ Achievement 2014/15 and the FSTE General Education Outstanding Teaching Award 2017. Her research interests lie in the areas of bilingual education, multimodal pedagogy, and content and language integrated learning.

Dr. Cecilia Fung-Kan Pun is a lecturer at the Division of Languages and Communication, College of Professional and Continuing Education, The Hong Kong Polytechnic University. She received her joint-university PhD from City University of Hong Kong and The University of Sydney. Her research interests include Systemic Functional Linguistics (SFL), text linguistics, academic writing, and discourse analysis.

Phoebe Siu is a lecturer at Division of Languages and Communication, College of Professional and Continuing Education, The Hong Kong Polytechnic University. Siu is a doctoral candidate (English Language Education) at The University of Hong Kong. Her research projects focus on multimodalities, content and language integrated learning, social semiotic awareness, and EMI higher education. Her conference papers were accepted at international academic conferences, including AERA, AAAL, AILA, EAC, and ISFC.

15 Implementing the Knowledge Framework in a Content-Based Language Teaching Classroom

Hong Ma and Jian Zhou

Abstract

From the perspective of Systemic Functional Linguistics (SFL), content is constructed through language. The Knowledge Framework (KF) inspires content-based language teaching (CBLT) by classifying different types of meaning constructed in social practices, including educational content areas, and specifying the semantic patterns of the discourse in each social practice. However, empirical efforts to implement the KF and evaluate the effectiveness of KF use in higher education remain scarce. This qualitative case study, contextualized in a college located in Southeast China, tracked 39 medical students throughout a one-semester course in which they received explicit instruction on the KF using prior theories on linguistic paths of knowledge. The models specify the hierarchical progression of different types of meaning and linguistic features in academic discourse. Analysis of students' writing samples composed before, during, and after the KF instruction suggested that the instruction was effective in urging students to produce language that mirrored higher levels of academic discourse. The findings of this study intend to raise awareness about adopting the KF and shed light on practical uses of the KF in higher education EFL contexts.

Keywords: Knowledge Framework; content-based language teaching; English for medical purposes; grammatical metaphor

Content-based language teaching (CBLT), an instructional approach to content teaching through the medium of a language that students are concurrently learning (Lyster & Ballinger, 2011), has long been adopted in various teaching contexts, ranging from content-driven total immersion programs to language-driven classes with content used for language practice (Met, 1998). It is widely acknowledged that the effectiveness of CBLT depends on meaningful communication about content (i.e., the meaning of a discourse) and intentional focus on language (i.e., the wording of a discourse) (Mohan & Beckett, 2003; Pica, 2000). Informed by a traditional view that sees language as a set of rules (Derewianka, 2001), CBLT facilitates students' language development by engaging them in the acquisition of correct forms (Long & Robinson, 1998). However, being able to talk scientifically and professionally entails more than just linguistic correctness.

Unlike using the well-established "focus on form" approach that fixes attention to problematical grammatical forms and elicits relevant form production (Day & Shapson, 1991), CBLT researchers taking a systemic functional linguistic (SFL) perspective have demonstrated, through discourse analysis research, that a functional approach is capable of scaffolding students' advanced language development by apprenticing the learners to conventional semantic patterns in a target discourse community (Mohan & Beckett, 2003; Mohan & Slater, 2004). More importantly, the theory of the Knowledge Framework (KF), developed from an SFL perspective, offers the possibility of teaching these semantic patterns in a systematic manner by dividing them into six knowledge structures (KSs), three at a general level (CLASSIFICATION, PRINCIPLES, and EVALUATION), and three at a specific level (DESCRIPTION, SEQUENCE, and CHOICE). Even though an increasing number of empirical studies have investigated how the KF could be implemented for language teaching, few researchers have focused on the explicit teaching of the KF in tertiary education. This study therefore intends to explore the effectiveness of teaching the KF explicitly in a medical English class offered at a college located in the southeast of China. Given the introductory level of this medical class and the genres of the assigned reading texts, only the KSs of DESCRIPTION, CLASSIFICATION, and PRINCIPLES were investigated in this current study.

Form-Meaning Relations and SFL

Despite the divergence of contexts, discussions on the effectiveness of CBLT have converged on the question of how to address content and language simultaneously and effectively (Hoare & Kong, 2008; Pica, 2000). Previous research investigating oral discourse in science classes contributes to our understanding of the relationship between content and language. Based on observations that the participants' difficulties in understanding academic discourse can be attributed to their unfamiliarity with its semantic patterns rather than with individual words, Lemke (1990) argued that meanings in science discourse are constructed through semantic patterns.

The relationship between content and language observed in previous research on science discourse can be addressed from the SFL perspective. According to SFL, three factors determine practical language use, including field ("the subject matter the activity is concerned with"), tenor ("the social roles and relationships between the people involved"), and mode ("the medium and role of language in the situation") (Mohan & Slater, 2005, p. 157). The ideational meaning in text, related to the field and closest to the everyday sense of content (Halliday, 1994), has been the focus of much SFL research. SFL research addresses the relationship between content and language by prioritizing the analysis of ideational meaning and establishing the connection between linguistic features in text and the ideational meaning created. SFL views wordings (lexicogrammar), an integration of grammar and lexis, as stratified realization of meaning (semantics) (Halliday & Matthiessen, 2004; Liardét, 2016). Specific to academic discourse, it is widely recognized that wordings generally move from spoken or unprepared language to noun-dominated written language (Liardét, 2016).

To capture the shift of wordings, Halliday (1998) proposed a "general drift of grammatical metaphor," which progresses from less grammatically metaphoric constructions in which processes are expressed using clauses, qualities are expressed using adjectives, circumstances are expressed using adverbs or prepositional phrases, and relations among these processes are expressed using conjunctions, to more grammatical metaphoric constructions, where processes, qualities, and even conjunctions are transformed into participants in clauses that relate one or more processes, qualities, and/or entities. An example that illustrates this more concretely from Halliday and Martin (1993, p. 66) is the movement from "*a* happens; so *x* happens" (with the process *happens* and the conjunction *so*) to "happening *a* is the cause of happening *x*, where the process *happens* has become a participant *happening* and the conjunction *so* has also become a participant, the cause of.

Researchers have also observed that there exists a hierarchy between various types of meaning. For example, by examining the interactions in a class conducting experiments between a teacher and two Chinese-Canadian students, Haneda (2000) found constructions of procedural meaning to be within what Vygotsky (1978) termed the students' "zone of proximal development," while constructions of explanatory meaning were beyond students' "zone of proximal development." The hierarchy between different types of meaning, as observed in Haneda's (2000) research, was systematically

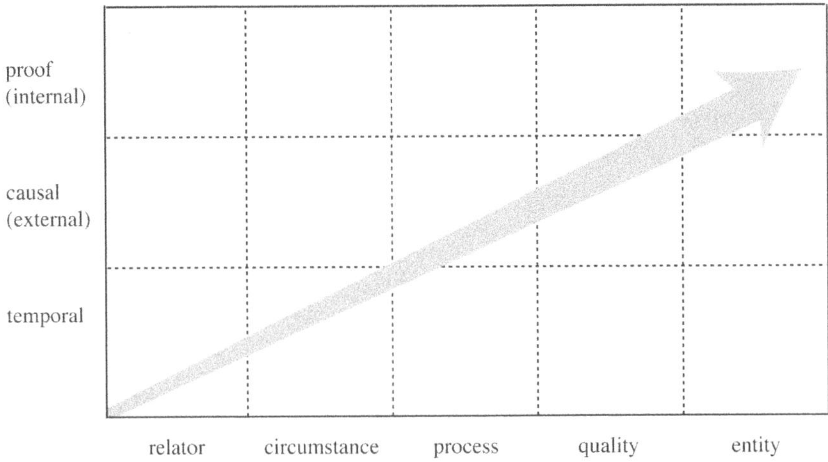

Figure 15.1 The developmental path of cause (Slater & Mohan, 2010)

investigated by Veel (1997) and Coffin (1997). Based on analysis of the main genres in secondary science textbooks, Veel (1997) identified an "idealized knowledge path" (p. 189) that progresses from procedural meaning, to scientific description and causal explanation, to persuasive discussion. Similarly, Coffin (1997) discovered that the written discourse of school history scaffolds students' exposure to the target discourse community from narration of past events to explanation or argumentation drawing upon historical events.

The two interrelated models, "the general drift of grammatical metaphor" and "the idealized knowledge path," were also unified in research on knowledge structures (KSs) with the proposal of "the developmental path of cause" (Slater & Mohan, 2010). As shown in Figure 15.1, the horizontal axis (the lexicogrammatical dimension) of "the developmental path of cause" illustrates that the sophistication of causal language "drifts" from relators through circumstances and processes to qualities and entities, in similar ways as does Halliday's (1998) general drift of grammatical metaphor. The semantic dimension (the vertical axis) moves sequentially from time to cause and proof, reflecting the evolution of "the preferred format for representing and explaining physical phenomena" (Halliday & Martin, 1993, p. 66).

Even though knowledge of the moves in the semantic dimension and the lexicogrammatical dimension have great potential for enlightening CBLT, little research has reported the effectiveness of explicitly teaching these moves. A review of discourse analysis research adopting a functional perspective has revealed that teachers of various content-based courses have implicitly apprenticed students in the use of semantic patterns of KSs by involving them in meaning-construction tasks and facilitating more sophisticated linguistic features appropriate for the content areas (Mohan & Beckett, 2003; Mohan & Slater, 2005, 2006; Slater & Butler, 2015). Practitioners may wonder about the effectiveness of teaching KF explicitly by incorporating knowledge on lexicogrammatical and semantic progressions in academic discourse. This study, therefore, intends to fill this gap by exploring the possibility of teaching the KF explicitly in an English as a foreign language (EFL) context.

CBLT in China

With the emergence of globalization and progressively closer intercultural communications in the 21st century, China has experienced a great shortage of "compound professionals," who excel in both their specialized fields and English communicative abilities (Wang, 2015). To cultivate talents with international competitiveness, the Ministry of Education in China has promoted educational reform offering 5% to 10% of all tertiary courses in a foreign language by issuing Official Document (2001) No. 4 concerning the Education Guidelines of Enhancing College Undergraduate Teaching Work (Zhu, Deng, & Li, 2014). An increasing number of content-based courses have thus mushroomed nationwide to simultaneously scaffold Chinese college students' development of content knowledge and language ability (Wang, 2015; Zhu et al., 2014).

Most content-based courses offered in Chinese tertiary education have been inspired by bilingual immersion programs in Canada, home to one of the most successful examples of second language teaching (Wang, 2015). A typical content-based course in China is delivered in English by a Chinese-speaking teacher who has studied related subjects in a foreign country or received a degree in a foreign language. In order to identify effective pedagogies for content-based courses in Chinese colleges, an increasing number of studies have detailed and reflected on the content-based teaching mode in various contexts (Kong, 2009; Wang, 2015; Zhu et al., 2014).

The implementation of this teaching mode in Chinese tertiary education has nevertheless encountered various challenges and difficulties, including "the availability of qualified teachers, sound curriculum planning and instructional organization, appropriate regular assessments and evaluations, pedagogy and cooperation between language and content teachers and approval and support from the educational administrations" (Wang, 2015, p. 111). Most importantly, the qualities and outcomes of these content-based courses have been questioned, since the relation between content and language had not been efficiently addressed, resulting in students' increased difficulty with following the instructions (Zhu et al., 2014). Among the various studies on CBLT in China, Kong (2009) is one of the few that has examined how teachers of content-based courses guide students in developing content and language knowledge. By comparing two content-trained teachers and two language-trained teachers' using CBLT pedagogies in their middle-schools located in two different Chinese contexts, Hong Kong and Xi'an, Kong (2009) found that only one content-driven teacher from Hong Kong devoted class time to form-function talk. The rest of the teachers either drew students' attention to grammatical errors or provided no language-focused talk whatsoever. Obviously, there is an urgent need to raise Chinese CBLT teachers' awareness of the content-language relations and a need to train students to produce appropriate language for specific discourse communities. Given that the KF is an appropriate tool to guide functional language teaching systematically, this study explores the effectiveness of teaching the KF in a college content-based course in China. The following question is addressed: In what ways does the explicit instruction of the KF guide students to draw upon more appropriate and sophisticated linguistic features to construct meaning?

Methodology

Participants and Context

The participants in this qualitative case study were 39 Chinese students—15 males and 24 females—registered in an English for medical purposes (EMP) course offered at a comprehensive university located in the southeast of China. This EMP course was designed as an adjunct support for undergraduate students majoring in Clinical Medicine with the specific aims of familiarizing them with word formation of English medical terms and developing students' communicative skills in an English-mediated medical context. Twelve students completed a bilingual course, Immunology, prior to this EMP course, while the other students had no previous experience taking medical courses delivered in English. The EMP course met two hours per week for eight weeks with each week devoted to a unit on one of the human body systems, including the musculoskeletal system, the nervous system, the urinary system, the endocrine system, the respiratory system, the digestive system, the circulatory system, and the reproductive system. Even though this course intended to prepare students for communication in English-mediated medical contexts, the majority of the in-class time was reserved for teaching the formation of medical terminology. Texts on different diseases related to human body systems covered in this class were assigned regularly in each unit to expose the students to English medical discourse.

The class teacher, one of the researchers, received a Master's degree in Applied Linguistics, and his research interest lies in EMP. To pursue his academic research, he took both applied linguistics and medicine courses during his graduate education. His interdisciplinary experience justified his qualification for teaching the EMP course. However, he admitted that there was little chance of applying his knowledge of EMP at the discourse level in practical teaching, because the majority of class time was devoted to explaining the formation of medical terms by introducing prefixes, stems, and suffixes that carry medical meaning.

Materials

The materials employed in this study include the reading texts, instructional handouts, and writing prompts used for collecting students' writing samples as well as the samples written by students over the semester.

The texts for reading. The assigned reading materials were selected from the books, *Medical English Course: Biological Medicine* (Hua, 2012) and *Innovative Medical English Textbook* (Li, 2008), and concerned different diseases related to the human body systems being focused on in each unit.

The instructional handouts. The instructional handouts presented the linguistic features used in the reading texts to construct different types of meaning, including cause-effect (PRINCIPLES), CLASSIFICATION, and DESCRIPTION. These linguistic features were presented in the form of a table aligning the KSs with their functions, linguistic contexts, and instructional comments that summarize instruction informed by progressions in the lexicogrammatical and semantic dimensions. Appendix A shows the instructional handout for the KSs that were selected from the reading text "Intestinal of Obstruction." Identical to instructional handouts designed for other reading texts, the "Notes/Explanations" column, encompassing a brief summary of the in-class lecture on the KF, emphasizes the grammatical metaphor that appears in the text. The grammatical metaphors in the text "Intestinal of Obstruction" include processes, such as "encroach on," "is aggravated by," and "lead to," and nominalizations such as "impairment," "manifestation," and "strangulation."

The writing prompts. The three writing prompts provided basic information about three medical issues (osteoarthritis, hyperthyroidism, and strokes) in phrases and organized the information in the form of a table. The information was categorized based on the KSs that the prompts intended to serve. Appendix B illustrates the presentation of the prompt for eliciting students' expositions of "stroke." Students were required to write a paragraph of at least 200 words on each of the diseases according to the information provided.

Procedure

The procedure for this study was divided into the following phases: a discourse analysis of the reading assignments adopting the KF, the elicitation and analysis of students' first writing samples, instruction of the targeted KSs (PRINCIPALS, CLASSIFICATION, and DESCRIPTION), and the collection and analysis of students' responses to the second and third prompts.

Discourse analysis of reading assignments. The medical discourse accessible to students was analyzed collaboratively by the researchers using the KF. For each reading text, the researchers first coded each clause with the KS and function that the clause was associated with. For example, the clause "It also accompanies inflammatory conditions of the abdomen..." is coded as "DESCRIPTION" (KS) and "describing symptoms" (function). The researchers examined the texts for sentences with grammatical metaphor and selected around 10 from each text to function as examples for the instruction of the KF, attempting to ensure a balanced coverage of the KSs and functions. Based on an analysis of the reading assignments, the texts generally incorporated three KSs (PRINCIPLES, CLASSIFICATION, and DESCRIPTION) serving six different functions, including "classifying a disease," "defining a disease," "describing symptoms," "describing high-risk populations," "explaining causes and effects of a disease," and "reasoning of treatment effects." Table 15.1 illustrates the KSs in texts, the functions they serve, and the clauses exemplifying the practical use of these KSs.

Elicitation of students' first writing samples. Prior to instruction on KSs, students were given 20 minutes to write a 200-word paragraph on osteoarthritis. The prompt was designed to elicit three types of KSs (PRINCIPLES, CLASSIFICATION, and DESCRIPTION) serving the six different functions aforementioned.

Instruction on KSs. In the first class, the instructor presented the KF to the whole class and introduced "the Developmental Path of Cause" as a demonstration for progressions in lexicogrammatical and semantic dimensions. For each category of causal resources, the instructor provided concrete examples. The instructor emphasized that the move toward processes and noun-oriented language is typical of academic discourse. The instructor then

Table 15.1 The functions and examples of KSs in texts

KSs	Functions	Example sentences
CLASSIFICATION	Classifying a disease	Early clinicians **distinguished between** bronchopneumonia **and** lobar pneumonia in pathological terms.
	Defining a disease	Osteoporosis, or "porous bone" **is a medical condition that** weakens bone by...
DESCRIPTION	Describing symptoms	**Other manifestations include** excessive sweating with an unpleasant odor, oily skin...
	Describing high-risk populations	Nosocomial pneumonia **is a particular problem in** post-operative patients...
PRINCIPLES	Explaining causes and effects of a disease	Osteoporosis **is a contributing factor in** as many as 1.5 million fracture each year.
	Reasoning of treatment effects	Lifestyle changes can **reduce** your risk of refracture.

presented the KSs appearing in the reading text for unit one, "The First Fracture May Be a Warning Sign," as a demonstration. As shown in Appendix C, to help students establish the connection between the KSs and the functions they serve, the KSs and their functions were paralleled in the table. Most importantly, for each example sentence, the instructor led the students to locate linguistic resources along the lexicogrammatical and semantic axis. For example, the instructor drew students' attention to the verb "strengthen" in the sentence "Participate in activities that will strengthen bone and muscle," and identified "strengthen" as "cause" semantically and "process" lexicogrammatically. This instructional model was adopted in a repetitive manner throughout the semester. During the instruction, the instructor deliberately avoided using SFL terms unfamiliar to college students. For example, "noun," "verb," "adverbial," and "conjunctions" were used to substitute "entity," "process," "circumstance," and "relator."

Instruction on KSs was provided in a cyclical manner with each week devoted to similar tasks. Students were asked to (1) complete the reading texts each week before the class, (2) identify the KSs serving different functions, and (3) fill in tables with KSs they identified in the assigned texts. The instructor, then, explicitly taught the KSs that appeared in the assigned texts by leading students to locate the linguistic features along the lexicogrammatical and semantic axis. After each class, students were provided with a complete table on the target KSs for reference with the "Notes/Explanations" column presenting the final product of in-class discussion, namely the semantic or lexicogrammatical categories of specific linguistic features.

Given the limited in-class time, instruction on the KSs was limited to 20 minutes in each class to guarantee the completion of teaching medical terms. The students were also required to finish two writing tasks on "hyperthyroidism" and "stroke" in the middle and at the end of the semester to experiment with productive use of KSs. They were granted 20 minutes of in-class time to finish each of the writing tasks.

Data Analysis

The Developmental Path of Cause (Slater & Mohan, 2010) functioned as our coding scheme for the analysis of cause-effect KSs, and students' improvement on causal resources was discussed with relating to the semantic and lexicogrammatical dimensions of the path. For the KSs of CLASSIFICATION (including definition) and DESCRIPTION, "the general drift of grammatical metaphor" (Halliday, 1998) and "the idealized knowledge path" (Coffin, 1997) were incorporated to evaluate students' production of KSs.

Linguistic resources provided in the prompts were excluded from our analysis. For example, in the sentence "Excessive intake of thyroid hormones may cause hyperthyroidism," "may cause" was identified and analyzed as the causal resource students produced. "Excessive intake," although a typical example for nominalization, was not considered in our analysis, since it appeared in the prompt.

Results and Discussion

This section discusses the evolution of students' practical use of KSs with reference to the progressions in the semantic and lexicogrammatical dimensions. The finding that students gradually produced an increasing number of linguistic features skewed toward the high end of the progressions undergirds the effectiveness of explicit instruction on the KF.

The KS of PRINCIPLES

An examination of causal resources in students' writing samples revealed that the explicit instruction of cause-and-effect discourse successfully scaffolded students' construction of causal meaning by helping students develop a variety of causal resources and guiding students to utilize causal resources approaching the more metaphoric end of the developmental path.

It was observed in the first writing samples that students generally failed to respond to the requirement of explaining the causes of diseases, or they resorted to using non-causal linguistic features suggesting that they may have encountered great difficulty in expressing causality. The syntactic structure "there-be" ranked among the most frequent non-causal linguistic features used by students. As seen in the following example sentences from the first writing samples, "there-be" structure indicated the existence of the causes but did not contribute to building causal relationship, instead representing the KS of CLASSIFICATION.

> Student 2: **There are many causes** or risk factors for the disease: obesity, repeated traumas or surgery…
>
> Student 23: **There are other factors** include obesity, repeated traumas or surgery to the joint, abnormal at birth, etc.
>
> Student 22: Meanwhile, **there are also many causes** that affect the osteoarthritis.

Consistent with the observation made in previous research (e.g., Ma & Slater, 2015, 2016), lower-level English students used descriptive or classificatory language, which ranks much lower than causal meaning along "the idealized knowledge path" to signify causality. Phrases for describing a high-risk population, such as "are at the risk of" and "is bound to," appeared more frequently in students' first writing samples to establish causality, as shown in the following examples.

> Student 13: The persons who have natural aging of the joint with water content of the cartilage increasing **are at the risk of** primary osteoarthritis.
>
> Student 12: It has two categories, one is primary Osteoarthritis which **is bound to** natural aging of the joint.

Students also relied heavily on the prompt for causal resources in their first writing samples, and thus produced sentences using the following formula: "The causes/risk factors of primary/secondary osteoarthritis + *be*-verb + a list of causes provided in the prompt." The *be*-verb was the only linguistic feature contributed by students in forming these causal sentences. This further strengthened our claim that students were not sufficiently equipped with appropriate linguistic features to establish cause-effect relationships before receiving instruction on the KF. In their second and third writing tasks, students used causal processes, such as "lead to," "result from," and "contribute to," much more frequently, causing a decrease in the use of the *be*-verb to form cause-effect sentences.

Student 14: The main causes of primary osteoarthritis **are** water content of the cartilage increasing... (writing 1) → Stroke **leads to** multiple complications including ... (writing 3)

Student 32: Pain and stiffness of the joints often long period of inactivity **is** often the normal reason. (writing 1) → Stroke can **result from** many causes like part of the brain loses flow and bleeding occurs within the brain. (writing 3)

Student 33: Primary Osteoarthritis's main risk factor **is** the natural aging of the joint ... (writing 1) → The former **contributes to** ischemic stroke while the last **contributes to** hemorrhagic stroke. (writing 3)

Student 34: The natural aging of the joint **is** a risk factor of primary osteoarthritis. (writing 1) → Bleeding occurs within the brain **contributes to** the development of hemorrhagic stroke. (writing 3)

Besides the typical causal processes previously mentioned, students also demonstrated greater flexibility in using processes to construct causal relationships by using an increasing number that infer indirect cause-effect meaning, such as "increase," "aggravate," and "interfere":

Student 15: Every reasonable effort should be made to ..., in order to counteract the effects of thyroid hormone to **increase** metabolism. (writing 2)

Student 17: Ischemic stroke **is aggravated by** the blood loss of part of the brain. (writing 3)

Student 25: Antithyroid drugs can **interfere** the development of the disease. (writing 3)

Students' responses to the three writing assignments also illustrate their efforts to produce more formal or sophisticated language to indicate causality. The process "make" dominated in students' early drafts and was gradually replaced by a wider variety of processes.

Student 9: ...which **makes** the higher water content and lower protein makeup of cartilage. (writing 1) → Excessive intake of thyroid hormones may **result in** hyperthyroid. (writing 2)
Student 15: Osteoarthritis can **make** some effect for body. (writing 1) → Every reasonable effort should be made to ..., in order to counteract the effects of thyroid hormone to **increase** metabolism. (writing 2)
Student 17: The thyroid gland "leaky" **make** the amount of thyroid hormone entering the blood increased. (writing 2) → Bleeding occurs within the brain **leads to** Hemorrhagic stroke. (writing 3)
Student 18: Thyroiditis ...**makes** the thyroid gland "leaky" (writing 2) → Ischemic stroke **results from** the blood loss of part of the brain. (writing 3)

The most grammatically metaphorical structure, nominalization, was almost absent in the students' first writing samples, but appeared in students' second and third writing samples (e.g. "complication," "development," and "likelihood"), especially in combination with causal process (e.g. "lead to," "interfere," "decrease," and "contribute to"):

Student 8: Strokes **lead to** multiple **complications** including difficult to speaking or understanding speech, difficult to balance, headache, and vomiting. (writing 3)
Student 25: Antithyroid drugs can **interfere** the **development** of the disease. (writing 2)
Student 26: Aneurysm clipping, hematoma can **decrease** the **likelihood** of the developing of hemorrhagic stroke. (writing 3)
Student 34: Bleeding occurs within the brain **contributes to** the **development** of hemorrhagic stroke. (writing 3)

Our results supported the idea that explicit instruction of the KF resulted in an increased variety of causal resources in students' second and third writings. The variety used in later texts reflected more than one category along the lexicogrammatical axis of the developmental path of cause. For example, student 15 used processes "make" and "cause" excessively in his first writing sample, but he used the causal circumstance "*to*-infinitive" followed by the causal process "increase" plus the nominalization "metabolism" in his second writing task. Student 18 added the entity "contributing factor" to his repertoire of causal resources exhibited in his final writing assignment, while in his previous two writing samples, he had used the process "make" multiple times:

Student 15: Osteoarthritis can **make** some effect for body. (writing 1) → Every reasonable effort should **be made to establish** a treating the symptoms…to **increase** metabolism. (writing 2)

Student 18: Thyroiditis is an inflammation of the thyroid gland which **makes** the thyroid gland "leaky." (writing 2) → Ischemic stroke **results from** the blood loss of part of the brain and the bleeding occurs within the brain is a **contributing factor** of hemorrhagic stroke. (writing 3)

As the above discussion of cause and effect language (i.e., the KS of principles) suggests, the ways that students constructed causal meanings expanded from a dependence on the existential "there be" form to a much wider variety of linguistic resources that reflect a more advanced sophisticated style of academic writing.

The KS of CLASSIFICATION

Similar to our findings on the language of cause and effect, students also made improvements semantically and lexicogrammatically when classifying and defining (the KS of CLASSIFICATION). As noted above, the "there-be" structure appeared frequently in students' first writings to introduce the classification of diseases; their usage decreased in students' second and third writing samples. Instead, processes such as "divide," "classify," and "distinguish," and entities (including nominalization) were increasingly used to indicate classification:

Student 7: **There are** two **types** for Osteoarthritis, primary or secondary. (writing 1) → The **classification** of stroke should be ischemic stroke and hemorrhagic stroke. (writing 3)

Student 8: **There are** two **kinds** of osteoarthritis, include primary osteoarthritis and secondary osteoarthritis. (writing 1) → Early clinicians **distinguished** between Ischemic stroke and Hemorrhagic stroke. (writing 3)

As can be seen, the simple entities of "kinds" and "types" in the first writing were replaced in later drafts by nominalizations of processes such as "classification" and Latin-based processes such as "distinguished."

As regards definitions, a decrease in the use of the "*be*-verb" was accompanied by an increasing use of processes, such as "define" and "refer to." The use of the entity "medical condition" instead of "disease," a more common word, as a general class was also adopted by more students in later writing samples:

Student 15: Osteopathic **is** a joint inflammation or joint disorder (writing 1) → Hyperthyroidism **refers to** a syndrome caused by excessive amount of thyroid hormones. (writing 2)

Student 25: [failed to define the disease in writing 1] →Hyperthyroidism **is defined** as an excessive amount of thyroid hormones. (writing 2)

Student 3: Osteoarthritis **is** a **disease** that will cause joint inflammation and disorder. (writing 1) → Hyperthyroidism **is** a **medical condition** in excessive amount of thyroid hormones. (writing 2)

The KS of DESCRIPTION

An analysis of descriptive language suggested that students' language production gradually advanced toward the metaphorical end of "the general drift of grammatical metaphor," showing more examples of qualities, processes, and nominalizations in later writings. In addition, after being instructed about the KF, students produced what we considered to be more characteristic of academic language. Student 8's writing samples is an example. "Dangerous" was the only expression of quality (i.e., adjectival description) used in her first writing sample, but the qualities "insidious," "present," and "susceptible" were used appropriately in her second and third written responses. Compared to student 8's first writing sample, one that used the *be*-verb dominantly with no nominalization, the use of process verbs increased noticeably: "be diagnosed with," "is associated with," "be directed against," and "is characterized by." The nominalization "manifestation" appeared in her later writing samples to refer to symptoms. Student 9 used "can be the cure of" to describe treatment in his first writing sample, but in his second writing sample, he shifted to the process "respond to" to achieve the same goal. Even though processes were used by student 9 to describe symptoms throughout all three writing tasks, he replaced "felt" (a common word with Old English roots) with "experienced" (a Latinate word) in the last writing task, creating what comes across as a more formal wording:

Student 8: Osteoarthritis **is** so **dangerous** and how to diagnosis it? (writing 1) → Hyperthyroidism has an **insidious** onset. (writing 2)
excessive sweating symptoms are **present** before a diagnosis. (writing 2)
Strokes being highly **susceptible** to that people who has high blood pressure... (writing 3)
Strokes **is characterized by** level of consciousness or confusion change acutely. (writing 3)
It **is associated with** half or part of the body weakens or paralyzes. (writing 3)

Student 9: Measures like joint replacement surgery can **be the cure of** osteoarthritis, which can reduce joint pain and inflammation. (writing 1) → Most cases of stroke **respond to** CAB. (writing 2)
Pain in the affected joints can **be felt** when you are in the condition of osteoarthritis. (writing 1) → Acute change of the level of consciousness or confusion would **be experienced** along with weakness... (writing 3)

As demonstrated through the evolution of the written responses, students' language appeared to shift from the lower left area of the developmental path of cause (See Figure 15.1) towards the higher right side of the semantic and lexicogrammatical axis. This shift was also apparent when looking at the KSs of CLASSIFICATION and DESCRIPTION, with students also using more formal (i.e., Latin-based) vocabulary and metaphorical constructions in their later texts. These findings suggest that explicit instruction of the KF helped students build up their repertoire of linguistic resources to construct key meanings in academic—and in particular medical—discourse.

Conclusion

This study investigated the effectiveness of introducing the KF to college students in an EFL context. Although this was a qualitative case study that cannot isolate the teaching of the KF as the sole variable producing the desired effect, the findings provide evidence to support the explicit introduction of the KF into tertiary-level content-based courses. Based on the analysis of students' written responses to three prompts, we can conclude that our explicit instruction of the KF, incorporating "the general drift of grammatical metaphor" and "the idealized knowledge path," was effective in helping students develop a greater variety of linguistic resources to produce more sophisticated academic language.

The data also highlighted several aspects that future studies could explore. As suggested above, the data, collected from a relatively small sample of the target population, may not be easily extrapolated to the wider context of ESP (English for specific purposes) offered in Chinese colleges. Differences between classes in terms of pedagogies, instructors, textbooks, and other factors may yield different results. More empirical effort, therefore, can be exerted to investigate the explicit instruction of the KF in various contexts.

Future research on the implementation of the KF into higher education content-based language courses could also incorporate activities that appeared to be useful for students' language development. In this specific class, the primary instructional activity was to draw students' attention to various linguistic features and to evaluate the sophistication of these linguistic features by bringing attention to the progression in semantic and lexicogrammatical dimensions. Students in our study received very little feedback delivered in the form of functional recasts, another approach that can lead to the appropriation of more academic constructions (see, e.g., Mohan & Beckett, 2003). Future studies on the implementation of the KF, if more in-class time can be given to this, could include functional recasts in an explicit manner by drawing students' attention to the semantic and lexicogrammatical aspects of the suggested expressions.

Teaching medical vocabulary and developing students' communicative skills in a Chinese English-mediated medical context requires a systematic approach to CBLT. This small qualitative case study suggests that by explicitly teaching the Developmental Path of Cause (Slater & Mohan, 2010), particularly focusing on Halliday's (1998) general drift of grammatical metaphor, instructors can help develop students' academic discourse within the context of medical meanings. In other words, the approach discussed in this chapter can help students use the medical vocabulary being taught in ways that can vastly improve their medical communication in English.

Acknowledgements

This research was supported by the Humanities and Social Sciences Fund of the Ministry of Education in China [grant number 21YJC740038].

References

Coffin, C. (1997). Constructing and giving value to the past: An investigation into secondary school history. In F. Christie & J.R. Martin (Eds.), *Genre and institutions: Social processes in the workplace and school* (pp. 196–230). Continuum.

Day, E.M., & Shapson, S. (1991). Integrating formal and functional approaches to language teaching in French immersion: An experiment study. *Language Learning, 41*, 25–58.

Derewianka, B. (2001). Pedagogical grammars: Their role in English language teaching. In A. Burns & C. Coffin (Eds.), *Analysis English in a global context: A reader* (pp. 240–269). Routledge.

Halliday, M.A.K. (1994). *An introduction to functional grammar (2nd ed.).* Edward Arnold.

Halliday, M.A.K. (1998). Things and relations: Regrammaticising experience as technical knowledge. In J.R. Martin & R. Veel (Eds.), *Reading science: Critical and functional perspective on discourses of science* (pp. 185–235). Routledge.

Halliday, M.A.K., & Martin, J.R. (1993). *Writing science: Literacy and discursive power.* The Falmer Press.

Halliday, M.A.K., & Matthiessen, C.M.I.M. (2004). *An introduction to functional grammar.* Hodder.

Haneda, M. (2000). Modes of student participation in an elementary school science classroom: From talking to writing. *Linguistics and Education, 10*(4), 459–485.

Hoare, P., & Kong, S. (2008). Late immersion in Hong Kong: Still stressed or making progress? In T. Fortune & D. Tedick (Eds.), *Pathways to bilingualism and multilingualism: Evolving perspectives on immersion education* (pp. 242–263). Multilingual Matters.

Hua, Z. (Eds.). (2012). *Medical English course: Biological medicine.* Shanghai Foreign Language Education Press.

Kong, S. (2009). Content-based instruction: What can we learn from content-trained teachers' and language-trained teachers' pedagogies? *The Canadian Modern Language Review, 66*(2), 233–267.

Lemke, J.L. (1990). *Talking science: Language, learning, and values.* Ablex Publishing Corporation.

Li, Y. (Eds.). (2008). *Innovative medical English textbook.* Shanghai Scientific & Technical Publishers.

Liardét, L.C. (2016). Nominalization and grammatical metaphor: Elaborating the theory. *English for Specific Purposes, 44*, 16–29.

Long, M.H., & Robinson, P. (1998). Focus on form: Theory, research and practice. In C. Doughty & J. Williams (Eds.), *Focus on form in classroom second language acquisition* (pp. 15–41). Cambridge University Press.

Lyster, R., & Ballinger, S. (2011). Content-based language teaching: Convergent concerns across divergent contexts. *Learning Teaching Research, 15*(3), 279–288.

Ma, H., & Slater, T. (2015). Using the developmental path of cause to bridge the gap between AWE scores and writing teachers' evaluations. *Writing & Pedagogy, 7*(2), 395–422.

Ma, H., & Slater, T. (2016). Connecting Criterion scores and classroom grading contexts: A systemic functional linguistic model for teaching and assessing causal language. *CALICO, 33*(1), 1–18.

Met, M. (1998). Curriculum decision-making in content-based language teaching. In J. Cenoz & F. Genesee (Eds.), *Beyond bilingualism: Multilingualism and multilingual education* (pp. 35–63). Multilingual Matters.

Mohan, B., & Beckett, G. (2003). A functional approach to research on content-based language learning: Recasts in causal explanations. *The Modern Language Journal, 87*, 421–432.

Mohan, B., & Slater, T. (2004). The evaluation of causal discourse and language as a resource for meaning. In J.A. Foley (Ed.), *Language, education, and discourse: Functional approaches* (pp. 255–269). Continuum.

Mohan, B., & Slater, T. (2005). A functional perspective on the critical "theory/practice" relation in teaching language and science. *Linguistics and Education, 16*, 151–172.

Mohan, B., & Slater, T. (2006). Examining the theory/practice relation in a high school science register: A functional linguistic perspective. *Journal of English for Academic Purposes, 5*, 302–316.

Pica, T. (2000). Tradition and transition in English language teaching methodology. *System, 28*, 1–18.

Slater, T., & Butler, I.J. (2015). Examining connections between the physical and the mental in education: A linguistic analysis of PE teaching and learning. *Linguistics and Education, 30*, 12–25.

Slater, T., & Mohan, B. (2010). Towards systematic and sustained formative assessment of causal explanations in oral interactions. In A. Paran & L. Sercu (Eds.), *Testing the untestable in language education* (pp. 256–269). Multilingual Matters.

Veel, R. (1997). Learning how to mean-scientifically speaking: Apprenticeship into scientific discourse in the secondary school. In F. Christie & J.R. Martin (Eds.), *Genre and institution: Social processes in the workplace and school* (pp. 161–195). Continuum.

Vygotsky, L.S. (1978). *Mind in society: The development of higher psychological processes.* Harvard University Press.

Wang, P. (2015). Looking beyond the ELT approach in China's higher education from the perspective of bilingual education: immersion, content-based instruction or something else? *International Journal of Bilingual Education and Bilingualism, 20*(1), 102–114.

Zhu, W., Deng, X., & Li, J. (2014). A case study on teaching business courses in English or bilingualism with Guangwai as an Example. *English Language Teaching, 7*(9), 156–164.

About the Authors

Hong Ma is currently an associate professor at Zhejiang University, China. She received her PhD in Applied Linguistics and Technology from Iowa State University. Her primary research interests are computer-assisted language learning, educational assessment, and educational data mining.

Jian Zhou is a lecturer at Hangzhou Normal University, China. He received his Master's Degree in foreign linguistics and its applications from HZNU and has been teaching EMP (English for Medical Purpose) in the same university since 2003.

Appendix A: An Example of Instructional Handouts

Intestinal of Obstruction (p. 66)			
Functions in English	**Linguistic Features**	**Sentences from the Reading Text**	**Notes/Explanations**
Define a disease	1.(a disease) ...designate...	1. Intestinal obstruction **designates** an impairment of movement of...	nominalization: impair->impairment, twist-> twisting
	2. (a disease) ...refer to...	2. Volvulus **refers to** a complete twisting of the bowel ...	
Describe symptoms	1. (a disease) ... accompanies... (symptoms)	1. It also **accompanies** inflammatory conditions of the abdomen...	
	2. The manifestation of... (a disease)	2. **The manifestation of** intestinal obstruction depend on...	
	3. With... (a disease), the onset is... (symptoms)	3. **With** acute/chronic obstruction, **the onset** is...	nominalization: manifest->manifestation
	4. The cardinal symptoms of ... are...	4. **The cardinal symptoms** of intestinal obstruction **are**...	
	5. (symptoms)... may appear along... (a disease/symptoms)	5. Visible peristalsis may **appear along** the course of the distended intestine.	
	6. ... are experienced along with...	6. Extreme restlessness and conscious awareness of intestinal movements **are experienced along with** weakness, perspiration, and anxiety.	

Explain causes & consequences of a disease	1. Major inciting causes include...	1. **Major inciting causes include** external hernia and postoperative adhesions.	S1(sentence 1) &S4 causal verbs: cause & effect.
	2. ... lead to...	2. **Strangulation** with necrosis of the bowel may occur and **lead to** perforation...	S2&S3 verb phrases for causality: lead to & result from
	3. ...result from... that encroach on ...	3. Mechanical obstruction can **result from** a number of conditions ...that **encroach on** the patency of the bowel lumen.	S3,S5&S6 verbs/ verb phrases for causality: encroach on, is aggravated by, & promote.
	4. The major effects of ... are...	4. **The major effects** of both types of intestinal obstruction are abdominal **distention** and...	S2,S5& S6 nominalization: strangulate-> strangulation, distend-> distention, accumulate-> accumulation.
	5. ... is aggravated by...	5. Distention **is** further **aggravated** by the **accumulation** of gases.	
	6. ...promotes...	6. This **promotes** rapid **growth** of bacteria within the obstructed bowel.	
Diagnosis/ treatment	1.(a diagnosis) ...reveal...	1. Abdominal x-ray studies **reveal** a gas-filled bowel.	
	2. Most cases of ... (a disease) ... respond to ...(treatments)	2. **Most cases of** a dynamic obstruction **respond to decompression** of the bowel through nasogastric suction...	nominalization: decompress->decompression, intervene -> intervention
	3. (a disease) ... require ...(treatments)	3. Strangulation and complete bowel obstruction **require** surgical **intervention**.	

Appendix B: Writing Prompt: Stroke

Stroke	Definition	Part of the brain loses its blood supply and stops working
	Types of strokes	Ischemic stroke Hemorrhagic stroke
	causes	1. Part of the brain loses blood flow => Ischemic stroke 2. Bleeding within the brain => Hemorrhagic stroke
	High-risk population	Those who 1. have high blood pressure, high cholesterol, diabetes 2. smoke 3. have heart rhythm disturbances
	Warning signs and symptoms	Partially loss of vision/Double vision Difficult speaking or understanding speech Difficult balancing Headache and vomiting.
	Diagnosis	Physical exam: assessing vital signs and wakefulness Neurologic exam: using the standardized stroke scale CT/ MRI: look for bleeding or masses in the brain and how much brain tissue is experiencing decreased blood supply. Blood tests: red blood cell count and platelets, kidney function, blood clotting function.
	Treatments	1. Ischemic stroke: thrombolytic therapy (tPA) (tissue plasminogen activator) tPA dissolves the clot that is blocking an artery in the brain and restore blood supply 2. Hemorrhagic strokes (tPA makes the symptoms worse): aneurysm clipping, hematoma evacuation or other techniques.

Appendix C: Handout for Demonstration

Functions	Linguistic Features	Sentences from the reading text
Define a disease	...is a medical condition that	Osteoporosis, or "porous bone" **is a medical condition that** weakens bone by ...
Describe symptoms	...be a warning sign...	A fracture may **be a warning sign that** you have osteoporosis.
Explain causes & consequences of a disease	...is a contributing factor in...	Osteoporosis **is a contributing factor in** as many as 1.5 million fracture each year.
	...cause...	Medical conditions other than osteoporosis can **cause** low bone density.
Describing/ signifying high-risk population	...have a higher risk for	Individuals with low bone density/ osteoporosis **have a higher risk for** fracture and refracture.
	...be at high risk for...	Many patients...**are at high risk for** premature death or loss of independence after the fracture.
	...occurs in...	Recent data indicates that osteoporosis **occurs in** all racial groups.
Reasoning of treatment effects	...reduce risk...	Lifestyle changes can **reduce** your risk of refracture.
	...strengthen...	Participate in activities that will **strengthen** bone and muscle.

16 Knowledge Structures as Designs: Tracing Patterns across Textual Trajectories

Diane Potts

Abstract

Drawing on examples from study abroad and foreign language higher education settings, this chapter examines use of Mohan's Knowledge Framework as a heuristic for curriculum design. It highlights the function of the framework during periods of textual instability, most significantly for addressing current concerns regarding (a) textual trajectories (the relations between texts across time and space), and (b) support for practices of textual critique and reflection literacy. The examples illustrate the possibilities for addressing these concerns while simultaneously targeting linguistic forms and the register demands of higher education. In the first example, a longstanding study abroad program for Japanese university students provides the context for examining how differences in knowledge structures' linguistic patterns can be harnessed to support students' understanding and use of projection/reporting verbs and to scaffold their interrogation of course content on intercultural communication. Similar attention to the sequencing of knowledge structures in curriculum development at a Korean university's English language institute makes it possible to draw students' attention to language's interpersonal metafunction and the dynamics of interlocutors' positioning in oral interaction. The chapter closes with a personal tribute to Mohan, whose scholarship consistently demonstrated respect for teachers and the demands they face.

Keywords: EMI; study abroad; higher education; foreign language education; curriculum design; SFL; reflection literacy; textual trajectories

In this chapter, I explore how Mohan's Knowledge Framework (Mohan, 1986)—also referred to in this chapter as simply "the framework"— functions as a heuristic for curriculum design in higher education, a heuristic that anticipated contemporary concerns with textual trajectories and continues to offer an entry point for exploring how meaning is made and remade across texts. I begin by briefly explaining the concept of textual trajectory as it is discussed in current research and its implications for language education. I then link that discussion to the ongoing challenges faced by English language educators in higher education and the value of the framework in addressing those challenges. To illustrate, I share two examples from my previous work as a post-secondary curriculum designer and educator. The first example is taken from a sheltered content course for third-year Japanese study-abroad students at the University of British Columbia, where the framework assisted in integrating targeted writing development activities and course content on intercultural communication. The second comes from my work at the language institute of a South Korean national university, where I was tasked with designing a new curriculum for the institute's flagship oral language program. In both contexts, the framework proved useful in designing curricula that attenuated students to available linguistic choices and the implications of those choices, thus supporting the metalinguistic awareness central to skilled language use. I close with a discussion of the complementarity of Mohan's Knowledge Framework and the concept of design, and the value of sensitizing students to texts' trajectories within programs of study.

The Concept of Textual Trajectories

Textual trajectory is not a concept Mohan employed in either his theoretical or practical explanations of the Knowledge Framework, despite his explicit interest in the organization of language experiences for pedagogic purposes (1986). Indeed, the concept of textual trajectories is a more recent concern. At its most simple, the term "textual trajectory" can be understood as "the changes, movements and directionalities of spoken, written and multimodal texts—and relationships between these—across social space and time" (Maybin, 2017, p. 416). It has emerged from complementary interests in textual dynamics in sociolinguistics, linguistic ethnography, discourse and literacies studies, and from corresponding discussions of the larger social implications of entextualization, recontextualization, and access to representational resources as observed across time. The focus on social and/or literacies practices is maintained but the emphasis shifts from microanalysis to examining the dynamic interplay of textual practices across time and context (see for example Prior & Hengst, 2010). Iedema's early multimodal analyses (2003) and more particularly his study of building a hospital extension (2001) are among the first to simultaneously trace: (a) the textual practices embedded within a project's decision-making processes and (b) their differential privileging and deprivileging of institutional stakeholders. Analysis of meeting transcripts, minutes, planning documents, and blueprints illustrate how (for example) control of the agenda allows the architect-planner to insert his views into a stakeholder consultation; how minutes of these consultations are subsequently accepted as facts on which future decisions can be based; and how project blueprints further solidify and advantage a set of interests. More recently, Lillis (2017) examined the trajectory of social work case files, the temporal orientations of those involved in their contiguous production, and the implications for those who make and remake knowledge across texts. The problematic transformation of information throughout the trajectory from client interviews to case reports to information serving as evidence for investigations and inquiries is traced. Here, too, issues of multimodality arise, this time in relation to digitalized casework forms that organize and constrain the flow of information. Long before this work began, however, the Knowledge Framework supported teachers in making chains of texts visible, and in encouraging examination of how knowledge is transformed across texts.

Research into textual trajectories attends to a range of semiotic resources employed, not only texts' oral and written dimensions, for "to understand the constantly transformative and innovative character of human meaning-making and learning therefore, then all means used in meaning-making will need to be recognized" (Bezemer and Kress, 2017, p. 528). Language educators are also focused on the intertwined relations of knowledge/meaning-making and semiotic resources, and texts' inherent multimodality is increasingly accounted for in research if not pedagogy (Early, Kendrick, & Potts, 2015; Harman, 2018; Potts, 2018; van Leeuwen, 2015). But while language education is moving beyond its inherent lingual bias, formal consideration of textual dynamics and more particularly the ways in which meanings are taken up and remade beyond the immediate interaction receives less attention. Mohan's focus on the organization of experience and corresponding interest in the language of knowledge structures remains a notable exception, and this aspect of the framework is one to which I will return.

Language education shares a second central concern with research on textual trajectories, that of the positioning of individuals within multiple conflicting ideologies (Lillis, 2017). Whether individuals are conceived of as decision-makers, meaning-makers, and/or agents, the interests of interlocutors are rarely in full alignment. As a result, conflict is inevitable in any flow of information and this has implications for education, more explicit in some research on textual trajectories than others. Perhaps the most significant implication is that learners must be supported in understanding the cascading effects of their choices, including choice of semiotic resources. Again, the argument resonates with previous research in language and literacy education. Not least, the call for greater attention to textual dynamics mirrors arguments for reflection literacy (Hasan, 1996, 2011), which put forth the need to prepare learners "to interrogate the wording and meaning of any utterance—why these words, what meanings are ascribed to them, how do they differ from the use of the word elsewhere, what do they achieve by the way they are used, contributing to whose loss and to whose benefit?" (2011, p. 229)

The question remains how such support can be provided. As Tusting (2017) points out, given that institutional processes are distinguished by fundamental differences in interest and purpose, those benefiting from current arrangements have little reason to open up processes or the associated textual trajectories for critique. If social participation is predicated on understanding the consequences of one's textual acts, and if access to such understandings is unevenly distributed, there are no easy routes for preparing learners to analyze and position themselves within institutional processes. A clear gap exists between what is called for in the research and the path to its achievement.

The gap is fundamentally pedagogic. Understanding the dynamics of decontextualization and entextualization, more particularly the across-time impact of semiotic choices, requires work. It requires work to expand the scope of long-established, critically oriented practices to include the temporal implications of one's choices. It requires work to develop a metalanguage that can cope with the instability of institutions and social formations in contemporary societies. It requires work to support learners' development as meaning-makers even when those assigning the work have a limited understanding of language itself. This work has been left to language educators, who are asked to reconcile institutional expectations and societal ambitions for greater critical interrogation of the norms, standards, and discourses that afford and/or restrict agency. In addition to this already daunting list, educators must also address the needs, wants, and desires of learners who have their own purposes for studying the English language and for expanding their repertoire of grammatical, lexical, and pragmatic resources. Students' priorities for acting, creating, and being in the world will not necessarily align with the priorities that others establish for them. The educator, any educator, stands amid these conflicts. Mohan's framework targeted the challenges faced by educators, and the framework's usefulness is what I hope to illustrate in this chapter.

Textual Trajectories and Curriculum Design

Research on textual trajectories calls for greater attention to the dynamic processes through which texts are made and remade across time, but most of a language educator's life in higher education is firmly rooted in the here and now. Entrance requirements, high-stakes assessments, and learners' struggles with disciplinary and/or occupational demands combine with scarce resources to focus attention on immediate needs. Somewhat surprisingly, though, prescribed learning outcomes and associated curriculum for English language education are rarely as clear-cut as they are for other disciplines in higher education. In part, this is a function of the range of institutional contexts in which English is taught: in English and non-English dominant contexts, in stand-alone institutes and mainstream classrooms, in for-credit and not-for-credit courses/modules, as a pre-condition and as an adjunct to disciplinary studies, and/or as a subject unto itself. Those who have worked in higher education will have taught in many of these settings, sometimes in combination and sometimes simultaneously. It is a world in which ideals smash up against the immediate educational, social, and emotional needs of learners and institutional realities.

Regardless of the setting, curriculum and materials are an issue. Commercial textbook providers modify their language products for national/regional contexts and (to a lesser extent) the demands of disciplinary settings, but higher education's increasingly specialized semiotic demands and the range of adult learners' needs can rarely be addressed with generic products. Research into second language writing and academic literacies highlights these realities. The substantial body of work on genre pedagogies and academic literacies, including research employing corpus methods, demonstrates the specificity of academic work (see for example Dreyfus et al., 2015; Gardner & Nesi, 2012; Gardner, Nesi, & Biber, 2018; Hyland, 2004, 2008; Hyland & Tse, 2004; Lillis & Scott, 2007; Martin, 2009). Hyland's many contributions to the field include problematizing assumptions a) that common academic language (e.g., analyze, process) holds similar meanings across disciplines (Hyland & Tse, 2007, 2009), and b) that academics' judgements of "good writing" mirror those of academic writing instructors (Hyland, 2013). Neither assumption holds true under the weight of evidence. Inevitably, the limitations of commercial products, the variability in institutional settings, and the increasing specialization of disciplinary demands lead language educators to fashion their own teaching materials. Language educators are designers not of choice but necessity.

Perhaps no one has illustrated these points better than Coffin and Donohue (2014) in a book-length treatment of their work at the United Kingdom's Open University. Combining what are effectively autoethnographic accounts of language teaching with detailed linguistic analyses of students' writing, they depict students' encounters with a dizzying array of hybrid genres that display far more variation than imagined in a traditional academic writing classroom. Although their primary purpose is to argue for a language as social semiotic (LASS) approach in higher education, Coffin and Donohue are particularly eloquent in describing the emotional plight of students who come up against linguistic and textual norms that are alien to their previous experiences. From a somewhat different angle, Johns (2008) is equally articulate in describing her attempts to address disciplinary demands while teaching in a university writing program. Although a firm advocate for genre pedagogies, she is nonetheless refreshingly clear-headed about the possibilities and limitations of such approaches when university programs are structured to supply generic writing support. Nor are non-English dominant contexts immune to these challenges. The rise of English as the medium of instruction (EMI) (Dearden, 2014), a policy without a pedagogy, requires academics across disciplines to teach in English. For language educators, this adds an additional challenge of supporting academics who may not have the linguistic confidence and/or proficiency to skillfully teach in a foreign language. Again, matters over which they have little control leave educators with significant challenges.

The Knowledge Framework

What do any of these challenges have to do with the work of Bernie Mohan? Frankly, everything. The Knowledge Framework and Mohan's subsequent research on language education have drawn on sophisticated theories of language, literacy, and philosophy as well as contemporary research on language education. Those who have benefited from discussions of his later work know that subsequent influences extend from Donald Schön to Charles Taylor. But his research was for the classroom, was conducted in dialogue with educators, and was crafted with the recognition that classroom-level change could make a meaningful difference even when educational systems appeared immovable. The trajectory of that research, including the ways educators have continued to take up and extend the work over the lifetime of their careers (see, for example, Early & Marshall, 2008), is beyond the scope of this chapter. There are, however, three facets of the framework relevant to higher education and to calls for greater attention to textual trajectories that I can attend to and then illustrate with my own work: the practicality of knowledge structures as a heuristic for identifying patterns, the usefulness of relations between knowledge structures for planning curricula, and the effectiveness of the framework in designing opportunities for discussing language's functions.

The Knowledge Framework has always functioned as a heuristic for discovering patterns in how language is used and reused across contexts. While it can be considered first and foremost a framework for pedagogic design, the language patterns it describes are generic patterns of language use. These patterns are the six knowledge structures: DESCRIPTION, SEQUENCE, CHOICE, CLASSIFICATION, PRINCIPLES, and EVALUATION. The structures exist as language and/or in combination with other semiotic resources, are recognizable by their grammatical, syntactic, and textual patterns, and correspond to different thinking processes. From a curriculum planning perspective, these affordances provide educators a means for setting complementary, pragmatically informed grammatical and text-level objectives; for analyzing teaching resources for their coherence and effectiveness and/or creating materials for the same; and for ensuring language learners are provided with support for engaging with a range of thinking processes. In essence, the framework provides educators with tools for checking (a) whether their pedagogic designs target the language students need to work with how knowledge is structured, and (b) whether the materials they design and use are effective in supporting development of that language. From a teaching perspective, the Knowledge Framework provides a rudimentary metalanguage for discussing what is happening in a text/textual phase (e.g., classification, explanation), a means of linking grammar and knowledge, and a basis for examining how knowledge is transformed across texts. In other words, the framework makes it possible to discuss language and its patterns of use in ways that are consistent with Hasan's call for reflection literacy.

This last point is critical to examining textual trajectories. A central issue raised by this research is the need to support individuals in understanding textual dynamics, including how their semiotic choices and the meanings they share may be taken up, reused, and/or recycled. This requires discussing what happens across talk, texts, and text types, in contrast to discussing what happens within a text, genre, or genre family. It also requires showing how topics and themes shift across texts in ways that may or may not serve an individual's interest. Pedagogically, it necessitates sequencing unit and/

or course content to spiral backwards and forwards so that students have multiple opportunities to see how shifts occur at the level of topic, text, and grammar. Following textbooks' traditional path from "simple" to "complex" knowledge is insufficient: rigid adherence to this sequence cannot reasonably be expected to support students in transferring their analytical and interpretative capabilities to contexts beyond the classroom. So then, what to do? Again, the framework serves as a useful reference. Relations between knowledge structures provide a theoretically informed basis for designing the sequence of units/courses. The knowledge structures of DESCRIPTION, SEQUENCE, and CHOICE are the structures of knowledge that accompany action (Mohan, 1986, p. 42); that is, attention is focused on specific objects, contexts, and/or decisions. The specific may be the description of an immediate problem within an organization, the process used to solve the problem, and the agreed upon solution. It may be a plot of land that is developed for a specific use and the development plans for the project. It may be the characters in a children's story, the story's plot, and a child's verdict of a character's actions. The same language patterns appear in all three. However, beyond the classroom, knowledge does not follow this sequence. People attempt to decide between two alternatives without clearly defining the problem or the organizational processes that will be followed. Novels begin—and we share narratives—without detailing who is involved in the story. Undergraduates read summaries of experimental outcomes with few details of the research design. We step into knowledge from different angles. Interrogating textual trajectories requires recognizing the door available to us and understanding our options once we enter in.

And CLASSIFICATION, PRINCIPLES, and EVALUATION? These are the theoretical dimensions of activity, the forms of knowledge that exist outside time or specific context. Classifications such as main and supporting character or hero and antagonist belong to the literary world, not the world of named characters in a specific novel. Principles, rules, and theorems linking gravity, time, and space must explain all known data and not merely one data point if they are to be credible in the scientific world. The criteria used to evaluate the robustness of such theories remain the same regardless of which theory is being evaluated. Dewey argues theories are also practical but are practical in relation to the world of ideas. CLASSIFICATION, PRINCIPLES, and EVALUATION belong to this second world.

In this world as well, the door to knowledge may open at any point. Critiquing textual trajectories involves challenging classifications (e.g. the representation of social actors) and the criteria for assessing "good" or "bad" outcomes (e.g. profitability vs. environmental impact), and not simply the relations of cause-effect. Again, the Knowledge Framework provides a door to discussing how knowledge is being organized, the extent to which the dominant discourse prevents or supports challenges to prevailing ideas, and the thinking required to move between action and theory. It does not tell educators what to teach. It does, however, support them in developing their design practices.

It is necessary at this point to highlight the concept of activity put forward in the framework, because it links the worlds of action and theory. It is perhaps the most contested concept in Mohan's work, at least among scholars who share his interest in social semiotics: the debates about activity and more importantly around differences in how context is theorized are unresolved in social semiotics/SFL more generally. So, while an educator can at least temporarily ignore these debates, it is important to know they exist. Still, the relation between action and reflection on action in the framework—between doing and theorizing—remains a useful one for curriculum planning. One can consider the relationship between DESCRIPTION and CLASSIFICATION; that is, between a text/textual phase that draws on a rich array of adjectives and verbs to describe a specific entity and a text/textual phase in which abstract nominals are defined using DESCRIPTION. Or point out to students the difference between a sequence (e.g., an experiment, a recount of a past event, a study plan) and the adverbials which help to identify it, and the same sequence remade to communicate causality or correlation, as in the often-mislabeled historical narratives. Within and across interactions and texts, we shift between action and theory with relative fluidity. However, executing those shifts often provides the subtle means through which knowledge is codified and power exercised. Planning for and highlighting such shifts, including their implications, is essential work for interrogating textual trajectories.

To be clear, the framework does not address every pedagogic decision an educator must make. It has one focus, knowledge structures, and that focus has applications across educational settings. However, I would argue that the value of Mohan's framework is also in what it is not. It is not a theory of language, it is not a theory of genre, and it is not capable of describing how language is used to negotiate interpersonal relations, whether between two speakers, a written text and its reader, or a human and a computer bot in any of its dynamic, multimodal forms. But sometimes knowing what you are not is useful, because it allows you to reach out to others and/or other resources for assistance. Hasan (2011) defines theories capable of this facility as exotropic and has written extensively on dialogues between Vygotskian theories of learning, Bernstein's sociology of education, and SFL. By extending this concept to pedagogic frameworks, we can reflect on their capacity to mutually inform teaching designs. The Knowledge Framework is open to SFL, to pragmatics, and to other fields addressing communicative practices. It leaves space for illustrating how these dimensions of the human experience are simultaneously negotiated alongside knowledge. It is also comfortable in dialogue with theories of genre and text types, a mainstay of academic writing programs. In other words, one valuable aspect of the framework is its openness to pedagogic theories that are epistemologically compatible, a valuable attribute in higher education when disciplines are increasingly turning their attention to teaching practices. This openness is illustrated in the two examples that follow, each of which draw attention to different facets of the framework's openness and flexibility.

Designing with the Framework

In what follows, I use two examples from my history in higher education to illustrate the framework's value in curriculum design, highlighting its relevance to issues associated with textual trajectories. In the first example, the framework was used in a three-credit third-year university course to design targeted language supports for Japanese study-abroad students. In this example, the framework was useful in designing knowledge flows between course content and students' experience, across the length of course, and (potentially) beyond the course to future academic studies. The link to issues of textual trajectories is clearer still in my work designing a new oral language curriculum for a language institute in South Korea (Potts & Park, 2007). Here, knowledge structures are the backdrop for activity/task designs that supported students in exploring how language is used to create, manage, and control relations between individuals, and between individuals and social institutions. In both settings, the framework functioned at the course, lesson, and activity level and supported decisions related to simultaneously controlling and varying patterns of language such that students could "see" what language was doing.

Designing for an Academic Study-Abroad Program

The teaching context. Each year, approximately one hundred students from a major Japanese university complete their third year of study at the University of British Columbia (UBC). Typically, they represent a cross-section of the humanities and social sciences and include a number of economics majors and/or students interested in business. At the time I taught in the program, the majority had written TOEFL scores in the neighborhood of 475 and 500;

a smattering had scores that permitted them to select from the full range of UBC's course offerings, and a very small number had scores below the program's theoretical admissions requirements.

All but a very few students took sheltered courses designed to provide additional language support. Although the courses were sheltered, the course content and assigned readings were consistent with other third-year courses across the university. Classes met three times a week for 4.5 hours/week over a total of 13 weeks. Formally, 3 hours were designated for lectures and 1.5 hours for seminars. Practically, lecturers had a reasonable amount of discretion in their course design. For the course on intercultural communication and language socialization, the first course I taught students each year, the reading list included peer-reviewed journal articles, UNESCO documents, and chapters from mainstream intercultural communication textbooks. Assessments included five short collaborative writing assignments, a multiple-choice exam focused on key concepts and research findings, and a final paper. Students received collaborative writing assignments on Fridays during the time budgeted for a seminar. During those classes, I reviewed the week's lectures and readings, linked them to the assignment, and provided language support tailored to the task at hand. Assignments were completed in a wiki hosted on PBWorks©, which was selected for its ease-of-use, security features, and integration of a wiki and forum on each page. The last point was key, as I wanted groups to analyze and discuss their written work on the same page (see below). Although collaborative assignments contributed to students' final marks, they were also designed as preparation for the more substantial final paper and for academic writing more generally: The thinking practices and grammatical resources needed for each assignment were structured for transfer beyond the immediate classroom context.

Linking practice and theory was a priority for this course on language socialization and intercultural communication, as it often is in intercultural communication courses. All sheltered courses in the program had been redesigned shortly before I began work in the program, and the course on language socialization and intercultural communication was intended to support students in remaking the experience of study abroad into transferable knowledge. Establishing links between practice and theory, however, is much more difficult than we often admit; literature on transfer suggests our assumptions that students can and/or do make connections is often false. Beyond linking theory and personal experience, I wanted to draw students' attention to the linguistic and conceptual relations between the two. The relation between action and reflection-on-action, a relation made explicit by the Knowledge Framework, was a productive tool for thinking how I might do this.

Designing curriculum. The design of the first collaborative assignment illustrates the richness of the support provided by the framework. Students received the assignment at the end of the second week of classes, after they had read and discussed Schieffelin and Ochs' seminal 1986 article on language socialization. The article was challenging—an unfamiliar genre with unfamiliar content in an unfamiliar register—and the assignment needed to be multidirectional if it was to help students make sense of this and subsequent readings. That is, it needed to support students in making meaningful connections between new ideas and their lives as Japanese students while simultaneously helping them see how research transforms everyday existence into theory. Because I was prioritizing connections between their lives as lived and what they read, I organized the assignment around the knowledge structures SEQUENCE and PRINCIPLES and blended personal narratives with explanation (Figure 16.1). (Note that the excised portions of the assignment were (a) directions for using the wiki and (b) due dates.)

My choice of SEQUENCE and PRINCIPLES linked to another of my design criteria for the assignment: I wanted to quickly and efficiently move beyond the quotidian concept(s) of culture students brought to the classroom and begin to have them think of culture as constantly remade by and across individuals, a perspective more consistent with theories and ideas at the heart of the course. I could have taught students about competing concepts of culture, and later in the course I provided several definitions from commercially successful textbooks on intercultural communication. However, providing classifications and definitions was unlikely to engage them in critically evaluating their current stances. What I needed was an activity that disrupted their current thinking. To do that, I had them think about becoming Japanese.

The very notion of becoming Japanese was strange to the students, for Japanese had always been what they were and not what they became. However, the assignment's linguistic demands required students to shift from describing culture and/or reiterating standard responses to classification questions

3. Reflect on becoming Japanese. Write your reflection on your group's page. Your reflection should be ~300 words (quality is more important than quantity) and you may include images, links to webpages, or other non-linguistic content if you like.
4. Post your individual reflection quickly - ASAP - before midnight Friday if you can. If you delay, you cannot have a good on-line conversation and your grade will be lower.
5. Use "Comments" and discuss each other's reflection. Ask questions. Explain how your experiences are similar or different. Expand or add to their ideas. Compliment them if their writing and/or ideas have helped you think and/or feel more deeply.

Figure 16.1 Assignment 1: Description (excerpt)

Criteria for Grading

1. Do you focus on practices of becoming Japanese? [Hint: The question is NOT "What is Japanese culture?"]
2. Do you reflect on specific examples?
3. Do you analyze as well as describe?
4. Do you build on others' ideas and examples?
5. Do you use a mix of mental processes in your writing?

Figure 16.2 Assignment 1: Grading criteria

(e.g. What are the characteristics of Japanese?) to something that was a process and a process that was contingent on their experiences. A Canadian university classroom provided neither the time nor a context in which they could "do" culture; that is, there was not an assignment that could address the action/theory as in Mohan's classic chess example (1986). But reflection requires retelling events, a classic act of sequencing. With reflection, I had both the sequence/action and cause-effect/reflection on action. The marking criteria reinforced the thinking processes that were critical to a successful assignment (Figure 16.2).

As stated earlier, the sheltered courses were designed to simultaneously meet the standards of a third-year UBC course and support language development. Here, the explicit relationship between language, knowledge structures, and thinking processes as set out in the framework was helpful as was the freedom to draw on SFL. One can see the linguistic emphasis in the grading criteria, most particularly in the criteria addressing mental processes. Analysis of previous cohorts' writing had shown almost no use of projection/reporting verbs, a key resource in academic writing. From this analysis but also from previous experience, I could also see that those students who had used reporting verbs limited themselves to a narrow range of options and had little apparent understanding of the nuances of their choices. My selection of the hybrid genre of reflection, which demands these grammatical resources, was informed by the Knowledge Framework. Importantly, the assignment gave me opportunities to provide feedback to students on their use of a critical academic language resource early in their program. I made my thinking explicit to students in the assignment's preamble (Figure 16.3).

Again, I was working with limited time. I had 1.5 hours to review the week's content, introduce the assignment, provide language support, teach students how to use the wiki and have them start work on their assignments so I could sort out any immediate problems. For that reason, I also provided a model text (Figure 16.4), an excerpt of which is provided below. With this, I could not only show how experience was transformed into data, I could show the language required to do this.

Task 1 - Becoming Japanese

Your first assignment involves writing a reflection. There are several reasons for having you reflect for your first assignment:

- A reflection is a personal opinion. Because there is no right or wrong, you can focus on thinking deeply. There is less stress about being "correct."
- It helps to begin the course with something familiar. Although you may never have thought about becoming Japanese, you are writing about you. You are the expert on you.
- This course focuses on practicing culture, not culture. A reflection is helpful activity for thinking about practices.
- The concept of voice is very important in academic writing. Academic English uses many different grammatical devices to create voice. One of them is your choice of mental processes. A reflection gives you the opportunity to practice using different mental processes, and to think deeply about the meaning that your words/grammar communicate. Thus, a reflection is a good place to begin because it helps you think about developing your academic voice.

Figure 16.3 Assignment 1: Preamble

So how can I write about becoming Canadian if we don't know what Canadian is? I can write instead about the **understandings** that guide my **decisions** as a Canadian, **understandings** which began to develop when I was very young and which developed without me realizing I was learning. **Experience** and stories taught these lessons. For example, my grandmother's mother (my great-grandmother) died when my grandmother was 8 years old. As a result, when my grandmother married and needed to learn to bake bread and buns, it was the owner of the Chinese cafe who taught her. Such acts of kindness carry forward. Eventually my grandmother taught my mother to bake the same buns. And later still, when my friends ate at my house, they often commented that my mother's buns were different than the buns/bread that their mothers baked. The **reason** for the difference became clear the first time I ate a Chinese barbequed pork bun. I laughed. The Chinese barbequed pork bun tasted just like my mother's baking!

Figure 16.4 Assignment 1: Model text (excerpt)

The model text did more than provide examples of projection. It also modeled nominalization; that is, it modeled categories (e.g., "the understandings" rather than "I understand"; "Experience and stories" rather than "I experienced") that predominate in analyses of applied linguistics and/or intercultural communication. Nominalization would be addressed in a later assignment and in separate writing workshops built into the program design. At this point, it was enough to show, not tell.

I should also highlight the importance of the online discussion on the reflections. For this assignment, students were organized in groups of three. Each group of three had a separate wiki page in which they wrote their reflection. These reflections were then discussed in a forum located below the wiki page. Effectively, students were required to reflect on reflections, moving the analysis one step further from experience. Again, the activity forced use of the targeted thinking, language forms, and course content. Again, the Knowledge Framework helped me to see possibilities for curriculum design that would have been difficult to identify otherwise.

Thus, this first assignment was not simple. It challenged students' conventional notions of culture and potentially their identity as Japanese. To at least some degree, it required thinking with ideas introduced in the Schieffelin and

Ochs' article. It required re-organizing experience into evidence and using that evidence to support an argument. It demanded analysis, an opaque term that has a meaning that shifts across disciplines. It also introduced the meta-language of mental processes and projection, metalanguage I could use in feedback and future discussions. This was a small assignment that students completed in 10 calendar days at the same time they were acclimating to Vancouver and working on other courses. It needed to achieve a lot with a little. Mohan's framework provided a basis for a design that coherently addressed the linguistic demands of the task while simultaneously and explicitly laying a foundation for continued use of these concepts and thinking and textual practices in subsequent classes.

I want to briefly comment on textual trajectories before moving to the next example. As may already be obvious, this and other assignments were designed to scaffold future academic writing in this course and others. But academic writing was not the only concern. The next week's readings covered second language socialization, so students were writing about their first language socialization as they read theory directly relevant to their current experience. Writing scaffolded future reading; readings scaffolded how they made sense of what they were experiencing in Vancouver and beyond. But more than that, understanding that their experiences were data provided a footing for critiquing what they read. Their experience could challenge and/or add greater nuance to readings on study abroad, on research on Japanese students and on cultural encounters. Their next assignments asked them to collectively author an explanation of language socialization, to compare and contrast first and second (or third) language socialization, to reflect on their processes of "becoming" in the Canadian communities they were encountering, and to explain the concept of cultural interaction as set out by UNESCO. Thus, the assignments were designed not only to interconnect with each other, but also to intersect with students' lives in Canada. They supported the study-abroad students in understanding how others made sense of them, as well as supporting them in making sense of their experience from a personal as well as academic perspective. By providing a basis for coherently linking the language of activity and the language of reflection on activity, Mohan's framework helped with that, too.

Designing in a foreign language setting

The teaching context. Designing in a foreign language setting brings its own complexities, not least the demands of meeting the needs of students who have studied English for many years but cannot or feel they cannot use the language. For these students, one question predominates before, during, and/or after a course—is this course useful? Language is for doing, thinking, and being in the world; the world of English is desirable because, for better or worse, English is currently the most influential and more powerful language. For a foreign English language learner, the value of a TOEIC/TOEFL course is assessed against changes in test scores; however, it is much more difficult for learners to assess a course when the goal is gaining access to the larger English-speaking world.

Students enrolled in the six-level oral language program at the Language Education Center (LEC) at Chonnam National University (CNU) in South Korea wanted access to the world. CNU is one of ten flagship national universities created by the South Korean government following the Korean War to further the nation's intellectual and economic development. In this highly educated country, English has been a compulsory subject from early primary school (Grade 3) for more than 20 years. The nation is frequently characterized as suffering from "English fever" and English proficiency is often used to screen job applications from recent university graduates, whether or not the position requires English. However, as in many East Asian contexts, there are frequent laments over individuals' ability to use English for business, professional, and/or political purposes. LEC students were caught in the bind of high expectations, limited opportunities for English language use outside the classroom, and real and immediate consequences if they did not develop their English language proficiency.

The oral language program, a core offering at LEC, aimed to support university students and public sector employees in addressing these concerns. Each course ran for seven weeks, five days a week, and one hour each day. Students were assessed on a pass/fail basis and a passing mark was required to advance to the next level. It was not uncommon for students to repeat Levels 4, 5, and/or 6 at least once; students who completed the program were allowed to participate in Level 6 indefinitely for free. In surveys and focus groups conducted in conjunction with the curriculum redesign, students expressed frustration with a self-perceived lack of progress; analysis linked these frustrations to lower enrollments and lower course evaluation scores in advanced modules (see Potts & Park, 2007). However, small changes I had made in my courses, changes informed by the Knowledge Framework, correlated with improvements in course evaluation outcomes, and those outcomes informed the management-level decision to revise the curriculum. What, then, were those changes and why did they matter?

Designing curriculum. Mohan's framework formed the backbone of my CNU teaching practices and the redesign of LEC's oral language program.

First, I used the framework to create coherence in theme-based units. Commercial textbooks were inadequate for the program's upper levels. Students "knew" a considerable amount about English: For many years, they had studied grammar, memorized word lists, and learned to write essays for high-stakes examinations. What they did not know was what to do with that knowledge. Conventional textbooks recycled grammar points from the students' earlier studies without targeting improvements in their sociolinguistic judgement. The same textbooks reused familiar themes with which students were already overly familiar from their elementary and high school studies. Without appropriate textbooks, language educators at LEC did what many language educators do, research and select materials from newspapers, government agency, and NGO websites, streaming radio, and so on, and then modify them for classroom use. However, non-Korean nationals who taught the oral language courses often had little to no experience in curriculum design, a challenge further exacerbated by the turnover of non-Korean staff. LEC needed to meet students' needs without requiring each instructor to design their courses from scratch. It needed the coherence created by curriculum, and the framework assisted with providing this coherence.

In the design of a coherent curriculum, the framework fulfilled its established role as a basis for organizing and sequencing engagement and experience. More importantly, it provided me with a basis for making the organization explicit. My process will be familiar to many educators. After a general plan setting out each level's language objectives had been established, I collected materials and scanned them for sub-themes, refining my ideas as I went. The process was iterative, with materials assessed against their potential for supporting students in describing, narrating, evaluating, and so on, and then further materials were sought out to address emerging gaps. In the final design of Levels 4 to 6, new themes were introduced in all but the first and final (seventh) weeks; in each of Weeks 2 to 6, the week's sub-themes followed an arc from personal to international. For example, in a week devoted to childhood, students spent the first day telling and retelling a memorable event from their childhood (SEQUENCE/narrative), a second discussing the concept of childhood in contemporary South Korean society (CLASSIFICATION), and a third examining the disjuncture between that concept of childhood and (then) South Korean adoption practices, which built to a discussion of Korean norms for ensuring children's welfare (PRINCIPLES). The week ended with an UN-authored document on the conditions facing former child soldiers and a discussion of the criteria that South Korea might use to evaluate its obligations to these youths (EVALUATION). In another unit on refugees, the week began with small groups discussing whether South

Korea should support international programs to aid refugees (CHOICE). When the lesson was first trialed, 20+ students answered with a unanimous no. But that confident and somewhat irritated response came undone when students confronted the consequences of a hypothetical failure of the North Korean regime and the flood of refugees into South Korea. The remainder of the week addressed definitions of humanitarian crises (CLASSIFICATION) and conditions which warranted international support (PRINCIPLES). Thus, while no two themes were identical, each began with an examination of an action situation and followed a general arc toward engagement with a more distanced and/or theoretical perspective. The six knowledge structures acted as building blocks that could be arranged and rearranged to create these weekly trajectories.

While the themes were topical and created bridges between students' experience and the larger world, these were language classes. Dominant knowledge structures were made explicit. As with the curriculum for study-abroad students, the repetition helped to illustrate how knowledge is remade across knowledge structures and texts; that is, the teacher-fronted portions at the beginning of each lesson highlighted how DESCRIPTION can be used to reinforce, extend, or challenge CLASSIFICATIONS, how personal narratives (SEQUENCE) can be combined with other sources of information to support an explanation (PRINCIPLES), and how careful consideration (EVALUATION) of decision-making criteria can lead to better choices. Further, the lessons addressed the linguistic patterns that identified these knowledge structures and (conversely) how knowledge could be structured and restructured in these patterns. But while the study-abroad program adopted a language and content approach, LEC students were focused on language proficiency. As the research indicated that these students were demonstrably at risk of not recognizing their progress, it was essential to provide them with better tools for self-assessment as well as systematic formative feedback. This is where the Knowledge Framework made its greatest contribution. But before I discuss assessment and its link to issues of textual trajectories, I want to explain how the framework helped me design language supports for negotiating interpersonal relations. To do that, I need to briefly revisit the framework's strengths.

The Knowledge Framework's support for the principled design of language curricula is threefold: the framework's knowledge structures are practical heuristics for identifying patterns; the relations between knowledge structures are useful for planning and sequencing courses, units, and activities; and the explicit link between knowledge structures and linguistic patterns facilitates discussions of language's functions. To the last point, the framework offers patterns of language, patterns associated with knowledge structures, that can be taught, noticed, repeated, reused, and reinforced by educators and students. But negotiating meaning requires more than organizing subject matter. It also requires negotiating relationships with interlocutors, and that requires attention to different patterns, patterns the framework is not designed to address. While the framework is silent on these dimensions of language, it continues to play an important role in this facet of curriculum development. Silence can be a strength.

No linguistically informed pedagogic framework exists for the negotiation of interpersonal relations, nothing that I could evaluate and potentially use alongside Mohan's knowledge structures. Thus, I turned to current issues of journals such as *Applied Linguistics, Discourse & Society* and *Discourse Studies* as well as books and workshop materials on interpersonal communication. Michael Byram's work on intercultural communication, including his work for the Council of Europe, has been widely recognized for its contribution to the field of intercultural communication in language education, but despite its ability to function in dialogue with Mohan's work, it does not provide a linguistically informed pedagogic framework for interpersonal communication that is equivalent to Mohan's knowledge structures. These interpersonal aspects of language use, which need to be explicitly taught, were targeted with more or less frequency at different levels in the program. For example, in Levels 5 and 6, a new pattern or concern was introduced each lesson. Additionally, in each lesson, students were expected to recycle and add to the repertoire of interpersonal resources they used in class discussions. By the end of each course, students had a checklist of linguistic resources they were expected to use and use purposefully in conversation, discussion, and dialogue. Some would be familiar to any language educator, such as gambits for signaling the degree to which one agreed/disagreed with group members' points-of-view. Others were more nuanced, such as the semantic differences between mental processes and/or reporting verbs, and differences in the evidence or support one might be expected to provide if remarks were prefaced by *I think* or *I feel* or *I believe*. Still others were more explicitly strategic, such as when and how to interrupt for different purposes. Always there was language—options, choices, chunks, and phrases—that would assist individuals in positioning themselves and their ideas. The overarching goal, which was clearly communicated to students, was that they would not be silenced.

But I would have had difficulty systematically addressing the negotiation of interpersonal relations without the Knowledge Framework. Recycling and repeating knowledge structures across and within courses created a consistent frame within which the interpersonal could be addressed. Across program levels, students described, classified, analyzed, and sequenced. They evaluated and made choices. The language for knowledge structures increased in complexity and the contexts for language use changed. However, regardless of the "what," there was a familiar structure that could be identified, named, and used. That allowed me to introduce the complexities of interpersonal relations without overburdening learners. It also supported unit and lesson designs that showed students that knowledge is not enough. By varying relations between interlocutors—shifting footing, hierarchies, roles, and so on—the lessons made the impact of interpersonal relations salient to students. Making knowledge structures explicit and using them as a constant variable created conditions that helped make this possible.

I have highlighted the frustration of students who could not sense improvement in their English. By itself, the Knowledge Framework could not address this concern. However, explicit, targeted instruction of usable language—useful language made usable through the design—*did* make a difference. As seen above, the framework benefited curriculum design by supporting the identification of such language and by assisting with the creation of contexts for its use. In turn, that opened up possibilities for formative assessment. In Levels 5 and 6, students took turns auditing classroom discussions for use of the targeted forms and/or gambits. In each small group, one person observed, took notes, and provided detailed feedback at the end of the class. In the curriculum as designed, the instructor also observed and jotted notes. Each class began with feedback from the instructor that built on students' observations from the previous day. That feedback was followed by short, targeted instruction that addressed common issues amongst the groups. Self-assessment tools were also designed into the curriculum, but the role of observer combined with daily feedback appeared to have the greatest impact. But the success of the observer's role depended on the observer having a clear purpose. Observers were listening for language, listening for how language was used, and observing the consequences of how language was deployed. In taking on the role of observer, observers advanced their reflection literacy as much or more than through their participation in discussions. In developing the curriculum, Mohan's framework helped to identify clear language targets. Those targets provided a basis for feedback loops. Those feedback loops assisted students in answering the question "Is this course useful?" for themselves.

Designing for impact

Mohan's framework provided considerable support for designing curricula in higher education in both contexts I have described. But did these designs have a positive impact on learning? For example, did the sequence of small assignments contribute to Japanese study-abroad students' comprehension of the course materials, support their capacity to interrogate how language learners are represented in the research literature, and assist students in using theory to find meaning in their study-abroad experience? Did the Korean university students gain confidence in their ability to communicate in English, enhance their capacity to access desired communities and not be silenced? I can only answer from the perspective of a lecturer, for there were no control groups, no pre- and post-tests, and no measures untainted by the range of experiences and influences that shaped students' lives during their period of study. However, if the use of targeted grammatical forms is any indication, the designs informed by Mohan's framework had a positive impact on the Japanese students' studies. Among the 60 to 70 students who took the language socialization and intercultural communication course in each of the three years I taught in the program, only one or two failed to use a range of mental processes in their first assignment; effective use of projection/reporting verbs continued across the remaining assignments and final papers, a marked contrast to papers from the previous two years. Over the length of the course, students sometimes struggled with journal and research articles, but surprised themselves with their ability to critique simplified concepts such as *culture shock* in intercultural communication textbooks. A year-end unmarked assignment required students to explain their (language) socialization without use of language. The students' translation of their understandings into video, art installations, board games, photo collages, and more demonstrated a depth of conceptual understanding. These students were not going to write grammatically perfect final papers after three and a half months of study, but their sophisticated thinking also showed in papers discussing their socialization into practices of racism, the shifting meanings of "sorry" in their everyday interactions, and the contrasting relations of clerks and customers in Japanese and Canadian convenience stores. I learned from multiple papers on *keigo*, the Japanese system of honorifics, in which students analyzed their language socialization into Japanese society at key points in their lives. Whether assessed against the calls of researchers on textual trajectories for enhanced understanding of how meaning transforms across texts, against the standards of reflection literacy which call for students to be supported in interrogating the wording and meaning of any utterance, or against the course objectives, the students were making gains.

And what of the Korean university students? How might their progress in the revised curriculum be assessed? I returned to Canada to complete my PhD not long after I completed work in the program, so I can again offer only anecdotes from my teaching. Scores on course evaluations improved and the gap between lower and upper courses disappeared. Courses in the upper levels began to fill less than 15 minutes after registration opened. Students shared stories of their English language use outside the classroom. A young woman who took up a researcher post in a laboratory emailed to tell me that visiting scholars sought her out at lunch because she spoke English better than other scientists and researchers. In what could be viewed as a compliment or a curse, a senior student was given responsibility for handling the most difficult study-abroad students because she had demonstrated a capacity for listening and sorting out problem situations. A PhD student in Economics described how the course assisted in handling the Q&A session after a conference presentation. In my last semester, two Korean nationals who had completed their MAs in Applied Linguistics/Language Education in North America asked to audit my Level 6 course so that they could better understand why students spoke so positively about it. There are more anecdotes, only anecdotes, but positive anecdotes nonetheless. Importantly, these anecdotes link to students' awareness of how language works and how they made use of that understanding beyond the walls of the classroom. Students found themselves able to speak, able to listen. They believed their studies had improved their capacity to share ideas, thoughts, and interests, and those ideas had been taken up by others. They faced limits and challenges, but a curriculum that drew on Mohan's framework was helping them work toward their goals.

Mohan's Framework and Textual Trajectories

The concept of textual trajectory has been forefront in my recent thinking about Mohan's framework. The oppressive hand of high-stakes standardized exams is omnipresent in language education and in my current context, England. Such exams rarely address thinking and reasoning, except to demand replication of acceptable arguments and forms of argumentation. Preparation for these assessments focuses on their immediate demands and not the demands individuals face after clearing the examination hurdle. Yet as we progress further into the evolution of information societies, our capacity to gain traction for our ideas and thinking becomes increasingly important. The work on textual trajectories follows the flow of ideas across texts and contexts; the pedagogic work associated with textual trajectories is preparing students to negotiate those flows. It demands attention to all texts, not only written. It demands attention to negotiating across contexts, not only within. It demands attention to the forms that knowledge takes, not only the knowledge itself. Mohan's *Language and Content* was written before these concerns dominated public discourse and it does not address them directly. But it was uncannily prescient in addressing the linguistic/semiotic transformations across knowledge structures and the thinking processes required in undertaking these transformations. It is a powerful beginning for work with students on textual trajectories and for research of the same.

My engagement with Mohan's work, however, has not been as a researcher. This volume is a testament to the impact of Mohan's contributions to the field of language education and applied linguistics more broadly, and many chapters approach Mohan's oeuvre from a research perspective. My own work has taken a somewhat different direction, although it is firmly grounded in social semiotics and undoubtedly shaped by the snatches of conversations I have had with Bernie over the years. My debt to Bernie, however, is the debt of an educator. As I have attempted to illustrate in my two examples from higher education, his work provides a powerful, practical basis for developing language curricula. Knowledge structures are a productive lens for examining how language is used, and the use of the Knowledge Framework as a design tool contributes to a curriculum's coherence, efficiency, and effectiveness. *Language and Content* was written before Halliday's first volume of *Introduction to Systemic Functional Grammar* and as an account of language, it is incomplete and partial. However, it was never intended to be an account of language. It is first and foremost research in the service of teachers, an account of pedagogic practice that continues to resonate with teachers and impact the lives of classrooms. It is a powerful testament to the intellect of Bernie Mohan, and a legacy that will continue to impact for many years to come.

References

Bezemer, J., & Kress, G. (2017). Continuity and change: semiotic relations across multimodal texts in surgical education. *Text & Talk, 37*(4), 509–530. doi: 10.1515/text-2017-0014

Coffin, C., & Donohue, J. (2014). *A language as social semiotic based approach to teaching and learning in higher education*. John Wiley & Sons Inc.

Dearden, J. (2014). *English as a medium of instruction—a growing global phenomenon*. Retrieved from the British Council website: https://www.teachingenglish.org.uk/sites/teacheng/files/pub_E484%20EMI%20-%20Cover%20option_3%20FINAL_Web.pdf

Dreyfus, S.J., Humphrey, S., Mahboob, A., & Martin, J.R. (2015). *Genre pedagogy in higher education: The SLATE project*. Palgrave Macmillan.

Early, M., & Marshall, S. (2008). Adolescent ESL students' interpretation and appreciation of literary texts: A case study of multimodality. *Canadian Modern Language Review, 64*(3), 377–397. doi: 10.3138/cmlr.64.3.377

Early, M., Kendrick, M., & Potts, D. (2015). Multimodality: Out from the margins of English language teaching. *TESOL Quarterly, 49*(3), 447–460. doi: 10.1002./tesq.246

Gardner, S., & Nesi, H. (2012). A classification of genre families in university student writing. *Applied Linguistics, 34*(1), 25–52. doi: /10.1093/applin/ams024

Gardner, S., Nesi, H., & Biber, D. (2018). Discipline, level, genre: Integrating situational perspectives in a new MD analysis of university student writing. *Applied Linguistics, 40*(4), 646–674. doi: 10.1093/applin/amy005

Harman, R. (Ed.) (2018). *Bilingual learners and social equity: Critical approaches to systemic functional linguistics.* Springer. doi: 10.1007/978-3-319-60953-9

Hasan, R. (1996). Literacy, everyday talk, and society. In R. Hasan & G. Williams (Eds.), *Literacy in Society* (377–424). Longman.

Hasan, R. (2011). Globalization, literacy and ideology. In J.J. Webster (Ed.), *Language and Education: Learning and Teaching in Society* (pp. 207–231). Equinox.

Hyland, K. (2004). *Disciplinary discourses: Social interactions in academic writing.* University of Michigan Press.

Hyland, K. (2008). Genre and academic writing in the disciplines. *Language Teaching, 41*(4), 543–562. doi: 10.1017/S0261444808005235

Hyland, K. (2013). Faculty feedback: Perceptions and practices in L2 disciplinary writing. *Journal of Second Language Writing, 22*(3), 240–253. doi: 10.1016/j.jslw.2013.03.003

Hyland, K., & Tse, P. (2004). Metadiscourse in academic writing: A reappraisal. *Applied Linguistics, 25*(2), 156–177. doi: 10.1093/applin/25.2.156

Hyland, K., & Tse, P. (2007). Is there an "academic vocabulary"? *TESOL Quarterly, 41*(2), 235–253. doi: 10.1002/j.1545-7249.2007.tb00058.x

Hyland, K., & Tse, P. (2009). Academic lexis and disciplinary practice: Corpus evidence for specificity. *International Journal of English Studies, 9*(2). Retrieved from https://revistas.um.es/ijes/article/view/90781

Iedema, R.A. (2001). Resemiotization. *Semiotica, 137*(1/4), 23.39. Accessed at http://hdl.handle.net/10453/9482

Iedema, R.A. (2003). Multimodality, resemiotization: Extending the analysis of discourse as multi-semiotic practice. *Visual Communication, 2*(1), 29–57. doi: 10.1177/1470357203002001751

Johns, A.M. (2008). Genre awareness for the novice academic student: An ongoing quest. *Language Teaching, 41*(2), 237–252. doi:10.1017/S0261444807004892

Lillis, T. (2017). Imagined, prescribed and actual text trajectories: The "problem" with case notes in contemporary social work. *Text & Talk, 37*(4), 485–508. doi: 10.1515/text-2017-0013

Lillis, T., & Scott, M. (2007). Defining academic literacies research: Issues of epistemology, ideology and strategy. *Journal of Applied Linguistics, 4*(1), 5–32. doi: 10.1558/japl.v4i1.5

Martin, J.R. (2009). Genre and language learning: A social semiotic perspective. *Linguistics and Education, 20*(1), 10–21. doi: 10.1016/j.linged.2009.01.003

Maybin, J. (2017). Textual trajectories: Theoretical roots and institutional consequences. *Text & Talk, 37*(4), 415–435. doi: 10.1515/text-2017-0011

Mohan, B. (1986). *Language and content.* Addison-Wesley.

Potts, D. (2018). Critical praxis, design and reflection literacy: A lesson in multimodality. In R. Harman (Ed.). *Bilingual Learners and Social Equity* (pp. 201–223). Springer.

Potts, D. & Park, P. (2007). Partnering with students in curriculum change: Students researching students' needs. In A. Rice (Ed.) *Revitalizing an Established Program for Adult Learners* (pp. 181–201). TESOL Press.

Prior, P. & Hengst, J.A. (Eds.) (2010). *Exploring semiotic remediation as discourse practice.* Palgrave Macmillan.

Schieffelin, B.B., & Ochs, E. (1986). Language socialization. *Annual Review of Anthropology, 15*, 163–191.

Tusting, K. (2017). Analyzing textual trajectories: Tensions in purpose and power relations. *Text & Talk, 37*(4), 553–560. doi: 10.1515/text-2017-0018

Van Leeuwen, T. (2015). Multimodality in education: Some directions and some questions. *TESOL Quarterly, 49*(3), 582–589. doi: 10.1002/tesq.242

About the Author

Dr. Diane Potts's research interest is pedagogies of difference and the semiotic demands confronting learners when remaking quotidian knowledge for academic purposes. Located at Lancaster University where she is Director of Studies for the Applied Linguistics and TESOL program, her work is informed by theories of social semiotics and multimodality.

Index